AN INTRODUCTION TO *Modern Philosophy*

THE MACMILLAN COMPANY
NEW YORK • CHICAGO
DALLAS • ATLANTA • SAN FRANCISCO
LONDON • MANILA

AN INTRODUCTION TO
Modern Philosophy

IN SIX PHILOSOPHICAL

PROBLEMS

by ALBUREY CASTELL PROFESSOR OF

PHILOSOPHY · UNIVERSITY OF OREGON

NEW YORK · *The Macmillan Company*

To my friend and colleague,
Joseph Warren Beach

There is nothing more wholesome for us
than to find problems that quite transcend our powers.

— Charles Peirce to William James, 1905

ACKNOWLEDGMENTS

A good portion of this book has been made possible only by the generosity of publishers who have graciously permitted the author to quote or paraphrase from works which they held in copyright. This debt of gratitude the author acknowledges to the following: Longmans Green, for permission to select from the writings of William James; The Macmillan Company, for permission to select from their translation of Kant; Harcourt Brace, for permission to select from Vaihinger's "Philosophy of the As If"; Charles Scribner's, for permission to select from the writings of George Santayana; and A. A. Knopf, for permission to select from Spengler's "Decline of the West." Only one who has wielded scissors and paste-pot can realize how co-operative and helpful publishers can be.

When this book was submitted for publication, it was reported on by persons unknown to the author. To the writers of these reports, especially the report which was so hard to take, the author wishes to acknowledge his gratitude. These "anonymous evaluators" are a marvellous institution, as anyone must realize, who has felt their praise or their censure.

To students who helped to make this book, by registering for "Phil I"; to colleagues who helped to make this book by patiently using it in mimeographed form; to its publishers who have put up with apparently endless delays, my sincere thanks!

ALBUREY CASTELL

MINNEAPOLIS, MINNESOTA
December, 1942

TABLE OF CONTENTS

AN INTRODUCTION TO *Modern Philosophy*

INTRODUCTION. AN ACCOUNT OF THIS BOOK

I

This book contains readings and comments on six philosophical problems. The problems, in the order presented here, are these: a problem in theology, a problem in metaphysics, a problem in epistemology, a problem in ethics, a problem in political theory, and a problem in philosophy of history. These somewhat academic expressions refer to very simple ideas.

1. *Theology* is the inquiry into the existence and nature of God. The term is derived from two Greek words meaning "God" and "discourse on." Within the general field of theology there are many problems. Of these, some are philosophical, some are not. Among those which are, attention is directed to the following: From our knowledge of the nature of things, is it possible to infer the existence of God? If not, why not? If so, can we go further and infer any of His attributes? If so, which? The attempt to answer these questions is called *natural* theology. It is to be distinguished from *revealed* theology on the one hand, and *mystical* theology on the other. With reference to the central problems of natural theology, we examine the views of Thomas Aquinas, Blaise Pascal, David Hume, John Stuart Mill, and William James.

2. *Metaphysics* is the inquiry into the nature of ultimate reality and the categories in terms of which it may be most fittingly described. The derivation of the word is curiously

accidental.   Among the writings of the Greek philosopher,
Aristotle, is a treatise in which he has analyzed the meanings
of some terms in Greek physics.   This treatise was lost after
his death, and recovered by a later scholar.   It bore no title.
Seeing the intended connection between this nameless monograph and Aristotle's general account of physics, the dis-
coverer bestowed upon it the rather laconic title, *ta-meta-ta-
phusika*, which is simply the Greek for "placed after the
physics," the word *meta* meaning "after."   The treatise became Aristotle's *metaphysics*.   The problems with which he
dealt, together with associated problems added by subsequent philosophers, came gradually to form the field of metaphysics.   Now, this field is large, and its problems exceedingly
abstract.   From among them, attention is directed to the
following: If we admit the distinction between a "reality"
and its "appearances," if we hold that things in *reality* are
so-and-so, whereas they *appear* to be otherwise, then what is
this reality?   And what is the relation between this reality
and its appearances?   For instance, it is possible these days
to read that everything is "really" energy.   This, however,
is not what things appear to be.   And what of energy?   Is it,
in turn, "really" something else?   If so, what?   With reference to this particular metaphysical problem we examine the
views of René Descartes, Thomas Hobbes, George Berkeley,
Arthur Schopenhauer, and William James.

3. *Epistemology* is the inquiry into the nature of knowledge.
The term is derived from two Greek words meaning "knowledge" and "discourse on."   In epistemology there are many
problems.   How does knowledge originate?   Has knowledge
any definable limits?   Wherein does it differ from error?
Wherein from opinion?   Wherein from speculation?   Suppose
a man turns from a page of natural theology or metaphysics
with the belittling remark, "Such stuff is mere speculation."
Clearly, he has a theory concerning the nature of knowledge,

in the light of which he discriminates between knowledge and speculation, and dismisses theology and metaphysics as speculation. What would his theory be? Many philosophers, both ancient and modern, have had views on the nature of knowledge. In some instances these views led them to repudiate theology and metaphysics as "mere speculation"; in some instances to include them within the scope of the term *knowledge*. With some representative studies in natural theology and metaphysics close at hand, attention is directed to the problem of knowledge in the writings of John Locke, David Hume, Immanuel Kant, Auguste Comte, and Hans Vaihinger. Each of these thinkers holds a theory concerning the nature of knowledge. Each of them uses it to discriminate between knowledge and speculation.

The first three topics — theology, metaphysics, epistemology — belong together. The transition from God and nature to appearance and reality, and then to knowledge and speculation is easily made. The second three topics form another loosely connected set. From God, reality, and knowledge, attention is directed to morals, politics, and history.

4. *Ethics* is the inquiry into the nature and conditions of the criticism we direct at action in such terms as *right-wrong, good-bad, ought-ought not*. We say an act was wrong, or that its results were bad. What is the principle upon which this right-wrong distinction rests? Can it be defended? With reference to this problem we examine the writings of five modern moralists: William Paley, Immanuel Kant, John Stuart Mill, Friedrich Nietzsche, and William James.

5. It is a short step from morals to *politics*. The great fact which is encountered here is the presence of an institution, the state, which dominates the field and generates most of the problems. The state differs from other institutions in the modern world. It alone issues absolute commands. It alone claims authority over life and death. It alone claims sover-

eign power. What is implied in this claim? Upon what grounds can it be shown to rest? Upon what grounds could it be challenged? Attention is here directed to James I of England, to Thomas Hobbes, to Jean Jacques Rousseau, to Edmund Burke, and to John Stuart Mill. A perusal of their writings as brought together here will lead us from the theory of the divine right of kings to the modern theory of government as resting eventually upon the consent of the governed.

6. Once in the field of politics, the transition to *history* is inevitable. Indeed, history has been described as "past politics." It may be more than that, but it is at least that. We deal here with what is usually described as "the philosophy of history." It arises thus: If one considers the enormous mass of details which constitute history, is there any pattern, any controlling regularity, any large movement within which the details find their place and significance? That there is, forms the first conviction of any thinker who professes to have a philosophy of history. One philosophy of history differs from another in respect to *what* the pattern is. Inasmuch as the pattern contains the meaning of the details, we can say that one differs from another in respect to the meaning of history. Attention is directed here to five great interpretations of history: the Augustinian, the rationalistic, the idealistic, the economic, and the cyclical. The first is drawn from the Middle Ages. It provides the best point of depature for considering the others. The remainder are from the writings of Immanuel Kant, Georg Wilhelm Friedrich Hegel, Karl Marx, and Oswald Spengler, respectively.

As far as feasible, I have quoted the actual words of each of the philosophers. But it should be clearly understood that this has not always been done. I have not hesitated to drop, or change the order of, words, phrases, clauses, sentences, where to do so seemed to make the meaning clearer. In extreme cases, I have resorted to paraphrases. It is therefore never safe to assume that any passage is, word for word, exactly as it would be found in the original. Literal textual accuracy has been subordinated wherever it seemed to me the author's *ipsissima verba* would get between him and the readers of this book. For this reason the citations are not enclosed in quotation marks, but merely printed in a smaller type.

II

There is little doubt that the first result of working through this large body of analyses and speculations will be profound confusion. The problems stand out clearly. The presence of rival alternative answers tends to unsettle one's mind. A sense of crosslights, of winding paths, not to say mazes, of claims and counterclaims, of assertion and denial, of proofs and disproofs, of principles and prejudices, and always the sense that finality may be apparent only is, to repeat, the first result of reading one's way through the authors brought together in this volume. Is *that*, then, the last word? Are persuasive alternatives the essentials of modern philosophy? Is suspended judgment its parting counsel? Four reflections present themselves at this point:

1. The first is this: Why not? If a survey of modern philosophical thought leaves a sense of bewilderment, not to say chaos, and if the survey has been made as representative as possible, what is gained by closing one's eyes to the fact? Modern philosophical thought appears to be chaotic, incoherent, confusing. Anyone who denies this is simply revealing his ignorance. I say it appears to be. This appearance may be deceptive, but it is at least the beginning of wisdom to allow for the possibility that this appearance may be a reality.

2. The second point is this: Past and present discord, no matter how deep and far-flung, are no grounds for asserting dogmatically that such must be the case in the future. How

old is the modern mind?   Three or four centuries; younger, in point of time lived, than any of its predecessors.   The only guarantee against further chaos and more "alternatives" is an invincible skepticism bred from a knowledge of past and present efforts and failures.

3. The third point is this: To turn over in one's mind the sequences of thoughts brought together in this book is an intellectual experience of the first order.   It is permissible for the present writer to say this because his own part in the book has been largely that of wielding the scissors and paste pot. To read and meditate upon Hobbes, Pascal, Rousseau, Hume, Mill, James, Berkeley, Schopenhauer, Kant, Comte, Vaihinger Nietzsche, Burke, Marx, and Spengler is to encounter large minds at moments when they are concerned with great issues. If this does not loosen the soil around the roots of a man's soul, and enable it to grow in wisdom, then philosophy was indeed misnamed "the love of wisdom."

4. The fourth point is this: Despite the disagreement and inconclusiveness which characterize modern philosophy, no person who is reflectively inclined can foreswear it.   The late Professor Schiller gave to one of his books the title, *Must Philosophers Disagree?*   The question suggests that indeed they must, and that the more's the pity of it.   It suggests that they need not, if only they will listen to Mr. Schiller.   It suggests that in the matter of disagreements, philosophers are unlike historians, speculative scientists, statesmen, poets, educators, and other depositaries of the contemporary Zeitgeist.   But, more important than these, it suggests a question, which is almost ruled out by the note of censure in the title of Schiller's book.   The question is this: "Must men philosophize?" And to that, given the nature of man and the nature of philosophy, the answer would seem to be, "Yes."   It would seem to be "Yes" even if the answer to Mr. Schiller's question were also "Yes."

By way of conclusion, I should like to emphasize two points The first is that an introduction to modern philosophy is not a modern introduction to philosophy.   This book is intended to say, in effect: These analyses and speculations are typical of what philosophers have been doing during the last three or four centuries.   The second is that a modern introduction to philosophy can be written and should be written.   Its central problem would be an inquiry into the nature, the varieties, and the presuppositions of criticism.   It would note that criticism is the fundamental activity of the human soul, but that the nature of this activity is far from clear.   It would note that criticism occurs in different forms, e.g., logical, ethical, political, aesthetic, etc.; but that the rationale of these varieties of critical experience is far from clear.   It would note that criticism has presuppositions, e.g., freedom, objectivity, communicability, etc., but that inquiry into these matters is difficult and obscure, once it attempts to go beyond the declaration of intuition.

These matters, however, call for another and quite different sort of book.

TOPIC ONE. A THEOLOGICAL PROBLEM

THE PROBLEM STATED

Men are religious. They do have beliefs about God. What is the rational foundation for these beliefs? It is customary to distinguish between *revealed* and *natural* or *rational* theology. Knowledge about God which rests upon revelations made directly to some man or group, and recorded in various sacred writings, constitutes *revealed* theology. Knowledge about God which is arrived at by a process of reasoning from the facts of nature constitutes *natural* or *rational* theology. It is named *natural* theology because it purports to be knowledge of God derived from our knowledge of nature. It is named *rational* theology because it purports to be knowledge of God derived by a process of reasoning from what we know about nature.

Our primary concern, in this topic, is with the central problem of natural or rational theology: Can a man, in an understanding of nature, find reasons for justifying a belief in the existence of God? With respect to revealed theology, it is possible to say very little. These limitations do not arise out of any inherent impossibility in the idea of God revealing His existence and nature to man. They arise out of the fact that a revelation, or the record of a revelation, is not open to the same kind of critical verification which we can make, for example, of the claim that the earth is round or that Napoleon was defeated at the battle of Waterloo. This impossibility of critical verification arises out of the fact that the revelation, or its record in sacred writings, has to be taken at its face

8

value. We cannot go "back" of it, to see whether its claims are true.

One turns, then, to the possibility of there being a natural or rational theology, which shall not rest upon the claim to be revealed directly by God. Natural theology, so understood, is at least as old as the writings of Plato in the fourth century B.C. In examining this matter, therefore, we are breaking into a long and venerable tradition reaching down to our own day in the writings of contemporary philosophical theologians. The problem remains much the same throughout its history.

The citations which follow these introductory remarks present five sets of reflections upon the problem of natural theology. The first set, in which the competence of human reason to prove God's existence is unquestioned, has been drawn from the writings of St. Thomas Aquinas. The second set, in which the competence of human reason to prove God's existence is sharply questioned, and the argument advanced that man's helplessness without God is the surest proof of His existence, is from the writings of Blaise Pascal. The third set, in which the incompetence of human reason to prove God's existence is carefully argued for, is from the writings of David Hume. The fourth set, in which the hypothesis of a finite or limited God is advanced as the most that human reason can defend, is from the writings of John Stuart Mill. The fifth set, in which the whole notion of an "appeal to reason" is rejected in favor of an appeal to the emotions, is from the writings of William James. These five sets span the modern period and provide examples characteristic of the analyses and speculations which this problem has evoked. Aquinas, the greatest of late medieval theologians, is included, from the thirteenth century, in order to provide the necessary background for those who follow. Pascal is seventeenth century; Hume is eighteenth century; Mill is nineteenth century; James is twentieth century. A careful perusal of what these men have said about this one problem should do two things: indicate the many sides which this problem presents when different minds make it the object of reflective analysis, and indicate the continuity of the problem over a period of several centuries.

1. THE PRINCIPLES OF NATURAL THEOLOGY — FROM ST. THOMAS AQUINAS

BIOGRAPHICAL NOTE. Thomas Aquinas was born in Italy in 1225 and died in 1274 at the age of forty-nine. The story of his life is soon told. (1) His father was a nobleman. At the age of five, Thomas was sent for his education to the Benedictine monastery of Monte Cassino, where his uncle ruled as abbot. He studied grammar, poetry, rhetoric, logic, and some elementary philosophy. From the monastery he attended the University of Naples. While there, or shortly after, he formed the design of becoming a monk in the order of St. Dominic. His mother objected, even going so far as to imprison him for two years. However, he escaped and entered the order in 1243. (2) During the next dozen years or so he pursued advanced studies in theology and philosophy at various European universities. In 1256 or 1257 he received the degree of "master of sacred sciences" and began a career of teaching and writing and controversy. (3) His writings are many. Among these the most important was his huge *Summa Theologica* in which he provided his generation with an extraordinarily systematic digest of Christian theology and much ancient philosophy. This great work, which was still unfinished at the time of his death, fills many volumes in its English translation. It begins with the question of God's existence, deals then with His attributes, traces the processes of things from God and the return of man to God through Christ by means of the sacraments which Christ instituted.

This *Summa* soon became, and still continues to be, the official presentation of Catholic theology and philosophy. (4) At the command of Pope Gregory X, Thomas undertook to be present at an ecclesiastical council to be held in Lyons. On the way he fell sick. He put up at a near-by monastery, but died after a few months' illness. In 1323, almost half a century after his death, Thomas was canonized by Pope John XXII. A recent translator remarks, "Whatever may be the proper statement of the grounds of his sainthood, his vast intellectual achievements are certainly events out of the natural order and appropriate to a miracle."

WHY THEOLOGY? It may be well to ask ourselves why we begin the study of philosophy with a set of chapters on theology; and why, among theologians, we begin with Saint Thomas Aquinas. The answers to these questions are very simple.

There are few methods better suited to introduce a student to philosophy than to spend a little time with theology. The reason is that in most ages men have sought to answer philosophical questions in terms of theological beliefs. "What shall I believe?" has frequently been answered by "The word of God." "What shall I do?" has frequently been answered by "Obey the Will of God." "Where did the world come from?" has frequently been answered by "It was created by God." "What happens to me when I die?" has frequently been answered by "You return to God." In these and countless other ways, the notion of God has entered into the very texture of men's thinking; and wherever it has entered, it has always been to answer some ultimate and highly critical question. We can generalize all of this by saying that the idea of God has functioned as an ultimate principle of explanation and an ultimate principle of criticism. Now, inasmuch as philosophy (literally, "the love of wisdom") is the systematic inquiry into our ultimate principles

of explanation and criticism, in every department of life
and thought, there has always been a close connection between it and theology.   If the answers to ultimate questions
of explanation and evaluation are to be found in theology,
it is a man's philosophical business to know this.   If there
is reasonable doubt about these matters, it is likewise a man's
philosophical business to inform himself that such is the case.

It is for this reason that theology provides a good beginning
in philosophy.   The questions which *define* philosophy have
frequently been answered by theology.   From a slight familiarity with the latter, therefore, we may at least expect to
discover what questions are philosophical in character.

Why Saint Thomas?   The answer to this second question
is that he is in many ways the prince among theologians.
His two great works, *Summa Theologica* and *Summa Contra
Gentiles* are, in many respects, the most elaborate and pains-
taking and influential of all theological writings.   If we read
Saint Thomas, we will confront ourselves with things which
are among the best which theology has to offer.   The full
text of his *Summa* runs to about a score of volumes.   We are
concerned with the first part of the first volume.   There
Saint Thomas poses, and endeavors to answer the questions,
Does God exist?   How do we know that He exists?   Can
this knowledge be demonstrated?

A MATTER OF INFERENCE.   Thomas's first claim is that the
existence of God is not something which we can know
directly; it is not given as, e.g., the color of this page is
given; it is not known by intuition; it is not known by
direct insight.   It is inferred or deduced.   In other words,
belief in the existence of God rests upon an argument, upon
discourse having the form If-then, where the If-part is something directly given and the then-part is something inferred
from what is directly given.   Such being the case, we are
naturally curious about the fact or facts, directly knowable,

from which Thomas will infer the existence of God. He proposes five facts. Each gives rise to its proper argument. These are known as the argument from change; the argument from cause; the argument from contingency; the argument from degrees of excellence; and the argument from design. In considering these five theological arguments, we shall not quote Saint Thomas's own words, since his manner of stating them would be rather elusive and foreign. In place of direct quotation, we shall paraphrase and describe what he says.

THE ARGUMENT FROM CHANGE. Change is an undoubted fact in nature. Wherever we look, things are changing. A-changing-into-B is a phrase which has a very wide application. How are we to explain or account for the fact of change? Any particular instance of change we can refer to some previous change; but this will not help us to account for the presence of change, as such. There are three possibilities: (a) We may accept change as an ultimate fact, neither requiring or permitting any explanation. (b) We may refer every case of change to some prior case, extending our reference backward to infinity. (c) We may postulate what Saint Thomas calls an Unmoved Mover, or Prime Mover, itself unchanging but the source from which all particular instances of change proceed.

The first two alternatives Thomas rejects. His reasoning is not so clear as one could wish it. He rejects the notion of change as an ultimate fact neither requiring nor permitting any explanation, because such a position would seem to be needless skepticism. Why *should* the fact of change in nature be allowed to fall outside the range of explanation? If there are going to be ultimate mysteries, why should change be among them? Is there any necessity in the claim that change is an ultimate, inexplicable fact? For these and similar reasons Thomas rejects the "skeptical" solution in favor of a more "rationalist" solution; that is, in favor of the claim that there is a reason for the fact of change.

He rejects the notion of explaining changes by referring them to prior changes, and so on back to infinity. His reasoning here seems to be that such an explanation is wrong in principle, and would hence break down and leave one in the first position of accepting change as an ultimate fact. The point here seems to be two-fold. First, that referring change to prior change is always to be left with change; whereas to be left with change is precisely the thing we are seeking to avoid. Second, the notion of an infinite regression is itself a highly unsatisfactory one. It involves the mind in many different puzzles and paradoxes which leave matters no better off than the skeptical solution. For these and similar reasons, Saint Thomas rejects the notion of infinite regression as required by the attempt to explain change by referring it to prior change.

If there is no fourth alternative, then he has a strong case for the remaining third explanation. If there are just three possibilities, and you show cause for rejecting two of them, you do not require any further justification for accepting the third. This, at any rate, seems to be Thomas's reasoning in respect to his argument from the fact of change to the existence of an Unmoved Mover, or Prime Mover, or God.

THE ARGUMENT FROM CAUSATION. These arguments in natural theology, as their name suggests, are inferences *from* some fact about nature *to* the existence of God. From the fact of change, Thomas argued to the existence of God. His second argument, known as the argument from causation, is similar in form, but begins with a different fact. This time the fact selected is causation. Like change, causation is a large, obvious, ubiquitous fact. When we examine nature, our minds seem to detect the fact of causation almost everywhere. We have many different words and phrases for expressing this fact. This causes that. This is causally connected with that. The principle of causality is illustrated between this and that.

Granted this fact about nature, Thomas's procedure is the same as in the case of change. How are we to explain or account for the fact of causation? Any particular instance of causation we can refer to some previous instance. Suppose B is the cause of A. We can refer B itself back to C, as its cause; and C itself back to D, as its cause, and so on. But this will not help us to account for the fact of causation as such. The question is not, Does this cause that? It is, Why does this cause that? Why does anything cause anything? Why is there causation in nature? As in the case of change, there are three possibilities: (a) We may accept causation as an ultimate fact, neither requiring nor permitting any explanation. (b) We may refer every instance of causing to some prior instance, extending our reference back to infinity. (c) We may postulate what Saint Thomas calls a First Cause, itself uncaused.

There is no need to retrace his argument in any detail. He rejects the notion that causation is an ultimate fact neither requiring nor permitting any explanation. He rejects the notion of an infinite regression. He is left with the notion of a First Cause.

THE ARGUMENT FROM CONTINGENCY. We have seen that Thomas's procedure is to select some obvious fact about nature, and to argue from the existence of this fact to the existence of God. From the fact of change, he argued the existence of God as unchanging First Mover. From the fact of causation, he argued the existence of God as uncaused First Cause. It will be noticed that these arguments begin with one sort of notion and conclude with the "opposite" notion. Thus from change, he argued an unchanging Being; from causation, he argued an uncaused Being. This inference from one sort of fact in nature, to God as an "opposite" sort of fact, characterizes Thomas's third argument.

The argument from contingency begins with the fact that in nature many things appear to be contingent, accidental, possible, dependent. A man is walking across a field. He encounters a stray bullet, fired by someone who was ignorant of his presence in that field. Death results. Speaking of this death, we say it was accidental. Among the things we mean when we say this is the notion that it did not *have* to happen. Matters might have been, could have been, otherwise. The man might have been elsewhere when the bullet came by. The shot might have been fired in some other direction. The compresence of the victim and the bullet, at just that time and place, was not necessary. The victim's presence, at just that time and place, did not necessitate the bullet's presence, at just that time and place. There were other possibilities. The way things actually happened did not exhaust all the possibilities. We have many different words and phrases which enable us to describe this sort of thing. We can say that his actual death was possible, but not necessary; that it was contingent or dependent upon the fact that he was there when the bullet came by; that it happened, but did not have to happen; that it was accidental, not necessary.

Like change and causation, contingency is an obvious fact about nature. Many things in nature exhibit this fact of contingency, or what Thomas sometimes calls "dependent being." It may be that *every* object and event in nature exhibits this fact of contingency. The question is, how are we to account for the fact of contingency in nature? The question is not, Was this contingent upon that? It is, Why are there contingent facts in nature? Why is anything contingent? We could put our question about contingency in the same form as our question about change and causation:

Why is there change in nature? Why is there causation in nature? Why is there contingency in nature?

Once the *sort* of fact is clear, the rest of the argument is easily grasped. We have again three possibilities: (a) We may accept contingency as an ultimate fact about nature, neither requiring nor permitting any explanation. (b) We may refer every instance of contingency to some prior instance, extending our reference back to infinity. (c) We may postulate what Thomas calls a Necessary Being, itself not contingent upon anything.

There is again no need to retrace his argument in detail. He rejects the notion that contingency is an ultimate fact neither requiring nor permitting any explanation. He rejects also the notion of an infinite regression. He is left with the notion of a Necessary Being.

THE ARGUMENT FROM DEGREES OF EXCELLENCE. Thomas's fourth argument differs slightly in character from the first three. If we examine the nature of things, we notice the fact of degrees of excellence. This is more excellent than that. What sort of excellence is in question does not matter. Saint Thomas seems to suggest that there are kinds or sorts or classes of things, and that particular cases exhibit varying degrees of excellence, each according to its kind. Thus, one horse may be more excellent than another; one tree more excellent than another; one man more excellent than another. Thomas does not seem to suggest that this notion of degrees of excellence cuts across kinds or classes. Thus, his idea is not that a horse is more excellent than a tree, but rather that one horse is more excellent than another. However this may be, nature exhibits degrees of excellence. Degrees of excellence, like change and causation and contingency, is a fact about nature.

Granted this fact, he urges that the notion of degrees of excellence implies the notion of perfection. Unless we have the notion of perfection, we could not say that something was more or less excellent. Imperfect being, of no matter what sort, implies perfect being of that sort. Evaluation of the actual, in terms of degrees of excellence, implies a grasp of the ideal. Now the totality of actuals, exhibiting their degrees of excellence, make up nature. Nature is the whereabouts of degrees of excellence. But what can we say of perfection? Its whereabouts is obviously not nature; nothing in nature is perfect after its kind.

It is easier to state Thomas's position here than it is to understand exactly what the words mean. What he seems to say is that nature is the realm of imperfect being, and God is the realm of perfect being. In nature, nothing is perfect. In God, all things are perfect. God is the whereabouts of perfect being, just as nature is the whereabouts of imperfect being. And our power to detect imperfect being (degrees of excellence) in nature implies our knowledge of perfect being in God. If knowing imperfect being entails the existence of imperfect being — if it did not exist you could not know it — then knowing perfect being entails the existence of perfect being.

This argument can be given the same formulation as we gave to the others. We can say, The fact in nature this time is degrees of excellence, or imperfect being. We have three possibilities: (a) We may accept this as an ultimate fact, neither requiring nor permitting any explanation. (b) We may refer every instance of a degree of excellence to some other instance of greater excellence, extending our reference to infinity. (c) We may postulate what Thomas calls Perfect Being, in whom all sorts of perfections live and move and have their being, and through knowledge of whom we are able to recognize the fact of imperfect being, or degrees of excellence, in nature.

The Argument from Harmony. Thus far, Saint Thomas has argued from nature as changing being to God as unchanging being; from nature as caused being to God as uncaused being; from nature as contingent being to God as necessary being; from nature as imperfect being to God as perfect being. In each instance we begin with nature as the whereabouts of a certain sort of fact, and argue from that to God as the explanatory ground of this fact.

In the fifth and last argument, Thomas selects the fact of what he calls "accord" or "harmony" in nature. We sometimes call it "adaptation." What he refers to is quite simple and obvious. Men require to see, and they have eyes; or, men have eyes and the nature of things is, in great part, visible to such eyes. There is "harmony" or "accord" or "adaptation" here. Polar bears require a covering to withstand arctic rigors, and they have a thick coat of fur; or, polar bears have a thick coat of fur, and arctic weather is, in great part, unable to penetrate such fur. There is adaptation here. A list of this sort of "accord" in nature could be extended indefinitely.

We have our fact, then. As in the other instances we have three possibilities: (a) We may accept adaptation as an ultimate fact, neither requiring nor permitting explanation. This is not to say that adaptation is to be "explained" by referring it to "chance," since such reference would either imply the legitimacy of the demand for explanation, or it would be only a covert way of denying the need or possibility of explanation. (b) We may refer each case of adaptation to some prior or some more general instance, extending our reference to infinity. (c) We may postulate what Saint Thomas calls "design"; that is, we may explain the fact of adaptation as the manifestation of intention or intelligence or foresight or providence.

THE NATURE OF GOD.   If we collect the conclusions to these five arguments, we have a general description of the nature of God. He is unchanging. He is uncaused. He is necessary. He is perfect. He is providential. We can add, by implication, that He is omnipresent and omnipotent: if He is present in all things as their cause, it must be the case that in some sense He *is* everywhere and *does* everything. So far, Thomas's argument has proceeded tolerably smoothly. At this point, however, it begins to generate problems. We may note two of these, namely, the problem of evil and the problem of freedom.

THE PROBLEM OF EVIL.   We have seen that natural theology proceeds by arguing from nature to God. Among the facts used by Saint Thomas were change, causation, contingency, degrees of excellence, and adaptation or "accord." One of these facts gives rise to a problem. It is this: If nature exhibits degrees of excellence, then it must be the case that nature is not perfect. Indeed, nature is, for Thomas, the realm of the imperfect. Here is a fact which needs to be accounted for. How account for the fact that nature is not perfect? On the hypothesis that nature is God's handiwork, it ought to be perfect. But it is necessary for Thomas to insist that nature is not perfect, otherwise the argument from degrees of excellence loses its point; moreover, he was too sensible to deny the fact of imperfection in nature. Hence the problem: how square the imperfection of the actual with the ideal perfection of the First Cause? If God is the omnipotent and perfect author of the actual, why is the actual imperfect?

Saint Thomas offers two lines of defense. Neither is satisfactory. The first is that we must ascribe the imperfections in nature to the materials with which the Great Artificer worked, as we might ascribe imperfections in a statue to the materials with which the human artist worked.

But this is to overlook the fact that the human artist did not create his materials. The second is that we must ascribe the imperfections in nature to the fact that they make possible some good things not otherwise possible, as we might say that trials are a necessary condition to the exercise and development of patience, and patience is a good thing. On the hypothesis that some good things require imperfections in order that they may come into being, Thomas argues that if all imperfections were excluded by divine providence, then the number of good things would be diminished. It does not seem necessary to criticize this argument. Thomas is in a dilemma, and there is no reason to prod him with the horns.

PROBLEM OF FREE WILL. Among the imperfections which are obvious to Saint Thomas is the fact of evil-doing, or sin, in the life of man. This sort of imperfection Thomas could dispose of by ascribing it to a man's free-will. However, if free-will is to be added to the facts of nature, we are obliged to ask how it is to be reconciled with the omnipotence of God. If God does *everything*, then in what sense does man do *anything*? If God's will governs all things, in what sense is man's will responsible for the evil acts which it performs? The argument would seem to require that Thomas sacrifice God's omnipotence to save man's freedom, if he proposes to use man's freedom to save God's righteousness. Thomas has three lines of defense, none of which are satisfactory. He says, in the first place, that the Scriptures tell us that God made man and left him in the hands of his own counsel, i.e., gave him free will to choose between good and evil. He says, in the second place, that man must have a free-will, since otherwise rewards and punishments would be inappropriate; i.e., if man's will is not free, then he is not responsible for his acts, and he should not be punished if those acts are evil, or rewarded if they are good. He says in the third place, that God made man rational, and that being rational includes having freedom of mind and will.   These arguments are all irrelevant.   The last two are good arguments in support of the thesis that man has a free will; but that was not Thomas's problem.   That problem was how man's free-will is to be reconciled with God's omnipotence.   The teaching of the Catholic Church is more forthright.   It says that moral evil is a fact, explainable by reference to man's free-will, but that man's free-will, while a fact, is also a mystery.

OF MAN'S LAST END.   These snags and bucklings are, it would seem, essential ingredients in the argument of Saint Thomas's natural theology.   However, once they have been noted one may pass on to further matters.   Of these, in the voluminous *Summas*, there are many.   One, selected here by way of conclusion, is the question of what Thomas calls man's last end.   By that he means man's highest good, the term "end" being used in the sense of goal or object.   Man's highest good, as set forth by Saint Thomas, is easily stated: it is the enjoyment of God.   What this means is less easily stated.   It is probably as follows: Man's last end is happiness.   Wherein is true happiness to be found?   It is to be found in those activities of the human psyche whereby man raises himself from a state of confusion and chaos about the world, to a grasp of the fact that the world's changeableness is rooted in God's unchangeableness; its causality rooted in God as first cause; its contingency rooted in God's necessity; its imperfection rooted in God's perfection; and its intelligibility rooted in God's intelligence.   As the Spanish proverb has it, these are major words.

Thomas's writings exemplify one type of natural theology and one approach to the central problem.   So long as the appeal to reason goes hand in hand with piety, his ideas are likely to be re-echoed in other men's minds, as in his mind they were echoes from classical Greek philosophy.   The essentials are simple.   God exists as the First Mover, the

First Cause, the Author of the order and harmony in nature. His attributes include perfection, omnipotence, omniscience, omnipresence, benevolence, justice, rationality, prevision, and so forth. How these are to be squared with man's free will and the world's great evils are nice theoretical problems. In God's ordering of things, man stands a little lower than the angels and exercises dominion over the animals and plant and inanimate orders. With his Creator he shares an intelligence and a power to know good from evil. In the knowledge and enjoyment of God man finds his only true and lasting happiness.

READING REFERENCES. Thomas's writings have been studied and written about almost continuously since their publication. In the year 1879 Leo XIII issued a papal encyclical in which he enjoined upon Catholics the wisdom of reading the writings of scholastics in general and Thomas in particular. It is a difficult task to point to two or three books and say, "Above all, do not fail to look into these." Much of the literature on Thomistic thought is in Latin or Italian or German or French. Of this, rather little has been translated. There are, however, two treatises, written by English scholars, which will repay any time spent on them: *The Conception of God in the Philosophy of Thomas Aquinas*, by R. L. Patterson, and *Thomas Aquinas* by M. C. D'Arcy. The same may be said for the translation of M. Gilson's *Le Thomisme*. Anyone who finds these books difficult should turn to the translation of M. Maritain's *Le docteur Angelique* or to G. K. Chesterton's charming little volume *Thomas Aquinas*.

READING QUESTIONS

1. Distinguish between revealed and natural theology.
2. Why is *rational* synonymous with *natural* in this connection?
3. Formulate the central problem of natural theology.
4. Why ignore the question of revealed theology?

5. How would you distinguish between theism and atheism?
6. How between atheism and skepticism?
7. What is the argument from change?   13
8. From causation?   14
9. From contingency?   16
10. From degrees of excellence?   17
11. From harmony?   19
12. Why does Thomas reject the idea of an infinite regression?   14
13. What qualities does Thomas ascribe to the Deity?   20
14. What is the problem of evil in natural theology?   20
15. Along what lines does Thomas seek to deal with it?   20, 21
16. What criticism is his position open to?   20, 21
17. What is the problem of free will in natural theology?   21
18. Do you see any connection between these two problems?
19. Why would Thomas hesitate to deny man's free will?
20. How does he seek to deal with this problem?   21, 22
21. What two attributes of Deity raise these two problems?
22. What does Thomas mean by man's last end?   22
23. Wherein does he believe man will find it?   22
24. Formulate one or more problems you would put to Thomas.

2. THE RELIGIOUS WAGER — FROM BLAISE PASCAL

FROM THOMAS TO PASCAL. Thomas Aquinas wrote in an age of Christian faith. His trust in reason to find out God was a trust shared by most of his contemporaries and readers. This, however, was in the thirteenth century. The Renaissance and the Reformation succeeded the Middle Ages. The new science of Copernicus, Kepler, Galileo, succeeded the old science of Aristotle, Ptolemy, and the medieval scholars. The new philosophy of Montaigne, Descartes, Hobbes, Bacon succeeded the old philosophy of Augustine, Anselm, Abélard, and Aquinas. It was only to be expected that the placid argumentation by which Thomas built up his *Summa* should be replaced by something more vibrant and uneasy. This change is seen most clearly in the religious writings of Blaise Pascal.

BIOGRAPHICAL NOTE. Pascal was born in 1623 and died in 1662 at the age of thirty-nine. It is convenient to consider his life in three periods. (1) He was educated at home. His parents, especially his father, were devout Catholics, pious but stern. Blaise early displayed a remarkable precocity in physics and mathematics; at the age of fifteen he was producing monographs on conic sections which were thought important enough to be read to "the most learned and scientific men in Paris." He was counted one of the outstanding physicists and mathematicians of his time. His discoveries were made during the years when most scientists are still mastering the known facts of their field. (2) The elder Pascal died in 1650 leaving a patrimony to Blaise and his sister Jacqueline. Jacqueline entered a convent; Blaise went off to Paris. During the next four years he lived among scholars, scientists, wits, and the nobility. On November 23, 1654, he had what is termed a mystical experience. That he had this experience, there is no reason to doubt; that it meant what he interpreted it to mean is perhaps more open to debate. (3) That hour, described for posterity in a note which was found sewn into the coat he was wearing at the time of his death, wrought a complete change in Pascal's life. Austerity, self-denial, boundless almsgiving, and absolute obedience to his spiritual director replaced his previous routine of scientist and man-about-town. He threw himself into the defense of the Cistercian abbey of Port Royal des Champs, which was being persecuted by the hierarchy for a number of real or supposed heresies. The case for the Port Royalists was stated by Pascal in his celebrated *Letters to a Provincial*. The closing years of his life were given to planning and sketching in what was to have been, had he lived to complete it, an apologia for the Christian faith in an age of unbelief and indifference. The book was never finished. It consists of hundreds of loosely grouped fragments, apho-

risms, jottings. It has always been known, in French, by
the title *Pensées;* in English, by the title *Thoughts*. The
citations which follow are drawn from this unfinished defense
of Pascal's religious beliefs.

THE ARGUMENT OF THE CITATIONS. The citations given
below do not trace the argument of Pascal's entire book.
Much of that volume deals with special topics, for example,
the relation of other religions to Christianity, the significance
of miracles, prophecy, revelation, etc. With these we are
not concerned. Our interest is limited to the question:
Can a man, by the use of his reason, argue the existence of
God from the existence of nature? To this question Thomas
had answered in the affirmative. Pascal, an equally devout
Christian and Catholic, answers in the negative. The movement of thought is as follows: Some persons are skeptical
or indifferent in matters of religious belief. Such persons are
to be pitied and scorned. But no appeal to reason, no natural
theology in the manner of Thomas, will avail to dissolve
their doubts, denials, indifference. This for two reasons:
They are too hardened, and in any case, human reason is
frankly unequal to the task of elaborating a rational theology.
Pascal soliloquizes at some length on the littleness of man
and the impotence of reason. If not through his rational
powers, then through what can the doubting and indifferent
soul be brought to a knowledge of God? Pascal's answer is
this: through his emotions. In a famous line he remarks:
"The heart hath its reasons, which the reason knows not of."
The utmost that reason can do is to pose and defend what
Pascal describes as a "wager," that is, a bet that God exists.
Man must see for himself that his happiness lies in belief in
and love of God. When he has seen this fact, his skepticism
and indifference will be replaced by faith and happiness and
true goodness.

He begins with those who have doubts about the existence of God and are not particularly worried over it:

Before entering on the proofs of the Christian religion, I find it necessary to set forth the unfairness of men who are indifferent to the search for truth in a matter which is so important to them and which touches them so nearly. Among all their errors, this most proves them to be fools and blind.

We know well enough how men of this temper behave. They believe they have made a great effort after their instruction when they have spent a few hours reading some book of Scripture and putting a few questions to some ecclesiastic. Whereupon they boast that they have "in vain consulted books and men." Such carelessness is intolerable.

Among unbelievers I make a vast distinction. I can have nothing but compassion for all who sincerely lament their doubt, who look upon it as the worst of evils, who spare no pains to escape it, who make these matters their chief and most serious occupation. But those who pass their lives without thinking of this ultimate end of existence, who neglect to examine whether these are matters which people receive through credulous simplicity or have a solid and impregnable basis, such persons I regard in a wholly different manner. Their negligence irritates me much more than it excites my pity. It astonishes and overwhelms me; it is for me something monstrous.

There are but three classes of persons: those who have found God and serve Him; those who have not found God, but do diligently seek Him; and those who have not found God, and live without seeking Him. The first are happy and wise. The second are unhappy, but wise. The third are unhappy and fools.

It is a sorry evil to be in doubt. It is an indispensable duty to seek when we are in doubt. Therefore he who doubts and neglects to seek to dispel these doubts, is at once in a sorry plight and guilty of great perversity. If he is calm and contented in his doubt, if he frankly avows it, if he boasts of it, if he makes it the subject of vanity and delight, I can find no terms with which to describe him.

How do men come by these sentiments? What delight is there

in such things?   What is there to be proud of in beholding ourselves in the midst of impenetrable darkness?   How can any rational
man reason in this way: "I know not who has put me in the world,
nor what the world is, nor what I am myself.   I am in terrible ignorance of all these things.   I view the awful spaces of the universe
that surround me, I find myself fixed to a corner of this vast extent,
I see nothing but infinities on every side enclosing me like an atom.
All that I know is that I must soon die.   Such is my state — full
of misery, weakness, obscurity.   And from this I conclude that I
ought to pass all the days of my life without thinking of what is
to happen to me hereafter.   It may be that I could find some answers
to my doubts; but I am unwilling to take the trouble."

Who would desire to have for a friend a man who discourses in
such a fashion?   Who would select such a person to be the confidant
of his affairs?   Who would have recourse to such a one in his afflic-
tions?   In fine, for what use in life could such a man be destined?
It is the glory of religion to have such irrational men for its enemies.
Such strange insensibility for the greatest things is something
monstrous.   It is an incomprehensible delusion.

There must be a strange revulsion in the nature of man, to make
him glory in such a state.   Most of those who are thus involved
are people who have heard that fine worldly manners consist in
what they call "throwing off the yoke."   This they try to imitate.
But, what good does it do us to hear a man say that he has "thrown
off the yoke," that he does not believe there is a God, that he is
answerable in his conduct to none but himself?   Is this a thing to be
said gaily?   On the contrary, is it not a thing to be said with sadness, as of all things the saddest?   It requires all the love of the
religion which they despise, not to despise such persons and abandon
them in their folly.

So much for perverse doubts and callous indifference.
Pascal knows that there is a long tradition of rational theolo-
gizing which, in its heyday, triumphed easily over such
skepticism and infidelity.   But that day has passed.   Since
then, Montaigne had written.   Doubt had taken too firm
a hold to be dislodged by appeals to man's reason in support

of religious belief. To what point, he seems to ask, to what point such intellectual circumgyrations as the argument from design, or the argument from first cause, when a man has really ceased to believe in God?

I wonder at the boldness of those who undertake to speak of God to the irreligious. Their first chapter is to prove the existence of God by reference to the works of nature. I should not be astonished if they addressed their argument to those who already believe; for those who have a lively faith in their heart see at once that all that exists is none other than the handiwork of God. But for those who are destitute of faith — to tell them that they need only look at nature around them in order to see God unveiled, to give them the course of the sun and the moon as the sole proof of this important matter, to imagine with such an argument we have proved anything, is only to give grounds for believing that the proofs of our religion are very feeble. Indeed, I see by reason and experience that nothing is more fitted to excite contempt.

This is what I see, and what troubles me. I look on all sides, and see nothing but obscurity; nature offers me nothing but matter for doubt. If I saw nothing in nature which marked a Divinity, I should decide not to believe in him. If I saw everywhere the marks of a Creator, I should rest peacefully in faith. But I see too much to deny, and too little to affirm; so my state is pitiful. A hundred times I have wished that God would mark His presence in nature unequivocally, if He upholds nature; or that nature would wholly suppress the signs which she gives of God, if those signs are fallacious; that she would either say all or say nothing, so I might see what part I should take. While in my present state, ignorant of what I am and of what I ought to do, I know neither my condition nor my duty.

The metaphysical proofs of God are so far apart from man's reason, and so complicated, that they are but little striking. If they are of use to any, it is only during the moment that the demonstration is before them. An hour afterwards they fear they have been mistaken. Therefore I do not here undertake to prove by natural reason the existence of God. I do not feel myself strong enough to find in nature proofs to convince hardened atheists.   All who seek God in nature find no light to satisfy them.   They fall either into atheism or into deism, two things which the Christian religion almost equally abhors.

What then?   Revealed theology, as Pascal well knows, is a dead horse when one is chasing doubters and deniers. Rational theology, in the sense of a reasoned appeal from nature to God, he has himself rejected as barren and unconvincing if a man does not already feel God in his heart.   His answer worked out bit by bit in the fragments of his unfinished *Thoughts*, comes to this: The strongest proof for the existence of God is the great need felt by the human soul for the sustaining presence of such a Being in an otherwise empty universe.

He begins by drawing attention to the immensity of the spatio-temporal universe in which man finds himself:

Let a man contemplate nature in her full majesty.   Let him extend his view beyond the objects which surround him.   Let him regard the sun.   Let him consider the earth whereon he lives as a point in comparison with the vast orbit described by the sun. Let him learn that this vast orbit is but a point compared with that embraced by the stars which roll in the firmament.   Let his imagination pass beyond.   All this visible cosmos is but a point in the ample bosom of nature.   In vain we extend our conceptions beyond imaginable spaces: We bring forth but atoms in comparison with the reality of things.   For the universe is an infinite sphere whose center is everywhere and whose circumference is nowhere.

From the vastness of things, he passes to the other extreme. Compared to the whole of nature, man may be a mere speck. But compared to the infinitely small particles which compose the material world, he is a colossus.

There is another aspect, equally astonishing.   Let a man seek things the most minute.   Let him consider a mite, in the exceeding smallness of its body: parts incomparably smaller, limbs with joints, veins in those limbs, blood in those veins, humors in this blood, globules in these humors, gases in the globules. Let him divide these globules. Let him exhaust his powers of conception. He will think perhaps that he has arrived at the minutest atom of nature. I will show him therein a new abyss. I will picture to him the inconceivable immensity of nature in the compass of this abbreviation of an atom. Let him view therein an infinity of worlds, each with its own firmament, its planets, its earth, in the same proportion as the visible world. Let him lose himself in these wonders, as astonishing in their littleness as the others in their magnitude. His body, which just before was imperceptible in the universe, is now a colossus in comparison with the infinitely small at which it is possible to arrive.

With this contrast in mind, he pauses to ask: What is man, amid all this? If Pascal had completed his argument, he would doubtless have used the words of the Psalmist, "What is man that Thou art mindful of him?" But at this point, that would be a flagrant begging of the question: It is precisely that "Thou" that is in question.

What is man, in the midst of these two infinities? A nothing compared with the infinitely large, all compared with the infinitely small. A mean between all and nothing, infinitely far from comprehending the extremes. Let us, then, know our range. Such is our true state. This is what renders us incapable, alike of absolute knowledge and absolute ignorance.

Nature confounds the skeptics, and reason confounds the dogmatists. What will become of you, O man, who would search out your true condition by your natural reason? You can avoid neither skepticism nor dogmatism; but, alas, you can live with neither!

Our intelligence holds the same position as our body, in the vast extent of nature. This middle state between two extremes is common to all our weaknesses: Our senses can perceive no extreme; too much noise deafens us, too much light blinds us, too far or too near interferes with our vision, too much brevity or too much prolixity obscures our understanding, too much truth overwhelms us, too much pleasure cloys on us, too many benefits annoy us, we feel neither extreme heat nor extreme cold, too much and too little teaching hinder our minds — in a word, all extremes are for us as though they were not. They escape us or we escape them.

Man is a creature full of natural error. Nothing shows him the truth, everything deceives him. His reason and his senses deceive each other. The senses trick the reason by false appearances; reason in turn avenges herself and deceives the senses. His emotions trouble his senses and make false impressions on him. Reason, senses, emotions, lie and deceive, outdoing each other.

What a chimera is man! Strange and monstrous! A chaos, a contradiction, a prodigy. Judge of all things, yet a weak earthworm. Depository of truth, yet a cesspool of uncertainty and error; the glory and the scrapings of the universe.

Who will unravel such a tangle? It is beyond the power of dogmatism, of skepticism, of philosophy. Man is incomprehensible by man. We grant that to the skeptics. Truth is not within our reach, nor to our taste; her home is not on earth.

We sail on a vast expanse of being, ever uncertain, ever drifting, ever hurried from one goal to another. If we seek to attach ourselves to any one point, it totters and fails us; if we follow, it eludes our grasp, vanishing forever. Nothing stays for us. This is our natural condition. Yet, it is the condition most contrary to our inclination; for we burn with desire to find a steadfast place and a fixed basis whereon we may build. But our whole foundation breaks up, and the abysses open before us.

When I consider the short duration of my life, swallowed up in an eternity before and after, the small space I fill engulfed in the infinite immensity of spaces whereof I know nothing, and which know nothing of me, I am terrified. The eternal silence of these infinite spaces alarms me. I wonder why I am here, rather than there, now rather than then. Who has set me here? By whose order and design have this place and time been destined for me?

When I see the blindness and misery of man; when I survey the whole dumb universe; when I see man left to himself without a light unto his path, lost in this corner of the cosmos, ignorant of who placed him here, of what he has come here to do, of what will overtake him when he dies, I fall into terror. And my terror is like that of a man who should awake upon a terrible desert island with no means of escape. And I wonder why men do not fall into despair. I see others around me, of like nature. I ask if they are better informed than I am; and they say they are not.

We may not, then, look for certainty or stability. Our reason is always deceived by changing shows. It matters not that man should have a trifle more knowledge of the universe; if he has it, he but begins a little higher; but he is always infinitely distant from the end. In regard to the infinities, all finites are equal, and I see no reason why we should fix our imagination on one more than on another.

Who would not think, when we declare that man consists of mind and matter, that we really understood this combination? Yet — it is the one thing we least understand. Nothing is more obscure than just this mixture of spirit and clay. Man is, to himself, the most marvelous object in nature, for he cannot conceive what matter is, nor what mind is, nor how a material body should be united to an immaterial mind. This is the crown of all his difficulties; yet it is his very being.

These are some of the causes which render man so totally unable to know nature. For nature has a twofold infinity, while he is finite. Nature is permanent, while he is fleeting and mortal. All things change and fail; he sees them only as they pass. All things have their beginning and their end; he sees neither the one nor the other. Things are simple and homogeneous. He is complex and composed of two different elements.

Not from space must I seek my dignity. I should have no more if I possessed whole worlds. By space the universe encompasses and swallows me as an atom. Man is but a reed, weakest in nature, but a reed which thinks. A thinking reed. It needs not that the whole universe should arm to crush him. A vapor, a drop of water is enough to kill him. But were the universe to kill him, man would still be more noble than that which has slain him, because he knows that he dies, and that the universe has the better of him. The universe knows nothing of this.

Know then, proud Man, how great a paradox thou art to thyself. Bow down thyself, impotent reason; be silent, thou foolish human nature.   Learn that man is altogether incomprehensible by man.

Let man now estimate his value.   Let him love himself, because he has a nature capable of good.   But let him not love the vileness which exists in that nature.   He has in himself the capacity of knowledge and happiness, yet he finds no last truth or satisfaction. I would lead him to desire it; to be freed from passions, to know how his passions obscure his knowledge and his achievement of happiness.   I would have him hate in himself the desires which bias his judgment, that they might neither blind him in choosing nor obstruct him when he has chosen.

The net result of all this is that man, of himself, is ignorant and helpless and alone.   The blind forces of nature offer him no haven.   The universe at large cares as little for his living as for his dying.   In his quest for happiness and goodness, he is confronted by an alien, indifferent, even hostile world. Pascal might have let it go at that.   Many have, for example, Schopenhauer and Thomas Hardy and Bertrand Russell.   Not so Pascal.   In such a plight, his soul could find no peace and rest.   So he picks up the argument again, reminding man that the conquest of true happiness is at stake:

All men seek happiness.   To this there is no exception.   Our will makes no step, except toward this object.   This is the motive of every action of every man.   And yet, after so many years no one has arrived, without faith, at the point to which all eyes are turned. All complain, rulers and ruled, nobles and commons, old and young, strong and weak, learned and ignorant, sound and sick, of all countries, all times, all ages, and all conditions.

A trial so long, so constant, so uniform, should have convinced us of our inability to arrive at our complete happiness by our own strength.   But example teaches us little.   We expect that our efforts will not be foiled on this occasion, as before.   Thus while the present never satisfies us, experience never teaches us; and from misfortune to misfortune we are led on to death, the eternal crown of our sorrows.

This desire, and this weakness, cry aloud to us that there is an empty space in man which he seeks vainly to fill from all that surrounds him, seeks vainly to find in things absent the happiness which he finds not in things present.

Peace of mind, happiness of soul, are nowhere within reach so long as these are sought for among the things of this world. Who can deny that? But who is prepared to let it go at that? Not Pascal, at any rate. It is at this point that his argument becomes a record of his personal findings:

Man finds his lasting happiness only in God. Without Him, there is nothing in nature which will take His place; neither the stars, nor heaven, nor earth, nor the elements; not plants, cabbages, animals, insects, calves, serpents, fever, pestilence, war, famine, vices, adultery, incest. Since man has lost track of his true happiness, all things appear equally good to him, even his own destruction, though so contrary to God, to right reason, and to the whole course of nature.

There is no good without knowledge of God. Only as we approach Him are we happy; and our ultimate good is to know Him certainly. We are unhappy, in proportion as we are removed from Him; and the greatest evil would be the certainty of being cut off from Him.

These reflections bring Pascal to the terms of his famous religious wager. It may be well to restate his position before proceeding: Some men doubt God's existence, and are indifferent to their doubts. For them Pascal has nothing to say. But others doubt, and are concerned. Like the man in the New Testament they cry, paradoxically: "Lord, I believe, help Thou my unbelief!" To those who feel this cry, Pascal addresses himself. They must recognize the futility of attempting a "rational" solution to their doubts; Renaissance skepticism, personified in Montaigne, has blown up that bridge. It remains to face squarely the utter loneliness and littleness of man. Left to himself, his hopes and joys and values and aspirations are doomed to extinction. In God alone, if there be a God, can he hope to find a friend and protector. But, good skeptic that he is, Pascal knows that there is a gap between the fact of our need for God and God's inferred existence to fill that need. Hence his genuine intellectual honesty. He is himself satisfied to argue from our need for God to the existence of God. But he does not ask his reader to follow him in that jump. He proposes a wager:

If there be a God, He is infinitely incomprehensible, since, having neither parts nor limits, He has no relation to us. We are, then, incapable of knowing either that He is or what He is.

Let us examine this point. "Either God is, or is not," we can say. But to which side shall we incline? Reason cannot help us. There is an infinite gulf fixed between creature and creator. What will you wager? It is like a game in which heads or tails may turn up. There is no reason for backing either the one possibility or the other. You cannot reasonably argue in favor of either.

If you know nothing either way, it might be urged, the true course is not to wager at all. But you must wager; that does not depend on your will. You are embarked in this business. Which will you choose?

Let us see. Since you must choose, your reason is no more affronted in choosing one way than the other. The point is clear. But what of your happiness? Let us weigh the gain and the loss in wagering that God does exist. If you wager that He does, and He does, you gain all; if you wager that He does, and He does not, you lose nothing. If you win, you take all; if you lose, you lose nothing. Wager then, unhesitatingly, that He does exist. This is demonstrable, and if men are capable of any truths, this is one.

If we ought to do nothing except on a certainty, we ought to do nothing for religion, because it is not a matter of certainty. But it is false to say, "We ought to do nothing except on a certainty." In a voyage at sea, in a battle, we act on uncertainties. If it be the case that we ought to do nothing except on a certainty, then we ought to do nothing at all, for nothing is certain.

You may object: "My hands are tied, my mouth is gagged. I am forced to wager, I am not free. But, despite this, I am so made that I cannot believe. What then would you have me do?"

I would have you understand your incapacity to believe. Labor to convince yourself, not by more "proofs" of God's existence, but by disciplining your passions and wayward emotions. You would arrive at faith, but know not the way. You would heal yourself of unbelief, yet know not the remedies. I answer: Learn of those who have been bound as you are. These are they who know the way you would follow, who have been cured of a disease you would be cured of. Follow the way by which they began, by making believe what they believed. Thus you will come to believe.

Now, what will happen to you if you take this side in the religious wager? You will be trustworthy, honorable, humble, grateful, generous, friendly, sincere, and true You will no longer have those poisoned pleasures, glory and luxury; but you will have other pleasures. I tell you that you will gain this life; at each step you will see so much certainty of gain, so much nothingness in what you stake, that you will know at last that you have wagered on a certainty, an infinity, for which you have risked nothing.

If my words please you, and seem to you cogent, know that they are the words of one who has thrown himself on his knees before and after to pray to that infinite Being to whom he submits all; know too that you also would submit to him your all for your own good and his glory, and that this strength may be in accord with this weakness.

Thus Pascal. Between the two of them, Thomas and this seventeenth-century religiously minded skeptic, they leave little more to be said on the question of natural theology. Hume, who follows in the eighteenth century only articulates more delicately the case against "reason" in these matters. Mill, in the nineteenth century, advances a startling hypothesis designed to save men like Thomas from the emotionalism of Pascal and the skepticism of Hume. James, in the twentieth century, comes full circle back to Pascal in a pragmatic approach to this perennial question.

READING REFERENCES.   Aldous Huxley, the English novelist, has written what amounts to a small book on Pascal.   It
is to be found in his volume of essays, *Do What You Will*.
In this study, Huxley attempts to "take Pascal to pieces"
to see just precisely what it is that "makes the wheels go
round."   The result is catastrophic — for Huxley, if you
agree with Pascal; for Pascal, if you agree with Huxley.
Such highly seasoned and partisan treatment should be
balanced by something more conventional and appreciative.
Several first-rate monographs exist.   Among these are *Pascal*
by Jacques Chevalier and *Pascal — the Life of Genius* by
Morris Bishop.   Bishop's volume is more suited to those
who come to the study of Pascal from Anglo-American
traditions.

READING QUESTIONS

Pascal differs significantly from Thomas;   in nothing,
perhaps, more than in that elusive thing called *spirit* or *mood*.
As one reads Thomas, one feels the presence of what is essentially a teacher, one who has the facts in hand and proposes to
impart them in an orderly and dispassionate manner.   One
result is that it is comparatively easy to cross-question one's
self on the points that are made and the general conclusions
reached.   It is otherwise with Pascal.   The man is articulat-
ing a mood, rather than calmly arguing a case.   To catch the
point it is more important to get *en rapport* with the author
than to bother much with the steps through which his
thought proceeds.   It is the difference, perhaps, between
reading a page of Euclid and a page of Shelley.

1. What "unfairness," "foolishness," and "blindness" does Pascal
   begin by noting?
2. Why does he think such "carelessness" is "intolerable"?
3. Into what three classes would he divide mankind?
4. What is his attitude toward religious doubt?

5. What is the "chief glory of religion" so far as concerns indifferent skeptics? 28

6. What spectacle requires "all the love of the religion they despise"? 28

7. What is his attitude toward natural or rational theology? 29

8. Why does he describe his state as "pitiful"? 29

9. To what end does he contrast man with the atom and the cosmos? 29

10. Wherein is man a paradox to himself? 29

11. Why does Pascal wish to show this? 32

12. What kinds of facts strike terror into his (Pascal's) heart? 32

13. Why does Pascal introduce an appeal to happiness as a first step in his wager? 34

14. In what, according to Pascal, does man find his true happiness? 35

15. State the terms of his religious wager. 36

16. Why does he urge wagering for God? 36

17. What advice does he offer the congenital doubter? 37

18. What advantages does he foresee from belief? 37

19. Formulate one or more questions you would put to Pascal.

3. A SKEPTICAL CRITIQUE OF NATURAL THEOLOGY — FROM DAVID HUME

FROM PASCAL TO HUME. The problem of natural theology continued to command men's attention. We have examined what is perhaps the most typical orthodox presentation of these matters. We have seen their unargued repudiation by Pascal; a repudiation, however, which left no bitter taste in the devout reader's mouth, since Pascal strove earnestly to restore with one hand what he had swept aside with the other. By the middle of the eighteenth century times and tempers had changed. The "Age of Reason" had set in. The French Revolution was drawing nearer. The sciences, from their small beginnings with Galileo and Bacon and Harvey in the seventeenth century, had come to exercise an almost unquestioned dominion over the imaginations of the intellectual classes. It was in this somewhat more chilly

climate of opinion that David Hume turned his critical attention to the central problem of natural theology.

BIOGRAPHICAL NOTE. Hume was born in Scotland in 1711
and died in 1776 at the age of sixty-five. Although he was
destined, along with Immanuel Kant, to mark the opening of
an as yet unclosed chapter in the history of philosophy, his
early life was passed in obscurity, and his fame, among his
contemporaries, was based principally upon his writings in
the field of political history. (1) He was intended by his
father for the law, and to that end was educated in Edinburgh.
Hume, however, abandoned the study of law and tried his
hand in a Bristol counting-house. This, too, proved uncon-
genial. He went to France, where he proceeded to write one
of the epoch-making books in modern philosophy, his
Treatise of Human Nature. The theme of this philosophical
masterpiece is simply stated in the form of a question: How
much of human knowledge, human emotional preferences and
aversions, human morality, is what it is for no better reason
than the fact that human nature is what it is? The suggestion, that once you have taken the "human" out of these
things there is nothing left over, was too much for his
generation to entertain. It contained too many skeptical
implications. The *Treatise* fell, as though stillborn, from the
press. (2) Hume now set about to find some employment
which would put him in a position of independence. He
applied, without success, for the chair of moral philosophy
in the University of Edinburgh. For two years he tutored
an almost insane Scottish marquis. He accompanied a
diplomatic expedition to France. He applied, again without
success, for the chair of logic in the University of Glasgow.
At last he secured the position of Keeper of the Advocates'
Library in Edinburgh. The access to books and original
authorities which this gave him, suggested the idea of
writing a work on history. This he proceeded to do, and

between the years 1754 and 1762, he produced his famous *History of England* which ranked, in that country, with Gibbon's *Decline and Fall of the Roman Empire*. (3) In the lean years before he became Keeper and turned historian, Hume continued reworking and expanding the ideas of his original philosophical treatise. These were published in a series of short monographs and collections of essays. In this form they gained a gradual acceptance. But it was still the historian who overshadowed the philosopher in the minds of his generation. He retired from active life in 1769, on a combined income and pension of £1,000 a year. He spent the remainder of his days, the recognized head of the intellectual and literary society in Edinburgh, admired by those who read his *History* and his miscellaneous essays, distrusted or misunderstood by those who tried their hand at his philosophy.

THE ARGUMENT OF THE CITATIONS. The selections which follow provide a skeptical examination of the principles of natural theology. They are, for the most part, from Hume's *Essay on Miracles* and *Dialogues Concerning Religion*. They presuppose, as a starting point, the general approach outlined in the chapter on Thomas Aquinas.

The position finally occupied by Hume is somewhat complex. It requires, therefore, a few words of introduction and summary. We may imagine Hume saying to himself: "Now, as to this matter of natural theology. Either we have knowledge of God's existence and nature, or we do not. If we do not possess such knowledge, there is no call for a skeptical examination of the beliefs which embody such knowledge. If, however, we do possess, or claim to possess, such knowledge, then it must rest on some sort of evidence. What is this evidence? It is formulated, usually, in three 'arguments.' There is the argument from miracles, the argument from design, and the argument from first cause.

A skeptical examination of the claims of natural theology will resolve itself finally into a skeptical examination of these three arguments. We shall advance two lines of criticism with respect to each: first, that the argument itself is very questionable; second, that even if it were accepted without question, it does not prove what it is claimed to prove." This outline of Hume's position is perhaps more systematic than the citations will at first suggest. But a careful study of what he says will, I think, leave some such general claim in one's mind. A word of caution: It is well to remember the limitations of the task which Hume sets himself to perform. He is not attempting to prove that God does not exist; that is, he is not stating the case for atheism. Nor is he seeking to discredit all belief in God. His claim is the more modest one, namely, that such belief, whether true or false is not susceptible of the traditional rational justification; that no appeal to reason, in the sense in which that appeal is made by Thomas, can be made in support of the claims of natural theology.

Belief in God has, in times past, been supported by what is called the *argument from miracles*. It is to this effect: Miracles, violations of natural laws, occur from time to time. An explanation of such events must therefore refer to something outside or beyond nature. That is, miracles point to a miracle-worker, namely, God. Hence Hume's interest in the question of miracles. His approach is indirect, as will be seen. He does not, as a well-known writer in the nineteenth century did, deny that miracles ever happen. He directs attention to the nature of the evidence upon which we believe that miracles happen and claims that the evidence in question is not strong enough to support any such belief. This rather oblique approach characterizes most of the man's writings and should, therefore, be watched carefully from the start.

I flatter myself I have discovered an argument which will be an everlasting check to all kinds of superstitious delusion, all accounts of miracles and prodigies sacred and profane.

A miracle is a violation of the laws of nature. Now, as a firm and unalterable experience has established our belief in those laws, the proof against miracles, from the very nature of the case, is as entire as any argument from experience can possibly be imagined. There must be a uniform experience against any miracle; otherwise it would not be so described. Now, as a uniform experience amounts to a proof, there is here a full proof against the occurrence of any miracle. Nor can such a proof against any miracle be weakened or destroyed, except by an opposite proof which would be superior to it.

The plain consequence is this: No testimony is sufficient to establish a miracle unless the testimony be of such a kind that its falsehood would be as miraculous as, or more miraculous than, the fact which it endeavors to establish. Even in that case there is a mutual destruction of arguments; and the superior only gives us an assurance suitable to that degree of evidential force which remains after deducting the inferior.

A man tells me he saw one dead restored to life. I ask myself: Is it more probable that he should deceive or be deceived, or that the fact which he relates should really have happened? I weigh one miracle against the other, and reject the greater. If the falsehood of his testimony would be more miraculous than the event which he relates, then (but not until then) can he command my belief.

There are two parts to Hume's criticism of the evidence for believing that miracles happen. The first, and most incisive, has been given already: Miracles purport to be violations of the laws of nature. Our evidence for believing in the uniformity of nature is very great; so great, in fact, that no evidence for doubting it could possibly be strong enough, since it would have to be stronger than the evidence for believing in nature's uniformity and this latter includes practically all our experience. Hume's point here is subtle, but important. He moves on to his second criticism:

We have supposed in the foregoing that the evidence for a miracle may be so strong that its falsehood would itself be a miracle. But it is easy to show that we have been a great deal too liberal in our concessions, and that no miracle has ever been established on so full an evidence.

First: There is not to be found in all history any miracle attested by a sufficient number of men of such unquestioned good sense, education, and learning, as to secure us against all delusion in themselves; of such undoubted integrity as to place them beyond all suspicion of any design to deceive others; of such credit and reputation as to have a great deal to lose in case of being detected in any falsehood; and, at the same time, attesting facts in such a manner and in so celebrated a place as to render that detection unavoidable.

Second: The many instances of mistaken or fraudulent miracles which have been detected show that mankind have a strong propensity to believe in the extraordinary and marvelous. This fact ought reasonably to beget a suspicion against all narratives concerning such matters.

Third: Reports of miracles abound chiefly among ignorant and barbarous peoples; or if such reports have been admitted by civilized and educated peoples they will be found to have received them from ignorant and barbarous peoples who transmitted them with that sanction and authority which, among such peoples, attends received opinions. This fact constitutes a strong presumption against all accounts of miracles.

Fourth: There is no *a priori* case in favor of the miracles peculiar to any one religion. The miracles of all religions stand on the same footing. If any such should be mutually incompatible, they simply cancel each other out. Nor is there any *a priori* case in favor of religious over secular miracles.

Fifth: The records of miracles in ancient times are not to be placed on an equal level with the records of nonmiraculous events in ancient times. Because some human testimony has the utmost force and authority in some cases, as when it relates to the battle of Philippi or Pharsalia, the assassination of Caesar or the execution of Socrates, it is not therefore reasonable that all kinds of testimony must, in all cases, have equal force and authority.

It appears, then, that no testimony for any kind of miracle has ever amounted to a probability, much less a proof. Experience only gives authority to human testimony, and it is experience which assures us of the laws of nature. When, therefore, these two kinds of experiences are contrary, we can only subtract the one from the other and embrace the opinion with that assurance which arises from the remainder. But, according to the measures of probability above established, this subtraction amounts to entire annihilation. Therefore no human testimony can have such force as to prove a miracle and make it a just foundation for any system of religion.

Mere reason is not sufficient to convince us of the miracles of the Christian religion. Whoever is moved by faith to assent to it, is conscious of a continued miracle in his own person, which subverts all the principles of his understanding and gives him a determination to believe what is most contrary to custom and experience.

The net result of what has been said thus far comes to this: Belief in God rests in part on belief in miracles. Belief in miracles rests on questionable grounds. Belief in God, therefore, insofar as it rests on belief in miracles, rests on questionable grounds. Hume's case against the argument from miracles ends at that point. He might have rounded out his argument with greater force. This was done by T. H. Huxley, Hume's biographer, in the next century. It amounts to this: Suppose the evidence for believing in miracles is left unquestioned. Suppose, that is, that we admit without argument, that miracles do take place. What follows? Belief in the Deity described by Thomas? It would seem not. For miracles are a very equivocal kind of evidence. They point frequently to a Deity who befriends some people at the expense of others. Consider, for example, the Old Testament miracle of the taking of Jericho. What kind of evidence would this be, in the eyes of a citizen of

Jericho? Or consider the miracle of the Gadarene swine recorded in the New Testament. What kind of evidence would this be, in the eyes of the unfortunate individual who owned those swine, or (to stretch a point) in the eyes of the still more unfortunate swine? These, and similar miracles, are not unequivocal testimony to Deity's universal benevolence. Moreover, if miracles are evidence of His benevolence, why do they fail to occur in so many cases where benevolence would seem to be very much in order, for example, when a vessel is sinking in a storm at sea? The point is a simple one and does not, perhaps, deserve elaboration. It is merely this: The fact of miracles, even if not disputed, does not provide us with decisive evidence one way or the other about the nature of God. And, when evidence points in opposite directions, it is wiser to omit it altogether.

Hume proceeds, in his examination of the principles of natural theology to a statement and refutation of the _argument from design_. This is one of his most famous pieces of destructive criticism. It demands, and repays, careful attention.

The chief argument for divine existence is derived from the order of nature. Where there appear marks of intelligence and design, you think it extravagant to assign for its cause either chance or the blind unguided force of matter. This is an argument from effects to causes. From the order of the work, you infer there must have been project and forethought in the workman.

Look around the world. Contemplate the whole and every part of it. You will find it to be nothing but one great machine, subdivided into an infinite number of lesser machines, which again admit of subdivisions to a degree beyond what human senses can trace and explain.

All these various machines, and even their most minute parts, are adjusted to each other with an accuracy which ravishes into admiration all men who have ever contemplated them. The curious adapting of means to ends, throughout all nature, resembles exactly, though it much exceeds, the productions of human contrivance, human design, human thought, wisdom, intelligence.

Anatomize the eye. Survey its structure and contrivance. Does not the idea of contriver immediately flow in upon you with the force like that of a sensation? Behold the male and female of each species, their instincts, their passions, the whole course of their life before and after generation. Millions of such instances present themselves through every part of the universe. Can language convey a more intelligible, more irresistible meaning than the curious adjustment of means to ends in nature?

Since the effects (natural productions and human productions) resemble each other, you are led to infer, by analogy, that the causes also resemble; that the author of nature is somewhat similar to the mind of man, though possessed of larger powers, proportioned to the grandeur of the work He has created.

You compare the universe to productions of human intelligence, to houses, ships, furniture, machines, and so forth. Since both terms of the comparison exhibit adaptation and design, you argue that the cause of the one must resemble the cause of the other.

The above citations give Hume's statement of the argument from design. It requires condensation, if we are to catch the point of his criticism. The argument from design, he says, is an argument from analogy. What he means is something like this: We examine a watch, a house, or a ship, and we conclude that such things were produced by beings possessing intelligence and controlled by purposes. We can, if we wish, verify this inference by acquainting ourselves with watchmakers, architects and shipwrights. We examine the universe, or parts of it, and conclude that it too must have been produced by a being possessing intelligence and controlled by purposes. Our reason for drawing this inference is that we do, as a matter of fact, find the universe, or parts of it, intelligible and answering to our needs and purposes. That is, we draw the analogy watch-watchmaker and universe-Deity. From the intelligibility and utility of a watch, we infer intelligence and purposiveness in the watchmaker. By analogy, from the intelligibility and utility of nature we infer intelligence and purposiveness in the author of nature. Hume's entire critique is directed toward undermining the strength of the proposed analogy between human-product-human-producer, on the one hand, and nature-author-of-nature on the other. "Is the analogy entire and perfect?" he asks and proceeds to show in what respects he thinks it is weak.

When two things (human intelligence and the products of human intelligence) have been observed to be conjoined, you can infer, by custom, from the one to the other. This I call an *argument from experience*. But how this argument can have place in the present case, may be difficult to explain. If you see a house, you can conclude it had an architect or builder because such effects, you have experienced, proceed from such causes.

But does the universe resemble a house so closely that we can with the same certainty infer a similar cause? Is the analogy entire and perfect? Can you pretend here to more than a guess, a conjecture, a presumption, concerning a similar cause? To ascertain such reasoning, it were necessary that you have had experience in the origin of the world. Have worlds ever been formed under your eye? Have you experienced the generation of the universe as you have experienced the building of a house?

If you survey a ship, you form an exalted idea of the ingenuity of the builder. You find him a stupid mechanic who imitated others, who copied an art which through a long succession of ages, after multiplied mistakes, corrections, deliberations, and controversies has been gradually improving. On your argument, then, many worlds might have been botched and bungled ere this one was arrived at; much labor lost; many fruitless trials made; a slow improvement during infinite ages in the art of world-making.

When you read a book, you enter into the mind and intention of the author, and have an immediate feeling and conception of those ideas which revolved in his imagination while employed in that composition. Is it thus when you read the book of nature?

By this argument from analogy, how prove the unity of Deity? Many men join in building a house or ship or city or commonwealth. Why may not several deities have combined in framing a world? This is only so much greater similarity to human affairs, to the operation of human intelligence. By dividing thus the work among several, you would get rid of that extensive power and knowledge which must be supposed in one deity.

Were one deity, who possessed every attribute necessary to the production of the universe, and not many deities, proved by this argument from analogy, it would be needless to suppose any other deity. But while it is still an open question whether all these attributes are united in one deity or dispersed among several independent deities, by what phenomena in nature can you pretend to decide the controversy? On this kind of argument from nature, polytheism and monotheism are on a like footing. Neither has any advantage over the other.

By this method of reasoning from analogy you renounce all claim to perfection in any of the attributes of the Deity. Imperfections in human productions you ascribe to imperfections in human producers. There are many inexplicable difficulties in the work of nature. Are you to ascribe these to the imperfections of the author of nature?

By representing Deity as so intelligible and comprehensible, so similar to a human mind, you make ourselves the model. Is this reasonable? The sentiments of the human mind include gratitude and resentment, love and hate, friendship and enmity, blame and approval, pity and scorn, admiration and envy. Do you propose to transfer such sentiments to a Supreme Being? Or suppose Him actuated by them? Do you propose to ascribe to Him only knowledge and power but no virtues?

The above citations bring out several difficulties in the proposed analogy which, Hume thinks, lie at the heart of the argument from design. The criticism continues, the point of attack being shifted slightly. From the nature of the product, you infer certain characteristics in the producer; from a man's handiwork you infer that the man is of such-

and-such character. Hume has no objection to this. His next point is merely that we should extend the same reasoning to the world and the maker of the world. What sort of place is this world, anyway? Is it such that we are obliged to argue that its author must have possessed the benevolent and providential attributes ascribed to him by traditional theology?

Can any man, by a simple denial, hope to bear down the united testimony of mankind? The whole earth is cursed and polluted. A perpetual war is kindled among all living creatures. Necessity, hunger, want, stimulate the strong and courageous; fear, anxiety, terror, agitate the weak and the infirm. The first entrance into life gives anguish to the newborn infant and to parent. Weakness, impotence, distress, attend each stage of many lives which are finished at last in agony and horror.

Is it not thus in nature? Observe the curious artifices of nature to embitter the life of living beings. The stronger prey upon the weaker, and keep them in perpetual terror and misery. The weaker, too, often prey upon the stronger. Consider these species of insects which are bred on the body of animals, or flying about, infix their stings into them. These insects have others, still more minute, which torment them. On every hand animals are surrounded with enemies which cause their misery and seek their destruction.

Why should man pretend to be exempted from the lot which befalls all other animals? Man is the greatest enemy of man. Oppression, injustice, contempt, slander, violence, sedition, war — by these men torment each other. The external ills of humanity, from the elements, from other animals, from men themselves, form a frightful catalogue of woes; but they are nothing compared with those that arise from conditions within. How many lie under the lingering torment of disease? How many suffer remorse, shame, anguish, rage, disappointment, fear, despair? How many suffer those deep disorders of mind, insanity, idiocy, madness? Who has passed through life without cruel inroads from these tormentors?

Were a stranger to drop into this world, I would show him, as a specimen of its ills, a hospital full of diseases, a prison crowded with malefactors, a battlefield strewn with carcasses, a fleet floundering in the ocean, a nation languishing under tyranny, famine, or pestilence. Labor and poverty are the certain lot of the far greater number, while the few who enjoy riches and ease never reach contentment or true felicity. All the good things of life taken together make a man very wretched indeed.

You ascribe an author to nature, and a purpose to the author of nature. What, I beseech you, is the object fulfilled by these matters to which attention has been drawn? Our sense of music, harmony, beauty, has some purpose. But what of gout, gravels, megrims, toothaches, rheumatisms? How does divine benevolence and purpose display itself here? Why argue for the power and knowledge of the Deity while His moral qualities are in doubt?

You say: But this world is only a point in comparison of the universe; this life is but a moment in comparison of eternity. Present evils are rectified in other regions and future times. And the eyes of men, being then opened to large views of things see the whole connection of general laws, and trace with adoration the benevolence and wisdom of the Deity through all the mazes and intricacies of his providence.

I answer: The only method of supporting divine benevolence is for you to deny outright the misery and wickedness of man; to say to me, "Your representations are exaggerated; your melancholy views are mostly fictitious; your inferences are contrary to fact and experience; health is more common than sickness; pleasure, than pain; happiness, than misery; for one vexation we meet, we attain a hundred enjoyments."

I add: Can such apologetics be admitted? Even allowing your claim that human happiness exceeds human misery, yet it proves nothing. For an excess of happiness over misery is not what we expect from infinite power coupled with infinite wisdom and infinite goodness.

The questions asked by Epicurus, of old, are yet unanswered. Is Deity willing to prevent evil, but not able? Then He is impotent. Is He able, but not willing? Then He is malevolent. Is He both able and willing? Then whence cometh evil? Is He neither able nor willing? Then why call Him Deity?

Evil and unhappiness are the rocks upon which all arguments for Deity must finally come to wreck. Why is there any misery and wickedness at all in the world? Not by chance, surely. From some purpose or cause then? Is it from the intention of the Deity? But He is perfectly benevolent. Is it contrary to his intention? But He is almighty. Nothing can shake the solidity of this reasoning, so short, so clear, so decisive; unless we agree that these matters lie beyond human capacity, that our human reason is not applicable to them. This is the counsel of skepticism that I have all along insisted on.

In the above citations Hume has been making capital out of the problem of evil which we meet with in Thomas' treatment of natural theology. He has, by this time, made his two principal criticisms of the argument from design: The analogy upon which it rests cannot be admitted; and even if it were admitted, it would come to grief over the problem of evil. However, he cannot let it go at that. The next seven citations give a different line of criticism. The point which they make is sufficiently self-evident to require little comment. From God as Designer, he turns to God as Soul, of the world.

You have argued, thus far, on the principle that like effects have like causes. But there is another you might try, based no less on experience: Where several known parts are observed to be similar, the unknown parts will also be found similar. Thus, if you see the limbs of a human body, you conclude that it is attended with a human head, though hid from you. If you see a small part of the sun, through a chink in the wall, you conclude that, were the wall removed, you should see the rest. Within the limits of experience, this method of reasoning is obvious and reliable.

Now I say, if you survey the universe, so far as it falls under your knowledge, it bears a great resemblance to an animal, or organized body, and seems actuated by a like principle of life and motion. A continual circulation of matter produces no disorder. A continual waste in every part is incessantly repaired. Each part, in performing its proper offices, operates both to its own preservation and that of the whole. From all this, why not infer that the world is an organism, an animal, and that Deity is the soul of the world, actuating it and being actuated by it?

If it be legitimate to argue thus by analogy from part to whole, I affirm that other parts of the world bear a greater resemblance to the structure of the world than do matters of human invention; and, therefore, should afford a better conjecture concerning the origin and nature of the whole. These parts are animals and vegetables. The world resembles more an organism than a clock or a knitting loom. Its cause, therefore, more probably resembles the cause of the former, namely, generation.

As a tree sheds its seed into neighboring fields, so the great system of the world produces certain seeds which, being scattered into the surrounding chaos, grow into new worlds. A comet, for instance, may be taken as such a seed. After it has been fully ripened, by passing from sun to sun and star to star, it is at last tossed into the unformed elements which surround this universe, and sprouts into a new system.

Or, for variety (for I see no other advantage), suppose this world to be an animal instead of a vegetable. A comet then would be an egg. And, in like manner as an ostrich lays its egg in the sand, which without any further care hatches the egg, so . . .

You protest: What wild, arbitrary suppositions are these? What data have I for such extraordinary conclusions? Is the slight resemblance of the world to a vegetable or animal sufficient basis for an argument as to further resemblances? You are right. This is what I have been insisting on, all along. We have no data, or insufficient data, for any such speculations. Our experience, from which alone we can argue safely, is so limited in extent and duration as to afford us no probable conjecture concerning the whole of things.

If you agree that our limited experience is an unequal standard by which to judge of the unlimited extent of nature, a too narrow stretch upon which to erect hypotheses concerning so vast a matter, you entirely abandon your case, and must admit of the absolute incomprehensibility of the author of nature.

The whole matter is summarized in the two following citations:

In a word, a man who follows this kind of argument from analogy, where one of the terms of the analogy lies beyond his experience, may perhaps be able to conjecture that the universe arose from something like design. But beyond that he cannot go, except by the utmost license of thought.

On this argument, for all you know to the contrary, this world may be a very faulty and imperfect copy compared to a superior standard; only the first rude essay of some infant deity who afterwards abandoned it, ashamed of his lame performance; only the work of some dependent, inferior deity, the object of derision to his superiors; only the product of old age and dotage in some superannuated deity, and ever since his death running on at adventures from the first impulse it received from him.

Thus far, the argument from miracles and the argument from design. It comes to this. The argument from the analogy of human producers led one to deny or left one unable to account for the facts of evil and misery, and led one to admit or left one unable to deny the absurd speculations which he suggested regarding the organic nature and origin of the world. If this *a posteriori* argument presented so many difficulties, would one fare better with the *a priori* argument from first Cause? By this argument could one prove the infinity, the unity, and the perfection, of the author of nature? Hume states this argument as follows:

The argument from first cause is this. Whatever exists must have a cause of its existence. Nothing can produce itself. In mounting up, therefore, from effects to causes, we must go on tracing an infinite regression without any ultimate cause, or must finally have recourse to an ultimate cause. Now, it is insisted, the conception of an infinite regression, of utterly no beginning cause to which all others can be traced, is absurd. We must, therefore, have recourse to a necessarily existent being, the first cause of all things, who carries the reason of His existence in Himself, and

whom we cannot suppose not to exist without embracing an absurdity. Such a being is the Deity.

His criticism is brief and to the point:

Wherein do we find the absurdity of an infinite regression? It
leads us beyond our powers of conceiving? So also does the conception of an infinite deity.

Let us admit its absurdity. Let us admit the necessity of a first
cause. Shall we then ask for a cause of this cause? If not, then
may we not argue a material first cause of this material universe?
If not, may we ascribe to the spiritual first cause the origin of evil
and misery and waste which we noted in our analysis of the argument from analogy? If not, to what cause then are they to be
traced? If so, wherein do we fare better with the argument from
the necessity of a first cause than from the probability of an intelligent designer?

His conclusion to the whole business is a frank plea for
skepticism in natural theology:

All religious systems are subject to insuperable difficulties. Each
disputant triumphs in his turn, exposing the absurdities, barbarities,
and pernicious tenets of his antagonist. But all of them prepare a
complete triumph for the skeptic who tells them no system ought
ever to be embraced with regard to such questions. A total suspense of judgment is here our only reasonable recourse.

The upshot of Hume's critique of natural theology is
skepticism. Its historical importance is to be seen along
several lines. In the first place, it was a nemesis visited upon
the Age of Reason; for what Hume showed his rationalistic
century was precisely the helplessness of reason to cope with
the problems of natural theology. In some minds this work
has never been undone. There is a sense in which Hume
administered a deathblow to the speculations at which he
directed his attention. Rational theology, in the grand
manner of Thomas and the seventeenth- and eighteenth-
century deists, has never been completely restored to its

former intellectual respectability. In the second place, Hume's handling of these questions led to an interesting attempt, by John Stuart Mill in the following century, to introduce into theology the conception of a finite God; in the twentieth century, to the pragmatic approach to these matters in the writings of the American, William James.

READING REFERENCES. Hume's skeptical examination of the principles of natural theology forms only one part of his general philosophy. He cultivated comparable doubts in other fields. The reading from Hume given in the third chapter of this book, the chapter dealing with epistemology, provides the premises from which he approached all problems. These will be looked at at that point, and some references noted. There are, however, one or two pieces of philosophical commentary which deal with Hume as critic of natural theology. These are worth reading. The first of these is A. E. Taylor's lecture, *David Hume and the Miraculous*. This lecture is published in the form of a little book, and again in a volume of philosophical essays. The second is Chapter 6, of Volume 2, of Sir Leslie Stephen's *English Thought in the Eighteenth Century*.

READING QUESTIONS

1. Why is Hume interested in a critique of the belief in miracles?
2. Formulate the argument from miracles in support of theism.
3. Why, according to Hume, must the evidence for miracles be unusually strong?
4. How strong, precisely, must it be?
5. For what five reasons, according to Hume, can it never be strong enough?
6. Why are miracles an equivocal kind of evidence for theism?
7. To what analogy does Hume reduce the argument from design?
8. "On this argument, many worlds might have been botched . . ." How so?

9. "By this argument, how prove the unity of the Deity?" Why not?

10. "By this argument you renounce all claim to perfection in the Deity." Why so?

11. "By this argument you make ourselves the model." Why so?

12. Why does Hume describe nature in such gloomy terms?

13. "Present evils are rectified in other regions and future times." What is his comment?

14. What trilemma did Epicurus formulate?

15. What is the argument "by analogy from part to whole"?

16. What absurdities does Hume develop, granted this analogy?

17. Why does he do this?

18. What follows, "for all you know to the contrary," on this argument?

19. What two criticisms does he make of the argument from first cause?

20. Are these decisive? Wherein do they fail to meet Thomas' presentation of this argument?

21. Formulate one or more questions you would put to Hume.

4. AN ARGUMENT FOR LIMITED THEISM—FROM JOHN STUART MILL

FROM HUME TO MILL. The student who has followed these readings thus far should find himself, by now, in possession of a considerable amount of natural theology. With Thomas, he examined the great tradition. With Pascal, he noted the appeal from reason to feeling and need. With Hume he reviewed skeptically the arguments from miracles, from design, and from first cause. This brings matters to the close of the eighteenth century. In the century which followed, several interesting variations were struck in philosophical theology. Not the least among these was John Stuart Mill's celebrated attempt to save natural theology from skepticism by advancing the challenging hypothesis that an appeal to reason might be made in support of belief in a finite or limited Deity.

BIOGRAPHICAL NOTE. John Stuart Mill was born in England in 1806 and died in 1873 at the age of sixty-seven. The late Lord Morley, in a review of Mill's life and work, referred to him as "the saint of Victorian rationalism." He might well have added "and of Victorian liberalism." For a great portion of Mill's contribution to modern liberalism is summed up in two propositions: that human reason applied to the data of human experience is the only source of human knowledge; and that a maximum of individual liberty of thought and action is the surest means of extending knowledge and increasing happiness. In the elaboration and defense of these claims he wrote book after book which came, in time, to form the staples of British liberalism in the nineteenth century. That all knowledge comes from experience is the thesis of his *System of Logic*. That the distribution of wealth is the fundamental problem in economics is the thesis of his *Principles of Political Economy*. That freedom of thought and action is the safest guarantee of individual and social well-being is the thesis of his essay *On Liberty*. That an act is right if, and only if, it produces more happiness than any other act possible, is the thesis of his *Utilitarianism*. That government by elected representatives is preferable to either constitutional monarchy or an enlightened aristocracy is the thesis of his *Considerations on Representative Government*. That women have as much right to votes and careers as men, is the thesis of *The Subjection of Women*. That the evils of a capitalistic economy give some point to the doctrines of socialists is the thesis of his *Socialism*. And that only so much as can be grounded in experience should be retained in a living theology, is the thesis of *Three Essays on Religion*. For further biographical material, see page 321.

THE ARGUMENT OF THE CITATIONS. In this chapter Mill seeks to establish (1) that Deity is a Being of "great but limited power"; (2) that He is a Being of "great and perhaps unlimited knowledge and intelligence"; (3) that benevolence but not justice is one of His attributes; (4) and that a theology centering in this conception has several things to recommend it over the more traditional views. The citations are from his essay on theism. The argument opens as follows:

The most important quality of an opinion on any momentous subject is its truth or falsity. It is indispensable that the subject of religion should be reviewed from time to time, and that its questions should be tested by the same methods, and on the same principles as any of the speculative conclusions drawn by physical science.

From this introductory remark, Mill passes at once to a consideration of the argument from design. He prefers it because it "is grounded wholly on our experience of the appearances of the universe"; that is, we can see order and harmony and adaptation of some sort by merely observing the nature of things, whereas we have no experience whatever of such things as first causes and unmoved movers.

Whatever ground there is to believe in an author of nature is derived from the appearances of the universe. The argument from design is grounded wholly on our experience of the appearances of the universe. It is, therefore, a far more important argument for theism than any other.

Mill's formulation of the argument from design, given in the next six citations, is somewhat more elaborate than we have met hitherto. His words bear close attention:

The order of nature exhibits certain qualities that are found to be characteristic of such things as are made by an intelligent mind for a purpose. We are entitled from this great similarity in the effects to infer similarity in the cause, and to believe that things which it is beyond the power of man to make, but which resemble the works of man in all but power, must also have been made by intelligence armed with a power greater than human.

The argument from design is not drawn from mere resemblances in nature to the works of human intelligence, but from the special character of those resemblances. The circumstances in which it is alleged that the world resembles the works of man are not circumstances taken at random, but are particular instances of a circumstance which experience shows to have a real connection with an intelligent origin; the fact, namely, of conspiring to an end or purpose.

To show this, it will be convenient to handle, not the argument from design as a whole, but some one of the most impressive cases of it, such as the structure of the eye or the ear. It is maintained that the structure of the eye proves a designing mind. The argument may be analyzed as follows:

1. The parts of which the eye is composed, and the arrangement of these parts, resemble one another in this very remarkable respect, that they all conduce to enabling the animal to see. These parts and their arrangement being as they are, the animal sees. This is the only marked resemblance we can trace among the different parts of the eye; beyond the general likeness in composition which exists among all other parts of the animal.

2. Now, the combination of the parts of the eye had a beginning in time and must therefore have been brought together by a cause or causes. The number of instances (of such parts being brought together to enable organisms to see) is immensely greater than is required to exclude the possibility of a random or chance concurrence of independent causes. We are therefore warranted in concluding that what has brought all these parts together was some cause common to them all. And, since the parts agree in the single respect of combining to produce sight, there must be some connection between the cause which brought the parts together, and the fact of sight.

3. Now sight, being a fact which follows the putting together of the parts of the eye, can only be connected with the production of the eye as a final cause, not an efficient cause; since all efficient causes precede their effects. But a final cause is a purpose, and at once marks the origin of the eye as proceeding from an intelligent will.

At this point we should expect Mill to proceed with his evaluation of the design argument. But he proposes, instead, to develop an alternative explanation covering the type of facts which would be explained by the hypothesis of God's existence if that hypothesis were accepted. This alternative to "creative forethought," or "intelligent will," is the hypothesis of "natural selection" suggested by Mill's contemporary, Charles Darwin. The important point to notice is the way in which natural selection, if granted as an hypothesis, would account for the type of fact which seems to demand explanation in terms of intelligent will.

Of what value is this argument? Is intelligent will, or creative forethought, the only hypothesis that will account for the facts? I regret to say that it is not. Creative forethought is not the only link by which the origin of the mechanism of the eye may be connected with the fact of sight. There is another connecting link on which attention has been greatly fixed by recent speculation. This is the principle of natural selection, of "the survival of the fittest."

This principle of the survival of the fittest does not pretend to account for the origin of sensation, or of animal or vegetable life. It assumes the existence of some one or more very low forms of organic life, in which there are no complex adaptations. It next assumes, as experience warrants us in doing, that many small variations from those simple types would be thrown out, which would be transmissible by inheritance, some of which would be advantageous to the creature in its struggle for existence and others disadvantageous. The forms which are advantageous would always tend to survive; and those which are disadvantageous, to perish. Thus there would be a constant, though slow, general improvement of the type as it branched out into many different varieties, until it might attain to the most advanced examples which now exist.

It must be acknowledged that there is something very startling, and *prima facie* improbable in this hypothetical history of nature.

With reference to the eye, for example, it would require us to suppose that the primeval animal could not see, and had at most such slight preparation for seeing as might be constituted by some

chemical action of light upon its cellular structure; that an accidental variation (mutation) would produce a variety that could see
in some imperfect manner; that this peculiarity would be transmitted by inheritance while other variations continued to take place
in other directions; that a number of races would thus be produced
who, by the power of even imperfect sight, would have a great
advantage over all other races which could not see and would in
time extirpate them from all places except perhaps from a few very
peculiar situations underground.   Fresh variations would give rise
to races with better and better seeing powers until we might at last
reach as extraordinary a combination of structures and functions as
are seen in the eye of man and of the more important animals.

Of this theory, when pushed to this extreme point, all that can
now be said is that it is not so absurd as it looks; and that the
analogies which have been discovered in experience, favorable to its
possibility, far exceed what anyone could have supposed beforehand.
Whether it will ever be possible to say more than this is at present
uncertain.

Leaving this remarkable speculation to whatever fate the progress
of discovery may have in store for it, I think it must be allowed that,
in the present state of our knowledge, the adaptions in nature
afford a large balance of probability in favor of creation by intelligence.   It is equally certain that this is no more than a probability.

Having noted these two hypotheses, creative forethought
and natural selection, and rejected the latter as less probable,
Mill turns to the question of the nature of the being whose
creative forethought is under consideration:

The question of the existence of a Deity standing thus, it is next
to be considered what sort of Deity do the indications point to?
What attributes are we warranted, by the evidence which nature
accords of a creative mind, in assigning to that mind?

The first attribute is great but limited power:

It needs no showing that the power, if not the intelligence, must
be so far superior to that of man as to surpass all human estimate.

but from this to omnipotence and omniscience there is a wide interval. And the distinction is of immense importance.

For I shall argue that the net result of natural theology, on the question of the divine attributes is this: a Being of great but limited power; how, or by what, limited we cannot even conjecture; of great, perhaps unlimited intelligence; who desires and pays some regard to the happiness of His creatures but who seems to have other motives of action for which He cares more, and who can hardly be supposed to have created the universe for that purpose alone.

Then follow the passages in which this claim is supported by a series of ingenious arguments:

Every indication of design in the cosmos is so much evidence against the omnipotence of the designer. For what is meant by *design?* Contrivance, the adaptation of means to end. But the necessity for contrivance, the need of employing "means" to achieve an "end," is a consequence of the limitation of power.

Who would have recourse to means, to attain his end, if his mere wish or word was enough? The very idea of *means* implies that the means have an efficacy which the direct action of the being who employs them has not. Otherwise, they are not means but an encumbrance.

A man does not use machinery to move his arms; unless he is paralyzed, i.e., has not the power to do so directly by his volition.

But, if the use of contrivance is a sign of limited power, how much more so is the careful and skillful choice of contrivance? Could we speak of "wisdom in the selection of means," if he who selects them could, by his mere will, have achieved the same results without them, or by any other means? Wisdom and contrivance are shown in overcoming difficulties, and there is no room for difficulties, and so no room for wisdom or contrivance, in an omnipotent being.

Any evidences of design in nature, therefore, distinctly imply that the author of nature worked under limitations; that he was obliged to adapt himself to conditions independent of his will, and to attain his ends by such arrangements as those conditions admitted of.

On this hypothesis, the Deity had to work out His ends by combining materials of given nature and properties. This did require
skill and contrivance; and the means by which it is effected are
often such as justly excite our wonder and admiration. But,
exactly because it requires wisdom, skill, contrivance, it implies
limitation of power.

It may be said: An omnipotent Creator, though under no necessity of employing contrivances such as man must use, thought fit to
do so in order to leave traces by which man might recognize his
Creator's hand.

The answer is: This equally supposes a limit to the Deity's
omnipotence, for it is a contrivance to achieve an end. Moreover,
if it was His will that man should know that they and the world
are His work, He, being omnipotent, had only to will that they
should be aware of it.

From the question of God's power, Mill turns to the question of His knowledge and wisdom. The claim here is that
there are probably no grounds for ascribing infinite knowledge
or intelligence to Deity:

Omnipotence, therefore, cannot be predicated of the Creator on
the evidences of design in nature. But what of omniscience? If
we suppose limitation of power, must we also suppose limitation of
knowledge and wisdom?

To argue that Deity possesses only limited power does not pre-
clude us from ascribing unlimited knowledge and wisdom to Him.
But there is nothing to prove it. The knowledge and wisdom
necessary to planning and arranging the cosmos are, no doubt, as
much in excess of human knowledge as the power implied is in
excess of human power. But nothing obliges us to suppose that
either the knowledge or the skill is infinite.

We are not even obliged to suppose that the contrivances and
arrangements were always the best possible. If we judge them as
we judge the work of human artificers, we find abundant defects.
The human body, for example, is one of the most striking instances
of artful and ingenious contrivance which nature offers. But we

may well ask whether so complicated a machine could not have been made to last longer, and not get out of order so easily and frequently.

We may ask why the human race should have been so constituted as to grovel in wretchedness and degradation for countless ages before a small portion of it was enabled to lift itself into the very imperfect state of intelligence, goodness, and happiness which we enjoy.

If, however, Deity, like human rule, had to adapt Himself to a set of conditions which He did not make, it is as unphilosophical, as presumptuous in us to call Him to account for any imperfections in His work; to complain that he left anything in it contrary to what (if indications of design prove anything) He must have intended.

Great but limited power. Great, perhaps unlimited, knowledge and intelligence. What moral attributes? To settle this question Mill suggests a consideration of the probable purposes of the author of nature. The idea here is that one's moral qualities will be embodied in, and therefore inferable from, whatever one devotes time and forethought to making or doing. The only conclusion Mill is able to reach is "some benevolence but no justice." The argument is as follows:

Assuming then, that while we confine ourselves to the evidences of design in nature, there is no ground for ascribing infinite power, and probably no grounds for ascribing infinite knowledge or intelligence to Deity, the question arises as to the same evidence afforded with regard to His moral attributes. What indications does nature give of the purposes of its author?

This question bears a very different aspect to us from what it bears to those who are encumbered with the doctrine of the omnipotence of Deity. We do not have to attempt the impossible problem of reconciling infinite benevolence and justice with infinite power and knowledge in such a world as this. The attempt to do so involves a contradiction, and exhibits to excess the revolting spectacle of a jesuitical defense of enormities.

To what purpose, then, do the expedients and contrivances in the construction of animals and vegetables appear to tend? These are the "adaptations" which most excite our admiration. If they afford evidence of design, of purpose, in nature, we can best hope to be enlightened by examining such parts of nature.

There is no blinking the fact that these animal and vegetable adaptations tend principally to no more exalted object than to make the structure remain in life and in working order for a certain time: the individual for a few years, the species for a longer but still limited period.

The greater part of the design or adaptation in nature, however wonderful its mechanism, is, therefore, no evidence of any moral attributes in the author of nature; because the end to which it is directed is not a moral end: it is not the good of any creature but the qualified permanence, for a limited period of the work itself.

The only inference that can be drawn from most of nature, respecting the character of the author of nature, is that He does not wish His work to perish as soon as created. He wills them to have a certain duration.

In addition to the great number of adaptations which have no apparent object but to keep the organism going, there are a certain number of provisions for giving pleasure and a certain number for giving pain. These, perhaps, should be included among the contrivances for keeping the creature or its species in existence; for both the pleasures and the pains are generally so disposed as to attract to the things which maintain existence and deter from the things which would destroy it.

When these matters are considered, a vast deduction must be made from the facts usually cited as evidence of the benevolence of the Creator; so vast, indeed, that some may doubt whether any remains.

Yet, viewing the matter impartially, it does appear that there is a preponderance of evidence that the Creator desired the pleasure of His creatures. This is indicated by the fact, which cannot itself be denied, that pleasure of one description or another, is afforded by almost all of the powers, mental and physical, possessed by the creature.

The author of these pleasure-giving and pain-preventing adaptations is no doubt accountable for having made the creature susceptible of pain. But this may have been a necessary condition of its susceptibility to pleasure: a supposition which avails nothing on the theory of an omnipotent creator, but is extremely probable in the case of a limited creator.

There is, therefore, much evidence that the creature's pleasure is agreeable to the Creator; while there is very little if any evidence that its pain is so. There is, then, justification for inferring that benevolence is one of the attributes of the Creator.

But to jump from this to the inference that his sole or chief purposes are those of benevolence, and that the single end and aim of creation was the happiness of his creatures, is not only not justified by any evidence but is a conclusion in opposition to such evidence as we have.

If the motive of the Deity for creating sentient beings was the happiness of those beings, His purpose, in our corner of the universe at least, must be pronounced to have been thus far an ignominious failure. If God had no purpose but our happiness, and that of other living creatures, it is incredible that He would have called them into existence with the prospect of being so completely baffled.

If man had not the power, by the exercise of his own energies, to improve himself and his circumstances, to do for himself and other creatures vastly more than God had in the first instance done, then He [God] would deserve something very different from thanks at his [man's] hands.

Of course, it may be said that this very capacity of improving himself was given to man by God, and that the changes which man will be able ultimately to effect will be worth purchasing by the sufferings and wasted lives.

This may be so; but to suppose that God could not have procured these blessings for man at a less frightful cost is to make a very strange supposition concerning the Deity. It is to suppose that God could not, in the first instance, create anything better than a primitive savage, and was yet able to endow this primitive savage with power of raising himself into a Newton or a Fénelon. We do not know the nature of the barriers which limit the divine omnipotence; but it is a very odd notion of them that they enable the Deity to confer on a primitive savage the power of producing what God Himself had no other means of creating.

Such are the indications respecting the divine benevolence. If we look for any other moral attribute, for example, justice, we find a total blank. There is no evidence whatever in nature of divine justice, whatever standard of justice we may hold. There is no shadow of justice in the general arrangements of nature. Whatever justice exists in human society is the work of man himself, struggling upwards against immense natural difficulties into civilization, and making to himself a second, and far better and more unselfish nature than he was created with.

Looking back, Mill summarizes his finding:

These, then, are the net results of natural theology on the question of the divine attributes. A Being of great but limited power, how or by what limited we cannot even conjecture; of great and perhaps unlimited intelligence; who desires, and pays some regard to the happiness of His creatures, but who seems to have other motives of action which He cares more for, and who can hardly be supposed to have created the universe for that purpose alone.

Such is the Deity whom natural religion points to; and any idea of God more captivating than this comes only from human wishes, or from the teaching of either real or imaginary revelation.

There are several considerations in favor of this hypothesis of a finite Deity. It eliminates the problem of evil and the problem of free will, as a moment's thought will show. These problems, it will be recalled, were raised by the claim that Deity combines in Himself the two attributes of omnipotence and complete benevolence. It keeps close to what experience actually tells us about the world we live in. And, by way of conclusion, it gives some semblance of meaning to the notion of helping or working with God:

This religious idea admits of one elevated feeling, which is not open to those who believe in the omnipotence of the good principle in the universe, the feeling of helping God — of requiting the good He has given by a voluntary cooperation which He, not being omnipotent, really needs, and by which a somewhat nearer approach may be made to the fulfillment of His purposes. This is the most invigorating thought which can inspire a human creature.

A contemporary of Mill had argued "that even if the investigation of the concept of God as the absolute, infinite, all-powerful, all-good Being, leads to self-contradiction, yet we must believe in such a Being, since neither human logic nor human ethics are applicable to such a being." To this Mill replied:

Convince me that the world is ruled by a being whose attributes are infinite, but what they are we cannot learn (except that the highest human morality which we are capable of conceiving does not sanction them) and I will bear my fate as I may. But when I am told that I must believe this, and at the same time call this being names that affirm the highest human morality, I say in plain terms that I will not. Whatever power such a being may have over me, there is one thing which he shall not do; he shall not compel me to worship him. I will call no being good who is not what I mean when I apply that epithet to my fellow creatures; and if such a being can sentence me to hell for not so calling him, to hell I will go.

READING REFERENCES. There are not many valuable commentaries on Mill's handling of this particular theological problem. The notion of a finite or limited deity did not originate with Mill; indeed, it is to be found as far back as Plato's *Republic* in the fourth century B.C. But Mill did set himself more deliberately to argue the case for the conception than any of his predecessors had done. Since his day, it has passed into the writings of William James and has been used by H. G. Wells as the theme of his little book, *God the Invisible King*.

When J. S. Mill was still exercising a great influence in England, his work was subjected to considerable critical overhauling by one of his fellow countrymen, F. H. Bradley. In the course of many years' study and writing Bradley declared himself upon most of the major themes in Mill's general philosophy. In a volume, *Essays on Truth and Reality*, he has a chapter "On God and the Absolute" which contains some suggestive remarks on the conception of a limited God. It is instructive to watch another philosopher at work on the idea. Moreover, in the concluding sentences, Bradley raises a point which forms, so to speak, the logical beginning of William James's pragmatic approach to this question. Says Bradley:

There is a fundamental inconsistency in religion. For, in any but an imperfect religion, God must be perfect. God must be at once the complete satisfaction of all finite aspiration, and yet on the other hand must stand in relation to my will. Religion (at least in my view) is practical, and on the other hand in the highest religion its object is supreme goodness and power. We have a perfect real will, and we have my will, and the practical relation of these wills is what we mean by religion. And yet, if perfection is actually realized, what becomes of my will which is set over against the complete good will? While, on the other hand, if there is no such will, what becomes of God? The inconsistency seems irremovable. . . .

An obvious method of escape is to reject the perfection of God. God will remain good, but in a limited sense. He will be reduced to a person who does the best that is in Him with limited knowledge and power. Sufficiently superior to ourselves to be worshipped, God will nevertheless be imperfect, and, with this admitted imperfection, it will be said, our religion is saved. . . .

Now certainly on such terms religion still can persist, for there is practical devotion to an object which is taken to be at a level far above our own. Such a religion even in one sense, with the lowering of the Deity, may be said to have been heightened. To help a God in His struggle, more or less doubtful and blind, with resisting evil, is no inferior task. And if the issue were taken as uncertain, or if even further the end were known to be God's indubitable defeat and our inevitable disaster, our religion would have risen thereby and would have attained to the extreme of heroism.

But on the other hand, if religion is considered as a whole and not simply from one side. it is not true that with the lowering of God religion tends to grow higher. A principal part of religion is the assured satisfaction of our good will, the joy and peace in that assurance, and the added strength which in the majority of men can come perhaps from no other source. To sacrifice altogether or in part this aspect means on the whole to set religion down to a lower level. And it is an illusion to suppose that imperfection, once admitted into the Deity, can be stopped precisely at that convenient limit which happens to suit our ideas. The assertor of an imperfect God is, whether he knows it or not, face to face with a desperate task or a forlorn alternative. He must try to show (how, I cannot tell) that the entire rest of the universe, outside his limited God, is known to be still weaker and more limited. Or he must appeal to us to follow our Leader blindly and, for all we know, to a common and overwhelming defeat. In either case, the prospect offered entails, I should say, to the religious mind, an unquestionable loss to religion.

And yet it will be urged that we have ourselves agreed that all other ways of escape are closed. For, if God is perfect, we saw that religion must contain inconsistency, and it was by seeking consistency that we were driven to a limited God. But our assumption here, I reply, is precisely that which we should have questioned from the first. Is there any need for our attempt to avoid self-contradiction? Has religion really got to be consistent theoretically? Is ultimate theoretical consistency a thing which is attainable anywhere? And, at all events, is it a thing attainable in life and in practice? That is the fundamental question upon which the whole issue depends. And I need not pause here to ask whether it is quite certain that, when God is limited, the universe becomes theoretically consistent. . . .

Viewed thus, the question as to what may be called religious ideas is seriously changed. To insist upon ultimate theoretical consistency, which in no case can we reach, becomes once for all ridiculous. The main question is as to the real nature and end of religion, and as to the respective importance of those aspects which belong to it. The ideas which best express our highest religious needs and their satisfaction, must certainly be true. Ultimate truth they do not possess, and exactly what in the end it would take to make them perfect we cannot know.

READING QUESTIONS

1. Why does Mill prefer the argument from design?
2. Restate concisely his version of the design argument.
3. What type of fact is the hypothesis of a creative designer used to account for?
4. Illustrate this point with reference to the human eye.
5. What is the distinction between a final and efficient cause?
6. How is the hypothesis of natural selection an alternative explanation for the type of fact noted in question 3?
7. Illustrate this point with reference to the eye.
8. What are Mill's own views on the tenability of this hypothesis?
9. By what lines of reasoning does Mill argue that God's power is "great but not infinite"?
10. What objection does he anticipate? How does he meet it?
11. On what grounds does he argue that God's knowledge may be limited?
12. "What indications does nature give of the purposes of its author?"
13. Why does he feel that he is in a better position to answer this than Thomas was?
14. Why does he deny complete benevolence to God?
15. Why does he nevertheless admit partial benevolence?
16. What bearing might Mill's hypothesis (limited theism) have on the problem of evil?
17. On the problem of free will?
18. What "elevated feeling" does he think his hypothesis admits of?
19. "There is a fundamental inconsistency in religion." State it.
20. What has he to say *for* the notion of a finite Deity?
21. What two things has he to say *against* it?

22. What "desperate task or forlorn alternative" does he note?
23. What is his final word on this question of God's finitude or infinitude?

§ *THE PRAGMATIC APPROACH TO NATURAL THEOLOGY — FROM WILLIAM JAMES*

FROM MILL TO JAMES. It will be recalled that Pascal, writing in the seventeenth century, repudiated the possibility of rational theology but clung to orthodox convictions. He rejected the appeal to reason in theology, but he retained the theology. John Stuart Mill, writing two centuries later, reversed the procedure. He clung to the idea of a rational theology, but repudiated the orthodox convictions. He rejected the orthodox theology, but he retained the appeal to reason. His hypothesis of a finite or limited Deity represented precisely that. The most man can rationally justify, he argued, is the belief in a finite God. Now, William James, writing toward the close of the nineteenth century and in the opening years of the twentieth century, combined Pascal's rejection of reason and Mill's hypothesis of a limited Deity. James must be envisaged as standing reflectively at the hither end of a long line of rational theologians stretching back to Thomas Aquinas and beyond. He knew his Thomas, his Pascal, his Hume, and his Mill. Dispassionate consideration convinced him that the appeal to reason in theology was bankrupt. No one had ever properly answered Hume on his own grounds. But James found himself believing wholeheartedly in the existence of God. That, he could not shake off. Accordingly, he sought to combine the two compromises offered by Pascal and Mill respectively: an appeal to emotional need in support of the belief in a finite God.

BIOGRAPHICAL NOTE. William James was born in 1842 and died in 1910 at the age of sixty-eight. He was educated at Harvard and in Europe. He was appointed to the teaching staff in Harvard in the department of physiology. From physiology he moved later to psychology, writing his brilliant and epoch-making *Principles of Psychology* and *Varieties of Religious Experience.* From psychology he moved finally to philosophy. His best-known and most readable books were written during his years as professor of philosophy. He gathered about him, at Harvard, what was perhaps the most brilliant group of teachers and writers ever assembled at any one time in any university in this country. His philosophical colleagues included Josiah Royce, George Herbert Palmer, George Santayana, and (in psychology) Hugo Münsterberg.

Although James was trained as physiologist and psychologist, he was essentially a moralist and theologian. His robust assurance that the good life, in the long run, provides the deepest and most lasting satisfaction; his passionately felt need for a "Friend" sustaining the universe and reaching out to man in his struggle for righteousness and truth, are convictions which pervade almost every chapter he has written. His three books, *The Will To Believe and Other Essays*, *The Varieties of Religious Experience*, and *Pragmatism*, contain the most popular and persuasive presentation of these views. They can and ought to be read by everyone professing interest in the human significance of the problems canvassed in this and succeeding topics.

THE ARGUMENT OF THE CITATIONS. The citations quoted hereunder are, for the most part, from James's essay, "The Will to Believe." He states somewhere that it might better have been called "The Right to Believe." His aim is to point out that, in certain cases, where the evidence is insufficient to justify belief on "rational" grounds, there may nevertheless be other grounds. In a word, sufficient evidence is not the only thing which justifies belief, is not the only thing which gives us a "right to believe." Clearly, there is an issue being raised here. Upon what does our right to believe rest? Upon what, especially, does it rest in instances where the evidence is insufficient? That is the central problem of the essay. James begins by a few remarks on hypotheses in general. The purpose of these remarks is gradually to define what he means by a "genuine option" between rival hypotheses. Where we are faced with a genuine option between rival hypotheses, neither of which is backed by sufficient evidence, upon what principle may we legitimately exercise our right to believe one and not the other? James then formulates the principle which, he thinks, justifies belief under such circumstances. We shall call this the "pragmatic principle." The question now is: Are there any hypotheses which present themselves for acceptance on this pragmatic principle? James notes that moral judgments are of this nature. However, and more important, the "religious hypothesis" is of this nature. He then states the terms of this hypothesis, using considerable care and deliberateness. In what follows, he deals with two possible lines of criticism which, he knows, will be directed against his position. The first of these is the objection of the skeptic, namely, that where evidence is insufficient to justify belief, we have no right to believe. James is good on this point and deserves close attention. The second objection is to the effect that once you set up any principle designed to justify belief on insufficient grounds, you have (in principle) obliterated the distinction between intelligent belief and any but the wildest superstition. James is not so good on this point. The reader must judge for himself. My own feeling is that he is hard pressed, if not actually in full retreat. Finally, in a few citations, we note his acceptance of Mill's limited theism.

He begins:

Let us give the name of *hypothesis* to anything that may be proposed to our belief. And, just as electricians speak of live and dead wires, let us speak of an hypothesis as either live or dead. A live hypothesis is one which appeals as a real possibility to him to whom it is proposed.

Next, let us call the decision between hypotheses an *option*. Options may be of several kinds. They may be living or dead, forced or avoidable, momentous or trivial.

A living option is one in which both hypotheses are live ones. If I say to you: "Be a theosophist or be a Mohammedan," it is probably a dead option, because for you neither hypothesis is likely to be alive. But if I say: "Be an agnostic or be a Christian," it is otherwise. Trained as you are, each hypothesis makes some appeal, however small, to your belief.

A forced option is one which arises when there is no standing outside of the alternative hypotheses. If I say to you: "Choose between going out with your umbrella or without it," I do not offer you a forced option. You can easily avoid it by not going out at all. But if I say: "Either accept this truth or go without it," I put on you a forced option, for there is no third alternative and no standing outside of these two alternatives.

A momentous option is one that is presented when the opportunity is unique, when the stake is significant, or when the decision is irreversible if it later prove unwise. If I were Dr. Nansen and proposed to you to join my North Pole expedition, your option would be momentous; for this would probably be your only opportunity, and your choice now would either exclude you from the North Pole sort of immortality altogether, or put at least the chance of it into your hands. *Per contra*, the option is trivial when the opportunity is not unique, when the stake is insignificant, or when the decision is reversible if it later prove unwise.

An option is genuine when it is of the living, forced, momentous kind.

So much for hypotheses and options. Suppose, now, that a man is confronted by a pair of rival hypotheses, neither of which can be said to rest on sufficient evidence to justify belief. What is he to do? Upon what principle can he justify himself in believing one or the other of these hypotheses? It is the following:

The thesis I defend is this: Our passional [emotion] nature not only lawfully may, but must, decide an option between propositions, whenever it is a genuine option that cannot by its nature be decided on intellectual grounds.

The essence of the matter is contained in this principle. Its full meaning should become clearer as we proceed. Whether it can be defended against criticism is a further question that lies ahead. Just now, however, we are curious to know where, among our many beliefs, we shall find some which call for acceptance on this pragmatic principle. The eye is at once struck by our moral beliefs, for example, that it is better to do this than that, better to be this sort of man than that, etc.

The question arises: Are there any such forced options in our speculative opinions? Are there some options between opinions in which this passional influence must be regarded both as an inevitable and as a lawful determinant of our choice?

Moral questions immediately present themselves. A moral question is a question not of what exists, but of what is good, or would be good if it did exist.

Science can tell us what exists; but to compare the worths, both of what exists and what does not exist, we must consult not science, but what Pascal calls our "heart," i.e., our passional nature. Science, herself, consults her heart when she lays it down that the infinite ascertainment of fact and correction of false belief are the supreme goods for man. Challenge the statement, and science can only repeat it oracularly, or else prove it by showing that such ascertainment and correction bring man all sorts of other goods which man's heart in turn declares desirable.

Moral beliefs. Is that all? While James is, I think, more fundamentally a moralist than a theologian in the whole of his work, he is, for the immediate occasion, more interested in theology than morality. So:

Let us pass to the question of religious faith. What do we mean by the religious hypothesis? Broadly it is this: Science says things are: morality says some things are better than other things: religion says that the best things are the more eternal things, the things in the universe that throw the last stone, so to speak, and say the final word: and that we are better off, even now, if we believe her first affirmation to be true.

Now let us consider what the logical elements of this situation are in case the religious hypothesis in both its branches be really true. We must admit that possibility at the outset.

We see, first, that religion offers itself as a momentous option. We are supposed to gain, even now, by our belief, and to lose by our nonbelief, a certain vital good.

We see, second, that religion is a forced option so far as that vital good is concerned. We cannot escape the issue by remaining skeptical, because although we do avoid error in that way if religion be untrue, we lose the good, if it be true. Skepticism, then, is not an avoidance of the option.

In these matters, the skeptic's position is exactly this: Better risk the loss of truth than the chance of error. But in this he is actively playing his stake as much as the believer is. He is backing the field against the religious hypothesis, just as the believer is backing the religious hypothesis against the field.

Now, to most of us, religion comes in a still further way. What I mean is this. The more perfect and more eternal aspect of the universe is represented in our religions as having a personal form. The universe is no longer a mere It, but a Thou, if we are religious; and any relation that may be possible from person to person might be possible here. We feel, too, as if the appeal of religion were made to our own active good will, as if evidence for its truth might be forever withheld from us unless we met the hypothesis halfway.

This feeling, forced on us we know not whence, that by obstinately believing that there are gods we are doing the universe the deepest service we can, seems part of the living essence of the religious hypothesis.

God is the natural appellation, for us Christians at least, for the supreme reality, so I will call this higher part of the universe by the

the name of God. We and God have business with each other; and in opening ourselves to His influence our deepest destiny is fulfilled. The universe, at those parts of it which our personal being constitutes, takes a turn genuinely for the worse or for the better in proportion as each one of us fulfills or evades God's demands.

God's existence is the guarantee of an ideal order that shall be permanently preserved. This world may indeed some day burn up or freeze up; but if it is part of His order, the old ideals are sure to be brought elsewhere to fruition, so that where God is, tragedy is only provisional and partial, and shipwreck and dissolution are not the absolutely final things.

Only when this farther step of faith concerning God is taken, and remote objective consequences are predicted, does religion, as it seems to me, bring hypothesis into play.

What is this but to say that religion, in her fullest exercise of function, is a postulator of new facts? The world interpreted religiously is not the materialistic world over again, with an altered expression. It must have, over and above the altered expression, a natural constitution different at some point from that which a materialistic world would have. It must be such that different events can be expected in it, different conduct must be required.

All this on the supposition that our passional nature may be prophetic and right: and that the religious hypothesis is a live hypothesis which may be true.

We are now in possession of the essentials of James's position. We know what he means by a genuine option between rival hypotheses. We know the principle by which he would justify belief in such circumstances. We know that he considers the religious hypothesis a case in point. We know, finally, what he means by this religious hypothesis. His defense of the whole position is still to be made. He deals first with the skeptic. The point here is this: It may be all very well to talk about the demands of our "passional nature," but, as a matter of fact, why is it not just as legitimate to refuse to believe either hypothesis when neither is

backed by sufficient evidence?   Why may a skeptic not take
the stand, in all conscience, that under the circumstances
stipulated by James, the proper attitude is one of suspended
judgment?   Let us hear, through James, the skeptic's statement of the case:

It does seem preposterous on the very face of it, to talk of our
opinions being modifiable at will.   Can our will either help or
hinder our intellect in its perceptions of truth? . . . Indeed, the
talk of believing by our volition seems from one point of view,
simply silly.   From another point of view it is worse than silly,
it is vile.   When one turns to the magnificent edifice of the physical
sciences, and sees how it was reared, what thousands of disinterested
moral lives of men lie buried in its mere foundations; what patience
and postponement, what choking down of preference, what submission to icy laws of outer fact are wrought into its very stones and
mortar; how absolutely impersonal it stands in its vast augustness —
then how besotted and contemptible seems every little sentimentalist
who comes blowing his voluntary smoke wreaths!   Can we wonder
if those bred in the rugged and manly school of science should feel
like spewing such subjectivism out of their mouths?   The whole
system of loyalties which grow up in the schools of science go dead
against its toleration; so that it is only natural that those who have
caught the scientific fever should pass over to the opposite extreme
and write sometimes as if the incorruptibly truthful intellect
ought positively to prefer bitterness and unacceptableness to the
heart in its cup.

Clough sings:
>   "It fortifies my soul to know
>   That, though I perish, Truth is so"

while Huxley exclaims: "My only consolation lies in the reflection
that, however bad our posterity may become, so far as they hold by
the plain rule of not pretending to believe what they have no reason
to believe, because it may be to their advantage so to pretend, they
will not have reached the lowest depth of immortality."

And that delicious *enfant terrible*, Clifford, writes: "Belief is dese-
crated when given to unproved and unquestioned statements for the

solace and private pleasure of the believer. Whoso would deserve well of his fellows in this matter will guard the purity of his belief with a very fanaticism of jealous care, lest at any time it should rest on an unworthy object, and catch a stain which can never be wiped away. If a belief has been accepted on insufficient evidence, even though the belief be true, the pleasure is a stolen one. It is sinful because it is stolen in defiance of our duty to mankind. That duty is to guard ourselves from such beliefs as from a pestilence which may shortly master our body and then spread to the rest of the town. It is wrong, always, everywhere, and for everyone, to believe anything upon insufficient evidence."

Now, all of this strikes one as healthy, even when expressed by Clifford with somewhat too much of robustious pathos in the voice. Willing and wishing do seem, in the matter of our beliefs, to be only fifth wheels to the coach.

How shall this indictment be answered? It will be noticed that James has been scrupulously fair to the skeptic in admitting the genuine possibility here of an ethical issue. The skeptic's claim is not, at its best, that we are merely foolish to believe on insufficient evidence. It is the more serious claim that we *ought* not to believe on insufficient evidence; that belief, in such cases, is positively immoral. That is the charge with which James is faced. The first move in his defense is to note that in this unique case of the religious hypothesis doubt is the equivalent of denial; and, the point is, denial is not suspended judgment. (It may be necessary to reread James's wording of the religious hypothesis, especially its *second* part, to follow his argument here.)

To preach skepticism in these matters is tantamount to telling us, when in the presence of the religious hypothesis, that to yield to our fear of its being false is wiser and better than to yield to our hope that it may be true.

As James points out, this puts a slightly different face on matters. Why is it "wiser and better" to refrain from belief on all occasions where the evidence is insufficient? It should be noted that, by developing the ethical case for skepticism, James is cleverly jockeying the skeptic into a "moral" question. He has already explained that moral questions must be decided on "emotional" grounds.

This is not a case of "intellect" against "passion." It is only intellect, with one passion — the dread or horror of believing what may be false — laying down its law — never to believe what may be false when there is no evidence that it may be true.

And by what, forsooth, is the supreme wisdom of this passion warranted? Dupery for dupery, what proof is there that dupery through hope is so much worse than dupery through fear? I, for one, can see no proof; and I simply refuse to imitate the skeptic's option in a case where my own stake is important enough to give me the right to choose my own form of risk.

And what it comes down to is this:

We may regard the case for truth as paramount, and the avoidance of error as secondary; or we may treat the avoidance of error as more imperative, and let truth take its chance. Clifford exhorts us to the latter course. Believe nothing, he tells us, keep your mind in suspense forever, rather than, by closing on insufficient evidence, incur the awful risk of believing lies. You, on the other hand, may think that the risk of being in error is a very small matter when compared with the blessings of real knowledge, and be ready to be duped many times rather than postpone indefinitely the chance of guessing true.

This being so, he knows where he stands:

For my own part, I have also a horror of being duped. But I can believe that worse things than being duped may happen to a man in this world. So Clifford's exhortation has to my ears a thoroughly fantastic sound. Our errors are surely not such awfully solemn things. In a world where we are so sure to incur them, a certain lightness of heart seems healthier than this excessive nervousness on their behalf.

If the religious hypothesis be true, and the evidence for it still insufficient, I do not wish, by putting a skeptical extinguisher upon my nature, to forfeit my sole chance of getting upon the winning side; that chance depending, of course, on my willingness to run the risk of acting as if my passional need of taking the world religiously might be prophetic and right.

When I look at the religious hypothesis, as it really puts itself to men, and when I think of all the possibilities which it involves, then the skeptical command to put a stopper on our heart and wait — acting meanwhile more or less as if religion were not true — wait till doomsday, or till such time as our intellect and senses may have raked in enough evidence — this command, I say, seems to me the queerest idol ever manufactured in the philosophic cave.

If the religious hypothesis were true, then pure intellectualism, with its veto on our willingness to make advances, would be an absurdity; and some participation of our sympathetic nature would be logically required. I, therefore, for one, cannot see my way to accepting the agnostic rules for truth seeking (never to believe any hypothesis when there is no evidence or insufficient evidence) or to willfully agree to keep my willing nature out of the game.

I cannot do so for this plain reason: A rule of thinking which would prevent me from acknowledging certain kinds of truth if those kinds of truths were really there, would be an irrational rule. That, for me, is the long and short of the logic of the situation.

The great empiricists are only empiricists on reflection; left to their instincts, they dogmatize like infallible popes. When the Cliffords tell us how sinful it is to be Christians on such "insufficient evidence," insufficiency is really the last thing they have in mind. For them the evidence is absolutely sufficient, only it makes the other way. They believe so completely in an anti-Christian order of the universe that there is no living option: Christianity, for them, is a dead hypothesis from the start.

As a kind of Parthian shot, James throws a question at the skeptics themselves:

Our belief in truth itself, for instance, that there is a truth and that our minds and it are made for each other — what is it but a passionate affirmation of desire in which our social system backs us up? We want to have a truth; we want to believe that our experiments and studies and discussions must put us in a continually better and better position toward it; and on this line we agree to fight out our thinking lives.

But if a skeptic asks us how we know all this, can our logic find a reply? It cannot. It is just one volition against another; we are willing to go in for life upon a trust or assumption which he, for his part, does not care to make. As a rule we disbelieve all facts and theories for which we have no use. Clifford's cosmic emotions find no use for Christian feelings. Huxley belabors the bishops because there is no use for sacerdotalism in his scheme of life. But Newman goes over to Romanism, and finds all sorts of reasons good for staying there, because a priestly system is for him an organic need for delight.

So Clifford notwithstanding, our nonintellectual nature evidently does influence our convictions. The state of things is far from simple, and pure insight and pure logic, whatever they may do ideally, are not the only things that really do produce our creeds.

If we had an infallible intellect, with its objective certitudes, we might feel ourselves disloyal to such a perfect organ of knowledge in not trusting to it exclusively, in not waiting for its releasing word. But if we believe that no bell in us tolls to let us know for certain when truth is in our grasp, then it seems a piece of idle fantasticality to preach so solemnly of our duty of waiting for the bell.

James has still to deal with another sort of critic, no less hostile in his way than the skeptic. The charge this time is not that where evidence is lacking it is wiser and better to suspend judgment. It is, rather, to this effect: If you start justifying belief (for example, in Christian convictions) on this pragmatic basis, where and how are you going to draw the line? The pragmatic justification is not, by its nature, the peculiar property of the man who desires to believe in God. It would seem to be equally available, as a principle of justification, for other beliefs as well, some of which (no doubt) might be incompatible with those beliefs which James used it to defend. A man who advances a principle which would justify belief in incompatible hypotheses has, to say the least, some explaining to do. James knew this. Although convinced that his argument was sound, he knew that others would not be. Thus:

> I confess I do not see how this logic can be escaped. But sad experience makes me fear that some of you may still shrink from saying with me that we have the right to believe at our own risk any hypothesis that is live enough to tempt our will.
>
> If this is so, however, I suspect it is because you have got away from the logical point of view altogether, and are thinking of some particular religious hypothesis which for you is dead. The freedom to "believe what we will" you apply to the case of some patent superstition; and the faith you think of is the faith defined by the schoolboy when he said: "Faith is when you believe something that you know ain't true."
>
> I can only repeat that this is a misapprehension of my position. The freedom to "believe what we will," for which I have been arguing, can only cover living options which the intellect by itself cannot resolve; and living options never seem absurd or superstitious to him who has them to consider.
>
> Where there is no such forced option, the dispassionately judicial intellect with no pet hypothesis, saving us, as it does, from dupery, at any rate, ought to be our ideal.

It would appear that James has only restated his difficulty. It is still open to anyone to point out: "Yes, what you have said, you have said. The point is, however, that what you have not said, you have not said. What about the man whose passional nature inclines him to embrace, as true, a proposition which is incompatible with one which your passional nature has inclined you to embrace? As between two passional natures having divergent inclinations, how do you decide?" A glance through the published letters of William James shows that he was mightily bothered by this point. Writing to his brother Henry, the novelist, he protests:

When I *say* that, *other things being equal*, the view of things that seems more satisfactory morally will legitimately be treated by men as truer than the view that seems less so, *they quote me as saying* that anything morally satisfactory can be treated as true, no matter how unsatisfactory it may be from the point of view of its consistency with what we already know or believe to be true about physical or natural facts, which is rot!!

Of course this is rot.   But the rot is on the side of James. So vague and ambiguous a phrase as "the view of things that seems more satisfactory morally" is in no better case than the phrase "demands of our passional nature."   It is a pinch of objectivity which his critics have been demanding. They could find none in "passional nature."   I suspect they found no more in "the view of things that seems satisfactory morally."   James has drawn a two-edged sword.   To vary the metaphor, his principle may be used to reinforce either theism or atheism, or for the matter of that, some third alternative equally removed from either, say skepticism or polytheism.   In the last analysis pragmatism merely reinforces the most deeply congenial belief; it does not state which belief is or ought to be the most congenial.   However, he is not done protesting.   Writing to an English philosopher, L. T. Hobhouse, he has much the same sort of thing to say:

Would to God I had never thought of that unhappy title for my essay.   What I meant by the title was the state of mind of the man who finds an impulse in him toward a believing attitude, and who resolves not to quench it simply because doubts of its truth are possible.   Its opposite would be the maxim: Believe in nothing which you can possibly doubt.

My essay hedged the license to indulge in private overbeliefs with so many restrictions and sign boards of danger that the outlet was narrow enough. It made of tolerance the essence of the situation. It defined the permissible cases. It treated the faith attitude as a necessity for individuals, because the total "evidence" which only the race can draw include their experiments among its data. It tended to show only that faith cannot be absolutely *vetoed*, as certain champions of "science" had claimed it ought to be.

I cry to heaven to tell me of what insane root my "leading contemporaries" have eaten, that they are so smitten with blindness as to the meaning of printed texts.

In my essay the evil shape was a vision of "Science" in the form of abstraction, priggishness and sawdust, lording it over all. Take the sterilest scientific prig and cad you know, compare him with the richest religious intellect you know, and you would not, any more than I would, give the former the exclusive right of way.

In these matters it is necessary to maintain a certain degree of detachment. One feels, readily enough, that James's "nature" would have led *him* to choose the "right hypothesis" for belief. But the world is full of persons who lack his powers of understanding. What about them? The root of this confusing problem lies, really, in James's initial skepticism. Following such traditions as Hume and Mill bespoke, James begins by admitting that reason is powerless to settle this question in natural theology; that there is no such thing as "rational" theology. From reason he turned to emotion. In this he resembled Pascal. And now he is attempting the somewhat difficult task of formulating a "reasonable" defense of his position. Once having thrown reason overboard, he might better have remained impervious to criticisms proceeding from persons who had, in fact, *not* made that initial concession.

There are two parts to any man's exposition of his ideas concerning God. In the first place, he should make clear why he believes that God exists. In the second, he should make clear what he conceives God's nature to be. In a phrase, the existence and nature of God. So far as God's existence goes, we know where James stands in this essay. "Why do I believe in God? Is it because I have experienced his presence? No; rather because I need it so that it must be true." Before quitting James and the whole question of natural theology, it is worth noting that he used his pragmatic principle to justify his belief in God's finiteness. Like Mill, and many other recent and contemporary theologians, James repudiated the celebrated "omni's" of traditional theology. His reasoning is much the same as Mill's.

I simply refuse to accept the idea of there being no purpose in the objective world. On the other hand, I cannot represent the existence of purpose except as based in a mind. The "not-me," therefore, so far as it contains purpose, must spring from a mind; but not necessarily a *One and Only* mind.

In saying God exists, all I imply is that my purposes are cared for by a mind so powerful as on the whole to control the drift of the universe. That is . . . merely a practical emotional faith.

The only difficulties of theism are the moral difficulties and meanness; and they have always seemed to me to flow from the gratuitous dogma of God being the all-inclusive reality. Once think possible a pluralism of which He may be one member, and piety forthwith ceases to be incompatible with manliness, and religious faith with intellectual rectitude.

In short, the only theism I defend is that of simple unphilosophic mankind. God, in the religious life of ordinary men is the name, not of the whole of things, heaven forbid, but only of the ideal tendency in things. . . . He works in an external environment, has limits, and has enemies. . . . If there be a God, how the devil can we know what difficulties he may have had to contend with? Possible difficulties! They save everything. But what are they if not limitations to the all-inclusiveness of any single being!

Having an environment, being in time, and working out a history just like ourselves, He escapes from the foreignness from all that is human, of the static, timeless, perfect absolute.

My God, being part of a pluralistic system, is responsible only for such things as He knows enough and has enough power to have accomplished. The "omniscient" and "omnipotent" God of theology I regard as a disease of the philosophy shop.

The line of least resistance, as it seems to me, both in theology and in philosophy, is to accept, along with the Superhuman Consciousness, the notion that It is not all embracing; the notion, in other words, that there is a God, but that He is finite, either in power or in knowledge, or in both at once.

READING REFERENCES. The best, the easiest, and the most continuously pleasing thing to do about William James is to read him. In so many respects, he is his own best commentary. The volume, *The Will to Believe and Other Essays*, from which this chapter has been largely drawn, is a delightful collection. But the time comes when one desires to know what other people think about an author whom one has read. The book here is Julius Bixler's *Religion in the Philosophy of William James*. The only complete account of James's life and times is to be found in R. B. Perry's two monumental volumes, *The Life and Thought of William James*. No one who once dips into this work will feel satisfied short of browsing through the whole of it. The chapter in which Perry gives an account of "The Will to Believe" will repay immediate perusal.

READING QUESTIONS

1. Can you trace the argument of natural theology from Aquinas through Pascal and Hume and Mill, to James?
2. What does James mean by an *hypothesis?*
3. How does he distinguish between a live and a dead hypothesis?
4. What does he mean by an *option?*
5. What by a living option? A forced option? A momentous option?
6. What by a genuine option?
7. Upon what principle does he propose to decide a genuine option which cannot be decided on intellectual (i.e., rational) grounds?

8. In what sense do moral questions present themselves for decision on this principle?
9. How does James state the religious hypothesis?
10. How does his statement make skepticism equivalent to denial?
11. Why does he proceed to develop the ethical case for skepticism?
12. What is the ethical case for skepticism?
13. Upon what grounds does he dismiss the skeptic finally?
14. Having disposed of the skeptic, what criticism does James turn to?
15. How does he deal with it?
16. Satisfactorily, do you think?
17. Having worked out the case for theism, on pragmatic grounds, why does James hold out for the conception of a limited deity?
18. Show how elements from Pascal and Mill are present in James.
19. Formulate one or more questions you would put to James.

TOPIC TWO. A METAPHYSICAL PROBLEM

One of the best-known remarks in the history of philosophy is ascribed to the Greek thinker, Thales. He is said to have held that "all things are made of water." On the face of it, this seems both unimportant and false. Whence its historical importance? Why has Thales been bracketed, along with Copernicus and Darwin, as having initiated a line of thought which marked an epoch in human speculation?

The reason is this. It required, in the first instance, a bold mind to conceive any proposition having the general form "All things are made of . . ."; because if there is one proposition which would appear to be justified by the facts of our everyday experience, it is that all things are not made of any one thing. Multiplicity and variety are the obvious facts about the everyday world. The effort of thought required to break down the testimony of the everyday world must have been considerable, as it certainly was subsequently fruitful.

Thales probably had his reasons. Such apparently diverse things as ice, snow, mist, vapor, steam are all "made of" water, if we use the term loosely. Why not other things too? Whatever his reasons may have been, his remark, once made, continued to re-echo in the minds of generations which came after him. "All things are made of . . ."

In fact, the problem is with us to this day. What are all things made of? What do we intend by the phrase *made of?* If we brush aside Thales' answer, what do we propose in place of it?   Speculations on this question constitute part of the general topic of metaphysics.   That is, metaphysics is, in part, an inquiry into the question what all things are "made of."

Suppose we consider a miscellaneous collection of things, a clay pipe, a bird's egg, a rainbow, a copy of *Hamlet*, an uprising in Central China, an act of mercy, a cry in the night, a new planet.   What are all these things made of?   Varying the words, to what common substance are these all reducible? Of what "underlying reality" are they all manifestations? Is this underlying reality itself further reducible?

The notion that the observed multiplicity and variety of the everyday world are reducible to something common and uniform and *not* given as part of the everyday world is not an unreasonable notion.   Few persons would care to deny it in principle, much as they might argue over what that something is to which all things are reducible.   Granted the propriety of the notion of an ultimate reality, it is necessary to go one step further.   In some sense or other, the everyday world is an appearance or a manifestation of it.   They are the appearances; it is the real.

It is then possible to restate our central problem: What is the nature of that ultimate reality of which the everyday world is but the appearance?

Answers to this question vary.   If it is held that there is *an* ultimate reality, we have what is called *monism* in metaphysics, the belief that ultimate reality is one in kind.   If it is held that there are at least two ultimate realities, we have what is called *dualism* in metaphysics, the belief that ultimate reality is two in kind.   If it is held that there are three or more ultimate realities, we have what is called *pluralism* in metaphysics, the belief that ultimate reality is three or more in kind.

Within these classifications others will occur.   You and I

might agree that monism is a true belief. Our agreement might extend no further. When we came to the question of the nature of this ultimate reality, we might differ. I might claim that it was matter; you might claim that it was mind; a third person might claim that it was neither, but something more ultimate of which both matter and mind are manifestations.

In this topic we are to be concerned with such inquiries. A metaphysical hypothesis is any belief about the nature of ultimate reality. In considering any such hypothesis, it will be helpful to ask: What is the belief? Is it a form of monism, or dualism, or pluralism? What reasons are given, or may be given, in support of it? What reasons against it? What consequences follow from it? Do these agree with common sense? Or do they make nonsense of it? Reflection upon the nature of ultimate reality is not the whole of metaphysics, but it is a large part of it. For a beginner in metaphysics, two things are of primary importance: to demand reasons for accepting any hypothesis, and to note consequences which follow from accepting the hypothesis.

The readings and comments which follow are grouped, in an historical way, around the problem stated above. They provide material for thinking about this problem, comparable to the readings and comments grouped around the theological problem in the sections which preceded. There are five sets of them: two from the seventeenth century (Descartes and Hobbes), one from the eighteenth century (Berkeley), one from the nineteenth century (Schopenhauer), and one from the twentieth century (James). These men have been chosen because, among them, they provide a varied gallery in which to roam. No two are alike. Each is convinced of his views and eager to spread them among "all rational minds." Each is a competent metaphysician in the sense that he realizes he must be prepared to argue his case. There is, among them, no appeal to emotions; at least, not intentionally. They are all, in this respect, "hardheaded rationalists." Here, for the eye which can detect it, is man's supreme intellectual sport insofar as he is a "rational" animal. Here are corrosive skepticism, caustic (if obscure) wit, resounding thwacks, closely built arguments, relentless determination to "begin at the beginning" and "think it through," and proud gestures directing attention to "positions established" and "positions overthrown." A taste for metaphysics and a flare for the practice of metaphysics are not widely diffused, but the genuine article, like a love for poetry or painting, is irrepressible once it has had a chance to take root.

The readings which follow are in chronological order, but the chronological order itself exhibits an interesting development. Conceive each of these five authors confronted with the inquiry: What is the nature of ultimate reality? The answer of Descartes is the most conventional. Reality consists of three substances, namely, God, human souls, and matter. The position taken up by Hobbes represents a selection of one of the elements argued for by Descartes. All things, runs the argument, are matter: materialism, as full blown as one could wish it. The position taken up by Berkeley represents a deliberate reaction from Hobbes's materialism. All things, runs the argument here, are mind or spirit. Hobbes's materialism and Berkeley's idealism, between them, account for an enormous amount of modern metaphysics. The term *voluntarism*, associated with Schopenhauer in metaphysics, covers the conviction that neither matter nor spirit but "will" is the ultimate substance, the ultimately real stuff, of which all things are merely manifestations. James's "pragmatic" approach to metaphysics with which this series concludes, represents an attempt to do two things: to formulate a radically new type of argument for metaphysical beliefs, and to place this type of argument at the disposal of James's own beliefs.

1. DUALISM AND ITS IMPLICATIONS — FROM RENÉ DESCARTES

In point of time, and with respect to content, one's acquaintance with modern metaphysics cannot begin more profitably than with the speculations of René Descartes. This, for two reasons: He lived in a "climate of opinion" which is still widely prevalent, despite the lapse of three centuries, and hence brings to his task the presuppositions which most persons still possess; and he has served as the point of departure for almost all metaphysicians since his day.

BIOGRAPHICAL NOTE. Descartes was born in France in 1596 and died in Sweden in 1650 at the age of fifty-four. His biography reveals three periods: years of education, years of wandering and learning, and years of maturity and production.

1. Descartes' formal education, from eight to sixteen, was received at the Jesuit college of La Flêche. Here he acquired the essentials of a "gentleman's education," a deposit which he subsequently devoted much time to erasing. Before he had turned seventeen he put aside his books and after a few lessons in fencing and horsemanship went to "the great world of Paris." Here he remained for about five years, living at first the usual life of gaiety and gambling, but retiring after a while to the quiet and seclusion of an obscure lodging house. His thoughtful temper reasserted itself. Habits of reflection acquired at La Flêche, and roused once more by a Catholic friend, one Father Mersenne, took possession of him again.

(2) In 1618 Descartes left Paris, determined to see the world. These were his true *wanderjahren*. He became a soldier, serving in three different European armies, in the Netherlands, in Bavaria, and in Hungary. It was a life which gave him much time for thought during the long months of idleness in winter quarters. He stuck to soldiering for three or four years, then resolved "no longer to carry a musket." Army days over, he continued his travels for five or six years more,

visiting Switzerland and Italy, until, in 1628, he decided that he had read enough in the "great book of the world."

(3) In 1629, his mind crowded with ideas demanding to be written down in books and essays and correspondence, he settled in Holland.   He was seeking quiet and seclusion once more, but this time in earnest.   His European retirement, as he called it, lasted twenty years.   These were the years of fruitful production.   Book followed book.   His reputation spread.   He had the intellectuals of his generation for his readers, and its rulers for his patrons and friends.   In rapid succession he wrote his *Quest for Truth*, his *Rules for the Direction of the Mind*, his *Discourse on Method*, his *Meditations on First Philosophy*, his *Principles of Philosophy*, his *Treatise on the Passions*, and many other volumes which soon became stock in trade for the philosophically minded of his day.   In 1649 he was invited by Queen Christina of Sweden to visit her at Stockholm and expound the principles of the "new philosophy."   After much hesitation, and against the advice of his friends, he agreed to go.   It cost him his life, for he caught a cold in his lungs which brought about his death within the following year.

THE ARGUMENT OF THE CITATIONS.   The following citations are taken for the most part from Descartes' little book *Meditations on First Philosophy*.   The thought of these six short soliloquies might be paraphrased as follows: I was given the usual gentlemen's education in my youth.   Presently I became skeptical of most of what had been taught me. Accordingly, I determined to abandon all my learning and begin again with a clean slate upon which no one but myself should write, and upon which nothing should be written that was not luminously clear and distinct to my mind.   I needed, as a starting point, something which could stand against all possible skepticism.   To that end I set about the cultivation of systematic doubt.   My doubts were brought to

an abrupt cessation at the fact of my own existence. The
fact that I was doubting entailed necessarily my own existence as a doubter.   From this indubitandum my reconstruction must proceed.   Could I use the fact of my own existence
to prove the existence of anything else?   Two great steps
were in order: to demonstrate the existence of God and the
existence of the material world.   The steps by which I
moved from doubts about things taught me at school, through
an elaborate process of systematic doubt to the demonstrated
existence of myself, God, and the external world, constitute
the theme of these *Meditations*.

The first group of citations puts one in possession of the
autobiographical facts with which Descartes wishes to begin.

I had been nourished on letters since my childhood, and since I
was given to believe that by their means a clear and certain knowledge could be obtained of all that is useful in life, I had an extreme
desire to acquire instruction.

But as soon as I had achieved the entire course of study at the
close of which one is usually received into the ranks of the learned,
I entirely changed my opinion.   I found myself embarrassed with so
many doubts and errors that it seemed to me that the effort to instruct myself had no effect other than the increasing discovery of
my own ignorance.   And yet I was studying at one of the most
celebrated schools in Europe, where I thought there must be men of
learning if such were to be found anywhere in the world.

I learned there all that others had learned.   Moreover, not being
satisfied with the sciences that we were taught, I even read through
all books which fell into my hands, treating of what is considered
most curious and rare.   Along with this, I knew the judgments
which others had formed of me, and I did not feel that I was esteemed inferior to my fellow students.   And finally, our century
seemed to me as flourishing, and as fertile in great minds, as any
which had preceded it.

These reflections combined to make me take the liberty of judging
all others by myself, and of coming to the conclusion that there

was no learning in the world such as I had formerly believed it to be.

That is why, as soon as age permitted me to emerge from the control of my tutors, I entirely quitted the study of letters. I resolved to seek no other knowledge than that which could be found in myself, or at least in the great book of the world. I employed the rest of my youth in travel, in seeing courts and armies, in intercourse with men of diverse temperaments and conditions, in collecting varied experiences, in testing myself in the various predicaments in which I was placed by fortune. In all circumstances I sought to bring my mind to bear on the things that came before it so that I might derive some profit from my experience.

For nine years I did nothing but roam hither and thither, trying to be a spectator rather than an actor in all the comedies which the world displays. Especially did I ask myself, in each matter that came before me, whether anything could make it subject to suspicion or doubt.

I considered the manners and customs of other men, and found nothing to give me settled convictions. I remarked in them almost as much diversity as I had formerly seen in the opinions of philosophies. So much was this so, that I learned to believe nothing too certainly of which I had been convinced only by example and custom. I thus concluded that it is much more custom and example that persuade us than any certain knowledge. And this despite the fact that the voice of the majority affords no proof of any value in matters a little difficult to discover. Such truths are like to have been discovered by one man, more than by a nation. But I could not, however, put my finger on a single person whose opinions seemed preferable to those of others.

I found I was constrained, so to speak, to undertake the direction of my own inquiries.

As regards all the opinions which, up to that time, I had embraced, I thought I could not do better than try once for all to sweep them completely away. Later on they might be replaced, either by others which were better, or by the same when I had made them conform to the uniformity of a rational scheme. I firmly believed that by this means I should succeed much better than if I had built on foundations and principles of which I had allowed myself to be persuaded in youth without having inquired into their truth. My design has never extended beyond trying to reform my own opinions and to build on a foundation which is entirely my own.

I was not seeking to imitate the skeptics, who only doubt for the sake of doubting and pretend always to be uncertain. On the contrary, my design was only to provide myself with good ground for assurance, to reject the quicksand and the mud in order to find the rock or clay.

These remarks give us the terms of his self-imposed task. It was twofold. On the one hand, to work himself free from the tangled mass of belief and opinion which he had accepted as part of a normal education; on the other, to avoid the flippant shallowness of the merely disillusioned skeptic. The execution of this design called for a deliberately formulated procedure. This Descartes outlines:

Like one who walks alone and in the twilight, I resolved to go slowly, to use so much circumspection that even if my advance was very small at least I guarded myself from falling. I did not wish to reject any opinion finally until I had planned out the task I had undertaken, and until I had sought out the true method of arriving at a knowledge of the things of which my mind was capable.

In my younger days I had studied logic and geometry and algebra — three sciences which, it seemed, ought to contribute something to the design I had in view.

But, in examining them, I observed in respect to logic, that syllogisms and the rest served better to explain those things which one already knows than to learn something new. As to geometry and algebra, they embrace only the most abstract matters, such as appear to have no actual use. This made me feel that some other method must be found exempt from their fault. So, in place of the many precepts of which logic is composed, and the many rules and formulae of which mathematics is composed, I settled on four rules for the direction of the understanding.

My first rule was to accept nothing as true which I did not clearly recognize to be so; to accept nothing more than what was presented to my mind so clearly and distinctly that I could have no occasion to doubt it. The second rule was to divide each problem or difficulty into as many parts as possible. The third rule was to commence my reflections with objects which were the simplest and easiest to understand, and rise thence, little by little, to knowledge of the most complex. The fourth rule was to make enumerations so complete, and reviews so general, that I should be certain to have omitted nothing.

Those long chains of reasoning which geometricians make had caused me to imagine that all parts of human knowledge might be mutually related in the same fashion; and that, provided we abstain from receiving anything as true which is not so, and always deduce one conclusion from some other, there can be nothing so remote that we cannot reach it, nor so recondite that we cannot discover it.

But what pleased me most, in this method which I was determined to follow, was that I was certain by its means to exercise my reason in all things; if not perfectly, at least as well as was in my power. I felt that, in making use of it, my mind would gradually accustom itself to think about its objects more accurately and distinctly.

The first of the above rules is perhaps the important one: to accept nothing as true which he did not clearly recognize to be so. It is one thing to lay this rule down. It is another to abide by it. The difficulty is in knowing where to start searching for one indubitable fact. But, the search is under way.

. . . it is necessary for me to reject as false everything as to which I can imagine the least ground of doubt, in order to see if anything remains that is entirely certain. So I set myself seriously and freely to the general upheaval of all my former opinions.

To that end it is not requisite that I examine each opinion in particular. That would be an endless undertaking. Owing, however, to the fact that the destruction of the foundations brings with it the downfall of the rest of the edifice, I shall only attack those principles upon which all my former opinions rested.

All that up to the present time I have accepted as most true and certain I have learned either from the senses or through the senses. But it is sometimes proved to me that these senses are deceptive. And it is wiser not to trust entirely to anything by which we have once been deceived.

But it may be objected that, although the senses sometimes deceive us concerning things which are hardly perceptible or are very far away, there are yet many things as to which we cannot reasonably have any doubt although we recognize them by their means. For example, there is the fact that I am here, seated by the fire, attired in a dressing gown, having this paper in my hand. And how could I deny that these hands and this body are mine?

At the same time I must remember that I am in the habit of sleeping, and in my dreams representing to myself the same things. How often has it happened that I dreamt I was in this particular place, dressed and seated near the fire, while in reality I was lying undressed in bed. On many occasions I have in sleep been deceived by similar illusions. In thinking carefully about this fact, I see that there are manifestly no certain indications by which we may clearly distinguish wakefulness from sleep.

Suppose we assume, then, that we are asleep; that all these particulars, e.g., opening our eyes, shaking our head, extending our hand, are but false delusions; that possibly neither our hands nor our body are such as they appear to us to be.

There is a point, however, which we must not overlook. We must admit that the things which are represented to us in sleep are like painted representations which can only have been formed as the counterparts of something real and true, i.e., not illusory. It would follow from this admission that those general things at least, i.e., eyes, head, hands, body, are not imaginary things but things really existent.

We are bound, at the same time, to confess that there are some objects yet more simple and universal than eyes, a head, a body, etc., namely, colors, shapes, size, number, etc., which are real and true. For, whether I am awake or asleep, red is not blue, two and three make five, squares have only four sides, and so on. It does not seem possible that truths so clear can be suspected of any falsity.

Nevertheless, I have long had fixed in my mind the belief that an all-powerful God existed by whom I have been created such as I am. But how do I know that He has not brought it to pass that there is no earth, no heaven, no extended body, no magnitude, no place; and that, nonetheless, I possess perceptions of all these things which seem to me to exist just exactly as I now see them?

It might be urged against this suggestion that God has not desired that I should be thus deceived. For is He not said to be supremely good? However, if it is contrary to His goodness to have made me such that I am constantly deceived, it would also seem to be contrary to His goodness to permit me to be sometimes deceived; and yet it cannot be denied that He does permit this.

Against the suggestion that I may be constantly deceived by God in the matter of what my senses tell me, I see no conclusive objection. In the end I feel constrained to admit that there is nothing, in all that I formerly believed to be true, of which I cannot in some measure doubt, not merely through want of thought or through facetiousness, but for reasons which are very powerful and maturely considered.

I shall suppose, then, that God, who is supremely good and the fountain of truth, is in reality some evil genius not less powerful than deceitful, employing His whole energies to deceive me. I shall consider that the heavens, the earth, colors, shapes, sounds, and all other external things, are nothing but illusions and dreams by which this evil genius has laid traps for my credulity. I shall consider myself as having no hands, no eyes, no flesh, no blood, nor any senses; yet falsely believing myself to possess all these things. I shall remain obstinately attached to this idea. If, by this means, it is not in my power to arrive at the knowledge of any truth, I may at least do what is in my power, namely, suspend judgment, and thus avoid belief in anything false and avoid being imposed upon by this arch deceiver, however powerful and deceptive He may be.

Determined to "doubt everything," until doubt becomes impossible of being pushed further, Descartes has had recourse to heroic measures. The senses have been discredited, and with them the credibility of the external world revealed by the senses. This, one might have thought, would have sufficed. But assurance must be made doubly sure. Hence the ingenious hypothesis of an omnipotent and malignant Deity. At this point the eagerly sought *indubitandum* begins to appear over the horizon.

I suppose, then, that all the things that I see are false. I persuade myself that nothing has ever existed of all that my fallacious memory represents to me. I consider that I possess no senses. I imagine that body, figure, extension, motion, and place are but the fictions of my mind. What, then, can be esteemed as true? Perhaps nothing at all, unless that there is nothing in the world that is certain.

But immediately I notice that while I wish to think all things false, it is nonetheless absolutely essential that I, who wish to think this, should truly exist. There is a powerful and cunning deceiver who employs his ingenuity in misleading me? Let it be granted. It follows the more that I exist, if he deceives me. If I did not exist, he could not deceive me. This truth, "I think, therefore I am; *cogito, ergo sum*," is so certain, so assured, that all the most extravagant scepticism is incapable of shaking it. This truth, "I am, I exist," I can receive without scruple as the first principle of the philosophy for which I am seeking.

I think, therefore I am. But what am I? I do not yet know; and hence I must be careful lest I imprudently take some other object in place of myself and thus go astray in respect of this knowledge which I hold to be the most certain of all that I formerly believed.

What then did I formerly believe myself to be? I considered myself as having a face, hands, arms, and all that system of members which I designate by the name of body. In addition to this, I considered that I was nourished, that I walked, that I felt, and that I thought.

But what am I, now that I assume that there is an evil and malicious genius who employs all his powers to deceive me? Can I affirm, with as much certainty as I can affirm my existence, that I possess any of the least of all those things which I have just now ascribed to myself? I pause to consider. I resolve all these things in my mind. I find none of the bodily attributes which I can ascribe to myself.

What of thinking? I find that thought alone is an attribute which cannot be separated from me. I am, I exist; that is certain. But this certainty reposes on the "I think" which preceded. I am trying here not to admit anything which is not necessarily true. To speak thus strictly, I am nothing more than a thing which thinks, that is, to say, a mind, an understanding. I am a real thing. I really exist. But what am I? I have answered: a thing which thinks.

I am a thing which thinks. And what more? What is a thing which thinks? It is a thing which doubts, understands, conceives, affirms, denies, wills, refuses, imagines, feels. Certainly it is no small matter if all these things pertain to my nature.

But why should they not so pertain? Am I not that being who now doubts nearly everything, who nevertheless understands certain things, who affirms that only one thing is true, who denies all other things, who desires to know more, who is averse from being deceived, who imagines many things, who perceives many things? Is there, in all this, anything which is less than that I exist? Indeed, it is so evident that it is I who doubts, who understands, who desires, and so on, that there is no reason here to add anything to explain it. From this time I begin to know what I am with a little more clearness and distinctness than before.

The argument begins to move rapidly now. Doubt has been explored and exploited. Self has been isolated as the single indubitable fact. The nature of self, a thinking thing, has been noted. Can this be used as a steppingstone? Does the fact of himself and his thoughts imply any other fact?

I shall now close my eyes; I shall stop my ears. I shall call away all my senses. I shall efface from my thoughts all images of material things — or, since that is hardly possible — I shall esteem them as vain and false. Thus holding converse only with my self, and considering my own nature, I shall try to reach a better knowledge of what I am.

I am a thing which thinks; that is to say, that doubts, affirms, denies, knows, is ignorant, wills, desires, imagines, perceives. For, as I remarked before, although the things which I perceive and imagine are perhaps nothing apart from me, yet the perceptions and imaginings certainly reside in me. And in the little that I have just said, I think I have summed up all that I really know, or was hitherto aware that I knew. To extend my knowledge further, I shall look around more carefully and see whether I cannot still discover in myself some other things which I have not hitherto perceived.

I am certain that I am a thing which thinks. But if I am indeed certain of this I must know what is requisite to render me certain of anything. I must possess a standard of certainty. In this first knowledge which I have gained, what is there that assures me of its truth? Nothing except the clear and distinct perception of what I state. This, indeed, would not suffice to assure me that what I state is true if it could ever happen that I should clearly and distinctly perceive to be true something which was in fact false. Accordingly, I can establish as a general rule that all things which I perceive very clearly and very distinctly are true.

All things which I perceive very clearly and very distinctly, are true. If I have heretofore judged that such matters could be doubted, it was because it came into my mind that perhaps a God might have endowed me with such a nature that I might have been deceived even concerning things which seemed to me most manifest. I see no reason to believe that there is a God who is a deceiver; however, as yet I have not satisfied myself that there is a God at all.

I must inquire whether there is a God. And, if I find that there is a God, I must also inquire whether He may be a deceiver. For, without a knowledge of these two truths, I do not see that I can ever be certain of anything.

Now, it is obvious that there must be at least as much reality in any cause as in its effect. For whence could the effect derive its reality, if not from its cause? From this it follows that something cannot proceed from nothing; and that the more or the greater cannot proceed from the less.

The longer and more carefully I investigate these matters, the more clearly and distinctly do I perceive their truth. But what may I conclude from it all, finally? It is this: If I have any ideas which I myself cannot be the cause of, it follows of necessity that I am not alone in the world, that there is some other being which exists as the cause of this idea. Have I any such idea?

There is the idea of God. Is this idea something that could have originated in, been caused by, me? By the name *God* I understand a being that is infinite, eternal, immutable, independent, all-knowing, all-powerful, by which I myself and everything else (if anything else does exist) have been created.

Now, all these qualities are such that the more diligently I attend to them, the less do they appear capable of originating in me alone. Hence, from what was premised above, we must conclude that God necessarily exists as the origin of this idea I have of Him. For, to consider but one point, the idea of a being or a substance is within me owing to the fact that I am myself a being or substance; nevertheless, I would not have the idea of an infinite being, since I am myself finite, unless it had proceeded from some being who was infinite.

I see nothing in all that I have just said which, by the light of nature, is not manifest to anyone who desires to think attentively on the subject. It only remains to examine into the manner in which I have acquired this idea from God.

I have not received it through the senses; nor is it a fiction of my mind, for it is not in my power to take from or add to it. The only alternative is that it is innate in me, just as the idea of myself is innate in me.

It is not strange that God, in creating me, placed this idea within me to be like the mark of the workman imprinted on his work. For, from the fact that God created me it is most probable that He has placed His image and similitude upon me. The whole strength of the argument which I have here used to prove the existence of God consists in this: It is not possible that my nature should be what it is, and that I should have in myself the idea of a God, if God did not exist. God, whose idea is in me, possesses all those supreme perfections of which our mind may have some idea but without understanding them all; is liable to no errors or defects, and has none of those marks which denote imperfection. From this it is manifest that He cannot be a deceiver, since fraud and deception proceed from some defect.

Before I pass on to the consideration of other truths which may be derived from this one, it seems to me right to pause for a while to contemplate God Himself, to ponder at leisure His marvelous attributes, to consider and to admire and to adore the beauty of His light. Faith teaches us that supreme felicity of the life to come consists in this contemplation of the Divine Majesty. Even so we continue to learn by experience that a similar meditation, though less perfect, causes us to enjoy the greatest satisfaction of which we are capable in this life.

Disillusionment. Systematic doubt. Existence of self as a thinking thing. Existence of God, no longer the deceiving genius of the early part of the argument. There remains only the external world, revealed by the senses. Can this be re-instated? Can its existence be shown to be part of the net-work, inextricably bound up with his own and Deity's nature and existence?

And so I see that the certainty and truth of all knowledge depends alone upon the knowledge of the true God. Before I knew Him, I could not have a perfect knowledge of any other thing. Now that I know Him I have the means of acquiring a perfect knowledge of an infinitude of things.

Nothing further now remains but to inquire whether material things exist. And first of all I shall recall those matters which I hitherto held to be true, as having perceived them through the senses; in the next place I shall examine the reasons which have since obliged me to place them in doubt; and in the last place I shall consider which of them I must now believe.

First of all, I perceived that I had a head, hands, feet, and all other members of which this body is composed. Further, I was sensible that this body was placed amid many others. In them, in addition to extension, figure, and motion, I remarked hardness, heat, light, color, scents, sounds, and so forth.

Considering the ideas of all these qualities which presented themselves to my mind, it was not without reason that I believed myself to perceive objects quite different from my thought, to wit, bodies from which those ideas proceeded. For I found by experience that these ideas of all these qualities presented themselves to me without my consent being needed. Thus, I could not perceive any object unless it were present to the organs of sense; nor could I help but perceive it, when it was present.

Furthermore, because these ideas which I received through my senses were clearer, more lively, more distinct, than any ideas I could myself frame in meditation or find in memory, it appeared as though they could not have proceeded from my mind. So, therefore, I concluded that they must have been produced in me by some other things. And, since I had no knowledge of these objects except the knowledge which the ideas themselves gave me, nothing was more likely to occur to my mind than that the objects themselves were similar to the ideas which were caused.

But afterwards many experiences destroyed, little by little, all the faith which I had rested in my senses. For example, I observed that towers, which from afar appeared to me to be round, seemed square when more closely observed; that colossal statues seemed quite tiny when viewed from a distance; that persons whose legs or arms had been cut off seemed to feel pain in the part which had been amputated; that my dreams, which could not be caused by outside objects, closely resembled my waking moments; and so on.

Now, however, that I begin to know myself better ("I am a thing which thinks") and to discover more clearly the author of my being, I do not think I should rashly admit all the things which the senses seem to teach me, nor do I think that I should doubt them all universally.

This much is certain, i.e., clear and distinct: There is in me the capacity to receive and recognize the ideas of sensible things. The active cause of these ideas which I passively receive cannot be in me, since those ideas are often produced in me without my contributing in any way to the same, often even against my will. It follows that the power which produces these ideas resides in some substance different from me. This substance is either a material object or God or some other creature.

But, I have argued already, God is no deceiver. He has given me a very great inclination to believe that my ideas of sensible objects are sent or conveyed to me by external material objects. I do not see how He could be defended from the accusation of deceit if these ideas were produced in me by any cause other than material objects. Hence we must allow that material objects exist.

Descartes' meditations have brought him the full circle. It is well to remember that he wrote in the seventeenth century. The significance attaching to Descartes' thinking lies in the gesture of impatience and sincerity with which he seeks to abandon old traditions and to start over again. The full weight of the Middle Ages was pressing upon him from the past. The rising sun of the new sciences and new world was beckoning him toward the future. A clean break with the past seemed required. The *Meditations* were an attempt to see what ideas of the past must be allowed for by the future.

READING REFERENCES. There is little point in trying to read an entire book on Descartes at this stage. Much of what he himself wrote is dated; however, there are some valuable secondary items. Short of attempting a thorough study of Descartes and his influence on later speculation, one does best to concentrate on the few ideas presented in the little books from which the citations in this chapter were taken, his *Meditations* and his *Discourse on Method*. These are still readable in their entirety. An old volume by a German historian of philosophy, Kuno Fischer, translated into English under the title *Descartes and His School*, is lively and interesting. In T. H. Huxley's volume of essays, *Method and Results*, there is a good study of Descartes as a thinker.

READING QUESTIONS

It cannot be repeated too often: Descartes repays study. Master him, and you are in a fair way to proceed to other thinkers. Study his way of thinking. It is typical of most others. Be sure that no turn in his total argument goes unnoticed.

1. Why did he quit the study of letters?
2. What did he thereupon resolve to do?
3. How did this lead him to the necessity of cultivating skepticism?
4. What four rules did he formulate for the direction of the understanding?
5. How does doubting his senses fail to carry him far enough?
6. What hypothesis concerning God does he introduce at this point?
7. What indubitandum does this lead him to? How?
8. "*Cogito, ergo sum.*" Explain.
9. How does he proceed from "self" to God?
10. Why could he not have recourse, at this point, to the design argument in natural theology?
11. How does he proceed from God to the external world?
12. Descartes is sometimes described as a "rationalist." What propositions express his unbounded faith in reasoning?
13. Formulate two or more problems you would put to Descartes.

2. MATERIALISM AND ITS IMPLICATIONS — FROM THOMAS HOBBES

FROM DESCARTES TO HOBBES. The problem we have been considering is stated in the question: What is the nature of ultimate reality? We have seen Descartes' answer. This, one suspects, is the metaphysics which is most congenial to the unsophisticated person. But not all men are unsophisticated in these things. There have therefore been several alternative metaphysical positions. One of the most familiar of these is a straight materialism: the belief, namely, that reality consists of particles of matter moving in space and time according to necessary laws. This metaphysical hypothesis came early to the fore, in the seventeenth century. and allowing for a certain quaintness of language, it has never received a more wholehearted exposition than is to be found in the pages of Thomas Hobbes, contemporary and friend and critic of Descartes.

BIOGRAPHICAL NOTE. Thomas Hobbes was born in England in 1588 and died in 1679 at the age of ninety-one. During a long and busy life he was a close student of revolutionary politics and the new physical sciences. His life's work was a sustained attempt to formulate a philosophy which, he felt, would be more adequate to the new times than either the medieval traditions persisting from St. Thomas and others or the somewhat compromising position adopted by Descartes and his followers. The story of his own life is crowded with interest, but it is a reflected interest arising largely out of the stirring times through which he lived. He was educated at Oxford. Thereafter he became tutor and secretary to the Earl of Devonshire. In this capacity he made the acquaintance of Francis Bacon, Ben Jonson, and other literary figures. He published a translation of Thucydides. When his patron died, Hobbes took over the education of his son with whom he took the Grand Tour, making the acquaintance of Galileo, Gassendi, and other scientific luminaries on the Continent. He returned to England to study politics. It was the time of England's civil war against Charles I. Hobbes was Royalist, siding against Cromwell. Circulation of his book, *The Body Politic*, obliged him to leave England and reside in Paris. This time he met Descartes and engaged him in metaphysical controversy. The exiled Prince of Wales, afterwards Charles II, was also in Paris. Hobbes became his tutor. He published again on the subject of politics, this time rousing the wrath of some of the Royalists. He returned to England and enjoyed such peace as obtained under Cromwell's regime, making friends with William Harvey, who discovered the circulation of the blood, with the poet Cowley, and others. Upon the restoration of Charles II to the English throne, Hobbes moved

once more to a place in the sun and on the pension list. He
was one of the most influential men of his day among persons
who were open to ideas. There is not space to outline his
position in seventeenth-century thought, but this much may
be summarized: He believed that matter is the ultimate
reality; that our sense organs are transformers, not revealers;
that man does not have a free will; that all human action is
motivated by complete selfishness; that an absolute sovereign
is needed, whether in the form of a monarch or a parliament,
to insure peace under law; and that religion is a "pill which
it is better to swallow without chewing."

THE ARGUMENT OF THE CITATIONS. The following citations
give a simple formulation of metaphysical materialism. From
a statement of the essential point, that all is matter moving
according to laws, the quotations follow Hobbes through the
principal turns of his belief. They present a development
and, in some cases, a defense of the implications of the fundamental belief. It should be remembered that Hobbes is
writing here as a philosopher, not as a scientist. In the strict
sense of the word, he was not a scientist, either by temperament or training. He is, where it is relevant, restating or
referring to the labors of Copernicus, Kepler, Galileo, Harvey,
and the rest. But the point of his writings, in effect, is this:
If what such men are finding out, is once accepted without
reservation, then over all we are committed to these more
comprehensive beliefs.

Think not, courteous reader, that the philosophy which I am
going to set in order is that which makes philosophers' stones. It
is the natural reason of man, busily flying up and down among the
creatures, and bringing back a true report of their order, causes,
and effects. Philosophy is therefore the child of the world and your
own mind. Like the world, its father, as it was in the beginning,
it is a thing confused. If you will be a philosopher in good earnest,
let your reason move upon the deep of your own cogitations and

experience; those things that lie in confusion must be set in order, distinguished, and stamped everyone with its own name.

Philosophy excludes theology, I mean the doctrine of God. It excludes the doctrine of angels and also such things as are neither bodies nor properties of bodies. It excludes history, natural as well as political, because such knowledge is but experience or authority and not reason. It excludes astrology and all such divinations. It excludes all such knowledge as is acquired by divine inspiration, or revelation, as not derived to us by reason but by some supernatural sense. Lastly it excludes the doctrine of God's worship as being not to be known by the light of natural reason but by the authority of the church.

I am not ignorant how hard a thing it is to weed out of men's minds inveterate opinions that have taken root there, and been confirmed by the authority of eloquent writers; especially since true philosophy rejects the paint and false colors, the ornaments and graces, of language. The first grounds of knowledge are not only not beautiful; they are poor and arid, and, in appearance, deformed. Nevertheless, there being some men who are delighted with truth and strength of reason, I thought I might do well to take these pains for the sake of even those few. I proceed therefore and take my beginning from the definition of philosophy.

With these preliminary observations, Hobbes closes in on his theme:

The subject of philosophy is every body [i.e., piece of matter] of which we can conceive any beginning, which we can compare with other bodies, or which is capable of composition and resolution; that is to say, every body of whose beginning or properties we can have any knowledge.

The definition of body may be this: a body is that which, having no dependence upon our thought, is coincident or coextended with some part of space.

The world — I mean the whole mass of things that are — is corporeal, that is to say, body; and that which is not body is no part of the universe. . . . The universe being the aggregate of all bodies, there is no real part thereof that is not also body.

The basic thesis once stated, Hobbes moves on to a series of implications, that is, propositions which follow from the fundamental position. The first of these is that <u>motion is the one thing that "really" takes place</u>; all else is mere appearance, thrown off, so to speak, by matter in motion.

There can be no cause of motion except in a body contiguous and moved.

Mutation, that is, change, can be nothing but motion of the parts of that body which is changed. We say that that which appears to our senses is otherwise than it appeared formerly. Both appearances are effects produced in the sentient creature; and, if they be different, it is necessary that some part of the agent which was formerly at rest is now moved, and so the mutation consists in the motion; or some part which was formerly moved, is now otherwise moved, and so the mutation consists in this new motion; or which, being formerly moved, is now at rest, and so again mutation is motion.

A second corollary is <u>rigid determinism, that is, the belief that everything happens of necessity, or inevitably</u>.

Whatever effect is produced at any time, the same is produced by a necessary cause. For whatsoever is produced had an entire cause, had all those things which, being supposed, it cannot be understood but that the effect follows; that is, it had a necessary cause. In the same manner, whatsoever effects are hereafter to be produced, shall have a necessary cause, so that all the effects that have been or shall be produced have their necessity in things antecedent.

From this determinism it would follow that, given enough knowledge of the past and present one could predict all future events in the greatest detail. Hobbes is aware of this claim. It has been made, off and on, ever since his time. Better than a century later the French astronomer, LaPlace, wrote:

We ought to regard the present state of the universe as the effect of its antecedent state and as the cause of the state that is to follow. <u>An intelligence, who for a given instant should be acquainted with</u>

all the forces by which nature is animated, and with the several positions of the beings composing it, if his intellect were vast enough to submit these data to analysis, would include in one and the same formula the movement of the largest bodies in the universe and those of the lightest atom. Nothing would be uncertain for him, the future as well as the past would be present to his eyes.

Before resuming the elaboration of his views, Hobbes pays his lip service to natural theology:

He that from any effect he seeth come to pass, should reason to the next and immediate cause thereof, and from thence to the cause of that cause, and plunge himself profoundly into the pursuit of causes, shall come at last to this, that there must be, as even the heathen philosophers confessed, one first mover, one first cause of things which is that which men mean by the name of God.

Having disposed of that, Hobbes turns back to the more congenial task of noting further implications of his materialism. All living organisms, it would follow, are just so many complicated machines:

Seeing that life is but a motion of limbs and organs, why may we not say that all automata (engines that move themselves by springs and wheels as doth a watch) have an artificial life? For what is the heart but a spring, and the nerves but so many strings, and the joints but so many wheels, giving motion to the whole body?

Hobbes continues. Materialism in metaphysics, he urges, implies sensationism in epistemology; implies, that is, that all knowledge originates in sensations.

The original of men's thoughts is sense, for there is no conception in a man's mind which hath not, totally or by parts, been begotten upon the organs of sense. The rest are derived from that original.

As I said before, whatsoever we conceive, hath been perceived first by sense, either all at once or by parts. A man can have no thought representing anything, not subject to sense.

Imagination is nothing but decaying sense. From whence it

followeth that the longer the time is after the sense, the weaker is the imagination.

Imagination being only of those things which have been formerly perceived by sense, it followeth that imagination and memory are but one thing which for divers considerations hath diverse names.

Materialism. Determinism. Mechanism. Sensationism. And now the doctrine of representative perception, that is, the belief that sensations represent but do not reveal the real nature of the external world. Hobbes labors this point at great length.

The cause of sense is the external object which presseth the organ proper to each sense either immediately or mediately. This pressure, by the mediation of the nerves and other strings and membranes, continues inward and causeth there a reaction or counter-pressure; which endeavor because outward, seemeth to be some matter without. This seeming is that which men call sense; and consisteth, as to the eye, in a light or colored figure; to the ear, in a sound; and so on. All which qualities, called sensible qualities, are, in the object that causeth them only so many several motions of the matter by which it presseth our organs diversely. Neither in us that are pressed, are they anything else but divers motions; for motion produceth nothing but motion. For if these sensible qualities (colors, sounds) were in the object which causeth them, they could not be severed from them as by mirrors and echoes they are.

The cause of perception consisteth in this: When the uttermost part of the organ is pressed, it no sooner yields but the next part within it is pressed also. In this manner the pressure or motion is propagated through all the parts of the organ to the innermost. Also, the pressure of the uttermost part proceeds from the pressure of some more remote body, and so continually till we come to the object. Sense therefore is some internal motion in the sentient organism, generated by some internal motion of the parts of the object, and propagated through all the media to the innermost part of the organ.

I shall endeavor to make plain these points: that the object wherein color is inherent is not the object seen; that there is nothing without us, really, which we call image or color; that color is but the apparition unto us of the motion, agitation, or change which the object worketh in the brain or some internal substance of the head; that as in vision, so also in the other senses, the subject of their inherence is not the object but the sentient creature.

As a color is not inherent in the object, but an effect thereof upon us, caused by motion in the object, so neither is sound in the thing we hear, but in ourselves. The clapper hath no sound in it, but action, and maketh motion in the internal parts of the bell; so the bell hath motion, and not sound, that imparteth motion to the air; and the air hath motion, but no sound, which it imparteth by the ear and nerve unto the brain; and the brain hath motion, but not sound.

From hence it followeth that whatsoever qualities our senses make us think there be in the world, they be not there, but are seeming and apparitions only; the things that really are in the world without us are those motions by which these seemings are caused. And this is the great deception of sense.

Hobbes is stopped by a rather ingenious problem. If the sensation, say the red color of a cherry, is really so much motion of particles in the observer's head, how can we explain the fact that it appears out there in space, located where the cherry is? As Hobbes asks, "Why doth the sensation appear as something situated without the organ?" His answer is as ingenious as his question:

Why doth the sensation appear as something situated without the organ? It is thus: There is in the whole organ, by reason of its own internal natural action some reaction against the motion which is propagated from the object to the innermost part of the organ. In the organ there is an endeavor opposite to the endeavor which proceeds from the object. That endeavor inwards is the last action in the act of sense. Then from the reaction, an idea hath its being, which by reason that the endeavor is now outward, doth always appear as something situated without the organ.

But though all sense be made by reaction, as I have said, it is not necessary that everything that reacteth should have sense. I know there have been philosophers, and those learned men, who have maintained that all bodies are endued with sense. Nor do I see how they can be refuted if the nature of sense be placed in reaction only.

The argument turns from the subjectivity of sensations to the question of desires. These too must be admitted to be merely so much matter in motion.

As that which is really within us, in sensation, is only motion caused by the action of external objects, so that which is really within us in appetite or desire is nothing but motion. But the appearance of that motion we call either pleasure or pain.

When appetites and aversions arise alternately concerning the same thing, so that sometimes we have an appetite to it and sometimes an aversion from it, then the whole sum of desires and aversions is what we call *deliberation*.

In deliberation, the last appetite or aversion, immediately adhering to the act or the omission thereof, is what we call *will*.

If this be the whole story of man's preferences and desires, Hobbes is in a position to make short shrift of any lofty moral idealism. This he proceeds to do:

Moral philosophy is nothing else but the science of what is good and evil in the conversation and society of mankind. Good and evil are names that signify our appetites and aversions; which in different tempers, customs, and doctrines of men, are different, and divers men differ not only in their judgment, on the sense of what is pleasant and unpleasant to the taste, smell, hearing, touch, and sight, but also what is conformable or disagreeable to reason in the actions of common life. Nay the same man, in divers times differs from himself and at one time praiseth, that is, calleth good what at another time he dispraiseth, that is, calleth evil.

Every man calleth that which pleaseth him, *good;* and that which displeaseth him, *evil.* Since every man differeth from another in constitution, they differ also from one another concerning the common distinction of good and evil. Nor is there any such thing as absolute goodness considered without relation.

Whatsoever is the object of any man's appetite or desire, that it is which he for his part calleth good; and the object of his hate and aversion, evil. For these words *good* and *evil* are ever used with relation to the person that useth them, there being nothing simply and absolutely so, nor any rule of good and evil to be taken from the nature of objects themselves; but from the man, where there is no commonwealth.

To the commitments adduced thus far, Hobbes adds one more: a categorical denial of man's free will:

I conceive that nothing taketh beginning from itself, but from the action of some other immediate agent without itself. Therefore, when a man hath an appetite or will to something, to which before he had no appetite or will, the cause of his will is not the will itself but something else not in his own disposing.

Neither is the freedom of willing or not willing greater in man than in other living creatures. For where there is appetite, the entire cause thereof hath preceded, and, consequently, the appetite could not choose but follow; that is, hath of necessity followed. Therefore such a liberty as is free from necessity is not to be found in the will.

If by *freedom* we understand the power, not of willing but of doing what we will, then certainly that freedom is to be allowed to both men and animals.

The ordinary definition of a *free agent* is that he is one that when all things are present which are needful to produce an effect, can nevertheless not produce it. This implies a contradiction that is nonsense, being as much as to say the cause of anything may be sufficient and yet the effect shall not follow. There is no such thing as an "agent," which when all things requisite to action are present, can nevertheless forbear to produce it. Or, which is all one, there is no such thing as freedom from necessity.

The essentials of Hobbes's materialism are now before us. The position bristles with difficulties. With unerring instinct Hobbes places his finger upon the one point which, more than any other perhaps, will be disputed. I mean the denial of man's free will. The following citations show Hobbes attempting to defend his determinism against anticipated objections:

To deny necessity is to destroy the power and foreknowledge of God Almighty. For whatsoever God hath purposed to bring to pass by man, or foreseeth shall come to pass, a man might frustrate and make not come to pass if he have freedom from necessity. Then would God foreknow such things as never shall be, and decree such things as shall never come to pass.

Liberty and necessity are consistent: as in the water, that hath not only liberty but a necessity to descend by the channel. So likewise in the actions men voluntarily do; which because they proceed from their will are termed *voluntary*. And yet, because every act of man's will and every desire and inclination proceedeth from some cause, and that from some other cause, in a continual chain, it proceeds from necessity. To him that could see the connection of those causes, the necessity of all men's voluntary actions would appear manifest.

The necessity of an action doth not make the laws that prohibit it unjust. Whatsoever necessary cause precede an action, yet if the action be forbidden, he that doth it willingly may justly be punished. For instance, suppose the law on pain of death prohibit stealing. Suppose there be a man who by the strength of temptation is necessitated to steal, and is thereupon put to death. Does not this punishment deter others from theft? Is it not a cause that others steal not? Doth it not frame and make their wills to justice? To make the law is therefore to make a cause of justice, and so to necessitate justice. The intention of the law is not to grieve the delinquent for that which is past and not to be undone; but to make him and others just who might otherwise not be so. It respecteth not the evil act past, but the good to come. But you will say, how is it just to kill one man to amend another, if what were done were necessary? To this I answer: men are justly killed, not because their actions are not necessitated, but because their actions are noxious. We destroy, without being unjust, all that is noxious, both beasts and men.

Repentance is nothing but a glad returning into the right way, after the grief of being out of the way. Even though the cause that made a man go astray were necessary, there is no reason why he should not grieve. So likewise, even though the cause that made a man return into the right way were necessary, there remaineth still the cause of joy. So that I say the necessity of actions taketh away neither of those parts of repentance, neither grief for the error nor joy for the returning.

As for praise and dispraise, they depend not at all on the necessity of the action praised or dispraised. For what is it to praise, but to say a thing is good? Good for me, good for someone else, or good for the commonwealth. What is it to say an act is good, but to say it is as I wish it, or as another wish it, or according to the law of the commonwealth? Can no action please me, or another, or the commonwealth, that should happen of necessity? Doth not praise and dispraise, reward and punishment, make and conform the will to good and evil by example?

Materialism is always with us. It is as old as the records of Western philosophy, having received an elaborate presentation in the fifth century B.C. among the Greeks. Our task is to grasp the meaning of materialism and its implications. To recapitulate: It is the belief that reality is moving particles of matter. Its adherents have usually felt committed to certain further claims, as, for example, all events are rigidly predictable; all organisms are only mechanisms; all knowledge, originating in sensations, is knowledge of appearances only, since sensations are entirely subjective; human conduct is strictly determined by antecedent and concomitant events; human motives are essentially egocentric; and the achievement of happiness, in the sense of the satisfaction of desire, is the only finally good thing. These assorted doctrines are not, of course, as logically interdependent as the materialist would have us believe. But they are temperamentally interdependent. They give expression to a mood or a temperament or a frame of mind which is sufficiently widespread to demand a courteous hearing.

READING REFERENCES. The best small book on Hobbes is by Sir Leslie Stephen. It is in the series, *English Men of Letters*. The literature on materialism itself is very large. One can only suggest a few things. A good beginning may be made in T. H. Huxley's volume mentioned already under Descartes, *Method and Results*. The third and fifth essays deal with phases of materialism. Hugh Elliot's *Modern Science and Materialism* is a competent and aggressive presentation of the case. Elliot has the virtue of *caring* whether his reader believes in materialism or does not. Santayana has remarked of himself that he is today perhaps the sole surviving materialist. The volume, *Reason in Science*, in his five-volume treatise, *The Life of Reason*, provides a statement of his materialism. It is also to be found in his later book, *The Realm of Matter*.

READING QUESTIONS

1. What does Hobbes begin by excluding from philosophy?
2. What does he propose to include?
3. How does he define his ultimate reality?
4. What account of change does he give?
5. How does this entail determinism?
6. What is his view regarding the nature of animal organisms?
7. What account of thought does he give? Of imagination?
8. What do you understand by representative perception?
9. How does Hobbes find himself committed thereto?
10. On what grounds does he defend the subjectivity of sensations?
11. "And this is the great deception of sense." What is?
12. How does he seek to account for the fact that we locate our sensations "out there"?
13. What account does he give of will? Its nature? Its freedom?
14. What account does he give of good and evil?

15. What objections to determinism does he formulate?

16. How does he seek to deal with these objections?

17. Formulate two or more questions you would put to Hobbes.

3. *IDEALISM AND ITS IMPLICATIONS — FROM GEORGE BERKELEY*

FROM HOBBES TO BERKELEY. It was inevitable that Hobbes's tough-minded materialism should provoke protest and criticism. Throughout the seventeenth and eighteenth centuries, it is not too much to say, materialism was the "specter" which haunted Western metaphysics. Some resorted to the simple expedient of ignoring such views. Some reviled the personal characters of those who held them. Some, less serene or less muddleheaded, attacked the premises and disputed the validity of the conclusions which comprised the materialist's position. Among these, in the eighteenth century, was George Berkeley, the founder of modern idealism, and one of the shrewdest metaphysicians of modern times.

BIOGRAPHICAL NOTE. George Berkeley was born in Ireland in 1685, and died in 1753 at the age of sixty-eight. He was educated at the Trinity College, Dublin, where while yet an undergraduate, he conceived the necessity of "refuting atheists and materialists." At the age of twenty-five he published *A Treatise Concerning the Principles of Human Knowledge*, and three years later his *Three Dialogues Between Hylas and Philonous*. These two small volumes, by the youngest and brightest philosophical mind of his generation, contain the statement and defense of his case against materialism and his case for idealism. For a while he was laughed at, as readers of Boswell's *Johnson* will remember. But the scattered ranks of those who had been troubled by the fashionable materialism launched by Hobbes and others in the preceding century soon closed to his support. Shortly after publication, Berkeley visited England and was received into the circle of Addison, Pope, and Steele. He traveled on the continent in various capacities, and on his return was appointed lecturer in divinity and Greek in Trinity College, Dublin. He received a D.D. He was made an ecclesiastical dean. He was promised aid to found a college in Bermuda for training clergymen for the colonies and missionaries for the Indians. He was made, finally, Bishop of Cloyne. He died at Oxford, beloved and respected, if not clearly understood, by all who knew him.

THE ARGUMENT OF THE CITATIONS. However much we may be left wondering about the metaphysical hypothesis which is advanced in the following citations, one thing cannot be ignored or denied. It is reached by an almost perfect embodiment of sound philosophical method. What I mean is this: Berkeley desires to establish the proposition that reality is ultimately spiritual in nature, that a man's mind provides him with a better example of the ultimately constituent "stuff" of things than is provided by a lump of matter. Now, this is strange doctrine at first notice, but the method by which Berkeley elaborates and defends his claim will repay the closest scrutiny. Once grasped, it will be seen to apply, *mutatis mutandis*, to many topics. The position to be established is idealism. The first step, therefore, must be a critique of materialism. This Berkeley proceeds to construct. Here, too, his method is sound. He starts from premises which the materialists themselves admit (any others would be irrelevant) and seeks to show that their conclusions (1) are either incompatible with these premises, or (2) do not follow from these premises. He then approaches materialism from another angle, seeking, this time, not to show its logical incoherence but to explain how, as a mere question of history, materialists have come to hold their "misguided" conclusions. Methodologically this procedure is above criticism. A communist might apply it to capitalism as the first step in a general statement of the case for communism. A free trader might apply it to protectionism as the first step in a general statement of the case for free trade. A liberal might apply it to conservatism as the first step in a general statement of the case for liberalism. To emphasize the fact that it is method and not doctrine to which attention is here directed, it should be noted that the same remarks are applicable to capitalists, protectionists, and conservatives.

The case against materialism stated, Berkeley's argument moves on to the case for idealism. The procedure is here equally sound. He formulates a few premises which anyone, he thinks, will admit. From these he seeks to deduce his idealism. He turns then to consider possible objections which might be urged against it before they are made.

The case against materialism stated, the case for idealism stated, the possible objections anticipated, he closes in on what, after all, he considers to be the most important part of the whole business, namely, an elucidation of the implications or commitments of his metaphysical idealism. By this I mean an enumeration of the propositions which, he thinks, are also true if his idealism is true.

The total argument begins as follows:

It is plain that the notion of what is called *matter* or *corporeal substance* involves a contradiction; so much so that I should not think it necessary to spend time exposing its absurdity. But belief in the existence of matter seems to have taken so deep a root in the minds of philosophers, and draws after it so many ill consequences, that I choose rather to be thought prolix and tedious than to omit anything that might conduce to the discovery and extirpation of that prejudice.

The following distinction between primary and secondary qualities and the claim that primary qualities are alone real, whereas secondary qualities are merely subjective, were familiar notions in Berkeley's day.

Some there are who make a distinction between primary and secondary qualities. By *primary qualities* they mean extension, figure, motion, rest, solidity, and number. By *secondary qualities* they mean sensible qualities, as colors, sounds, tastes, and so forth.

Our ideas of secondary qualities they acknowledge not to be the resemblances of anything existing without the mind or unperceived. But they will have our ideas of the primary qualities to be patterns or images of things which exist without the mind in an unthinking substance which they call *matter*. By *matter*, therefore, we are to understand an inert, senseless substance in which extension, figure, and motion do actually exist.

Colors, sounds, heat, cold, and such like secondary qualities, they tell us, are sensations existing in the mind alone, depending on and occasioned by the different size, texture and motion of the minute particles of matter. This they take for an undoubted truth, which they can demonstrate beyond all exception.

By *materialism*, then, Berkeley proposes to mean the belief in an inert, senseless substance possessing primary qualities in its own right but not possessing secondary qualities in the same intimate fashion. His first criticism of this belief is as follows:

But can anyone conceive the extension and motion of a body without any of its secondary qualities? It is not in my power to frame an idea of a body extended and moving but I must withal give it some color or other secondary quality which is acknowledged to exist only in the mind. In short, primary qualities abstracted from secondary qualities are inconceivable. Where therefore the secondary qualities are, to wit, in the mind and nowhere else, there must the primary qualities be also.

His second criticism is this:

Great and small, swift and slow, degrees of extension and motion, are allowed to exist only in the mind, being entirely relative, and changing as the frame or position of the sense organs varies. The extension therefore which exists independently of the mind is neither great nor small; the action, neither swift nor slow. That is, they are nothing at all.

His third criticism is this:

Number is entirely a creature of the mind. Even though the other primary qualities be allowed to exist without, it will be evident that the same thing bears a different denomination of number as the mind views it with different respects. Thus the same extension is one, or three, or thirty-six, according as the mind considers it with reference to a yard, a foot, or an inch. Number is so visibly relative and dependent on men's understanding that it is strange anyone should give it an absolute existence without the mind.

His fourth criticism is this:

One argument whereby modern philosophers would prove that secondary qualities do not exist in matter but in our minds may be turned likewise against primary qualities. Thus, it is said that heat and cold are affections only of the mind and not at all qualities of real things; for the same body which appears cold to one hand seems warm to another. Thus, too, it is proved that sweetness is not really in the sapid thing; because, the thing remaining unaltered, the sweetness is changed to bitterness, as in the case of a fever or otherwise vitiated palate.

Now, why may we not as well argue that figure and extension are not real qualities existing in matter? To the same eye at different stations, or to eyes of a different texture at the same station, they appear various. By parity of reasoning, therefore, they cannot be ideas of anything settled and determinate without the mind.

In short, those arguments which are thought to prove that secondary qualities (colors, tastes, etc.) exist only in the mind, may with equal force be brought to prove the same thing of primary qualities (extension, figure, motion, etc.).

His fifth criticism is this:

Suppose it were possible that material substances possessing only primary qualities do exist independent of the mind. Yet how is it possible for us to know this? Either we know it by our senses or by our reason. As for our senses, by them we have knowledge only of our sensations: but they do not inform us that things exist independent of the mind, or unperceived by the mind, like to those which are perceived. This the materialists themselves acknowledge; nay, insist.

It remains, therefore, that, if we have any knowledge at all of material substances, it must be by our reason inferring their existence from what is immediately perceived by sense. But I do not see what reason can induce us to believe in the existence of bodies independent of the mind, from what we perceive, since the very patrons of matter themselves do not pretend there is any necessary connection betwixt them and our ideas.

His sixth criticism is this:

It may be thought easier to explain the production of our sensations by supposing external bodies, rather than otherwise; and so it might be at least probable that there are such things as bodies that excite ideas in our minds. But neither can this be said. For, though we give the materialists their "external bodies," they by their own confession are no nearer knowing how our ideas are produced, since they own themselves unable to comprehend in what manner body can act upon spirit (or mind) or how it could imprint any idea in the mind.

Hence it is evident that the production of ideas or sensations in our minds can be no reason why we should suppose matter or corporeal substances; since their production is acknowledged to remain equally inexplicable with or without this particular supposition. If therefore it were possible for bodies to exist without the mind, yet to hold that they do so must needs be a very precarious opinion. In short, if there were external bodies, it is impossible we should come to know it; and if there were not, we might have the very same reasons to think there were that we have now. Which consideration were enough to make any reasonable person suspect the strength of whatever arguments he may think himself to have, for the existence of external bodies independent of the mind.

His conclusion is this:

It is on this, therefore, that I insist, to wit, that the absolute existence of unthinking things are words without a meaning, or which include a contradiction. This is what I repeat and inculcate, and earnestly recommend to the attentive thoughts of the reader.

He turns now to an exploration of the probable reasons which led men "to suppose the existence of material substance":

It is worth while to reflect on the motives which induced men to suppose the existence of material substance; so that having observed the gradual ceasing and expiration of those motives, we may withdraw the assent that was grounded on them.

First, it was thought that the sensible qualities did really exist without the mind. And for this reason it seemed needful to suppose that some unthinking substratum or substance wherein they did exist, since they could not be conceived to exist by themselves.

Then, in process of time, men being convinced that secondary qualities had no existence without the mind, they stripped this substratum or material substance of those qualities, leaving only the primary ones, which they still conceive to exist without the mind and consequently to stand in need of a material support.

But now, it having been shown that none even of these can possibly exist otherwise than in a spirit or mind which perceives them, it follows that we have no longer any reason to suppose the being of "matter," nay, that it is utterly impossible that there should be any such thing so long as that word is taken to mean an unthinking substratum or substance for qualities wherein they exist without mind. It is an extraordinary instance of the force of prejudice that the mind of man retains so great a fondness, against all the evidence of reason, for a stupid, thoughtless Somewhat as a support of the qualities we perceive.

Thus Berkeley on materialism. One is moved to ponder its probable effect upon Thomas Hobbes, could that doughty old metaphysician have revisited the scene of his former labors. A grim smile perhaps, or an even grimmer sharpening of his tireless controversial quill as he prepared to do battle with this newcomer. His comment upon what remains would be even more interesting. For Berkeley, having "dethroned" matter, sets about to "enthrone" spirit. His first step is to secure one or two propositions which "any rational man" would admit.

It is evident to anyone who takes a survey of the objects of human knowledge, that they are either ideas imprinted on the senses; or such as are perceived by attending to the passions and operations of the mind; or lastly, ideas formed by help of memory and imagination — compounding, dividing, or merely representing those originally perceived in the aforesaid ways.

As several such ideas are observed to accompany each other, they come to be marked by one name, and so reputed as one thing. Thus a certain color, taste, smell, figure, and consistence having been observed to go together, are accounted one distinct thing, signified by the name *apple*. Other collections of ideas constitute a stone, a tree, a book, and the like.

Besides the ideas or objects of knowledge, there is something which knows or perceives them, and exercises divers operations as willing, imagining, remembering, about them. This perceiving active being I call *mind, spirit, soul,* or *myself*.

The existence of an idea consists in its being perceived. Its *esse* is *percipi*. The table I write on I say "exists"; that is, I see and feel it; and if I were out of my study, I should say it "existed"; meaning that if I was in my study, I might perceive it, or that some other spirit actually does perceive it. There was an odor, that is, it was smelt; there was a sound, that is, it was heard; there was a color or figure, that is, it was perceived by sight or touch. That is all I can understand by these and like expressions. Their *esse* is *percipi*. Nor is it possible they should have any existence out of the minds which perceive them.

All our ideas and sensations are visibly inactive. There is nothing of power or agency included in them. One idea or sensation cannot produce or alter another. The very being of an idea implies passiveness and inertness in it; insomuch that it is impossible for an idea to do anything, or be the cause of anything.

We perceive a continual succession of ideas. Some are excited anew, others are changed or totally disappear. There is therefore some cause of these ideas, whereon they depend, and which produces and changes them.

Having premised the above facts, Berkeley proceeds to argue from them:

It is clear, from what hath been said, that this cause cannot itself be any idea or sensation since all such are passive and inert. It must therefore be a substance. But it has been shown that there is no corporeal or material substance. It remains therefore that the cause of our ideas and sensations is an incorporeal active substance, or spirit.

I find I can excite some of my ideas in my mind at pleasure, and vary and shift the scene as oft as I think fit. This making and un-making of ideas doth very properly denominate the mind active. Thus much is certain and grounded on experience. But when we talk, as do materialists, of unthinking substances producing ideas, we only amuse ourselves with words.

But whatever power I have over some of my ideas, I find that others have not a like dependence on my will. When, for example, I open my eyes in broad daylight, it is not in my power to choose whether I shall see or no, nor to determine what I shall see. It is likewise as to hearing and the other senses. The ideas imprinted on them are not creatures of my will. There is, therefore, some other will or mind or spirit that produces them.

These ideas which I cannot control, these ideas of sense are more strong, more lively, more distinct than those which I can control. They have, likewise, a steadiness, order, and coherence which belong not to those that are the effects of my will. They speak themselves the products of a Mind more powerful and wise than human minds.

Some truths there are so near and obvious to the human mind that a man need only open his eyes to see them. Such I take this impor-tant one to be, namely, that all the choir of heaven and furniture of the earth, in a word, all those bodies which compose the mighty frame of the world, have not any subsistence without a mind; that their being is to be perceived or known; that, consequently, so long as they are not actually perceived by me, or do not exist in my mind or the mind of any other created spirit, they must either have no existence at all or else subsist in the mind of some Eternal Spirit. For it is unintelligible to attribute to any single part of them an existence independent of (perception by a) Spirit.

Until his premises are effectively questioned, or his reasoning from these premises shown to be fallacious, Berkeley may now survey his work with satisfaction; however, he prefers first to look about him. Are there any loopholes? The citations which follow show Berkeley at work on this question. They should be studied carefully. They reveal a mind of penetration and persistence, seeking honestly to detect any flaws in its work.

Before we proceed any farther, it is necessary that we spend some time in answering objections which may probably be made against the principles we have hitherto laid down. In this, if I seem too prolix, I desire I may be excused, since all men do not equally apprehend things of this nature; and I am willing to be understood by every man.

It might be objected, Berkeley thinks, that:

By the foregoing principles all that is real and substantial in nature is banished out of the world. All things that exist, it will be said, exist only in the mind, that is, are purely notional. What therefore becomes of the sun, moon, and stars? What must we think of houses, rivers, mountains, trees, stones, nay even of our own bodies? Are all these but so many chimeras and illusions?

To this objection he has a ready answer:

We are not deprived of any one thing in nature. Whatever we see, hear, feel, or any wise conceive or understand remains as secure as ever, and is as real as ever. I do not argue against the existence of any one thing that we can apprehend either by sense or reflection. That the things I see with my eyes and touch with my hands do really exist, I make not the least question. The only thing whose existence I deny is that which philosophers call *matter*. There are minds which will or excite ideas in themselves at pleasure. Other ideas, which they do not so excite, speak themselves the effects of a mind more powerful and wise than human spirits. These latter are said to be more real than the former. In this sense the sun I see is the real sun. In this sense, everything in the world is as much a real being by our principles as by any other. If the word *substance* be taken for a combination of sensible qualities, we cannot be accused of denying its existence.

It sounds harsh to say we eat and drink ideas, and are clothed with ideas. But, in common discourse, the word *idea* is not used to signify the several combinations of sensible qualities which are called *things*. But this concerns not the truth of the proposition, which says no more than that we are fed and clothed with those things which we perceive immediately by our senses. The sensory qualities which, combined, constitute the several sorts of victuals and apparel, have been shown to exist only in the mind that perceives them. This is all that is meant by calling them *ideas*. If you agree that we eat and drink and are clad with the immediate object of sense, which cannot exist unperceived, I shall readily grant that it is more conformable to custom that they should be called *things* rather than *ideas*.

"I will still believe my senses and will never suffer any argument, how plausible soever, to prevail over the certainty of them." Be it so. Assert the evidence of your senses. We are willing to do the same. That what I see, hear, feel, etc. doth exist, I no more doubt of than I do of my own being. But, I do not see how the testimony of sense can be alleged as a proof for the existence of anything which is not perceived by the senses. We are not for having any man turn skeptic and doubt his senses.

Again, it might be objected that:

From these principles it follows that things are every moment annihilated and created anew. The objects of sense exist only when they are perceived. The trees are in the garden, the chairs in the parlor, only while there is someone there to perceive them. Upon shutting my eyes it is all reduced to nothing, and upon opening them it is again created.

His answer to this:

It is thought absurd that, upon closing my eyelids, all the visible objects around me should be reduced to nothing. Yet, is not this what my very critics and opponents commonly acknowledge when they agree on all hands that light and color, which are the immediate objects of sight, are mere sensations, mere "subjective states" which exist no longer than they are perceived?

Indeed we hold the objects of sense to be nothing else but ideas which cannot exist unperceived. Yet we may not hence conclude that they have no existence except only when they are perceived by us; there may be some other spirit that perceives them though we do not. It would not follow, hence, that bodies are annihilated and created every moment, or exist not at all during the intervals between our perception of them.

It might be objected that:

If primary qualities exist only in the mind, it follows that mind is extended, since extension is a primary quality of things.

The answer is clever, even if it does seem to beg the question rather subtly:

It no more follows that the mind is extended because extension is in it alone, than that it is red or blue because those qualities exist in it alone and nowhere else. Yet my opponents admit that secondary qualities exist in the mind alone; i.e., are "subjective."

It might be objected, once more that:

There have been a great many things explained by matter and motion. Take these away and you destroy the whole atomic theory, and undermine those principles of mechanics which have been applied with so much success to account for things. In short, whatever advances have been made in the study of nature, do all proceed on the supposition that "matter" doth exist.

To which Berkeley replies:

To "explain" things is all one as to show why, upon such and such occasions, we are affected with such and such ideas. But, how "matter" operates on mind, or produces any idea in it, is what no philosopher will pretend to explain. Of what use is it, therefore? Besides, things are accounted for by figure, motion and other qualities; not by "matter." Such qualities are no more than ideas, and therefore cannot be the cause of anything, since ideas cannot be the cause of anything.

It might be objected:

Does it not seem absurd to take away "natural causes" and ascribe everything to the operation of spirit? To say, not that fire heats or water cools, but that a spirit heats or a spirit cools, etc. Would not a man be deservedly laughed at who should talk after this manner?

To which Berkeley rejoins:

In such things we ought to think with the learned and speak with the vulgar. Those who are convinced of the truth of Copernican astronomy do nevertheless say "the sun rises," and "the sun sets." Yet it doth not. But if such persons affected a contrary style in common talk, it would appear ridiculous. It is the same with our tenets.

It might be objected:

Is not the universal assent of mankind an invincible argument on behalf of matter? Must we suppose the whole world to be mistaken? If so, what cause can be assigned of so widespread and predominant an error?

To which Berkeley responds:

It will perhaps not be found that so many do really believe in the existence of "matter." Strictly, to believe that which involves a contradiction, or has no meaning, is impossible. I admit men act as if the cause of their sensations were some senseless, unthinking being. But, that they clearly apprehend any meaning thereby, that they have formed a settled speculative opinion, is what I am not able to conceive.

Adding, too:

Even though we should grant a notion to be universally and stead-
fastly held to, yet that is but a weak argument for its truth. A
vast number of prejudices and false opinions are everywhere embraced by the unreflecting part of mankind. There was a time
when the antipodes and the motion of the earth were looked upon
as monstrous absurdities even by men of learning.

It is demanded that we assign a cause of this prejudice that matter
exists and is the cause of our sensations. I answer: Men, knowing
they perceived several ideas whereof they themselves were not the
author, nor depending on their wills, first maintained that those
ideas had an existence independent of and external to the mind.
But, seeing that the immediate objects of perception do not exist
except they are being perceived, they then argued that there are
objects, distinct from the colors, etc. immediately perceived by the
mind, of which those latter are images or resemblances or effects
imprinted on us by those objects. So the notion of an imperceived
and unthinking "matter" owes its origin to the consciousness that
we are not the authors of our sensations, which must therefore have
some cause distinct from our minds upon which they are imprinted.

It might be objected:

You say: Though the ideas themselves do not exist without the
mind, yet there may be things like them whereof they are copies
or resemblances, which exist without the mind in an unthinking
substance.

To which Berkeley counters:

It is indeed an opinion strangely prevailing among men that
houses, mountains, rivers, in a word, all sensible objects, have an
existence distinct from their being perceived by the understanding.
But this principle involves a manifest contradiction. For what
are the aforementioned objects but the things we perceive by sense?
And what do we perceive besides our own ideas or sensations?
Could any of these exist unperceived? There was an odor, that is,
it was smelt; there was a sound, that is, it was heard; there was
a color or figure, that is, it was perceived by sight or touch. That

is all I can understand by these and like expressions. Their *esse* is *percipi*. Nor is it possible they should have any existence out of the minds which perceive them.

An idea can be like nothing but an idea; a color can be like nothing but a color. It is impossible for us to conceive a likeness except only between our ideas.

I ask whether the supposed originals or external things, of which our ideas are pictures or representations, be themselves perceivable or no? If they are, then they are ideas, and we have gained our point. If they are not, I appeal to anyone whether it be sense to say a color is like something which is invisible; to say hard or soft is like something intangible; and so of the rest.

It might be objected:

Let us admit that the notion of "matter" as the cause or support of the perceived qualities of things, is not needed. Yet there may perhaps be some inert, unperceiving substance, as incomprehensible to us as colors to a man born blind; supporting, it may be, qualities of which we know nothing because we have no senses adapted to them, but which, if we had other senses we should know of.

To which Berkeley replies:

If by *matter* you mean the unknown (and unknowable) cause or support of unknown (and unknowable) qualities, I see no point in affirming or denying its existence. I see no advantage in disputing about something we know not what and we know not why.

And adds:

If we had those other senses, they could only furnish us with new ideas or sensations. In which case we should have the same reason against their existing in an unperceiving substance that has been already offered with relation to such qualities as we do perceive: They would exist only in a mind perceiving them. This is true not only of ideas we are acquainted with at present but likewise of all possible ideas whatsoever.

The case is by now almost completed. He has stated and refuted materialism. He has stated and established idealism. He has anticipated and parried every objection which he can imagine. He proceeds to draw the conclusions which, in all justice, he feels are his due.

Having posed and met possible objections, we proceed to take a view of our principles with regard to their consequences. After what hath been premised, I think we may lay down the following conclusions.

First: It is plain that men amuse themselves in vain when they inquire for any natural cause distinct from a mind or spirit.

Second: Since the whole creation is the workmanship of a wise and good Agent, it should seem to be in order to employ our thoughts about the final causes, or purposes of things. This not only discovers to us the attributes of the Creator and Sustainer, but may also direct us to the proper uses and applications of things.

Third: The natural immortality of the soul is a necessary consequence of these principles. To assert natural immortality is not to assert that it is incapable of annihilation by the Creator who first gave it being but only that it is not liable to be broken or dissolved by the laws of nature or motion. Bodies are ideas in the mind or soul. The latter is indivisible, incorporeal, unextended, and consequently indissoluble. Changes, decays, dissolutions, which we see in bodies cannot affect a spirit which hath none of their properties. Such a being, a mind or soul or active spirit, is therefore indissoluble by the forces of nature.

Fourth: From what hath been said, it is plain that we cannot know the existence of other minds or spirits otherwise than by their operations or the ideas excited by them in us. I perceive combinations of ideas, and changes thereof, that inform me that there are agents like myself which accompany them and concur in their production. But the knowledge I have of these other spirits or minds is hence indirect; not as is the knowledge of my ideas, but depending on the intervention of ideas by me referred to minds as spirits distinct from myself.

Fifth: Though there be some things (i.e., combinations of sensations) which convince us that human agents are concerned in producing them, yet it is evident that nature, that is, the far greater part of the ideas or sensations perceived by us, is not produced by or dependent on the wills of men. There is therefore some other Spirit that causeth them. But if we consider the regularity, order, and concatenation of natural things, the surprising magnificence, beauty, and perfection of the larger, and the exquisite contrivance of the smaller parts of creation, we shall clearly perceive that the attributes One, Eternal, Infinitely Wise, Good, and Perfect, belong all of them to the aforesaid Spirit, who "works in all" and "by whom all things consist."

Hence it is evident that God is known as certainly and immediately as any other mind or spirit, distinct from ourselves. We may even assert that the existence of God is more evident than the existence of men; because the effects of nature are more numerous and considerable than those ascribed to men. There is not any one mark which denotes a man, or effect produced by him, that does not more strongly evince the being of that Spirit which is the author of nature. A human spirit is not perceived by sense: when we perceive the color, size, etc. of a man, we perceive only sensations or ideas excited in our own minds. These being exhibited to our view in sundry distinct collections, serve to mark out unto us the existence of finite spirits like ourselves. And after the same manner we see God. All the difference is that whereas some one finite and narrow assemblage of ideas denotes a particular human mind, on the other hand wherever we direct our view we perceive manifest tokens of the Divinity, "in whom we live and move and have our being."

It will be objected here that monsters, untimely births, fruits blasted in the blossom, rains falling in desert places, waste, miseries incident to human life, and so on, are evidence that the whole frame of nature is not actuated and superintended by a Spirit of infinite wisdom and goodness. If, that is to say, God is the author of all things, is He not the author of evil and undesirable things? Is this coherent with His infinite wisdom and goodness?

I answer: The very blemishes and defects of nature are not without their use. They make an agreeable variety and augment the beauty of the rest of creation, as shadows in a picture serve to set off the brighter parts.

I add: We do well, before we tax the author of nature with wastefulness, to examine whether such accusation be not the effect of prejudice contracted by our familiarity with impotent and saving mortals. In man, thriftiness with what he cannot easily secure may be wisdom. But, an Omnipotent Spirit can produce everything by a mere fiat. Hence nature's splendid profusion should not be interpreted as wastefulness in the author of nature. Rather is it an evidence of the riches of His power.

I add: As for the pain which is in the world, pursuant to the general laws of nature and the actions of finite imperfect Spirits, this is indispensably necessary to our well-being. We consider some one particular pain and account it an evil. But our view is too narrow. If we enlarge our view, so as to comprehend the various ends, connections, and dependencies of things, we shall be forced to acknowledge that those particular things which, considered in themselves, appear to be evil, have the nature of good when considered in connection with the whole system of beings.

From what hath been said, it will be manifest that it is merely for want of attention and comprehensiveness of mind that there are any atheists or Manichaeans. Little and unreflecting souls may indeed burlesque the works of Providence, the beauty and order whereof they have not the capacity or will not be at the pains to comprehend. But those who are masters of any justness and extent of thought can never sufficiently admire the traces of wisdom and goodness that shine through the economy of nature.

Since it is downright impossible that a soul pierced and illumined with a thorough sense of the omnipresence, holiness, and justice of that Spirit, should persist in a remorseless violation of His laws, we ought therefore earnestly to meditate on those important matters, that so we may attain conviction without scruple.

For, after all, what deserves the first place in our studies, is the consideration of God and duty; which to promote, was the main drift and design of my labors.

What is to be said of this flight of the metaphysical imagination? A generation later it caught the roving eye of the skeptically minded David Hume. He observed, somewhat tartly, "The speculations of the ingenious Dr. Berkeley — they admit of no refutation, but they produce no conviction," and proceeded to deal with idealism as Berkeley had dealt with materialism. But of that, more later. Meanwhile, one does well to study the argument. It has served, to this day, as a kind of rallying point for the like-minded in each generation. By this I would not be understood as saying that Berkeley produced no criticism, even among his followers. But he performed a greatly needed service. He provided an apparently coherent case against the "specter" of materialism. He gave articulation to that perennial temperament which dreads and despises and mistrusts the "appeal to matter." For his premises, others have been substituted. To his conclusions, especially his repudiation of materialism, little of importance or variety has been added.

READING REFERENCES. The citations in this chapter have been taken from Berkeley's *Principles of Human Knowledge* and his *Dialogues*. The latter are enjoyable reading. There the case for idealism is worked out in much more elaborate detail. Berkeley was an able and plausible writer. His dialogues are almost as lifelike as Plato's. A great number of books and chapters have been written about and against the philosophical position taken up by Berkeley. Any one of these will satisfy curiosity stirred up by this chapter. Perhaps mention might be made of four items. The first is a book by T. H. Huxley, *Hume, with Helps to the Study of Berkeley*. The "helps" part of this book is interesting and illuminating, inasmuch as Huxley is ordinarily credited with views which fall short of Berkeley's religiously motivated idealism. The second is a book by John Wild, *George Berkeley, a Study of His Life and Philosophy*. This is, by all odds, the most careful and elaborate exposition of Berkeley available anywhere in English. The third is the chapter on Berkeley in Mary Whiton Calkins' book, *The Persistent Problems of Philosophy*. The fourth is G. E. Moore's well-known essay, "The Refutation of Idealism," contained in his book, *Philosophical Studies*.

READING QUESTIONS

1. Enumerate the four large steps in Berkeley's argument.
2. Why does he concern himself with the case against materialism?
3. Why does he base his criticism of materialism on facts admitted or claimed by materialists?
4. From whom did he get the distinction between primary and secondary qualities?
5. And the claim that the latter are subjective?
6. What use does he make of this distinction and claim?
7. Condense into six propositions his criticism of materialism.
8. Why does he turn from refuting materialism to accounting for it?
9. On what hypothesis does he account for it?
10. Enumerate the premises upon which his idealism rests.
11. What does he mean by *"esse* is *percipi"*? To what does it apply?
12. What part does this idea play in his argument for idealism?
13. Enumerate the steps by which he proceeds from his premises to his conclusion.
14. The objections should be studied carefully. Be prepared to state each one in a single proposition. Be prepared to state his answer to each one, in a single proposition.
15. Do any of the objections seem more serious than others?
16. Are any of his answers less convincing than others? For example, his answer to the objection if primary qualities exist only in the mind, then the mind is extended?
17. What consequences, according to Berkeley, follow from his position?
18. How is he led to deal with the theological problem of evil?
19. How does he deal with it?
20. Formulate two or more questions you would put to Berkeley.

4. VOLUNTARISM AND ITS IMPLICATIONS — FROM ARTHUR SCHOPEN-HAUER

FROM BERKELEY TO SCHOPENHAUER. It is sometimes argued that metaphysics is a question of temperament. There is a half truth in the claim. What it comes to is something like this: Descartes was an eminently commonplace individual, inclined both by nature and training to safe, middle-of-the-road opinions. This is abundantly reflected in his quite orthodox metaphysics of God, human souls, and matter. Hobbes was a rather hardheaded, realistically minded individual, inclined both by nature and training to discount flights of imagination and to stick to the "facts." What more natural, then, than his unvarnished materialism? Berkeley was a devout and genial Anglican cleric, inclined both by nature and training to share the pious aspirations enshrined in the institution for which he was a spokesman. Why not an idealism, under these circumstances? Why not the firm conviction that this world is, in the last analysis, but the manifestation of a Supreme Mind? Hume was a canny, skeptically minded Scot, impressed, above everything else, with man's seemingly boundless credulity. What more natural than his carefully reasoned refutation of Descartes, Hobbes, and Berkeley? And so one might continue, seeking to "psychologize" away any claim of metaphysics to rational consideration. There is just one fatal flaw in this notion. It is this: No explanation in terms of nature and training, of why any man believes anything, has any relevance to the question of whether the beliefs are true or false. It is well to raise this point here for two reasons: (1) One's first introduction to a variety of alternative metaphysical hypotheses is usually marked by a sense of confusion and a ready ear to the dissolving suggestion that, "After all, it's only a question of temperament." The best reply is that the truth of an opinion has nothing to do with the temperament of the man who holds the opinion. (2) In the case of Arthur Schopenhauer, there is a great tendency to "explain away" his doctrine by reference to his biography. It is well known that in life he was bitter, disillusioned, cynical, pessimistic. It is also well known that his metaphysical views amount to the claim that the nature of ultimate reality is such as to justify his cynicism and pessimism. The result has too often been that persons who reject his metaphysics, with something approaching abhorrence, do so on the ground that "his temperament explains his views." Perhaps it does, but that is not the important point. What one should ask is, "Does the nature of things justify his views?"

BIOGRAPHICAL NOTE. Arthur Schopenhauer was born in Germany in 1788 and died in 1860 at the age of seventy-two. His life was filled with selfishness, suspiciousness, and bitterness. He spent some time in a commercial house before going to the universities at Göttingen, Jena, and Berlin. He left his business career in disgust. He berated most of his fellows and teachers at the universities. Upon the death of his father, his mother had moved to Weimar. Schopenhauer followed her, quarreled with her, and took separate lodgings; met Goethe, quarreled with him, and left town to settle a while in Dresden. Here he wrote his great work, *The World as Will and Idea*. As soon as it was published, he left for Italy. There he fumed jealously over the reputation and the gallantries of Lord Byron. He returned to Germany to find his book almost unnoticed. He stamped and raged at the obtuseness of his contemporaries and set himself up as a Privatdocent at the university in Berlin. Here he was outclassed by the famous Hegel, whom he denounced as a "windbag," and left Berlin for Frankfort. In Frankfort, despite squabbles with persons who shared his rooming house, he spent the remaining years of his life writing brilliant essays on various themes in his own philosophy, compiling a scrapbook of all articles and notices dealing with his work, preparing for a second and third edition of his treatise, and watching his doctrines and fame spread slowly over the whole of the Western world.

THE ARGUMENT OF THE CITATIONS. Schopenhauer's metaphysics is called *voluntarism*. It may be contrasted with materialism and idealism. It is the belief that will, not matter and not spirit, is the ultimate reality of which all things are manifestations. The following citations, in which this metaphysical hypothesis is set forth, fall into two groups. The first, given immediately below, without any comment, comprises what might be called the *data*. The second sets forth what might be called the *theory*. The first group requires no elucidation. Collectively, they might be inscribed "cynicism and pessimism." They are random reflections on the rottenness of things. As I read him, Schopenhauer would have these disconnected observations on nature and life fall, like so many drops of acid, into the reader's mind, preparing him to understand and appreciate the metaphysical theory which is to follow. "See," he seems to say, "see — these are the facts. Think them over. Then, but not until then, I'll give you a theory that will fit them."

Unless suffering is the direct and immediate object of life, our existence must entirely fail of its aim. It is absurd to look upon the enormous amount of pain that abounds everywhere in the world, originating in needs and necessities inseparable from life itself, as serving no purpose, as being the result of mere chance.

Let us consider the human race. Here life presents itself as a task to be performed. Here we see, in great and in small, universal need, ceaseless wars, compulsory activity, extreme exertion of mind and body. Millions united into nations, striving for a common good, each individual on account of his own. But thousands are sacrificed. Now silly delusions, now intriguing politics, excite them to wars. Then sweat and blood must flow to carry out someone's ideas or expiate someone's folly. In peace time it is industry and trade. Inventions work miracles, seas are navigated, delicacies are brought from the ends of the earth, waves engulf thousands. The tumult passes description. And all to what end? To sustain life through a brief span, and then to reproduce and begin again.

From whence did Dante take the materials for his hell but from our actual world? And a very proper hell he was able to make of it.

When, on the other hand, he came to describe heaven and its delights, he was confronted with a difficulty, for our world affords no materials for this.

In early youth we are like children in a theater before the curtain is raised, sitting in high spirits and eagerly waiting for the play to begin. It is a blessing we do not know what is actually going to happen . . . the longer you live, the more clearly you feel that life is a disappointment, nay, a cheat.

We are like lambs in a field, disporting under the eye of the butcher who chooses first one and then another. In our good days we are unconscious of the evil which fate may have in store for us — sickness, poverty, mutilation, blindness, insanity, and so on.

It is folly to try to turn this scene of misery into a garden of pleasure. It is folly to aim at joy and pleasure instead of the greatest possible freedom from pain. There is some wisdom in taking a gloomy view of things, in looking upon the world as a kind of hell and in confining one's efforts to securing a little room not too exposed to the fire.

Human life? It is like a drop of water seen through a microscope, teeming with infusoria; or a speck of cheese full of mites invisible to the naked eye. We laugh as they bustle about, and struggle. It is only in the microscope that our life looks so big. It is an almost invisible point, drawn out and magnified by the powerful lenses of time and space.

Unrest is the mark of human existence. We are like a man running down hill who cannot keep on his legs unless he runs on. We are like a pole balanced on the tip of one's finger, or like a planet which would crash into its sun the moment it should cease to hurry on its way.

As far as real physical pleasure is concerned, man is no better off than the brute. The higher possibilities of his brain and nervous system make him sensitive to more and intenser kinds of pleasure, but also to more and intenser kinds of pain. Boredom is a form of suffering unknown to brutes, except perhaps when they are domesticated. Whereas, in man it has become a scourge. Of a truth, need and boredom are the two poles of human life.

In every man there dwells, first and foremost, a colossal egotist who snaps the bands of right and justice with consummate ease. Newspapers show it every day. History shows it on every page. Does not the need of a balance of power in Europe demonstrate it? If it were egotism only, it would be bad enough. But to the egotist in man is joined, in every other human breast, a fund of hatred, anger, envy, rancor, malice, accumulated like the venom in a serpent's tooth.

I have been reading a book on the condition of the slaves in the southern states. This book constitutes one of the heaviest indictments against the so-called human race. No one can put it down without a feeling of horror. Whatever you may have heard will seem small when you read of how those human devils, those bigoted, church-going, Sabbatarian rascals treated their black brothers whom they had gotten into their clutches.

What is our civilized world but a big masquerade, where you meet knights, priests, soldiers, scholars, lawyers, clergymen, philosophers and so on? But they are not what they pretend to be. They are only masks, and behind the masks, as a rule, you will find moneymakers. It is merchants and moneylenders alone who, in this respect, constitute an honest class.

Formerly faith was the chief support of a throne. Now it is credit. The pope himself is scarcely more concerned over the faithful than over his creditors. In times past it was the guilty debt of the world which was lamented. Now it is the financial debt which arouses dismay. Formerly it was the Last Day which was prophesied. Now it is the great repudiation, the bankruptcy of nations.

Leibnitz, you know, argued that this is the best of all possible worlds. Those who agree with him are optimists. If I could conduct a confirmed optimist through hospitals, infirmaries, operating rooms, asylums; through prisons, torture chambers, and slave kennels; over battlefields, places of execution and sudden death; if I were to open to him all the dark abodes where misery hides from cold curiosity — he might come finally to understand the nature of this "best of all possible worlds."

Nature has appointed that the propagation of the species shall be the business of men who are young, strong, and handsome; so that the species may not degenerate. There is no law older or more powerful than this. Woe to the man who sets up claims and interests that conflict with it; they will be unmercifully crushed at the first serious encounter.

If we contemplate life, we behold a turmoil where most are occupied with want and misery, straining to dodge or ward off its multifarious sorrows. In the midst of this tumult, we see the stealthy glance of two lovers. Why so fearful, so secret? Because — unrealized by them, perhaps — these lovers are traitors who seek to perpetuate whole sordid rounds of want and drudgery which would otherwise come to an end.

If children were brought into the world by an act of pure reason, would human life continue to exist? Are not most of us trapped into life? Would not a man rather have so much sympathy with the coming generation that he would spare it the burden of existence?

Kant speaks much of the dignity of man. I have never seen it. It seems to me that the notion of dignity can be applied to man only in an ironical sense. His will is sinful. His intellect is limited. His body is weak and perishable. How shall a man have dignity whose conception is a crime, whose birth is a penalty, whose life is toil, whose death is a necessity?

Human life must be some kind of mistake. Else why is man a compound of needs and necessities so hard so satisfy? And why, if perchance they should be satisfied, is he thereby abandoned to boredom? This is direct proof that existence has no real value. For what is boredom but the feeling of the emptiness of life? The fact that this most perfect manifestation of life, the human organism, with the infinite cunning and complex working of its machinery, must oscillate between need and boredom and finally fall to dust and extinction, this fact, I say, is eloquent to him who has the mind to understand it.

Disillusion is the mark of old age. By that time the fictions are gone which gave life its charm and spurred on the mind to activity. By that time the splendors of the world have proved themselves null and vain. Its pomp, grandeur, ideals, and enthusiasms are faded. Not till a man has attained his three score years and ten does he quite understand the first verse of Ecclesiastes.

The world and man is something that had better not have been. This may sound strange. But it is in keeping with the facts. And it reminds us of that which is, after all, the most necessary thing in life — the tolerance, patience, regard, love of neighbor, which everyone needs and which everyone owes to his fellow.

You need only look at the way woman is formed to see that she is not meant to undergo great labor either of mind or body. She pays the debt of life not by what she does but by what she suffers: by the pains of childbearing, by caring for the child, by submission to her husband to whom she should be a patient and cheering companion.

That woman is meant by nature to obey may be seen by the fact that every woman who is placed in the unnatural position of complete independence immediately attaches herself to some man by whom she allows herself to be guided and ruled. If she is young, it will be a lover; if she is old, it will be a priest or a lawyer.

The institution of monogamy, and the marriage laws which it entails, bestow upon women an unnatural position of privilege by considering her as the full equivalent of a man, which is by no means the case. Seeing this, men who are shrewd and prudent often scruple to make so great a sacrifice and to acquiesce in so one-sided an arrangement.

The nobler and more perfect a thing is, the later and slower it is to mature. A man reaches the maturity of his reasoning powers hardly before the age of twenty-eight; a woman at eighteen — and then it is only reason of a sort, very niggard in its dimensions.

This weakness of woman's reasoning power explains why she shows more sympathy for the unfortunate than men do; present circumstances have a stronger hold over her, and those concrete things, that lie directly before her eyes, exercise a power which is seldom counteracted to any extent by abstract principles of thought, by fixed rules of conduct, or in general by consideration for the past and the future.

Women are dependent, not upon strength but upon craft. Hence their instinctive capacity for cunning and their inveterate tendency to say what is not true. For as lions are provided with claws and teeth, elephants with boars and tusks, cuttlefish with clouds of inky fluid, so nature has equipped woman with the arts of dissimulation. Therefore a perfectly truthful and straightforward woman is perhaps an impossibility. It may indeed be questioned whether women should be allowed to take an oath in court.

It is only the man whose intellect is clouded by his sexual impulses that could give the name of "fair sex" to that undersized, narrow-shouldered, broad-hipped, short-legged race. For the whole beauty of women is bound up with that impulse.

Nature proceeds with her usual economy. Just as the female ant, after fecundation, loses her wings which are then superfluous, nay, a danger to the business of breeding; so, after giving birth to one or two children, a woman generally loses her beauty; probably for similar reasons.

What can you expect of women, when you consider that the most distinguished intellects among them have never produced a single achievement in the fine arts that is really great, genuine, and original. Not even in painting, where mastery of technique is as much within their power as within man's, and where they have diligently cultivated it. The case is not altered by a few partial exceptions. Taken together, women are and remain thorough Philistines and incurable.

There is no proportion between the troubles of life and the gains of life. In the lives of the brute creation, the vanity of life's struggle is easily grasped. The variety and ingenuity of adaptation contrasts sharply with any lasting aim. Only momentary comfort, only fleeting pleasures conditioned and succeeded by want, much suffering, long strife, war of all against all as Hobbes has it, each one a hunter and a hunted, everywhere pressure, need, anxiety, shrieking, howling, and sudden death. And this, *in secula seculorum* or till once again the crust of the planet breaks.

The bulldog ant of Australia affords us a most instructive example. If it is cut in two, a battle begins between the head and the tail. The head seizes the tail with its teeth; the tail defends itself by stinging the head. The battle may last for half an hour, until they die or are dragged off by other ants.

Yunghahn relates that he saw in Java a plain, as far as the eye could reach, entirely covered with skeletons. He took it for a battlefield. They were, however, merely the skeletons of large turtles which come out of the sea to lay their eggs and are then attacked by wild dogs who drag them over onto their backs, strip off the small shell from the stomach, and devour them alive. For this, these turtles are born. Thus life preys upon itself, and in different forms is its own nourishment.

Under the firm crust of the planet dwell powerful forces of nature. Some accident affords them free play. The crust is destroyed, with every living thing on it. The earthquake of Lisbon, the destruction of Pompeii, are only playful hints of what is possible.

The only thing that reconciles me to the Old Testament is the story of the Fall. In my eyes, that is the only metaphysical truth in the book, even though it appears as an allegory. There seems to me no better explanation of our existence than that it is the result of some false step, some sin for which we are paying the penalty.

Vanini, whom his contemporaries burned, finding that easier than refuting him, put the same matter in a very forcible way: "Man is so full of misery that, if it were not contrary to the Christian religion, I should say that evil spirits, if there are any, have passed into human form and are now atoning for their crimes."

Tragedy is the summit of poetical art. The pain and wail of humanity, the triumph of evil, the mastery of chance, the fall of just and innocent, are here presented for us. And in it lies a significant hint of the nature of the world and man: the strife of the will against itself comes here into prominence. It is shown in the sufferings of men due to chance and error, reaching sometimes even the appearance of design. This we are led to see in the noblest works of the tragic muse.

Religious teachers tell us that suicide is cowardice, that only a madman could be guilty of it, and other insipidities of the same kind. Or else they make the nonsensical remark that suicide is wrong, when obviously there is nothing to which every man has a more unassailable title than to his own life and person.

The ancients did not regard the matter in that light. Pliny says "Life is not so desirable as to be protracted at any cost. Whoever you are you are sure to die, even though your life has been full of abomination and crime. The chief remedy for a troubled mind is the feeling that there is no greater blessing than an opportune death; and that every one can avail himself of."

Two Chinamen traveling in Europe paid their first visit to the theater. One of them spent all his time studying the machinery. He succeeded in finding out how it was worked. The other tried to get at the meaning of the piece being presented, in spite of his ignorance of the language. There you have the scientist and the philosopher.

The citations thus far have been expressions of Schopenhauer's pessimism and cynicism. They form a necessary prolegomenon to his metaphysical voluntarism. His general argument is to this effect: Metaphysical voluntarism is the only hypothesis which will account for the many facts upon which I base my cynicism and pessimism. The next four citations set forth his fundamental thesis.

I teach that the inner nature of everything is will.

That which makes itself known to us in the most immediate knowledge as our will is also that which objectifies or manifests itself at different grades in all the phenomena of the world.

If we observe the unceasing impulse with which the waters hurry to the ocean, the persistence with which the magnet turns to the pole, the readiness with which iron flies to the magnet; if we see the crystal take form, the attraction and repulsion of bodies; if we feel how a burden which hampers us by its gravitation toward the earth presses and strains in pursuit of its one tendency — if we note all these things, it requires no great effort of the imagination to recognize in nature what is will in us.

As the magic lantern shows many different pictures made visible by one and the same light, so in all the multifarious phenomena which fill the world, or throng after each other as events, only one will manifests itself, of which everything is the visibility, the objectivity, the manifestation. It is that which is identical in all this variety and change.

To throw his position into bolder relief, Schopenhauer contrasts it with pantheism, the belief that reality is God Himself manifested in everything.

Pantheism is the belief that God is the world — a belief which has always puzzled me. Taking an unprejudiced view of the world as it is, who would regard it as a god? A very ill-advised god, surely, who knows no better than to turn himself into such a world as ours, such a mean, shabby world; there to take the form of countless millions who are fretted and tormented, who live only by preying upon one another. What a pastime for a god!

With the pantheist, I have that One-in-All in common; but my One is not God. I do not go beyond experience, taken in its widest sense; and still less do I fly in the face of the facts which lie before me. The "God" of pantheism is, and must ever remain, an unknown "X." The will, on the other hand, is the one thing known most immediately in experience and therefore exclusively fitted for the explanation of the rest. What is unknown should always be explained by what is better known, not conversely.

The "God" of pantheism manifests himself to unfold his glory. What glory! Apart from the vanity here attributed to him by pantheism, there is immediately created the obligation to sophisticate away the colossal evil of the world. With me, there is none of this. With me alone, the evil of the world is honestly confessed in its whole magnitude. I alone have no need to have recourse to palliatives and sophistries.

From pantheism, he turns to the more orthodox alternative of theism, the belief, namely, that nature is God's handiwork:

There are two things which make it impossible to believe that this world is the successful work of a wise, good and all-powerful Being. The first is the misery which abounds everywhere. The second is the obvious imperfection of its highest product, man, who is a burlesque of what he should be.

In its explanation of the origin of the world — creation by God — Judaism is inferior to any other form of religious doctrine professed by a civilized people. That Jehovah should have created this world of misery and woe, because he enjoyed doing it, and should then have clapped his hands in praise of his own work, declaring everything to be good — that will not do at all!

I shall be told that my philosophy is comfortless — because I speak the truth. People prefer to be assured that everything the Lord has made is good. Go to the priests, then. Or go to your university professors; they are bound to preach optimism; and it is an easy task to upset their theories.

These matters of contrast noted, he resumes the exposition of his own metaphysical thesis:

That which, in us, pursues its ends by the light of knowledge, strives in nature blindly and dumbly in a one-sided and unchangeable manner. Yet in both cases it may be brought under the conception of will; just as the first dim light of dawn must share the name of sunlight with the rays of full midday.

The lowest grades of the objectification of the will are to be found in those most universal forces of nature which partly appear in all matter, as gravity, impenetrability, and so on, which it is the work of physics and chemistry to discover. They are the simplest modes of its objectification.

The conception of "will" has hitherto been subordinated to the conception of "force." I reverse the matter. I desire that every force in nature be understood in terms of will. This is not mere quibbling. For at the basis of the conception of force, as of all conceptions except will, there lies the sense-perceptual knowledge of the objective world, and the conception is constructed out of this. It is hence an abstraction from what is given in sense-perception. We have no direct experience of "forces" in nature, only of connections and sequences. The conception of will, however, is of all conceptions the one which does not have its origin in sense perception, in ideas of things. It comes from within, and proceeds from our immediate consciousness. If therefore, we refer the conception of will to the conception of force we have referred the better known to the less known.

From inanimate nature, Schopenhauer passes to the world of living things. It, too, is only a higher manifestation of the same underlying will:

Every species of animal is a <u>longing of the will-to-live</u>. For instance, the will is seized with a longing to live on trees, to hang from their branches, to devour their leaves. This longing becomes objectified in the sloth. It can hardly walk, being only adapted for climbing. It is helpless on the ground, agile on trees, looks like moss so as to escape its pursuers.

The will is active in nature where no knowledge guides it. This we see in the <u>instincts</u> and mechanical skills of animals. The ends toward which they strive are to them unknown. <u>The bird of a year old has no idea of eggs for which it builds a nest.</u> The young spider has no idea of the prey for which it spins its first web. Ants, marmots, bees, lay in provision for the winter they have never experienced. Insects deposit their eggs where the coming brood finds future nourishment. The larva of the stag beetle makes the hole in the wood, in which it is to await its metamorphosis, twice as big if it is going to be a male beetle as it would if it were going to be a female beetle — so that there will be room for the horns which no female beetle possesses. Has it knowledge thus in advance? The point is merely this: Knowledge is not necessary to guide will. It acts instinctively at some levels.

The instincts of plants and animals give us the best illustration of what is meant by teleology in nature. <u>An instinct, is an action like that which is guided by a purpose, and is yet entirely without this purpose.</u> So all constructions of nature resemble that which is guided by an aim, and yet is entirely without it. What we think to be means and end is, in every case, the manifestation of the unity of the one will.

Everywhere in nature pervading this adaptation we see strife. In this we can recognize that variance with itself which is essential to the will. Every grade of objectification fights for the matter of the others. The permanent matter must continually change its form. This strife may be followed through the whole of nature. It is most visible in the animal kingdom. For animals have the whole of the vegetable kingdom for their food, and within the animal kingdom one order is the prey and food of another. Thus the will everywhere preys upon itself and in different forms is its own nourishment.

From the lower forms of animal life, Schopenhauer turns to consider the higher levels at which instinct and impulse are somewhat modified by the emergence of intellect and knowledge.

From grade to grade, yet still without consciousness, as an obscure striving force, the will rises through matter and the vegetable kingdoms to the point at which the individuals in whom it is manifested can no longer receive food through mere movement following upon stimuli. The chances of the individual that is moved merely by stimuli would be too unfavorable. Its food must be sought out and selected. For this purpose movement following upon motive, and therefore consciousness, becomes necessary.

Consciousness, called in at this stage for the conservation of the individual, appears. It is represented by the brain, just as every other effort of the will is represented by an organ. With this new addition, the "world as idea" comes into existence at a stroke, with all its forms and categories, its subject and object, its time and space and causality and multiplicity. The world now shows its second side.

Till now mere will, it becomes now also idea, object to a knowing conscious subject. Up to this point the will followed its tendency in the dark with unerring certainty. But at this grade it kindles for itself a light as a means to an end, as an instrument needed to deal with the throng and complication of its prior manifestations; a need which would have accrued precisely to its highest manifestation.

The hitherto infallible certainty and regularity with which will worked in unorganized and vegetable matter, rested upon the fact that it alone was active in its original nature as blind impulse, as unconscious will, without interruption from a second and entirely different world, the world of perception. But with consciousness, its infallible certainty comes to an end. Animals are thereby exposed to deception and error. They have, however, only ideas arising out of perception. They have no conceptual powers, no reflective powers, and are therefore bound to the present.

This "knowledge without reason" becomes insufficient. When

the will has attained to the highest grade of its objectification, the kind of knowledge which arises out of mere perception confined to what is immediately present to the senses, does not suffice. That complicated and many-sided imaginative being, man, with his many needs, exposed to innumerable dangers, must, if he is to exist, be lighted by a double knowledge. A higher power than mere perception must be given him.

With this new power of reasoning, of framing and using abstract conceptions, there has appeared reflection, surveying the past, anticipating the future, deliberation, care, premeditated action, and finally the full and distinct awareness of one's own deliberate volition as such.

With mere knowledge of perception there arose the possibility of illusion and error, by which the previous infallibility of the blind striving of the will was done away with. With the entrance of reasoning powers that certainty and infallibility are almost entirely lost. Instinct diminishes. Deliberation, supposed to supplant everything from physical causation to instinctive reaction, begets irresolution and uncertainty. Errors become widely possible, and in many cases obstruct the will in action.

Thus knowledge, rational as well as sensuous, proceeds originally from the will itself, belongs to the inner being of the higher grades of its objectification as an instrument of selection and adaptation, a means of supporting the individual and the species like any other organ. Destined to forward the aims of the will, it remains almost entirely subject to its service. It is so in all brutes and in almost all men.

In all grades of its manifestations, from the lowest inorganic forms to the highest organic forms, the will is controlled by no final goal or aim. It always strives, for striving is its sole nature which no attaining can put to an end. Therefore it is not capable of any final satisfaction, but only of obstruction. This endless striving, of the will-to-be, the will-to-live, the will-to-conquer, the will-to-reproduce, we see everywhere, and see hindered in many ways. Wherever blocked, we see suffering. So if there be no final aim and no final satisfaction, there are no measure and end of suffering.

We ask: For what purpose does all this torment and agony exist? There is only one consideration that may serve to explain. It is this: The will-to-live, which underlies the whole world of phenomena, must satisfy its cravings by feeding on itself. This it does by forming a graduated scale of phenomena in which one level exists at the expense of another. Note two animals, one of which is engaged in eating the other.

By now man's place in nature has been indicated. Two citations conclude this somewhat evolutionary account.

In the life of man all this appears with greatest distinctness, illumined by the clearest knowledge. As the manifestation of the will rises higher, the suffering becomes more apparent. In the plant there is no sensibility and therefore no pain. In the lowest forms of animal life, a small degree of suffering may be experienced. As the level rises, sensitivity becomes wider and deeper. It appears in a high degree with the complete nervous system of backboned animals, and increases as intelligence develops. Thus, as knowledge increases, as consciousness attains to greater distinctness, pain also increases, and reaches its highest degree in man. And the more intelligent and finely formed a man is, the more pain he is open to.

Every human being is only another short dream of that endless spirit of nature, the persistent will-to-live; only another fleeting form carelessly sketched on an infinite page, and obliterated to make room for new. And every one of these fleeting forms must be paid for with many deep and long-drawn sufferings, and finally with a relentless death. Do you wonder why the sight of a corpse is never funny?

From the vantage point of his metaphysical hypothesis Schopenhauer feels himself in a position to account, in a general way, for the futility, the restlessness, the unhappiness and boredom which mark human life. If mankind is nothing but an objectification of a blindly striving universal will, what else could be expected?

Man's appetites are insatiable. Every satisfaction he gets lays the seeds of some new desire. There is hence no end to the wishes of any

individual will.   Why is this?   The reason is simple.   Will is the
lord of all worlds.   Everything is but a manifestation of will.
Therefore no one single thing can ever give it satisfaction.   Only the
totality of things — which is endless.

The basis of all willing and striving is need, deficiency, pain.
Thus the nature of man is subject to pain originally and in its essence.   If, on the other hand, it lacks objects of desire, a terrible
void and boredom comes over it.   Thus man's life swings like a
pendulum, backwards and forwards, between uneasiness and boredom.   (Hence, in his speculations, after man had transferred all
pains to hell, there remained nothing over for heaven but
boredom.)

Real boredom is by no means an evil to be lightly esteemed.   In
the end it depicts on the countenance a real despair.   It makes
beings who love each other so little as men do, seek each other
eagerly.   Like its opposite evil, famine in every form, it provokes
us to elaborate precautions.   People require *panem et circenses* —
bread and circuses.   As want is the constant scourge of the lower
classes, boredom is the lash laid across the back of the fashionable
world.   In the great middle classes, boredom is represented by
Sunday and want by the six weekdays.

Thus, between desiring and attaining, all human life flows on.
The wish is, in its nature, uneasiness.   The attainment soon begets
satiety.   The end was only apparent, and possession drives away
the charm.

It should be added to this that satisfaction, or what is commonly
called *happiness*, is never positive.   It is not something original,
growing out of itself, so to speak;   but must always be the satisfaction of some wish or longing.   The wish, the want, the need,
the desire, these are the positive things;   and these precede, condition, and follow every satisfaction.

The life of every individual, surveyed as a whole, is a tragedy.
Here and there in detail, it may have the character of a comedy.
The restless irritations of a moment, the needs and vexations of a
day, the mishaps and fears of a week, are scenes in a comedy.   But
the overarching, never-satisfied wishes, the frustrated efforts, the
crushed and abandoned hopes, the deep errors of a whole life, with

increasing pain or boredom, and death at the close, are always a tragedy. As if the fates would add derision to the miseries of our existence, our life must contain all the ingredients of a tragedy while in detail it will have the foolish look of a comedy.

That happiness is not something positive, that it is merely the satisfaction of some want, to be followed by another or by ennui, finds support in art, that true mirror of the world and life. Every epic and dramatic poem can only represent struggle, effort, fight for happiness; never-enduring and complete happiness. It conducts its heroes through a thousand difficulties and dangers to the goal. But, as soon as this is reached, the curtain falls, for now there remains nothing for it to do but show that what lured the hero on as happiness, materialized as disappointment.

Everyone who has awakened from the first dream of youth will realize, if his judgment is not paralyzed, that this world is the kingdom of chance and error, of folly and wickedness. Hence, everything better only struggles through with difficulty. What is noble and wise seldom attains to expression. The absurd and perverse in thought, the dull and tasteless in art, the wicked and deceitful in action, assert a real supremacy broken only by brief interruptions. In vain the sufferer calls on his gods for help. This irremediable evil is only the mirror of the will, of which himself is the objectification.

To me, optimism, when it is not merely the thoughtless verbalizing of those who have nothing but words under their low foreheads, is not merely absurd; it is wicked. It is a bitter mockery of the unspeakable misery of mankind. To me, as to the writers of the Gospels, the *world* and *evil* are almost synonymous terms.

Thus far Schopenhauer the metaphysician. Now Schopenhauer the moralist. The latter directs the argument from this point to its despairing conclusion. In our own day Thomas Hardy has expressed in poetry what Schopenhauer, up to this point, has been arguing in prose.

Given this view of things, what message does Schopenhauer deliver to mankind? It is one of pity and self-mortification. His argument turns to these matters, beginning with an explanation of the origin of humanity's pervasive egoism and selfishness, working around gradually to counsels of despair.

What I have been saying comes to this: In the whole of nature, at all the grades of the objectification of the will, there is a necessary and constant conflict, expressing the inner contradiction of the will with itself. This phenomenon exhibits itself with greater distinctness at the highest level of the will's objectification, namely in man. What I propose now is to trace to its source that egoism which is the starting point of all conflict.

The will everywhere manifests itself in separate individuals. But this separateness does not concern the will as it is in itself. The will itself is present, whole and undivided, in every one of these — as the color red is present, whole and undivided, in any red object — and beholds around it the innumerably repeated images of its own nature. Therefore everyone desires everything for himself, and would destroy whatever would oppose it. Every individual feels himself the center of the world, has a primary and inextinguishable regard for his own existence and well-being.

This disposition, which I call *egoism*, is essential to everything in nature. It is by reason of this primary fact that the inner conflict of the will with itself attains such terrible proportions. Yet this egoism has its being and continuance in that opposition of the microcosm and the macrocosm, in the fact that the objectification of the will has individualization as its form, in the fact that it manifests itself in the same way in innumerable individuals. In the highest grade of consciousness all this appears in its sharpest form.

We see the consequences of this basic fact everywhere in human life, in small things and great. We see its terrible side in the lives of great tyrants and miscreants, and in world-desolating wars. We see its absurd side in conceit, vanity, and minor selfishness. We see it writ large in history, which is the record of struggles ranging from vast armies to pairs of human alley cats. We see it when any mob of men is set free from law and order and restraint. Then that "war of all against all" which Hobbes has described so admirably, shows itself. This is the highest expression of egoism.

This "primary and ineradicable egoism" is the fact upon which Schopenhauer proceeds to build a moral philosophy, an ethics of pity and despair.

Out of this primary and ineradicable egoism arise both misery and wickedness. Do we desire to know what men so constituted, are worth in moral terms? We have only to consider their fate as a race. This is want, wretchedness, affliction, misery, and death. There is a species of eternal justice in it all. In this sense the world is the judgment of the world. Could we lay the misery of the world in one scale of the balance, and the guilt of the world in the other, the needle would point to the center.

I referred to an eternal justice in the scheme of things. To him who has grasped in all of its ramifications the thought which I have been developing, this will be evident. The world, in all its parts is the manifestation of one will. The will is free. The will is almighty. The world is its mirror. As the will is, so is the world. It alone bears the responsibility for what comes into being.

However, the world does not stand thus revealed to the knowledge of him whose mind is still bound to the service of his will, as it does to him who has risen to an entirely objective contemplation. The vision of the uncultured individual is clouded. He does not see the reality behind the phenomenon in time and space. He sees not the inner unity and identity of things, but only its separated, individualized, disunited, opposed, manifestations. For him pleasure is one thing and pain another. He sees one manifestation of the will live in abundance and ease, while at his door another dies of want and cold. He asks, "Where is Justice?"

But the vision of eternal justice is beyond him. He sees no inner connection. He sees the wicked flourish and the oppressed suffer. He cannot rise above these individual differences. Hence he does not understand the nature of this world's justice. That man only will grasp and comprehend eternal justice who raises himself above particular things, who sees through the individualizations of the real. He alone sees that the difference between him who inflicts suffering and him who bears it, is phenomenal only and concerns not the will as thing-in-itself. The inflicter of suffering and the sufferer are one. If the eyes of both were opened, the inflicter of suffering would see that he lives in all that suffers pain. The sufferer would see that all the wickedness in the world proceeds from that will which constitutes his own nature.

The comprehension of this eternal justice, of the tie that unites the evil of my crime with the evil of your misery, demands the power to rise above the limits of individuality. Therefore it will always remain unattainable by most men.

What I have been arguing is this: Hatred and wickedness are conditioned by egoism, and egoism rests on the entanglement of knowledge in the principle of individuation, in the fact that the will realizes itself in separate individuals.

If this penetration of the principle of individuation, this direct knowledge of the identity of the will in its diverse manifestations, is present in a high degree of distinctness, it will show an influence upon the will of the individual who has achieved this insight. If the veil is lifted from his eyes so that he no longer makes the egotistical distinction between his self and other selves, then he will regard the infinite suffering of all sufferers as his own.

To such a man no suffering is any longer strange to him. All the miseries of others work upon his mind like his own. It is no longer the changing joy and sorrow of his own person that he has in view. All lies equally near him. He knows the ultimately real, and finds that it consists in a constant passing away, a vain striving, an inward conflict, a continual suffering. Wherever he looks he sees suffering humanity and a world in passage. But all this now lies as near him as his own person lies to the man who is still in bondage to egoism.

The moralist, backed by the metaphysician, is now in a position to ask pointedly: Why should man, with this knowledge of ultimate reality, accept life on such terms? Why should man be a yea-sayer? Why not a nay-sayer?

Why should he, now, with this knowledge of ultimate reality, assert this very life through constant acts of will? Knowledge of the nature of the thing-in-itself becomes a quieter of the individual will. The individual will now turns away from life, now shudders at the pleasures in which it once recognized the assertion of life, now attains to voluntary renunciation, resignation, indifference, will-less-ness.

If we compare life to a course which we must run, a path of red-hot coals with here and there a cool spot, then he who is still entangled in the egoistic delusion is consoled by the cool places and sets out to run the course. But he who sees through individualization to the one will which is identical in all, is no longer susceptible to such consolation. He sees himself in all places at once, and withdraws. His will turns round, no longer asserts itself, but denies.

This denial of the will by an individual manifestation of it follows the recognition of the real nature of the thing-in-itself. It is the transition from virtue to asceticism. This is to say, when a man has once seen, it no longer suffices for him to love others as himself. There arises within him a horror of that will of which he is himself a manifestation.

Nothing but a manifestation of the will, the individual ceases now to will anything. His body he denies. His health he is indifferent to. His desires he ignores. He desires no gratification of any appetite in any form.

More concretely, what is meant by this exhortation to suppress and deny the will-to-live? Schopenhauer is clear enough about it all. Upon unhappy man he urges a program of chastity, asceticism, self-chastisement, and ultimate starvation:

Voluntary and complete chastity is the first step in asceticism, the first move in the denial of the will-to-live. It denies the assertion of the will which extends beyond the individual's own life. It gives assurance that the life of this body, the will whose manifestation it is, ceases.

Asceticism shows itself further in voluntary and intentional poverty; not only *per accidens* as when possessions are given away to mitigate the sufferings of others, but directly to serve as a constant mortification of the will, so that the satisfaction of desires, the sweet things of life, shall not rouse the will of which a penetrating self-knowledge has conceived a horror.

Asceticism extends further as humility and patience. He who denies the will as it appears in his own person will not resist if another does wrong to him. Suffering, insult, ignominy, he will receive gladly, as the opportunity of learning that he no longer stands behind his will. Patience and meekness will replace impatience and pride and anger.

Asceticism culminates in self-chastisement, fasting, and starvation. By constant privation and suffering he who has seen the nature and source of the evil of life in the will-to-live, is able more and more to break down and destroy that manifestation in himself; to crush in himself that which he recognizes and abhors as the source of his own and humanity's misery and wickedness.

When death comes to such a one, it is most welcome. Here it is not, as in the case of others, merely the manifestation of the will that ends in death. The inner nature of the will has long been restrained, denied, crushed. The last slight bond is now broken. For him who ends thus, the world also ends.

With a backward glance over the whole argument of his metaphysics and moral philosophy, Schopenhauer concludes:

What I have described here with feeble tongue and only in general terms, is no philosophical fable. It is the moral of the life of saints and ascetics in all ages and all religions. The inner nature of holiness, self-renunciation, mortification, is here expressed, abstractly and free from mythology, as the denial of the will-to-live, appearing after the complete knowledge of its own nature has become a quieter of all volition.

Before us there is certainly only nothingness. We look with deep and painful longing upon the perfect calm of the spirit which has strangled and subdued the will-to-live. Beside it, the misery and evil of life is thrown into clear contrast. Yet, only when we have recognized the incurable suffering and endless wickedness which follows upon the assertion of the will, and have ordered our days to its denial, do we attain any lasting consolation. To those in whom the will has turned against itself, this world of planets, suns, and milky ways is nothing.

READING REFERENCES. In a book by R. A. Tsanoff, *The Nature of Evil*, will be found a good, brief account of Schopenhauer's life and thought. Tsanoff writes on a gallery of pessimists, but his tenth and eleventh chapters are on Schopenhauer alone. A book by V. J. McGill, *Schopenhauer: Pessimist and Pagan*, is a popular biographical study. There is an edition of Schopenhauer, by Will Durant, which contains the best selections. There is a single-volume collection of essays, *Essays of Schopenhauer*, in which seven small volumes are bound in one. These are more easily read than the selections from *The World as Will and Idea*. Much criticism of Schopenhauer is either narrowly technical, in which case the whole point of the man is somehow overlooked, or is so pious and horror-stricken that one feels that after all there must be something to what Schopenhauer says. An exception to this might be found in the "Pessimism" chapter of Paulen's *System of Ethics*. A valuable little book, *Thomas Hardy's Universe*, by Ernest Brennecke, will show the way in which Schopenhauer's metaphysics forms a basis upon which Hardy's poems, tales, and novels can be understood.

READING QUESTIONS

1. Explain the point involved in Schopenhauer's references to the following: (*a*) Dante, (*b*) slavery, (*c*) Leibnitz, (*d*) Kant, (*e*) woman, (*f*) monogamy, (*g*) the bulldog ant, (*h*) wild dogs in Java, (*i*) the Fall, (*j*) tragedy, (*k*) suicide, (*l*) the two Chinamen.
2. What metaphysical hypothesis does he propose?
3. Wherein does he contrast his position with pantheism?
4. Wherein with theism?
5. Wherein does he consider his hypothesis as being superior to the hypothesis of force?
6. What account does he give of intelligence?
7. Between what alternatives does human life swing?
8. What has he to say of optimism?

9. What does he mean by *egoism?*

10. How does he pass from it to his conception of eternal justice?

11. What conclusions does he draw, with respect to the conduct of life?

12. Formulate two or more questions you would put to Schopenhauer.

5. THE PRAGMATIC APPROACH TO METAPHYSICS — FROM WILLIAM JAMES

FROM SCHOPENHAUER TO JAMES. Our problem remains: Granted a distinction between appearance and reality, what is the nature of reality? We have seen dualism in Descartes, materialism in Hobbes, idealism in Berkeley, and voluntarism in Schopenhauer. The case for any metaphysical hypothesis is, in the end, its power to account for the everyday world. Any hypothesis in metaphysics which makes the everyday world an unaccountable puzzle; any hypothesis which, if followed out, would require some other sort of everyday world than the one we have — any such hypothesis is unsatisfactory. In metaphysics, as elsewhere, the function of an hypothesis is to account for the facts, and the everyday world is, here, the "facts." Which hypothesis being true, would go furthest to account for our everyday world? Descartes'? Hobbes'? Berkeley's? Schopenhauer's? There is, no doubt, something to be said for each. It would be odd, indeed, if one of these historic hypotheses should turn out to have *no* power to account for the everyday world.

This notion, that an hypothesis in metaphysics stands or falls by its power to account for the everyday world, is the central claim made by William James. We must conceive James as thinking over the possible alternatives in metaphysics and asking himself the perennial question, "How estimate the value of each one? How justify the acceptance or rejection of any one of these?" We may proceed at once to examine his argument.

BIOGRAPHICAL NOTE.   See under "A Theological Problem," page 73.

THE ARGUMENT OF THE CITATIONS.   James first explains what he means by *pragmatism*, or the *pragmatic approach*, in metaphysics.   It is a way of dealing with metaphysical hypotheses.   He applies it, then, to several hypotheses, to show what he means.   He begins as follows:

The pragmatic method is primarily a matter of settling metaphysical disputes that otherwise might be interminable. Is the world one or many?   Fated or free?   Material or spiritual?   Here are notions either of which may or may not hold good of the world, and disputes over such notions are unending.

A glance at the history of the idea will show you what *pragmatism* means.   The term is derived from the same Greek word *pragma* meaning "action," from which our words *practice* and *practical* come.   It was first introduced into philosophy by Charles Peirce in 1878, in an article entitled "How to Make Our Ideas Clear."   After pointing out that beliefs are really rules for action, Mr. Peirce said that to develop a thought's meaning we need only determine what conduct it is fitted to produce; that conduct is its sole significance.

A few years ago the German chemist, Ostwald, wrote to me: "All realities influence our practice, and that influence is their meaning for us.   I am accustomed to put questions to my classes in this way: In what respects would the world be different if this alternative or that were true?   If I can find nothing that would become different, then the alternative had no sense."   This is genuine pragmatism.

Metaphysics has usually followed a very primitive kind of quest. The universe has always appeared to the natural mind as a kind of enigma, of which the key must be sought in the shape of some illuminating word or name, like *God, Matter, Reason, the Absolute,* or *Energy.*

The pragmatic method in such cases is to try to interpret each notion by tracing its respective practical consequences.   What difference would it practically make to any one if this notion, rather than that notion were true?

If no practical difference whatever can be traced, then the alternatives mean practically the same thing, and all dispute is idle. Whenever a dispute is serious, we ought to be able to show some practical difference that must follow from one side or the other's being right.

But if you follow the pragmatic method, you must bring out of each word its practical cash value, set it at work within the stream of your experience. It appears more as a program for further work than as a solution. Theories thus become instruments, not answers to enigmas, in which we can rest.

To attain perfect clearness in our thoughts of an object, then, we need only consider what conceivable effects of a practical kind the object may involve — what sensations we are to expect from it and what reactions we must prepare. Our conception of these effects is for us the whole of our conception of the object, so far as that conception has positive significance at all.

Pragmatism does not stand for any special results. It is a method only. It is an attitude of orientation. The attitude of looking away from first things, principles, "categories," supposed necessities; and of looking toward last things, fruits, consequences, facts. It has no dogmas and no doctrines save its method.

It lies in the midst of our theories like a corridor in a hotel. Innumerable chambers open out of it. In one, you may find a man writing an atheistic volume; in the next, someone on his knees praying for faith and strength; in a third, a chemist investigating a body's properties; in a fourth, a system of idealistic metaphysics being excogitated; in a fifth, the impossibility of metaphysics is being shown. But they all own the corridor, and all must pass through it if they want a practicable way of getting into or out of their respective rooms.

It is astonishing to see how many philosophical disputes collapse into insignificance the moment you subject them to this simple test of tracing their concrete consequences.

So much, then, for the meaning of pragmatism in metaphysics. There are two questions, it seems, which one should ask of any metaphysical hypothesis: (1) What sort of everyday world would there be, if it were true?" (2) "What sort of conduct would be required of me, as an intelligent being, in the everyday world, if it were true?" James was not the first person to take metaphysics thus seriously. Berkeley, it will be remembered, was not oblivious to the demands on conduct made by his hypothesis. Schopenhauer was even more explicit. William James proposes to begin by applying his pragmatic test to the question of substance and quality:

I will begin with what is driest. The first thing I shall take will be the problem of substance. Every man uses the old distinction between substance and attribute. Here is a bit of blackboard crayon. Its attributes or properties are whiteness, friability, cylindrical shape, insolubility in water, etc. But the bearer of these attributes is so much chalk, which thereupon is called the "substance" in which they inhere. So the attributes of this desk inhere in the substance "wood," those of my coat in the "wool," and so forth. Chalk, wood, and wool show again, in spite of their differences, common properties, and insofar forth they are themselves counted as modes of a still more primal substance, matter, the attributes of which are space-occupancy and impenetrability.

Now it was very early seen that all we know of the chalk is the whiteness, friability, etc., all we know of the wood is the combustibility and fibrous structure. A group of attributes is what each substance is known as. They form its sole cash value for our actual experience. The substance is in every case revealed through them; if we were cut off from them, we should never suspect its existence; and if God should keep sending them to us in an unchanged order, miraculously annihilating at a certain moment the substance that supported them, our experiences themselves would be unaltered.

Nominalism is the opinion that substance is a spurious idea due to our inveterate human trick of turning names into things. Phenomena come in groups — the chalk group, the wood group, etc. — and each group gets its name. The name we then treat as in a way supporting the group of phenomena. The low thermometer today, for instance, is supposed to come from something called *climate*. Climate is really only the name for a certain group of days, but it is treated as if it lay behind the day, and in general we place the name, as if it were a being, behind the facts it is the name of.

But the phenomenal properties of things, nominalists say, surely do not really inhere in names, and if not in names then they do not inhere in anything. They adhere, or cohere, rather, with each other, and the notion of a substance inaccessible to us, which we think accounts for such cohesion by supporting it, as cement might support pieces of mosaic, must be abandoned. The fact of the bare cohesion itself is all that the notion of the substance signifies. Behind that fact there is nothing.

The notion of a substance which underlies certain observed qualities is, by now, a familiar one. We have met it in previous chapters. What difference, we might have asked, does it make whether there *is* such a thing as substance so conceived? What difference, furthermore, does it make *how* we conceive this thing? James draws attention to a point in Catholic theology which makes the notion of substance, under some circumstances, very important indeed:

Scholasticism, that is, philosophy in Christian Europe in the Middle Ages, has taken the notion of substance from common sense and made it very technical and articulate. Few things would seem to have fewer pragmatic consequences for us than substances, cut off as we are from every contact with them. Yet in one case scholasticism has proved the importance of the substance-idea by treating it pragmatically.

I refer to certain disputes about the mystery of the Eucharist. Substance here would appear to have momentous pragmatic value. Since the accidents of the wafer don't change in the Lord's supper, and yet it has become the very body of Christ, it must be that the change is in the substance solely. The bread substance must have been withdrawn, and the divine substance substituted miraculously without altering the immediate sensible properties. But though those don't alter, a tremendous difference has been made, no less a one than this, that we who take the sacrament, now feed upon the very substance of divinity. The substance notion breaks into life, then, with tremendous effect.

From medieval, James turns to modern theology:

Material substance was criticized by Berkeley with such telling effect that his name has reverberated through all subsequent philosophy. Berkeley's treatment of the notion of matter is so well known as to need hardly more than a mention. So far from denying the external world which we know, Berkeley corroborated it. It was the notion of a material substance unapproachable by us, behind the external world, deeper, and more real than it, and needed to support it, which Berkeley maintained to be the most effective of all reducers of the external world to unreality. Abolish that substance, he said, believe that God, whom you can understand and approach, sends you the sensible world directly, and you confirm the latter and back it up by his divine authority.

Berkeley's criticism of "matter" was consequently absolutely pragmatistic. Matter is known as our sensations of color, figure, hardness, and the like. They are the cash value of the term. The difference matter makes to us by truly being is that we then get such sensations; by not being, is that we lack them. These sensations then are its sole meaning. Berkeley doesn't deny matter, then; he simply tells us what it consists of. It is a true name for just so much in the way of sensations.

These by way of historical illustrations. James is not interested, primarily, in the history of metaphysics. He has other business to attend to. Says he:

The mention of "material substance" naturally suggests the doctrine of materialism, in the wider sense of explaining higher phenomena by lower ones, and leaving the destinies of the world at the mercy of its blinder parts and forces.

In this wider sense of the word, materialism is opposed to theism. The laws of physical nature are what run things, materialism says. The highest productions of human genius might be ciphered by one who had complete acquaintance with the facts, out of their physio-

logical conditions. This is the completion of present-day materialism, which may better be called *naturalism*. Over against it stands
theism, which says that mind not only witnesses and records things,
but also runs and operates them: the world being thus guided, not
by its lower, but by its higher element.

Let us apply the pragmatic method to the question. What do
we mean by *matter*? What practical difference can it make now that
the world should be run by matter or by spirit? I think we find
that the problem takes with this a rather different character.

In every genuine metaphysical debate some practical issue, however conjectural and remote, is involved. To realize this, revert
with me to our question, and place yourselves this time in the world
we live in, in the world that has a future, that is yet uncompleted
whilst we speak. In this unfinished world the alternative of
"materialism or theism" is intensely practical; and it is worth
while for us to spend some time in seeing that is so.

This, then, is the meaning of *materialism*, abstractly stated.
What of this, pragmatically considered?

You all know the picture of the last state of the universe which
science foresees. I cannot state it better than in Mr. Balfour's words:
"The energies of our system will decay, the glory of the sun will be
dimmed, and the earth, tideless and inert, will no longer tolerate
the race which has for a moment disturbed its solitude. Man will
go down into the pit, and all his thoughts will perish. The uneasy
consciousness which in this obscure corner has for a brief space
broken the contented silence of the universe, will be at rest. Matter
will know itself no longer. 'Imperishable monuments' and 'immortal deeds,' death itself, and love stronger than death, will be as
if they had not been. Nor will anything that is, be better or worse
for all that the labor, genius, devotion, and suffering of man have
striven through countless ages to effect."

That is the sting of it. In the vast driftings of the cosmic weather,
though many a jeweled shore appears, and many an enchanted
cloud bank floats away, long lingering ere it be dissolved — even
as our world now lingers, for our joy -- yet when these transient
products are gone, nothing, absolutely nothing remains to represent

those particular qualities, those elements of preciousness which they may have enshrined. Dead and gone are they, gone utterly from the very sphere and room of being. Without an echo; without a memory; without an influence on aught that may come after, to make it care for similar ideals. This utter final wreck and tragedy are of the essence of materialism as at present understood. The lower and not the higher forces are the eternal forces, or the last surviving forces within the only cycle of evolution which we can definitely see.

The true objection to materialism is not positive but negative. It would be farcical at this day to make complaint of it for what it is, for "grossness." Grossness is what grossness does — we now know that. We make complaint of it, on the contrary, for what it is not — not a permanent warrant for our more ideal interests, not a fulfiller of our remotest hopes.

The purpose is to contrast materialism with theism. We have seen what the former amounts to, pragmatically considered. What of theism?

The notion of God, on the other hand, however inferior it may be in clearness to these notions so current in philosophy, has at least this practical superiority over them, that it guarantees an ideal order that shall be permanently preserved. A world with a God in it to say the last word, may indeed burn up or freeze, but we then think of Him as still mindful of the old ideals and sure to bring them elsewhere to fruition; so that, where He is, tragedy is only provisional and partial, and shipwreck and dissolution not the absolutely final things. This need of an eternal moral order is one of the deepest needs of our breast. And those poets, like Dante and Wordsworth, who live on the conviction of such an order, owe to that fact the extraordinary tonic and consoling power of their verse.

Here then, in these different emotional and practical appeals, in these adjustments of our concrete attitudes of hope and expectation, and all the delicate consequences which their indifferences entail, lie the real meanings of materialism and theism — not in hairsplitting abstractions about matter's inner essence, or about the metaphysical attributes of God. *Materialism* means simply the denial that the moral order is eternal, and the cutting off of ultimate hopes. *Theism* means the affirmation of an eternal moral order and the letting loose of hope. Surely here is an issue genuine enough for anyone who feels it; and, as long as men are men, it will yield matter for a serious philosophic debate.

Possibly some of you may still rally to the defense of those who belittle such disputes. Even whilst admitting that theism and materialism make different prophecies of the world's future, you may pooh-pooh the difference as something so infinitely remote as to mean nothing for a sane mind. The essence of a sane mind, you may say, is to take shorter views, and to feel no concern about such chimaeras as the latter end of the world.

Well, I can only say that if you say this, you do injustice to human nature. Religious melancholy is not disposed of by a simple flourish of the word *insanity*. The absolute things, the last things, the overlapping things, are the truly philosophic concerns; all superior minds feel seriously about them, and the mind with the shortest views is simply the mind of the more shallow man.

The central metaphysical problem is this: What is the nature of ultimate reality? We have seen how an answer to this question may carry certain corollaries along with it. Thus Hobbes, a materialist in metaphysics, is also a determinist in psychology, denying that man has any free will. James, for pragmatic reasons, rejects materialism. Where does he stand on the question of determinism? From a consideration of materialism, he turns his attention to free will. Says he: "Let me take up another well-worn controversy, the free-will problem." Why, he asks, why have men been concerned to affirm or deny free will? Because, largely, they feel that questions of moral accountability and responsibility, moral praise and blame, depend upon it. Thus:

You know how large a part questions of accountability have played in ethical controversy. To hear some persons, one would suppose that all that ethics aims at is a code of merits and demerits.

Thus does the old legal and theological leaven, the interest in crime and sin and punishment abide with us. Who's to blame? Whom can we punish?

So both free will and determinism have been inveighed against and called absurd, because each, in the eyes of its enemies, has seemed to prevent the "imputability" of good or bad deeds to their authors. Queer antinomy this! Free will means novelty, the grafting onto the past of something not involved therein. If our acts were predetermined, if we merely transmitted the push of the whole past, the free-willists say, how could we be praised or blamed for anything? We should be "agents" only, not "principals," and where then would be our precious imputability and responsibility?

But where would it be if we had free will? Rejoin the determinists. If a "free" act be a sheer novelty, that comes not from me, the previous me, but *ex nihilo*, and simply tacks itself on to me, how can I, the previous I, be responsible? How can I have any permanent character that will stand still long enough for praise or blame to be awarded? The chaplet of my days tumbles into a cast of disconnected beads as soon as the thread of inner necessity is drawn out by the preposterous indeterminist doctrine.

So it goes, or has gone, James finds. With this way of stating the case for free will, he will have nothing to do. If the sole, or main reason for believing that man has a free will lies in the fact that we cannot otherwise censure him for his misdemeanors, then James has no interest in the question. Such reasoning, from either party, he says, "is pitiful." Thus:

I ask you, quite apart from other reasons, whether any man, woman, or child, with a sense for realities, ought not to be ashamed to plead such principles. Instinct and utility between them can safely be trusted to carry on the social business of punishment and praise. If a man does good acts, we shall praise him, if he does bad acts we shall punish him — anyhow, and quite apart from theories as to whether the acts result from what was previous in him or are novelties in a strict sense.

To make our human ethics revolve about the question of "merit" is a piteous unreality — God alone can know our merits, if we have any. The real ground for supposing free will is indeed pragmatic, but it has nothing to do with this contemptible right to punish which has made such a noise in past discussions of the subject.

What, then, *is* the case for free will? It is this: Granted that men have free will, i.e., *can* mold their own destinies in part, there is some ground for the hope that they will, since they *can*, improve the general conditions of life.

Free will pragmatically means novelties in the world, the right to expect that in its deepest elements as well as in its surface phenomena, the future may not identically repeat and imitate the past. That imitation *en masse* is there, who can deny? The general "uniformity of nature" is presupposed by every lesser law. But nature may be only approximately uniform; and persons in whom knowledge of the world's past has bred pessimism (or doubts as to the world's good character, which become certainties if that character be supposed eternally fixed) may naturally welcome free will as a melioristic doctrine. It holds up improvement as at least possible, whereas determinism assures us that our whole notion of possibility is born of human ignorance, and that necessity and impossibility between them rule the destinies of the world.

Free will is thus a general cosmological theory of promise, just like the Absolute, God, Spirit, or Design. Taken abstractly, no one of these terms has any inner content; none of them gives us any picture; and no one of them would retain the least pragmatic value in a world whose character was obviously perfect from the start. Elation at mere existence, pure cosmic emotion and delight, would, it seems to me, quench all interest in these speculations, if the world were nothing but a Lubberland of happiness already.

Our interest in free will arises from the fact that our empirical future feels to us unsafe, and needs some higher guarantee. If the past and present were purely good, who could wish that the future might possibly not resemble them? Who could desire free will? Who would not say, with Huxley, "Let me be wound up every day like a watch, to go right fatally, and I ask no better freedom."

"Freedom" in a world already perfect could only mean freedom to be worse, and who could be so insane as to wish that? The only possibility that one can rationally claim is the possibility that things may be better. That possibility, I need hardly say, is one that, as the actual world goes, we have ample grounds for desiderating.

Free will thus has no meaning unless it be a doctrine of relief. As such, it takes its place with other religious doctrines Between them, they build up the old wastes and repair the former desolations. Our spirit, shut within this courtyard of sense experience, is always saying to the intellect upon the tower: "Watchman, tell us of the night, if it aught of promise bear," and the intellect gives it then these terms of promise.

Other than this practical significance, the word *free will* has none. Yet dark though it be in itself, or intellectualistically taken, when we bear it into life's thicket with us the darkness there grows light about us. If you stop, in dealing with such words, with their definition, thinking that to be an intellectual finality, where are you? Stupidly staring at a pretentious sham! Pragmatism alone can read a positive meaning into it, and for that she turns her back upon the intellectualist point of view altogether.

James has, by now, done these things: He has explained what is meant by the *pragmatic* approach to questions in metaphysics. He has illustrated his point by reference to two historical digressions. He has used the method to justify his own stand on the questions of materialism and determinism. It remains for him to commend his doctrine to his readers:

See then how all these ultimate questions turn, as it were, upon their hinges; and, from looking backwards, see, I say, how pragmatism shifts the emphasis and looks forward into facts themselves.

The really vital question for us all is, What is this world going to be? What is life eventually to make of itself? The center of gravity of philosophy must therefore alter its place. The earth of things, long thrown into shadow by the glories of the upper ether, must resume its rights.

It will be an alteration in "the seat of authority" that reminds one almost of the Protestant Reformation. And as, to papal minds, Protestantism has often seemed a mere mess of anarchy and confusion, such, no doubt, will pragmatism often seem to ulta rationalist minds in philosophy. It will seem so much sheer trash, philosophically. But life wags on, all the same, and compasses its ends, in Protestant countries. I venture to think that philosophic Protestantism will compass a note of dissimilar prosperity.

I fully expect to see the pragmatist view of truth run through the classic stages of a theory's career. First a theory is attacked as absurd; then it is admitted to be true but obvious and insignificant; finally it is seen to be so important that its adversaries claim that they themselves discovered it.

READING REFERENCES. The best thing to read on William James is more by William James. He is a delightful and inspiring author. If his breeziness and buoyancy should pall, turn to an essay by G. E. Moore in his *Philosophical Studies*. The essay is simply named "William James's Pragmatism." Or read the essay, "William James," in Santayana's *Character and Opinion in the United States*. In an earlier chapter I mentioned R. B. Perry's *The Life and Thought of William James*. In *Studies in the History of Ideas*, Volume Two, there is a good article by John Dewey on the history of pragmatism. It should be read by anyone proposing to see James in an historical perspective.

READING QUESTIONS

1. What does he say pragmatism is?
2. By whom was it first introduced into philosophy?
3. How does he define *pragmatism* more closely?
4. What has this in common with his test proposed in "The Will to Believe"?
5. "Pragmatism does not stand for any special results." Meaning?
6. Develop his corridor analogy.
7. Explain what you understand by nominalism.

8. What use does James make of the doctrine of the Real Presence to illustrate his point?

9. What does he say of Berkeley's idealism?

10. What is the meaning of materialism as James conceives it?

11. Does this differ substantially from Hobbes?

12. To what end does he quote A. J. Balfour?

13. What is James's pragmatic criticism of materialism?

14. What is his pragmatic justification of theism?

15. "Pragmatism does not stand for any special results." Explain. Illustrate. State whether you agree or disagree.

16. On what grounds, according to James, have men accepted the free-will doctrine?

17. Why does he reject these grounds?

18. What is the pragmatic case for free will?

19. In what respect does James compare pragmatism to Protestantism?

20. Through what stages does he expect pragmatism to pass?

TOPIC THREE. AN EPISTEMO-
LOGICAL PROBLEM

THE PROBLEM STATED

The word *epistemology* is derived from two Greek words meaning "knowledge" and "the rationale of." It means an inquiry into the nature of knowledge. If the derivation were carried out, it would provide us with a somewhat complicated conception, namely, knowledge of the nature of knowledge. How, it may well be asked, did philosophers ever find themselves launched upon so subtle an inquiry? Its full subtlety might escape notice, unless one paused to realize precisely what is intended. Suppose we refer to the sciences as theories about the nature of things. Thus we have, in astronomy, a theory of the universe at large; in economics, a theory of the production and distribution of wealth; in psychology, a theory of the mind and its relation to the body; and so forth. These are all theories of things. But in the conception of epistemology, knowledge turns in upon itself and seeks to formulate a "theory" of itself. Here knowledge is itself made the object of investigation.

From an acquaintance with the theological and metaphysical speculations which comprise the first two divisions of this book, one can see in a general way how epistemology came about. There is a cautious turn of mind to which all such speculations seem to be of doubtful value. Such a mind is impressed finally with the futility of such matters, and with the confusion which emerges when men seek to clarify their beliefs about such things. Out of this attitude toward speculation, two widely different things have resulted. There have come, in the first place, the genial and undisciplined doubts of such persons as Montaigne and Anatole France. Here the procedure is largely one of banter and ridicule. But that has not been the doubter's only defense against the speculator. For, in the second place, there has come the demand that flights of speculation be put aside until a preliminary inquiry is made into the nature of knowledge itself, and the question faced: Can it be shown, from an analysis of the nature of knowledge itself, whether such speculations are legitimate, whether they lie within the actual or possible grasp of the mind?

The chapters that follow may, therefore, be considered as five approaches to a single problem: Can we make an inquiry into the nature of knowledge? From the findings of such an inquiry can we say anything about the scope or reach of human knowledge? Can we show that some speculations carry the quest for knowledge beyond a legitimate possibility?

The authors chosen for consideration are John Locke, from the seventeenth century; David Hume and Immanuel Kant, from the eighteenth century; Auguste Comte, from the nineteenth century; and Hans Vaihinger, from the twentieth century.

1. THE APPEAL TO EXPERIENCE — FROM JOHN LOCKE

Epistemology is by no means a modern inquiry. Indeed, one of the finest pieces of epistemological analysis ever written may be found in Plato's dialogue "The Theaetetus"; but not all of Plato was continuously read by the generations which came after him, with the result that much that appeared in the early modern centuries was taken to be new. It is in this sense that John Locke is described as the founder of modern epistemology. Questions of priority aside, however, there is no reasonable doubt that the enormous literature which has grown up around this problem owes its inspiration, directly or indirectly, to Locke's epoch-making *Essay Concern-*

ing Human Understanding. This famous old book is very long, very wordy, and very repetitious, but its historical importance is exceedingly great, for it drew attention, from the year it was published, to the central place in all philosophy of the problem of knowledge. What it said, in so many words, was this: Before any man launches into speculation, he should pause to inquire concerning the human understanding itself. What things is it capable of knowing? How does knowledge arise? Are there not some questions to which the answers lie beyond the reach of human understanding? Would not a cool hour spent in a reflective consideration of the nature of knowledge reveal precisely this sort of fact?

BIOGRAPHICAL NOTE. John Locke was born in England in 1632 and died in 1704 at the age of seventy-two. His life may be divided into three periods: years of education and educating, years of politics and governmental affairs, years of authorship. (1) He was educated at Westminster School and at Oxford University. After graduation he was made lecturer on Greek, and two years later, lecturer on rhetoric. While still a student, he had turned from the ancient and medieval authors and doctrines which then formed the basis of a university education. From Aristotle and the medieval schoolmen, for example, he felt drawn to Hobbes, Descartes, Bacon, and the new experimental sciences. These were the great molders of progressive opinion in his day. (2) In 1664 he left his work at the university and accepted the post of secretary to an Embassy to Brandenburg. This was the beginning of a long political and governmental career. The great political event of the times was the "bloodless" revolution of 1688. Locke allied himself, through the house of Shaftesbury, with the party which was to engineer the deposition of King James and the invitation to King William of Holland. (3) The revolution took place in 1688. Thereafter John Locke shared the prestige which attached to those who were instrumental in bringing it about. He was now a man of fifty-six, widely read, widely traveled, widely respected. He turned to publishing a series of treatises which gave expression to the ideas and aspirations of British liberalism in education, in politics, in religion, in philosophy. He had been writing these books for many years, but had not thus far ventured to publish. Now in rapid succession he issued *Letters Concerning Toleration, Essay Concerning Human Understanding, Two Treatises of Government, Some Thoughts Concerning Education, The Reasonableness of Christianity*. These volumes were published between 1689 and 1695. In six years, near the close of his life, Locke produced books which were destined to influence liberal thought for the next century.

THE ARGUMENT OF THE CITATIONS. The citations which follow pose the modern problem of knowledge. They do not solve it, but they point to the need for a solution, and they express the spirit in which this inquiry has been carried on. Locke begins by explaining why an inquiry concerning human understanding is important. He then asks the primary question: How does the human mind come by its knowledge? He pauses to state and refute one answer to this question current in his century, the hypothesis of innate ideas. He returns then to propound his own thesis: All knowledge comes from experience. This is known in philosophy as *empiricism*. He elaborates this claim in some detail. From the question of the origin of knowledge, he turns to the question of its limits. If knowledge arises in experience, how far can it reach? He distinguishes, to begin with, between intuitive and demonstrative knowledge. This suggests a further distinction between demonstrative and probable knowledge. With these distinctions made, Locke's theory of knowledge is complete; however, there were some who talked of a kind of knowledge, namely, *revelation*, which appeared not to fall anywhere within his scheme. His argument closes with some reflections on revelation and its relation to knowledge obtained through experience.

The argument begins with a series of reflections on the value of an inquiry into the nature of mind and knowledge:

> Since it is the understanding that sets man above the rest of sensible beings, and gives him all the advantage and dominion which he has over them, it is certainly a subject, even for its nobleness, worth our labor to inquire into.

This therefore is my purpose: to inquire into the original, certainty, and extent of human knowledge, together with the degrees of belief, opinion, and assent. It is worth while to search out the bounds between opinion and knowledge, and examine by what measures in things, whereof we have no certain knowledge, we ought to regulate our assent and moderate our persuasions.

If I can discover the powers of the understanding, how far they reach, to what things they are in any degree proportionate, and where they fail us, I suppose it may prevail with the busy mind of man to be more cautious in meddling with things exceeding its comprehension; to stop when it is at the utmost extent of its tether; and to sit down in a quiet ignorance of those things which, upon examination, are found to be beyond the reach of our capacities.

I shall imagine I have not wholly misemployed myself, if, in this historical, plain method, I can give any account of the ways whereby our understandings come to attain those notions of things we have, and can set down any measures of the certainty of our knowledge, or the grounds of those persuasions which are to be found among men, so various, different, and wholly contradictory.

We should not then perhaps be so forward, out of an affectation of an universal knowledge, to raise questions and perplex ourselves and others with disputes about things to which our understandings are not suited, and of which we cannot frame in our minds any clear or distinct perceptions, or whereof we have not any notion at all.

If we can find out how far the understanding can extend its view, how far it has faculties to attain certainty, and in what cases it can only judge and guess, we may learn to content ourselves with what is attainable by us in this state.

When we know our own strength, we shall the better know what to undertake with hopes of success.   When we have well surveyed the powers of our own mind, and made some estimate of what we may expect from them, we shall not be inclined either to sit still and not set our thoughts on work at all, in despair of knowing anything;   or, on the other side, question everything and disclaim all knowledge because some things are not to be understood.

It is of great use to the sailor to know the length of his line, though he cannot fathom all the depths of the ocean with it.   It is well he knows that it is long enough to reach the bottom at such places as are necessary to direct his voyage and caution him against running upon shoals that may ruin him.

So much for purpose and plan.   Before proceeding, Locke pauses to narrow and sharpen the inquiry:

Thus much I thought necessary to say concerning the occasion of this inquiry into human understanding.   But, before I proceed to what I have thought on this subject, I must here in the entrance beg pardon of my reader for the frequent use of the word *idea*.   It being that term which, I think, serves best to stand for whatsoever is the object of the understanding when a man thinks, I have used it to express whatever it is which the mind can be employed about in thinking;   and I could not avoid frequently using it.

I presume it will be easily granted me that there are ideas in men's minds.   Everyone is conscious of them in himself, and men's words and actions will satisfy him that they are in others.

Our first inquiry shall be how ideas come into the mind.

The problem has been brought to a focus: How does the mind come by its ideas?   Before advancing his own hypothesis, Locke glances at an alternative explanation:

It is an established opinion amongst some men that there are in the understanding certain innate principles, primary notions, characters as it were stamped upon the mind of man, received in its very first being, brought with it into the world.

This "established opinion" to which Locke refers will be found in the writings of several of his predecessors.   The most typical example is perhaps Lord Herbert of Cherbury, the author of a book, *On Truth*. In this book Lord Herbert lays it down that there are certain "common notions." Some of these common notions are formed without any assistance from experience or reason; others are developed by experience and reason, but do not originate therein. The former group is distinguished by certain marks or tests. Of these tests some are logical (such as independence, necessity, etc.); others are psychological (such as priority in time and universality). These common notions were supposed to yield the first principles of morality and religion. His book emphasizes in particular five common notions which Locke has in mind at this point. They were the notions (1) that there is a supreme Deity; (2) that He ought to be worshiped; (3) that the chief part of divine worship is virtue combined with piety; (4) that men should repent of their sins and turn from them; (5) that reward and punishment follow from the goodness and justice of God, both in this life and hereafter. With these historical references in mind, we may return to Locke's paragraphs:

> It would be sufficient to convince unprejudiced readers of the falseness of this supposition if I should only show how, barely by the use of their natural faculties, men may attain to all the knowledge they have without the help of any innate impressions, and may arrive at certainty without any such original notions or principles.
>
> But, because a man is not permitted without censure to follow his own thoughts in the search for truth when they lead him ever so little out of the common road, I shall set down the reasons that made me doubt the truth of the supposition of innate ideas.

Locke's refutation of the hypothesis of innate ideas is too long to be reproduced here. It comes to this: (1) It is a useless hypothesis, since the steps to knowledge are all discoverable. If this be the case, why assume innateness for some ideas? (2) Many ideas for which innateness is claimed are not perceived by infants.   How account for this?   If any ideas are genuinely innate, one would expect very young children to be in conscious possession of them.   (3) Many ideas for which innateness is claimed are not known till the person "comes to the use of reason."   How account for this? Why do some ideas, said to be innate, require for their discovery or recognition the use of powers which develop comparatively late in the organism's life?   (4) Many ideas for which innateness is claimed are said to be "self-evident"; and their self-evidence is advanced as proof of their innateness. Locke objects.   It is risky to claim self-evidence for any ideas.   Self-evident to whom?   Moreover, granting self-evidence, what of it?   "Self-evident" is not the same as "innate"; and who shall say, without assuming the point at issue, that it is evidence of innateness?   Further, are all self-evident ideas (for example, $2 + 2 = 4$) to be taken as innate? If not, by what do we distinguish, among self-evident ideas, which are innate?   (5) The "universal assent of mankind" to some ideas is advanced as evidence of their innateness. Locke objects again.   To what ideas do all men give assent? One genuine dissenter would be enough to spoil the argument from consensus.   Moreover, that all men assent to an idea is one thing; that the idea is therefore innate is another thing. Upon what grounds are we justified in arguing from the one to the other?   (6) Finally, Locke suspects that this whole notion of innate ideas has arisen from men's anxiety to place some ideas, particularly moral and religious ideas, beyond the scope of reasonable inquiry and doubt.   Having disposed thus of the arguments in support of the hypothesis of innate ideas, he resumes his original inquiry:

Let us then suppose the mind to be, as we say, white paper, void of all characters, without any ideas.   How comes it to be furnished? Whence comes it by that vast store which the busy and boundless tancy of man has painted on it with an almost endless variety? Whence has it all the materials of reason and knowledge?

To this I answer in one word: experience. All our knowledge is founded in experience, and from experience it ultimately derives itself.

This experience is of two sorts. Our observation is employed either about external sensible objects or about the internal operations of our mind, perceived and reflected on by ourselves. This observation supplies our understandings with all the materials of thinking. These two are the fountains of knowledge from whence all the ideas we have, or can naturally have, do spring.

First, our senses, conversant about particular sensible objects, do convey into the mind several distinct perceptions of things, according to those various ways wherein those objects do affect them: and thus we come by those ideas we have of yellow, white, heat, cold, soft, hard, bitter, sweet, and all those which we call sensible qualities. This great source of most of our ideas I call *sensation*.

Secondly, the other fountain from which experience furnisheth the understanding with ideas, is the perception of the operations of our own mind within us. Such operations are perceiving, thinking, doubting, believing, knowing, willing, and all the different actings of our own minds. We, being conscious of these operations, do from them receive into our understandings ideas as distinct as we do from bodies affecting our senses. As I call the other source *sensation*, so I call this *reflection*, the ideas it affords being such only as the mind gets by reflecting on its own operations within itself.

These two, I say, namely, external material things as the objects of sensation, and the operations of our own minds within as the objects of reflection, are to me the only originals from whence all our ideas take their beginnings. The understanding seems to me not to have the least glimmering of any ideas which it doth not receive from one of these two.

Having satisfied himself that all knowledge consists of ideas, that all ideas are derived from experience, that all experience is either sensation or reflection, Locke settles down to map out the entire field. His argument, at this point, becomes too detailed to permit of adequate reproduction by citation. Highly condensed, it comes to the following:

Considered with reference to their origin, ideas come to the mind either by way of sensation or reflection, or a combination of the two. From sensation, the mind gets ideas of the primary qualities of objects, e.g., solidity, extension, figure. These are qualities of the objects perceived. From sensation the mind gets also ideas of the secondary qualities of objects, e.g., sounds, tastes, colors, smells. These are not qualities of the objects perceived in the same sense that primary qualities are: they are effects, arising out of the operation of the object on the senses. From reflection the mind gets ideas of its operations. These operations include perceiving, retaining, discerning or discriminating, comparing, compounding or enlarging, abstracting, willing.

Considered with reference to their objects, ideas are either simple or complex. By *simple ideas* Locke means such qualities as coldness, hardness, sweetness, redness, as perceived in some particular object on some particular occasion. These simple ideas, either of sensation or reflection, are "the materials of all our knowledge." These simple ideas are sheer data, given to the mind in experience: "The mind can neither make nor destroy them." In the reception of simple ideas, the mind is passive.

By *complex ideas*, Locke means combinations of simple ideas; made by the mind out of its simple ideas, by repeating, combining, abstracting, etc. Complex ideas "may all be reduced under three heads: modes, substances, relations."

Modes are complex ideas which "do not contain in them the supposition of subsisting by themselves, but are considered as depending on or affections of things." Such are "ideas of triangle, gratitude, murder, etc." The point is, modes exist as properties or accidents or qualities of things, not in their own right. There are triangular things, grateful persons, murderers, etc., but none of these qualities exists independently.

Substances are "collections of qualities existing together" considered as "inhering" in some one thing. Thus, the color, shape, taste, weight, and other qualities of an apple exist together and "inhere" in the apple as a substance. The notion of substance causes Locke great perplexity and distress. It corresponds to no simple idea. It is nowhere given in experience. He refers to it as "something we know not what." "The idea to which we give the name *substance* is nothing but the supposed unknown support of those qualities we find existing, which, we imagine, cannot subsist without something to support them. We call that support *substance*." The need for the category is obvious. Its justification is obscure. He adds: "Whether anyone has any other clear idea of substance, beyond certain simple ideas coexisting together, I appeal to everyone's own experience." To repeat: "Because we cannot conceive how various sensible qualities, of which we have ideas, could exist alone, or in one another, we suppose them existing in and supported by some common subject which we denote by the name *substance*, though it is certain we have no clear or distinct idea of that thing we suppose a support."

Relations, the third kind of complex ideas, are many and various. Examples are identity and diversity, cause and effect, time and place, owner and owned, father and son, larger and smaller, and so on. Relations are described as "the work of the mind." Locke examines them at great length, classifies them, arranges them, defines them. They occur between two things at least. All things are capable of some kind of relation. Relations are often clearer than the things related. Relations terminate in simple ideas. Relations may change when the relata remain unchanged, and so on.

Having surveyed ideas with reference to their origin, i.e., sensation and reflection, their objects, i.e., modes, substances, relations, Locke turns to a consideration of the nature and degrees of human knowledge. Here we may resume our citations:

Since the mind, in all its thoughts and reasonings, hath no other immediate object but its own ideas, which it alone does or can contemplate, it is evident that our knowledge is only conversant about them.

Knowledge, then, seems to me to be nothing but the perception of the agreement or disagreement, connection or repugnance, of any of our ideas. In this alone it consists. Where this perception (of agreement or disagreement of our ideas) is, there is knowledge; where it is not, we come short of knowledge.

Locke's argument may be recapitulated. All knowledge may be analyzed into ideas. All ideas arise in experience. None are innate. Ideas are either simple or complex, the latter being combinations of the former. In knowing, the mind notes only ways in which its ideas agree or disagree. Upon the basis of this general analysis, Locke proceeds to discriminate between intuitive and demonstrative knowledge:

I have said that all knowledge consists in the view the mind has of its own ideas. It may not be amiss to consider a little the degrees of its evidence. The different clearness of our knowledge seems to me to lie in the different ways of perception the mind has of the agreement or disagreement of any of its ideas. There are three different ways.

1. Sometimes the mind perceives the agreement or disagreement of two ideas immediately, without the intervention of any other. Thus the mind perceives that white is not black, that a circle is not a triangle, that three are more than two, and so on. This we may call *intuitive* knowledge, for in this the mind is at no pains of proving or examining, but perceives the truth, as the eye doth light, merely by being directed toward it.

This intuitive kind of knowledge is the clearest and most certain that human frailty is capable of. On this kind of knowledge depends all the certainty and evidence of all our knowledge. He that demands a greater certainty than this, demands he knows not what, and shows only that he has a mind to be a skeptic, without being able to be so. In the next degree of knowledge, which I call *demonstrative*, this intuitive knowledge is necessary in all the intermediate ideas.

2. The next degree of knowledge is where the mind perceives the agreement or disagreement of any ideas, but not immediately. Thus, the mind being willing to know the agreement or disagreement in bigness between the three angles of a triangle and two right angles, cannot by an immediate view and comparing them do it. The three angles of a triangle cannot be brought at once and be compared with two right angles. In this case the mind is fain to find out some other angles, to which the three angles of a triangle have an equality, and, finding those equal also to two right angles, comes to know their equality to two right angles. And so, of the equality of the three angles of a triangle, to two right angles, the mind does not have immediate, intuitive knowledge. This mediated kind of knowledge we may call *demonstrative* knowledge.

When the mind cannot bring two ideas together in immediate comparison, to perceive their agreement or disagreement, it is fain, by the intervention of other ideas, to discover the agreement or disagreement which it searches. This is what we call *reasoning*. Those intervening ideas which serve to show the agreement or disagreement of any two others, are called *proofs*. Where the agreement or disagreement is by this means clearly perceived, it is called *demonstration*. A quickness in the mind to find out these intermediate ideas (that shall discover to it the agreement or disagreement which it searches) is called *sagacity*.

In every step which reason makes in demonstrative knowledge, there is an intuitive knowledge of that agreement or disagreement it seeks with the next intermediate idea which it uses as a proof. Without this intuitive knowledge of each step in reasoning, there would be no knowledge produced. If the connection between each step be perceived immediately, it is intuitive knowledge; if not,

there is need of some intervening idea. This knowledge by inter·
vening proofs, though it be certain, is thus not so clear and bright,
nor assent so ready, as in intuitive knowledge.

These two, intuition and demonstration, are the degrees of our
knowledge. Whatever comes short of these, with what assurance
so ever embraced, is but faith or opinion.

Had Locke stopped at this point, or been satisfied merely to
develop it in more detail, all might have been well. But he
stumbled upon a further distinction which led him deeper and
deeper into difficulties which he was never able finally to
clear up. The next five citations are included merely to
suggest something of what is meant.

3. There is, indeed, another perception of the mind, which I shall
call _sensitive_ knowledge. It is the perception of the existence of
particular things about us, e.g., the sun, a rose, a fire, a table.
I think we may add this knowledge of particular external objects,
that by perception and consciousness we have of the actual entrance
of ideas from them, to the two former sorts of knowledge, and allow
these three, namely, intuitive, demonstrative, sensitive.

There is a difficulty connected with sensitive knowledge of the
existence of external objects. It is this. There can be nothing
more certain than that the idea we receive from an external object
is in our minds. Of this fact we have intuitive knowledge. But
whether there be anything more than barely the idea in our minds;
whether we can thence certainly infer the existence of anything
without us, which corresponds to that idea; of this some men think
there may be a question made. They think so because men may
have such ideas in their minds when no external thing exists, when
no object affects their senses.

I think we are provided with an evidence that puts us past doubting. For I ask anyone, whether he be not invincibly conscious to
himself of a different perception when he looks on the sun by day
and thinks on it by night; when he actually tastes wormwood or
smells a rose and thinks on that savor or odor? We find the difference between an idea revived in our mind by our memory and one

actually coming into our minds by our senses, as plainly as we do between any two distinct ideas.

If any one say, a dream may do the same thing, and all these ideas may be produced in us without any external object; he may please to dream that I make him this answer: (1) Where all is dream, reason and argument are of no use, truth and knowledge nothing; so it is no great matter whether I remove this scruple or no. (2) He will allow a very manifest difference between dreaming of being in the fire, and actually being in it.

If he be resolved to appear so skeptical as to maintain that what I call "being actually in the fire" is nothing but a dream, and that we cannot certainly know that any such thing as fire actually exists without us, I answer: We certainly find that pleasure or pain follows upon the application of certain objects to us, whose existence we perceive or dream we perceive. The certainty with which we know this is as great as the pleasure or the pain. Beyond this we have no concernment to know or to be. So, I think, we may add sensitive knowledge of external objects to the two former kinds of knowledge.

Locke returns to the main argument of his inquiry. He has traced knowledge to experience. He has distinguished between intuitive and demonstrative knowledge: The former is the basis of the latter. There is, however, another possibility. Knowledge may fall short of demonstrative rigor, in which case it is "probable knowledge." Thus:

The understanding being given to man, not barely for speculation but also for the conduct of life, man would be at a great loss if he had nothing to direct him but what has the certainty of true knowledge. For that being very short and scanty, as we have seen, he would be often utterly in the dark had he nothing to guide him in the absence of clear and certain knowledge.

The faculty which supplies the want of clear and certain knowledge, in cases where it cannot be had, is judgment. In judgment the mind takes its ideas to agree or disagree (or, which is the same, any proposition to be true or false) without perceiving a demonstrative evidence in the proofs. The mind sometimes exercises this judgment out of necessity, where demonstrative proofs are not to be had; and sometimes out of laziness, unskillfulness, or haste even where demonstrative proofs are to be had.

As demonstration is showing the agreement or disagreement of two ideas by the intervention of one or more proofs, so probability is nothing but the appearance of such an agreement or disagreement by the intervention of proofs. For example, we may have a demonstration of the equality of the angles of a triangle to two right angles, or we may take the word of some mathematician that it is so, in which case the foundation of our judgment or assent is the probability of the thing.

Probability is likeness to be true. The entertainment the mind gives this sort of proposition is called *belief, assent, opinion.* Herein lies the difference between proability and certainty: In all the parts of certainty there is intuition, each step has its visible connection; in belief, not so. That which makes me believe is something extraneous to the thing I believe, something not evidently joined on both sides to those ideas that are under consideration.

Probability, being to supply the defect of our knowledge and to guide us where that fails, is conversant about propositions whereof we have no certainty but only some inducements to receive them for true. The grounds of probability are two: conformity with our own experience, or the testimony of the experience of others.

The propositions which we receive upon inducements of probability are of two sorts: concerning some particular existence falling under observation and hence capable of human testimony; concerning things which, being beyond our senses, are not capable of any such testimony.

Concerning the first of these, the concurrent experience of all other men with ours produces assurance approaching to knowledge; failing this, the concurrence of unquestionable testimony with our experience produces confidence; failing for the most part this, fair testimony in support of a proposition having no great initial improbability. When, however, experience and testimonies clash, the degrees of probability vary indefinitely.

The above probabilities are only such as concern things capable of observation and testimony. There remains that other sort, where the things are not capable of such testimony. In these matters, analogy is the only help we have, and it is from this alone that we draw all our grounds of probability.

One large question remains. Locke lived in an age when men traced some of their most valued knowledge, not to experience, but to revelation. This is not to be confused with the doctrine of "innate ideas." Many who held to revelation as a source of knowledge would take no stock in innate ideas. Locke was himself a devout person. He realized the important role which revealed knowledge played in the religious life of his friends and contemporaries. It was, however, not compatible with a thoroughgoing empiricism. Hence his rather grudging remarks:

Besides those we have hitherto mentioned, there is one sort of proposition that challenges the highest degree of our assent upon bare testimony. I mean where the testimony is of God Himself. This is called by a peculiar name, *revelation;* and our assent to it, *faith.*

Properly understood, faith is a settled and sure principle of assent and leaves no manner of room for doubt. Only, we must be sure (1) that it is a revelation from God, and (2) that we understand it aright. Otherwise we shall expose ourselves to all the error of wrong principles and all the extravagance of enthusiasm if we have faith in what is not divine revelation. Our assent, therefore, can be rationally no higher than the evidence of its being a revelation, and that we do understand the meaning of the expression by which it is delivered. If the evidence of its being a revelation, or that we do understand its true meaning, be only on probable proofs, our assent can rise no higher than that probability.

From these things thus premised I think we may come to lay down the measures and boundaries between faith and reason; the want whereof may possibly have been the cause of great disputes and perhaps mistakes in the world. For, till it be resolved how far we are to be guided by reason and how far by faith, we shall in vain dispute and endeavor to convince one another.

I find that every sect, as far as reason will help them, make use of it gladly; and where it fails them, they cry out, "It is a matter of faith and above reason." And I do not see how they can argue with anyone, or ever convince a gainsayer who makes use of the same plea, without setting down strict boundaries between faith and reason.

Reason I take to be the discovery of the certainty or probability of such truths as the mind has got by sensation or reflection, or has arrived at by deduction from such ideas. Faith is the assent to any proposition not thus arrived at but accepted upon the credit of the proposer as coming from God in some extraordinary way of communication. This way of discovering truths to men we call *revelation.*

First, I say that no man inspired by God can by any revelation communicate to others any new simple ideas which they had not before from sensation and reflection. For whatsoever impressions he himself may have received from the immediate hand of God, if it be of new simple ideas, cannot be conveyed to another either by words or any other signs; because words and other signs recall to our minds those ideas only which to us they have been wont to be signs of. They cannot introduce any new and formerly unknown simple ideas.

For our simple ideas, then, which are the foundation and sole matter of all our notions and knowledge we must depend wholly upon our natural faculties; and can by no means receive them from traditional revelation. I say traditional revelation, in distinction to original revelation. By the former I mean those impressions delivered over to others in words; by the latter I mean that first impression which is made immediately by God on the mind of any man, to which we cannot set any bounds.

Second, I say that the same truths may be discovered and handed down by revelation which are discoverable to us by reason. So God might by revelation discover the truth of any proposition in geometry, as well as men might make the discovery themselves.

Third, I say nothing can, under title of revelation, shake or over-rule plain knowledge, or rationally prevail with any man to admit for true anything directly contradictory to the clear evidence of his own understanding. A proposition supposed revealed which contradicts our knowledge or reason will always have this objection hanging to it, namely, that we cannot conceive that to come from God, the bountiful author of our being, which, if received for true, must overturn all the principles and foundations of knowledge He has given us, render our faculties useless, wholly destroy the most excellent part of His workmanship (our understandings), and put a man in a condition wherein he will have less light than the beast which perisheth.

If anything shall be thought revelation which is contrary to the plain principles of reason and the evident knowledge the mind has of its own ideas, there reason must be hearkened to. And this because a man can never have so certain a knowledge that a proposition contradictory to reason was divinely revealed, or that he understands rightly the words wherein it is delivered, as he has that the contrary is true. So he is bound to consider it, and judge of it, as a matter of reason, and not swallow it, without examination, as a matter of faith.

In all things, therefore, where we have clear evidence from our ideas and principles of knowledge, reason is the proper judge. Revelation may, in consenting with it, confirm it; yet it cannot in such cases invalidate it. Nor can we be obliged, where we have the clear and evident sentence of reason, to quit it for the contrary opinion under the pretense that it is a matter of faith.

Fourth, I say that things werein we have imperfect notions or none at all, being beyond the discovery of our natural powers and above reason, are, when revealed, the proper matter of faith. Thus, that some of the angels rebelled against God, and thereby lost their first happy state; that the dead shall rise and live again — these and the like, being beyond the discovery of reason, are purely matters of faith. With them reason has nothing to do.

Thus John Locke on the problem of knowledge. A few paragraphs gather up the threads of his argument:

If, then, knowledge lies in the perception of the agreement or disagreement of any of our ideas, it follows that we can have knowledge no farther than we have ideas; and no farther than we can have perception of their agreement or disagreement.

It follows from this that we cannot have an intuitive knowledge that shall extend itself to all our ideas because we cannot examine and perceive all the relations they have one to another by an immediate comparison. Some knowledge, at least, must always remain mediated.

It follows also that our demonstrative knowledge cannot reach to the whole extent of our ideas because between two different ideas we cannot always find such intervening ideas as we can connect one to another with an intuitive knowledge. Wherever that fails, we come short of demonstrative knowledge.

From all which it is evident that the extent of our knowledge comes not only short of the reality of things, but even of the extent of our own ideas.

Nevertheless, I do not question but that human knowledge, under the present circumstances of our beings and constitutions, may be carried much farther than it has hitherto been, if men would sincerely, and with freedom of mind, employ all that industry and labor in improving the means of discovering truth which they employ to support a falsehood, to maintain a system, interest, or party they are once engaged in.

These ideas should be studied and thought about carefully. Their very simplicity tends to lull one's critical faculties. All seems too straightforward and inevitable. Only here and there does the argument show signs of getting out of hand. But, as subsequent chapters in the history of the problem were to show, these difficulties pointed to problems from which epistemology is still seeking to extricate itself.

READING REFERENCES. John Locke's *Essay Concerning Human Understanding* had both a popular and a technical influence. In this respect it was comparable in philosophy to Adam Smith's *Wealth of Nations* in the field of economic theory. It was widely read by the educated laity, not only in Great Britain, but also on the continent and in the Ameri-

can colonies. Its influence, for example on Voltaire in France
and on Jonathan Edwards in the colonies, is a matter of common knowledge. It was made the subject of an extended
chapter-by-chapter commentary by Locke's contemporary,
the German philosopher Leibniz. It exercised the minds of
Berkeley, Hume and Kant, to mention only a few outstanding
names in the history of eighteenth-century philosophy. To
the general reader it brought clarification and emancipation.
For the philosopher, as will be seen, it raised difficult problems. The history of this two-fold influence has not yet been
adequately studied. Suggestions of its manifold variety may
be gained by reading, e.g., Gibson's *Locke's Theory of Knowledge*
or Hefelbower's *Locke and English Deism*, or Leibniz's *New
Essays*. An interesting and valuable article by F. J. E. Wood-
bridge, "Locke's Essay," is to be found in the third volume of
the Columbia University *Studies in the History of Ideas*. The
standard two-volume life is by Fox Bourne. Good general
accounts of Locke's life and writings are to be found in
Aaron's *John Locke*, in Fraser's *Locke*, and in Fowler's *Locke*.

READING QUESTIONS

1. What value does Locke see in an inquiry into human knowledge?
2. What was the hypothesis of innate ideas?
3. By whom was it held?
4. What items were so described?
5. What motive would Locke have in criticizing such a doctrine?
6. What criticisms does he offer?
7. What alternative hypothesis does he advance?
8. What does he mean by *simple* in contrast to *complex* ideas?
9. What by *modes, substances,* and *relations?*
10. What problem does he note in connection with substances?
11. What is his distinction between intuitive and demonstrative
    knowledge?
12. What is the relation between them?
13. What does he have in mind by sensitive knowledge?

14. What problem does he note in this connection?
15. Is his reasoning here open to any criticism?
16. How does he distinguish between demonstrative and probable knowledge?
17. What does he say about probable knowledge?
18. Why is he called upon to deal with the doctrine of revelation?
19. How would you distinguish it from the doctrine of innate ideas?
20. What four points does he make with respect to revelation?
21. Why would you expect Locke's empiricism in epistemology to ramify into a general liberalism in other fields, e.g., politics, religion, education?
22. Formulate two or more questions you would put to Locke.

2. EMPIRICISM INTO SKEPTICISM — FROM DAVID HUME

FROM LOCKE TO HUME. Epistemology is an inquiry into the nature of knowledge. It is an inquiry which is motivated by the desire to discover, from an analysis of knowledge, what range and scope we may ascribe to knowledge. All this was set forth in the previous section. For most readers, during the closing years of the seventeenth and most of the eighteenth century, the problem of knowledge meant John Locke's *Essay Concerning Human Understanding*. His general common-sense tone, his homely appeal to experience, his determination not to be led into unverifiable speculations, all combined to secure for him a wide circle of readers and followers. It was only natural, therefore, that the next stage in the development of epistemological theory should take the form of an attempt to "begin where Locke left off." His position briefly was this: All knowledge may be analyzed into ideas. All ideas come to us from experience. All experience is by way of the senses. This *empiricism*, as it is called, was Locke's contribution to epistemological theory. His successor in these matters, David Hume, wrote for a generation which was familiar with the problem as Locke had stated it, and the appeal to experience as Locke had formulated it. Hume set himself a simple task: to deduce more rigorously the implications of Locke's widely accepted position.

BIOGRAPHICAL NOTE. See under "A Theological Problem," page 40.

THE ARGUMENT OF THE CITATIONS. Hume will be remembered, from an earlier chapter in these readings, as the critic of natural theology. His method there was to show what happens in natural theology if one sticks closely to the terms laid down by traditional speculation in these matters. He applies the same method in expistemology. It is proposed to make an appeal to experience, he writes; let the appeal be made, then, and not abandoned because it is found to lead to inconvenient consequences. The argument of his position is simple and direct. All knowledge may be analyzed into impressions and ideas. All ideas are derived from earlier impressions. We have certain metaphysical ideas, such as "matter," "mind," "causal connection," "free will," "the uniformity of nature." These ideas play a large part in human thinking and speculating. In fact, they are the fundamental terms in the modern man's general reflections upon the world about him. What are they worth? From what "impressions" are they derived? What corresponds to them in that actual experience to which Locke proposed to appeal? In each case Hume's answer is "they have no basis in experience." They are unjustifiable knowledge claims, and any speculation which incorporates them is mere waste of ink and paper. He begins, in the manner of Locke, by explaining that an inquiry into the nature of knowledge is directed toward eliminating as mere speculation all abstruse ideas which clutter up human thinking:

The only method of freeing learning from abstruse questions is to inquire seriously into the nature of human understanding and show, from an exact analysis of its powers and capacity, that it is by no means fitted for such subjects.

The premises of his theory of knowledge are to be the following:

We may divide all perceptions into two classes: impressions and ideas. By impressions I mean all our perceptions when we hear, see, feel, love, hate, desire, etc. Ideas are those less lively perceptions of which we are conscious when we reflect on any of those sensations mentioned above.

All ideas are copies of impressions. . . . Even those ideas which seem most wide of this origin are found, upon a nearer scrutiny to be derived from it. . . . We shall always find that every idea is copied from a similar impression . . . it is impossible for us to think of anything which we have not antecedently felt by our senses.

The test of all ideas is to be "show me the impression":

When we entertain any suspicion in a philosophical term, we need but inquire from what impression is that supposed idea derived. If it be not possible to assign any, this will serve to confirm our suspicion that it is employed without meaning. . . . By this means we can throw light upon ideas and render them precise. Produce the impressions or originals from which the ideas are copied.

The first idea to be tested by the appeal to impressions is the now familiar idea of substance or matter:

Some philosophers found much of their reasonings on the distinction of *substance* and *quality*. I would fain ask them whether the idea of substance be derived from impressions of sensations or impressions of reflection? Does it arise from an impression? Point it out to us, that we may know its nature and qualities. But if you cannot point out any such impression, you may be certain you are mistaken when you imagine you have any such idea.

If the impression from which we derive our idea of substance be conveyed to us by our senses, I ask, by which of them? If by the eyes, it must be a color. If by the ears, it must be a sound. If by the palate, it must be a taste. And so of the other senses. But I believe none will assert that substance is either a color, a sound, or a taste.

Is the idea of substance, then, derived from an impression of reflection [i.e., introspection]? But impressions of reflection resolve themselves into our feelings, passions, and emotions, none of which can possibly resemble a substance. We have, therefore, no idea of substance, apart from that of a collection of qualities.

The idea of substance is nothing but a collection of ideas of qualities, united by the imagination and given a particular name by which we are able to recall that collection. The particular qualities which form a substance are commonly referred to an unknown something in which they are supposed to "inhere." This is a fiction.

We may well ask what causes us to believe in the existence of body [i.e., matter]. 'Tis certain there is no question in philosophy more abstruse. By what argument can it be proved that perceptions must be caused by external objects entirely different from them? By an appeal to experience? But here experience is and must be entirely silent. The mind has never anything present to it but its perceptions and cannot possibly have any experience of their connection with objects. The supposition of such a connection is, therefore, without any foundation in reasoning.

Philosophers distinguish betwixt *perceptions* and *objects*. The perceptions are supposed to be caused by the object, and to be interrupted, perishing and different at different times and for different people. The objects are supposed to cause the perceptions, and to be uninterrupted, continuous, and identical. But, however this new view may be esteemed, I assert that there are no principles, either of the understanding or the fancy which lead us to embrace this opinion of the double existence of perceptions and objects.

This hypothesis of the double existence of perceptions and objects has no primary recommendation to reason. The only existences of which we are certain are perceptions. Being immediately present to us by consciousness, they command our strongest assent, and must be the foundation of all our reasonings. But, as nothing is ever present to the mind but perceptions, it follows that we can never observe any "object," or any connection, causal or otherwise, between perceptions and objects.

The idea of substance as something underlying a set of qualities is unable to produce its credentials.   Away with it, then.
As Hume rather picturesquely remarks of all such ideas,
"Commit it to the flames."   From material substance he
turns to the idea of mind or spiritual substance:

There are some philosophers (e.g., Berkeley) who imagine we are
every moment intimately conscious of what we call our *self;* that
we feel its existence and its continuance in existence, and are certain
of its identity and simplicity.

Unluckily all these positive assertions are contrary to that very
experience which is pleaded for them.   Have we any idea of a self?
From what impression could it be derived?   It must be some impression that gives rise to every idea.   But self or person is not any one
impression.   If any impression gives rise to the idea of one's self,
that impression must continue to be the same, since one's self is
supposed to continue to be the same.   But there is no such continuing, constant impression.

For my part, when I enter most intimately into what I call my
self, I always stumble on some particular perception or other, of
heat or cold, light or shade, love or hatred, pain or pleasure, color or
sound, etc.   I never catch my self, distinct from some such perception.

If anyone thinks he has a different notion of his self, I must confess
I can no longer reason with him.   He may perceive something simple
and continued which he calls his *self;* though I am certain there is
no such principle in me.

Setting aside metaphysicians of this kind, I may venture to affirm
of the rest of mankind that they are nothing but a bundle or collection of different perceptions which succeed each other with an
inconceivable rapidity and are in a perpetual flux and movement.
Our eyes cannot turn in their sockets without varying their perceptions.   Our thoughts are still more variable.   And all our other
senses and powers contribute to this change.

The mind (or self) is a kind of theater where perceptions make
their appearance, pass, repass, glide away, and mingle in an infinite
variety.   But there is no simplicity, no one simple thing present or

pervading this multiplicity; no identity pervading this process of change; whatever natural inclination we may have to imagine that there is. The comparison of the theater must not mislead us: it persists, while the actors come and go. Whereas, only the successive perceptions constitute the mind.

The idea of mind or self or Spirit fails to reveal any basis in immediate impressions. That seals its fate. But the question persists: Why do we entertain such a notion? It is one thing to show that an idea is a mere fiction. It is another thing to account for its widespread presence in human thinking.

Why do we ascribe an identity amid these successive perceptions, and suppose our selves possessed of an invariable and uninterrupted existence through the whole course of our life? The identity which we ascribe to minds and selves is only a fictitious one, but why do we ascribe it?

Suppose we could see clearly into the mind of another, and observe that succession of perceptions which constitutes his mind. Suppose, too, that he always preserves the memory of a considerable part of past perceptions. It is evident that nothing could more readily contribute to bestowing a relation between these successive perceptions. Would not the frequent placing of these remembered perceptions in the chain of thought convey our imagination more easily from one to another? And so make the whole seem like the continuance of one object?

As memory alone acquaints us with the continuance and extent of a succession of perceptions, it is to be considered, on that account chiefly, as the source of personal identity. Had we no memory, we should never have any notion of that succession of perceptions which constitutes our self or person. But having once acquired this notion from the operation of memory, we can extend the same beyond our memory and come to include times which we have entirely forgot. And so arises the fiction of person and personal identity.

Matter, in the usual sense of the term, is gone.   Mind ditto
is gone.   Hume turns to more serious business, namely, the
notion of causal connection between events.   I say "more
serious business" because he is here proposing to invade the
very citadel of eighteenth-century science, a structure which
was believed to rest squarely on the notion of causal connection.   Hume's handling of this idea should be observed
closely.   His first question is: What do people mean by the
idea of causal connection?   His answer is, By causal connection they mean necessary connection; they believe that there
is a necessary connection between a cause and its effect.   His
next question is the inevitable one: What evidence, open to
our senses, have we for believing that there is any necessity
in causal connection? His answer is: None whatever.

There is no idea in metaphysics more obscure or uncertain than
necessary connection between cause and effect.   We shall try to fix the
precise meaning of this term by producing the impression from which
it is copied.

When we look at external objects, and consider the operation of
causes, we are never able, in a single instance, to discover a necessary
connection;   any quality which binds the effect to the cause, and
renders the one a necessary consequence of the other.   We find only
that the effect does, in fact, follow the cause.   The impact of one
billiard ball upon another is followed by the motion of the second.
There is here contiguity in space and time, but nothing to suggest
necessary connection.

The scenes of the universe are continually shifting, and one object
follows another in an uninterrupted succession.   But any "force" or
necessary connection pervading the whole machine never discovers
itself in any of the sensible qualities of body.   We know that heat
is a constant attendant of flame.   But as to any necessary connection
between them, we have no room so much as to conjecture or imagine.

In single instances of causal connection we never, by our utmost
scrutiny, discover anything but one event following another.   We
detect no necessary connection between the cause and its effect.   All

events seem loose and separate. One event follows another. But we observe no tie between them, beyond contiguity in space and time. They are contiguous, thus; but never connected. As we can have no idea of anything of which we have had no correspondent impression, the conclusion seems to be that we have no idea of necessary connection, and that these words are absolutely without meaning.

We are apt to imagine that we could discover effects from their causes by the mere operation of our reason, without experience. We fancy that, were we brought on a sudden into this world, we could have inferred that one billiard ball would communicate motion to another upon impact; and that we need not have waited for the event, in order to pronounce with certainty concerning it.

Knowledge of this relation arises entirely from experience. We find that particular objects are constantly conjoined with each other. Knowledge of this relation is not, in any instance, attained by reasonings a priori. Causes and efforts are discoverable by experience, not by reason. Every effect is a distinct event from its cause. It could not, therefore, be discovered in the cause (prior to experience of their conjunction). Without the assistance of observation and experience, we should in vain pretend to determine any single event or infer any cause or effect. A man must be very sagacious who could discover by reasoning that ice is the effect of cold, without being previously acquainted with the operation of these qualities.

Hence no philosopher who is rational and modest has ever pretended to assign the ultimate cause of any natural operation. Ultimate springs and principles (causes) are totally shut off from human curiosity and enquiry.

As in the case of our idea of mind or self, Hume pauses to inquire why we ascribe to the connection between cause and effect something which is not revealed in experience.

Why do we imagine a necessary connection? From observing many constant conjunctions? But what is there in a number of instances which is absent from a single instance? Only this: After a repetition of similar instances the mind is carried by habit, upon the appearance of the cause, to expect the effect. This connection, which we feel in the mind, this customary and habitual transition of the imagination from a cause to its effect, is the impression from which we form the idea of necessary connection. There is nothing further in the case.

When we say a cause is necessarily connected with its effect, we mean, therefore, that they have acquired a connection in our thought: a conclusion which is somewhat extraordinary, but seems founded on sufficient evidence.

Every idea is copied from some impression. In all single instances of causal connection there is nothing that can suggest any idea of necessity. But when many instances have been experienced, we begin to entertain the idea. We then feel a new impression, to wit, a customary transition in our thoughts or imagination between the cause and its effect. This impression is the original of that idea which we seek for. For, as this idea arises from a number of similar instances, it must arise from that circumstance in which the number of instances differ from each single instance. This customary transition is the only circumstance in which they differ.

His rejection of the idea of cause as necessary connection suggests at once that he may be in a position to say something about the long-standing controversy over free will and determinism. That dispute arises because men hold (*a*) that human acts are caused, and (*b*) that causes are necessary connections. Hume's claim, here is not that he can solve the problem but that he can dissolve it.

The question of man's free will has been long disputed among philosophers. Does man have freedom of will? Or are his acts determined? If motives determine acts, are motives themselves determined? This dispute has been much canvassed on all hands, and has led into such labyrinths of obscure sophistry that a sensible reader inclines to turn a deaf ear to the question, expecting neither instruction nor entertainment. I hope to make it appear that the whole controversy has hitherto turned merely upon words.

We ascribe necessity to matter. The degree and direction of every motion are prescribed with exactness. Do we similarly ascribe necessity to persons? Are the degree and direction of every action prescribed with exactness?

Two circumstances form the whole of the necessity we ascribe to matter: a constant conjunction between cause-events and effect-events, and a consequent inference in our minds from the one to the other. Beyond these two circumstances we have no notion of any necessity in the motion of matter.

Do not these two circumstances take place in the voluntary actions of men? Are not similar motives followed by similar actions? Are there not detectable uniformities in human action? Is it impossible to collect any general observations concerning mankind? Has experience of human affairs, however accurately digested by reflection, no purpose?

The most irregular and unexpected resolutions of men may be accounted for by those who know every particular circumstance of their character and situation. A genial person, contrary to expectation, may give a peevish answer, but he has a toothache or has not dined. Even when, as sometimes happens, an action cannot be accounted for, do we not put it down to our ignorance of relevant details?

Thus it appears that the conjunction between motive and action is as regular and uniform as between cause and effect in any part of nature. In both cases, constant conjunction and inference from one to the other.

Though constant conjunction and customary transition be all that is discoverable between a cause and an effect in nature, men believe they perceive something like a necessary connection. Then, when they consider the operations of their own wills and feel no such necessary connection between motive and action, they suppose there is a difference between the cause-effect relation and the motive-action relation. And are hence led to say that man's will, unlike matter, is free.

But our knowledge of causation, like our knowledge of motivation, is merely of a constant conjunction and a consequent inference in our minds from one to the other. It is the same in both cases. It is different only if it be pretended that the mind can perceive, in the operation of matter, some other connection between cause and effect than has place in the voluntary actions of intelligent beings. It is incumbent on those who pretend thus to make good their assertion. So long as we rashly suppose that we have an idea of some necessity in the operations of external nature, beyond constant conjunction and an habitual inference in our minds; and, at the same time, admit we can find nothing such in the voluntary actions of the mind, we shall continue in confusion.

Thus far Hume has examined the ideas of substance, of mind, of causal connection, of free will. Of each in turn he has asked one question: Upon what impression, received by the senses, does it rest? From each in turn he has received only silence for an answer. One more idea remains, namely, the idea of a uniformity of nature, the unquestioned premise of all our inductions and generalizations from nature. Why do we believe, so unquestioningly, that the "future will resemble the past"? Why do we argue, for instance, that fire will always melt ice, when our only grounds for this belief is the fact that it has done so in the past?

All our conclusions from experience proceed on the supposition that the future will resemble the past. To prove that the future will resemble the past, by arguing from experience, is evidently going in a circle, and taking that for granted which is the very point in question.

As to past experience, it can be allowed to give direct and certain information of those precise objects only, and that precise period of time only, which fell under its cognizance. But why this experience should be extended to future times and other objects, is the question on which I would insist. So to extend it is a process of mind or thought of which I would willingly know the foundation.

Not by an argument from experience can we prove this resemblance of the past to the future, for all such arguments are founded on the supposition of that resemblance. Let the course of things be allowed hitherto ever so regular. That alone, without some new inference, does not prove that for the future it will continue so.

My practice, you say, refutes my doubts. But you mistake the purport of my question.   In practice I am satisfied.   As a philosopher, who has some share of curiosity, I will not say skepticism, I want to learn the foundation of this inference.   No reading, no inquiry, has yet been able to remove my difficulty.   Upon what grounds can we argue that the future will resemble the past?   Upon what grounds expect similar effects from causes which are similar?

Geometry (or any mathematics) when taken into the assistance of science, is unable to remedy this defect.   Every part of applied mathematics proceeds on the supposition that certain laws are established by nature in her operations.   Mathematical reasonings are employed to assist experience in the discovery of these laws, or to determine their influence in particular instances.   But the discovery of the law itself is owing merely to experience, and all the mathematical reasoning in the world could never lead one step toward the knowledge of it.

In all reasonings from experience, then, there is a step taken by the mind (that the future resembles the past) which is not supported by any argument.   Nevertheless, we take this step.   There must therefore be some other principle (than rational or demonstrative argument).

Though none but a fool or madman will ever pretend to dispute the authority of experience, it may surely be allowed a philosopher to have so much curiosity as to examine the principle of human nature which gives authority to experience.

This principle is custom, or habit.   Wherever repetition produces a propensity to renew the same act, without being impelled by any reasoning, we say this propensity is the effect of custom or habit.   That habit or custom is the ultimate principle of all our conclusions from experiences, seems to be the only hypothesis which explains why we draw from many instances an inference which we are not able to draw from one instance that is in no respect different from them.

All inferences from experience are, therefore, effects of habit or custom, not of reasoning.   The conclusions which we draw, based on reasoning, from considering one circle, are the same which we would draw from surveying all circles.   But no man, having seen only one body impelled by another, could infer that every other similar body would move after a like impulse.

Custom, then, not reason, is the great guide of human life. It is that principle alone which renders our experience useful to us, and makes us expect, for the future, a similar train of events with those which have appeared in the past. Without the influence of custom, we should be entirely ignorant of every matter of fact beyond what is immediately present to the memory or the senses.

What, then, is the conclusion of the whole matter? A simple one, though, it must be confessed, pretty remote from the common theories of philosophy. All belief concerning matters of fact or real existence, is derived merely from some object present to the memory or the senses, and a customary conjunction between that and some other object. Having found, in many instances, that two kinds of objects have been conjoined (say, flame and heat), the mind is carried by custom to expect the same in the future. This is the whole operation of the mind in all our conclusions concerning matters of fact and existence.

Here, then, is a kind of pre-established harmony between the course of nature and formation of our beliefs. Custom or habit is the principle of human nature by which this correspondence, so necessary to the subsistence of our species and the regulation of our conduct, has been effected. Did not the presence of an object excite in us the ideas of other objects commonly conjoined with it, all human knowledge would be limited to the narrow sphere of our memory and senses. Those who delight in the discovery of purposes in nature have here ample subject to employ their wonder and admiration.

As this operation of the mind, whereby we infer like effects from like causes, is so essential to human life, it is not probable that it could be trusted to the fallacious deductions of our reason, which is slow in its operation and extremely liable to error and mistake. It is more conformable to the ordinary wisdom of nature to secure so necessary an act of the mind by some instinct or mechanical tendency which may be infallible in its operations and independent of all the labored deductions of understanding.

Hume is now at the end of his review:

By way of conclusion to these reflections on diverse questions: When we run over libraries, persuaded of the principles here expounded, what havoc must we make? If we take in hand any volume, of divinity or metaphysics, for instance, let us ask: Does it contain any reasoning concerning quantity or number? No. Does it contain any experimental (probable) reasoning concerning matter of fact? No. Commit it then to the flames: for it can contain nothing but sophistry and illusion.

I am at first affrighted and confounded with that forlorn solitude in which I am placed by my philosophy, and fancy myself some strange uncouth monster, utterly abandoned and disconsolate. Fain would I run into the crowd for shelter and warmth. I call upon others to join me. But no one will hearken to me. Everyone keeps at a distance, and dreads that storm which beats upon me from every side. I have exposed myself to the enmity of all metaphysicians, logicians, mathematicians, and theologians. Can I wonder at the insults I must suffer? I have declared my disapprobation of their systems. Can I be surprised if they should express a hatred of my ideas and my person? When I look about me, I foresee on every hand, dispute, contradiction, anger, calumny, detraction. When I turn my eye inward, I find only doubt and ignorance. Every step I take is with hesitation; every new reflection makes me dread an error and absurdity in my reasoning.

READING REFERENCES. It would be advantageous to consult the pages on Hume in B. A. G. Fuller's *History of Philosophy*. They form a section in a chapter on Locke, Berkeley, Hume. The Hume portion should be read straight through. It brings together his critique of natural theology and his theory of knowledge. T. H. Huxley's little book on Hume, recommended elsewhere, is noted again here. Time given to C. W. Hendel's *Studies in the Philosophy of David Hume* will be well spent.

READING QUESTIONS

1. What is the historical relation between Locke and Hume?
2. What does Hume propose to free learning from? How does he propose to do it?
3. Into what two elements does he analyze knowledge? How does he relate the two?
4. What test does he propose for all ideas?
5. Enumerate the ideas to which he applies this test.
6. Summarize the steps by which he criticizes the idea of material substance.
7. Summarize the steps by which he criticizes the idea of spiritual substance.
8. By what hypothesis does he seek to account for the idea of spiritual substance?
9. What alternative terms can you give for *spiritual substance?*
10. Summarize the steps by which he criticizes the idea of necessary connection.
11. By what hypothesis does he seek to account for this idea?
12. Can you suggest any reason why Hume's critique of the idea of necessary connection should have caused such consternation at that time and since?
13. "Hume does not solve the problem of free will; he merely dissolves it." Explain.
14. Upon what "supposition" do "all our conclusions from experience proceed"?
15. Summarize Hume's criticism of this supposition.
16. "My practice, you say, refutes my doubts." Elucidate.
17. What is his answer to this objection?
18. "Those who delight in the discovery of purposes in nature have here ample subject to employ their wonder and admiration." Where?

3. MIND AND THE WORLD ORDER — FROM IMMANUEL KANT

FROM HUME TO KANT. The problem of knowledge was, to all intents and purposes, posed for modern times by John Locke in his *Essay Concerning Human Understanding*. That problem, stated simply, was this: To suggest a theory of the nature and origin of knowledge, and from that theory to indicate the limits of human understanding. The problem persisted. It is with us yet. It has come, indeed, to occupy the center of philosophy. Hume and Kant, between them, have been, in large measure, responsible for this fact. For that reason it is important to grasp clearly what these two thinkers sought to accomplish.

Locke, it will be remembered, was led to pose the problem of knowledge as a measure of caution. His words reveal this motive:

> If by this inquiry into the nature of the understanding I can discover the powers thereof, how far they reach, to what things they are in any degree proportionate and where they fail us, I suppose it may be of use to prevail with the busy mind of man to be more cautious in meddling with things exceeding its comprehension, to stop when it is at the utmost extent of its tether, and to sit down in a quiet ignorance of those things which, upon examination are found to be beyond the reach of our capacities.

Nothing could be more straightforward than that. From an insight into the nature of knowledge, to recognize that some things lie beyond its reach. The hypothesis which Locke advanced was this: All knowledge comes from experience and all experience is by way of the senses. This was in the seventeenth century.

By the middle of the eighteenth century, in Hume's writings, things had undergone a subtle change. Indeed, it would perhaps be more accurate to say that they had come to something of an impasse. What Hume did, in effect, was to take Locke's appeal to experience and push it to its "logical conclusion." This conclusion was that much of the familiar furniture of man's world was dissolved into a series of question marks. The metaphysical notions of matter and spirit were declared to be so much verbiage. No appeal to experience showed any grounds for believing in their existence. The psychological notions of mind and will went the same way. Only the come-and-go of impressions and ideas remained. The generally accepted notions of cause and uniformity of nature met a like fate; they were mere habits, mere effect of custom. The theological notions of God as first cause and designer were weighed and found wanting. Hume tried, indeed, to undermine the credibility even of mathematics, by arguing, for example, that such geometrical notions as straight line, circle, equal angles, etc., were "mere notions" to which nothing discoverable in experience could be said to correspond. Hume's own consternation at this reduction of Locke's empiricism was genuine. His words will be recalled:

I am at first affrighted and confounded with that forlorn solitude in which I am placed by my philosophy, and fancy myself some strange uncouth monster, utterly abandoned and disconsolate. Fain would I run into the crowd for shelter and warmth. I call upon others to join me. But no one will hearken to me. Everyone keeps at a distance, and dreads that storm which beats upon me from every side. I have exposed myself to the enmity of all metaphysicians, logicians, mathematicians, and theologians. Can I wonder at the insults I must suffer? I have declared my disapprobation of their systems. Can I be surprised if they should express a hatred of my ideas and my person? When I look about me, I foresee on every hand, dispute, contradiction, anger, calumny, detraction. When I turn my eye inward, I find only doubt and ignorance. Every step I take is with hesitation; every new reflection makes me dread an error and absurdity in my reasoning.

These conclusions, which filled Hume with grave doubts about the whole epistemological enterprise, were meanwhile being read and digested by the German philosopher, Immanuel Kant. They did not fill his mind with any fright and confusion. Their effect was, to quote his well-known words, "to rouse me from my dogmatic slumbers." Where Hume was "affrighted and confounded," Kant was stimulated and enlightened. For he detected an element of irony in the whole affair. Here was Hume, in the name of a theory of knowledge denying that there is any knowledge. Knowing that it is the function of a theory to account for that of which it is a theory, not to deny it, Kant was moved to say, in effect, "So much the worse for Hume's theory." If the appeal to experience will not serve as a satisfactory hypothesis, by means of which to account for the fact of knowledge, then so much the worse for the appeal to experience; surely, not so much the worse for knowledge. This was the point of his remark about being "roused from his dogmatic slumbers." He had been satisfied to assume dogmatically that empiricism would account for knowledge. Hume's conclusions served only to convince Kant that unrelieved empiricism must somehow be a mistaken hypothesis.

That is the first fact to be kept in mind with respect to Kant. There is another fact, equally important. It was this: Kant believed firmly in the existence of God, in the freedom of the will, and in the immortality of the soul. But, being also a man of wide reading in modern philosophy he knew that his age, the Age of Reason, was unsympathetic with such convictions. The age was willing, in theory, that a man should entertain these convictions as a matter of faith. But it would not in practice let it go at that. It was inclined to challenge, even to ridicule, such faith. It urged an appeal to reason, confident that in such an appeal faith would come off second best. Everything was to be tried at the "bar of reason." Kant's answer to all this was to carry the war into the enemies' country. He determined to put reason itself on trial. To this end he wrote his large and epoch-making treatise, *Critique of Pure Reason*. The thesis of this book, in one sentence, was this: An examination of reason itself will show that it is powerless to deny, to challenge, or to ridicule the beliefs which devout men hold on faith.

Kant's handling of the problem of knowledge was motivated, then, by these two considerations. First, a theory of knowledge was required to replace the empiricism of Hume. Second, a theory of knowledge was required to deflate the appeal to reason which was placing obstacles in the way of religious convictions. What Kant proposed was this: to replace the appeal to experience and the appeal to reason by a critical analysis of the function of reason in experience.

BIOGRAPHICAL NOTE. Immanuel Kant was born in Germany in 1724 and died in 1804 at the age of seventy-nine. His parents were members of a German sect known as Pietists. What this meant, for Kant, was that he was given a very devout turn of mind from earliest infancy. This devotion to the "fundamentalism" of his parents did not outlast his adolescence, but it was succeeded by an equally rigorous adherence to the fundamentals of morality. His early education was intended to direct his thoughts toward the church. University years directed them along more secular lines. He graduated in classics, mathematics, science, and philosophy. At the age of thirty-one he became a privat-docent in the University at Königsberg. Here, for fifteen years, he provided coaching in mathematics, physics, physical geography, logic, and metaphysics. During these years he was gradually awakened to the dilemmas of the modern mind. These repay a moment's consideration. He took his mathematics and his natural sciences with great seriousness; he found, on the one hand, that the kind of world to which they pointed was "incompatible" with his belief in God, free will, immortality, and the supremacy of a high-minded morality; and he found, on the other, that the unquestioned appeal to experience among progressive minds cast grave doubts on the reliability of mathematics and the sciences. This was not the only respect in which the "modern mind" was at sixes and sevens with itself.   In the fields of theology and metaphysics, confusion reigned supreme.   In the name of reason there were claims and counterclaims; theism, atheism, skepticism with respect to Deity; dualism, materialism, idealism, skepticism, with respect to the nature of ultimate reality.   All these eddies and cross-currents met in the mind of this young man whose business was to provide instruction in science and philosophy.   The thought which gradually took shape in his speculations was this: The modern mind appears to be divided against itself.   Used in one field, it has provided us with the beauties and achievements of mathematics and science; used in another field, it has created endless confusion in which unverifiable speculation is met with unverifiable denial.   He looked into his own mind and found two unshakable convictions: on the one hand, mathematics and the sciences must be "saved" from the skeptics; on the other, the normal beliefs of a conscientious and God-fearing soul must be "saved" from both the sciences and the skeptics.   As these various dilemmas clarified themselves, he saw his task: What was required, apparently, was an examination of the human mind itself.   His thoughts began to shape themselves along these lines.   He was, at the age of forty-six, appointed to the chair of philosophy in his university.   In his inaugural address he communicated to his fellow professors his intention of devoting himself to a critical analysis of the mind's power to know.   For the next eleven years he did just that, and in 1781, at the age of fifty-seven, published his long-awaited *Critique of Pure Reason*.

THE ARGUMENT OF THE CITATIONS.   Kant's problem, in its general outlines, was clear enough.   The only point was where to begin.   He must find a sort of "Achilles' heel" at which to direct his first line of attack.   This he found in the distinction between *a priori* and *a posteriori* knowledge.   Both he held to be undoubted facts, but the current appeal to experience would account only for the latter; the former it either ignored or sought to deny. This little point gave Kant just the opening he required. It is time to let him speak for himself. As the citations begin, he is reflecting upon metaphysics. As his thoughts move around, he hits upon the strategic distinction between *a priori* and *a posteriori* knowledge.

My object is to persuade all those who think metaphysics worth studying, to pause, and, neglecting everything that has been done, to propose the preliminary question: Is metaphysics possible?

How does it come about that metaphysics, unlike other sciences, cannot obtain universal and permanent recognition? It seems almost ridiculous that, while every other science is continually advancing, we should, in metaphysics, move constantly around on the same spot gaining a single step. We do not find men, confident of their ability to shine in other sciences, venturing their reputation here. And so its followers have melted away.

Time was when metaphysics held a royal place among all the sciences. If the will were taken for the deed, the importance of her subject matter might well have secured her that place of honor. But at present it is the fashion to despise her; and like Hecuba, she languishes forsaken and alone. Time was when her rule was despotic. But intestinal war and anarchy broke out. The skeptics, a kind of nomad tribe, despising all settled cultivation of her lands, broke up all civil society. Fortunately their number was small; they could not prevent the old settlers from returning to till the ground afresh. But the old settlers returning had no fixed plan or agreement. At present there reign in metaphysics weariness and indifference, the mother of chaos and night. Near-reforms, ill-applied study, have rendered her counsels dark, confused, and useless.

It is vain, however, to assume a kind of artificial indifference with respect to inquiries to which human nature cannot be indifferent. Nay, even those who pretend indifference, if they think at all, fall back inevitably into those very metaphysical dogmas which they profess to despise.

Nevertheless, this widespread indifference to metaphysics is worth attention and consideration. It is, clearly, not the result of carelessness but of matured judgment. Our age will no longer rest satisfied with the mere appearance of knowledge in these matters. Its patience has run out. This fact constitutes a powerful challenge, a powerful appeal to reason to undertake anew the most difficult of her duties, to institute a court of appeal which, while it will protect her own rights, will dismiss all groundless claims. This court of appeal is no other than a critique of pure reason.

By a *critique of pure reason* I do not mean a criticism of books and systems. I mean a critical analysis of the power of reason itself, touching that whole class of knowledge which it may strive after unassisted by experience. This must decide the question: Is metaphysics possible or impossible?

Since the origin of metaphysics nothing has ever happened which was more decisive to its fate than the attack made upon it by David Hume. He started from a single, but important concept, namely causal connection. He challenged reason, which pretends to have given birth to this idea, to tell him by what right she thinks anything to be so constituted that it is necessarily connected with something else; for that is the meaning of causal connection. He demonstrated, beyond refutation, that it is impossible for us to see why, in consequence with the existence or occurrence of one thing, another thing must necessarily exist or occur also.

Hence he inferred that reason was deluded with reference to this conception of causal connection; that she erroneously considered it one of her children; that, in reality, it was nothing but a bastard child of imagination impregnated by experience; that a subjective necessity of habit was mistaken for an objective necessity arising from insight. I frankly confess, the suggestion of David Hume was the very thing which, many years ago first interrupted my dogmatic slumber, and gave my investigations in the field of speculative philosophy quite a new direction.

Hume's question was not whether the conception of causal connection was right, useful, even indispensable for our knowledge of nature. This he had never doubted. His question was whether that conception could be thought, by reason, *a priori;* whether it thus possessed an inner truth, independent of all experience. That was Hume's problem. It was, as we see, a question concerning the origin of the conception, not its indispensability.

I tried whether Hume's objection could not be put in a general form, and soon found that the conception of causal connection was by no means the only idea by which the understanding thinks the connection of things *a priori.*

It may be advisable to interrupt the movement of Kant's thought at this point. He has already used this fundamental term *a priori* twice. He is going to explain what it means, give an illustration of its use, and contrast it with its antonym, *a posteriori.* But, since the entire argument of his position revolves around this idea, it may be well to try to fix its meaning for ourselves. If we say that some fact is known, or can be known, *a priori,* we mean that it is known or can be known in advance of experience of it. Thus, we might say, "I don't know whether there are any triangles on the far side of the moon; but if there are, I can say *a priori* that the sum of their interior angles will equal two right angles." Or, we might say, "I don't know whether a slave economy was the cause of the fall of the Roman Empire, but I can say *a priori* that there was a cause." Or, we might say, "I don't know whether there are two chairs in the next room, and two in the hall; but if there are, I can say *a priori* that they will add up to four chairs." Or, we might say, "I don't know what happened either before or after I ate my dinner, but I can say *a priori* that something happened both before and after." These illustrations could be extended indefinitely. As Kant will indicate, the problem which they present is this: How does it happen that we can know certain sorts of facts *a priori?*

It is a question worth investigating, whether there exists any knowledge independent of experience and all sense impressions.

Such knowledge is called *a priori* and is distinguished from *a posteriori* knowledge which has its sources in experience. That there is genuine *a priori* knowledge, that we can advance independent of all experience, is shown by the brilliant example of mathematics.

This term *a priori* requires closer definition. People are wont to say, even with regard to knowledge derived from experience, that we have it or might have it *a priori*. They mean we might derive it from a general rule. Thus, of one who undermines the foundations of his house, they would say he might have known *a priori* that it would tumble down; know it, that is, from the general rule that unsupported bodies fall. But this general rule has itself been derived from experience. Whoever knows this general rule had first to learn it from experience. He could not have known this entirely *a priori*. (This Hume has shown.) In what follows, we shall use the term more strictly. We shall understand by *a priori* that which is absolutely independent of all experience, and not of this or that experience only. Opposed to this is *a posteriori* or empirical knowledge, such as is derived from experience.

Experience tells us what is, but not that it must necessarily be as it is. It therefore never gives us any necessary, *a priori*, knowledge. Experience never imparts to its judgments any strict universality, but only relative universality (by means of induction) so that we ought always to say, "so far as we have experienced, there is no exception to this or that rule." Necessity and universality are criteria of the *a priori*. If, therefore, a judgment is thought with strict universality and necessity so that no exception is admitted as possible, it cannot have been derived from experience.

We have here a mystery. We must discover the ground of *a priori* judgments. We must understand the conditions which render them possible. The real problem is contained in the question: How is *a priori* knowledge possible? That metaphysics has hitherto remained in so vacillating a condition of ignorance and contradiction is due entirely to the fact that this problem has been ignored.

David Hume, who among all philosophers approached nearest to this problem, arrived at the conclusion that *a priori* knowledge is impossible. According to his reasoning everything we call metaphysics would turn out to be mere delusion. But if he had grasped clearly the problem of the *a priori* he would never have thought of an assertion which destroys all metaphysics, because he would have seen that, according to such an argument, neither was mathematics possible (since it contains *a priori* judgments). And from such an assertion his good sense would probably have saved him.

It is to be noted that our problem is not: Are *a priori* judgments possible? For there are enough of them to hand, of undoubted certainty, that we need not argue for their possibility. (What is actual must be possible.) We must inquire into the grounds of the possibility of their existence. <u>The proper problem, upon which all depends, when expressed precisely is this: How are *a priori* propositions possible?</u>

It again seems advisable to break in upon Kant's meditations. The justification must be this: He is saying things quite calmly which cut very deep. He began by admitting a sort of bankruptcy on all hands in matters philosophical. He added, however, that no philosopher worth his salt would therefore feel justified in crying quits. He realized that Hume had been an important factor, despite his negative conclusions. He wants, above all, a toe hold, some fact upon which he can take a stand. His eye catches sight of this apparently neglected distinction between *a priori* knowledge and *a posteriori* knowledge. He fastens on this, realizing that this may have important implications. He sees, also, that the fact of the *a priori* raises a problem. The *a priori* is a fact. The problem is how to account for it.

Although all our knowledge begins with experience, it does not follow that it arises entirely from experience. For it is quite possible that our empirical knowledge is a compound of that which we receive through impressions and that which our own faculty of knowing (incited by impressions) supplies from itself — a supplement to impressions which we do not distinguish from that raw material (i.e., impressions) until long practice has roused our attention and rendered us capable of separating one from the other.

Hitherto it has been supposed that all our knowledge must conform to the objects, but, under that supposition, all attempts to establish any knowledge about them *a priori* have come to nothing.

The experiment therefore ought to be made, whether we should not succeed better by assuming that objects must conform to our forms of knowledge. For this would agree better with the required possibility of an *a priori* knowledge of objects; that is, with the possibility of settling something about those objects before they are given us in experience.

We have here the same case as with the first thought of Copernicus. Not being able to explain the movements of the heavenly body so long as he assumed that the stars moved around the spectator, he tried assuming the spectator to be turning around and the stars to be at rest. A similar experiment may be tried in metaphysics, so far as our knowledge of objects is concerned. If our knowledge has to conform to the nature of objects, I do not see how we could know anything *a priori*. But if the object of knowledge has to conform to the constitution of our power of knowing, I can very well conceive the possibilities of such *a priori* knowledge.

If Copernicus had not dared, by an hypothesis which contradicted the senses, to seek the observed movements in the spectator instead of in the heavenly bodies, the laws of planetary motion would have remained for ever undiscovered. I propose my own view, which has so many analogies with the Copernican hypothesis, as, at first, an hypothesis only.

Kant's argument at this point becomes too complicated for reproduction in quotation. For that reason, the next passages are mere descriptions of his argument, not selections or paraphrases from his *Critique*. Thus far, what he has been saying comes to this: Metaphysical speculation is in disrepute. Hume's criticism seems to have put an end to it. His conclusions followed from his dogma that all knowledge comes from experience. Since, on this premise, he could not account for *a priori* knowledge, he denied it. But a theory of knowledge which issues in a denial of knowledge is a poor theory. *A priori* knowledge is a fact to be accounted for, not an illusion to be denied. Since the appeal to experience has failed, something else must be tried. A new theory of knowledge is required to account for the fact of *a priori* knowledge. Kant's hypothesis is this: That knowledge is a joint product of mind and external world, arising in experience. This hypothesis raises the following problem: If knowledge is a joint product of mind and external world, then what part of the joint product is contributed by the mind? Kant answers by distinguishing between the form and the content of knowledge. <u>The form of knowledge is contributed by the mind.</u> <u>The content is contributed by the external world.</u> In the production of knowledge the mind acts to impose form on content supplied by the external world. This leads to a new problem: If knowledge is a joint product of mind and world, and mind's contribution is the form, can these formal elements in knowledge be isolated and analyzed? What, in other words, is the form which mind contributes?

Kant answers by distinguishing between perceptual, conceptual, and speculative knowledge. <u>To our perceptual knowledge, mind contributes the forms of space and time. These</u> Kant calls *forms of sensibility*. <u>To our conceptual knowledge mind contributes the forms of quantity, quality, relation, and modality.</u> These, when further analyzed, he calls *categories of understanding*. To our <u>speculative knowledge, mind contributes the forms of self, universe, and God.</u> These he calls *ideas of reason*. I shall refer to them as *forms of speculation*. Space and time are forms of perception, not things perceived. Things are always perceived spread-out-and-strung-along, are always perceived in a background-foreground and a before-and-after setting. This invariable spatial and temporal character is the form of all perceptual knowledge. On Kant's hypothesis, it is due to the "diffracting" action of mind or consciousness. Except as forms of consciousness, these words have no meaning. They are forms of awareness, not things of which we are aware. In Kant's words, space and time are "empirically real, but transcendentally ideal," that is, real in experience but otherwise only ideal. Quotations are here possible once more:

Space does not represent any property of things in themselves, nor does it represent them in their relation to one another. . . . Space is nothing but the form of all appearances of outer sense. It is the subjective condition of sensibility under which alone outer perception is possible for us.

Since the capacity to be affected by objects must precede all perceptions of these objects, it can readily be understood how the form of all appearances (i.e., space) can be given prior to all perceptions, and so exist in the mind *a priori;* and how, as a pure intuition, in which all objects must be determined, it can contain, prior to all experience, principles which determine the relations of these objects. It is, therefore, solely from the human standpoint that we can speak of space, of extended things. If we depart from the subjective, the representation of space stands for nothing whatsoever.

This predicate (i.e., space) can be ascribed to things only insofar as they appear to us, that is, to objects of sensibility. Since, however, we cannot treat the special conditions of sensibility as conditions of the possibility of things, but only of their appearances, we can indeed say that space comprehends all things that appear to us as external, but not all things in themselves. For we cannot judge in regard to the perceptions of other kinds of thinking beings, whether they are bound by the same conditions as limit us.

The proposition that all things are side by side in space is valid under the limitation that these things are viewed as objects of our perception. Our exposition claims the reality, the objective validity, of space in respect of whatever can be presented us; but also, at the same time, the ideality of space in respect of things when they are considered in themselves, that is, without regard to the constitution of our sensibility.

We assert, then, the empirical reality of space, as regards all possible outer experience, and, at the same time, its transcendental ideality, i.e., that it is nothing at all, immediately we withdraw the said condition, namely limitation to possible experience, and look upon it as something that underlies things in themselves.

The transcendental conception of appearances in space is a critical reminder that nothing perceived in space is a thing in itself; that space is not a form inhering in things in themselves as their intrinsic property; that objects in themselves are nothing but mere representations of our sensibility, the form of which is space. The true correlate of sensibility, the thing in itself, is not known, and cannot be known, through these representations; and in experience no question is ever asked in regard to it. DAS DING AN SICH

Kant's remarks on the status of time, which parallel, roughly, his remarks on the status of space, may be quoted in part:

Time is not an empirical conception that has been derived from any experience. For neither coexistence nor succession (the two modes of time) would ever have come within our perception, if the representation of time were not presupposed as underlying them *a priori*.

Time is not something which exists of itself or inheres in things. Were it a determination (i.e., property) of things in themselves, it could not be known *a priori*. But such *a priori* knowledge is quite possible if time is nothing but the subjective condition under which alone perception can take place in us. For, that being so, this form of intuition can be represented prior to the objects and therefore *a priori*.

Time is a purely subjective condition of our human perception, and, in itself, apart from the subject, is nothing. . . . What we are maintaining is the empirical reality of time, its objective validity of all objects which allow of ever being given to our senses. Since our perception is always sensible (i.e., by the senses), no object can ever be given to us in experience which does not conform to the condition of time. On the other hand, we deny to time any claim to absolute reality; that is to say, we deny that it belongs to things absolutely, as their condition or property independently of any reference to the form of our perception. Properties that belong to things in themselves can never be given to us through the senses.   This, then, is what constitutes the ideality of time.

What we mean by the *ideality of time* is this: If we abstract from the subjective conditions of sensuous perception, time is nothing, and cannot be ascribed to the objects in themselves apart from their relation to our perception, neither in the way of subsistence nor of inherence.

By *categories* Kant means such forms of understanding things as unity and plurality, substance and quality, cause and effect, and so on.   He enumerates twelve.   The number is not so important as his recognition that conceptual knowledge has form as well as content, and his hypothesis that the form is mind's contribution.   Thus, to consider one of these categories, causation is a form of understanding, not a reality in its own right.   When a drop in temperature causes the water to freeze, there are not three things, namely, dropping temperature, freezing water, and a cause connecting the two. Rather, there are two things understood in terms of a category. Our understanding of anything involves many such categories.   Kant's point is the simple, but revolutionary suggestion that categories of understanding are not objects of knowledge but forms of knowledge; not things known but ways of knowing.   Our understanding of things given in experience is conditioned by the categories in terms of which our minds work.   These categories are forms of understanding what is given in experience; they are, themselves, not given in experience.

Speculation is the attempt to carry understanding beyond the limits of experience.   Since the categories are only forms to which experience gives content, any such attempt is deemed to fail.   To use a common expression, it can never be anything more than "mere speculation."   Kant notes, and condemns, three forms of speculation, three ways in which the mind perennially seeks to transcend the limits of experience.

The first of these is <u>the attempt to speculate on the nature of the mind itself,</u> to seek to understand the nature of that which contributes form to knowledge. Beyond detecting the forms, we cannot go. The mind itself is outside of experience. It is, itself, never given in experience. It can never be content for its own forms. The attempt to formulate a rational psychology, that is, to gain an understanding of the mind, soul, self, ego, is, on Kant's theory of knowledge, to attempt the impossible. We cannot pierce beyond the stream of consciousness, to a knowledge of the factors which make it to be the kind of thing it is. That there is a mind, beyond the stream of consciousness, Kant is prepared to argue, as against Hume. His reason for refusing to stop short with Hume is simple. The latter, it will be recalled, "reduced" mind to a succession of awarenesses. To this Kant has a rejoinder. The fact to be accounted for, he points out, is not a succession of awarenesses, but an awareness of succession. If that which is aware passed with the awareness, there could be no awareness of succession. But there is precisely this, namely, <u>awareness of succession.</u> Time indeed is one of the forms of knowledge.

The second attempt to extend knowledge beyond experience, is <u>to speculate on the nature of the whole of things, beyond what is given piecemeal in experience</u>. The attempt to formulate a rational cosmology, that is, to extend the categories beyond experience is to attempt the impossible. The mind's categories are valid only within experience. As the universe comes within the grasp of experience, it becomes understood in terms of the categories. Beyond that, as in the case of rational psychology, is "mere speculation."

The third attempt to extend knowledge beyond experience is <u>to speculate on the nature of God.</u> For reasons which will appear later, Kant believed in the existence of God, but he is prepared to argue that such belief is not to be confused with knowledge. To attempt to formulate a rational theology, that is, to know God as we know things which fall within our experience, is to attempt the impossible. Kant reiterates and extends Hume's destructive criticism of the grounds for theism. Like rational psychology and rational cosmology, rational theology is "mere speculation." A quotation from Kant is possible here:

> Human reason begins with principles which, in the course of experience it must follow. With these again, according to the necessities of its nature, it rises higher and higher to more remote conditions. Thus it becomes involved in darkness and contradictions. It may conclude that errors must be lurking somewhere, but it is unable to discover them because the principles which it follows go beyond all limits of experience and so beyond all experimental verification. Metaphysics is the battlefield of these endless controversies.

Kant contrasts the forms of sensibility and the categories of understanding with these three ideas of speculation. The two former are constitutive of knowledge. That is, within the limits of experience, they enter into and contribute to genuine knowledge. The latter, however, are merely regulative. This distinction between constitutive and regulative forms of knowledge is important. The ideas of self, cosmos, and God are regulative goals toward which knowledge moves but to which it never attains.

Kant's distinction between *phenomena* and *noumena*, between things as known and things-in-themselves, follows as a corollary from this general theory of knowledge. It arises thus: Knowledge is a joint product of mind and external world arising in experience. There are here two contributing factors: the mind and external world. The latter "appears" through the forms and categories of the former. The word *phenomena* is derived from a Greek word meaning "that which appears." Hence reality as known is appearance, is phenomenal, is to be contrasted with reality as it is, which is noumenal. As Kant sweepingly remarks, "We only know phenomena."

We are now in a position to return to the one basic fact which this elaborate theory was invoked to account for, namely, *a priori* knowledge. Our *a priori* knowledge is formal only, and arises out of the dual origin of knowledge. We know *a priori* that things perceived will be perceived as spread-out-and-strung-along. We know *a priori* that things will be understood as effects of causes. We know *a priori* that things will be understood as qualities inhering in substances. We know *a priori* that things will be understood in terms of part-whole relations. And so on through the categories. But this knowledge is purely formal. We do not know *a priori* what the content of future experiences will be. We know that it will exhibit the various forms referred to, because, by hypothesis, knowledge is a joint product of mind-imposed forms filled with experience-given content. Thus did Kant "answer" Hume. At this point we can resume quoting directly from his writings.

I must, therefore, even before objects are given me in experience, presuppose the "rules of the understanding," or the "principles of knowledge" as existing within me *a priori*. These rules are expressed in *a priori* concepts to which all objects of experience must necessarily conform and to which they must agree. By thus changing our point of view, the possibility of *a priori* knowledge can well be explained.

After a superficial view of this work, it may seem that its results are negative only, warning us against venturing beyond the limits of experience. Such is no doubt its primary use. But its results are seen to be positive, when we perceive that it leads inevitably to a narrowing, a limiting, of the employment of reason; to the impossibility of going by it beyond the frontier of possible experience.

But thus and thus alone can we cut away the very root of materialism, idealism, skepticism, fatalism, atheism, fanaticism, and superstition. If governments ever think proper to interfere with the affairs of the learned, it would be consistent with their wise regard for science and society, to favor the freedom of such a criticism as can establish the labors of reason on a firm footing.

To deny that this service, setting limits to the speculative use of reason, is a positive advantage, would be the same as to deny that the police confer any positive advantage on us in preventing that violence which citizens have to fear from citizens. The police protection enables each to pursue his vocation in peace and security. The critique of reason does as much for the powers of the mind.

To illustrate this, let us suppose that the necessary distinction, established in our critique, between things as phenomena and things-in-themselves, had not been made. In that case the principle of causality, and with it the mechanical interpretation of nature, would apply to all things and not to their appearances only. I should then not be able to say of one and the same thing, for instance, the human soul, that it is both free and subject to necessity, without involving myself in a contradiction.

If, however, we may legitimately take an object in two senses, namely, as phenomenon and as thing-in-itself; and if the principle of causality applies to things only as phenomena and not as noumena, then we can, without any contradiction, think one and the same thing when phenomenal as necessarily conforming to the principle of causality and so far not free, and yet, in itself not subject to that principle and therefore free.

Suppose morality necessarily presupposed freedom of the will while speculative reason had proved that such freedom cannot even be thought. In such case freedom, and with it morality, would have to make room for the mechanical interpretation of nature. But our critique has revealed our inevitable ignorance of things-in-themselves, has limited our knowledge to mere phenomena. So, as morality requires only that freedom should not entail a contradiction, there is no reason why freedom should be denied to the will, considered as thing-in-itself, merely because it must be denied to it as phenomenon. The doctrine of morality may well hold its place, and the doctrine of nature too; which would have been impossible without our theory of the nature and limitations of knowledge.

If I cannot deprive speculative reason of its pretensions to trans-cendent insight, I cannot even assume freedom of will, not even in the interests of morality. I had, therefore, to remove the possi-bility of knowledge of what lies beyond experience, in order to make room for faith. This question of free will is but one of many which derive positive advantage from the limitations imposed by my theory of knowledge, on the speculative reach of pure reason beyond ex-perience.

Let any reader who finds these inquiries obscure consider that not every one is bound to study metaphysics; that many minds will suc-ceed very well in the exact sciences more closely allied to practical experience while they cannot succeed in investigations dealing ex-clusively with abstract conceptions. In such cases men should apply their talents to other subjects.

The following citations from John Dewey's *Quest For Certainty* describe rather pointedly the motive and the main turns of Kant's theory of knowledge:

Kant's position bristles with points of internal difficulty; many of these are objects of controversy. Ignoring these, however, it can fairly be asserted that the main characteristic of his position is a division of territory between the objects of cognitive certitude and the objects of equally complete moral assurance.

He aims in the first place to make secure, on rational *a priori* grounds, the foundation of natural knowledge; in the second, to perform a like office for the foundations of moral and religious con-ceptions. Science is limited to phenomena in space and time in order that the world of higher and noumenal realities may be ap-propriated by ideals and spiritual values. Each has complete jurisdiction and undisputed sovereignty in its own realm.

His argument in justification of the certitude of the foundations of knowledge is couched at every point so as to indicate the necessity of a higher although intellectually unapproachable realm. There was nothing factitious, in Kant's own conception, in the way in which the two kingdoms excluded each other and yet made each other necessary. On the contrary, the neat way in which the ele-ments of each dovetailed into those of the other was to him a convincing proof of the necessity of the system as a whole. If the dove-tailing was the product of his own intellectual carpentry, he had no suspicion of the fact.

He thought he had disposed, once for all, of many of the most per-plexing problems of earlier philosophy. Upon the scientific side he was concerned to provide a final philosophical justification, be-yond the reach of skepticism, for the Newtonian science.

His conception of space and time as necessary forms of the possi-bility of perception was the justification of the application of mathe-matics to natural phenomena. Categories of thought, necessary to understand perceived objects — and understanding necessary to science — supplied the foundation of permanent substances and causal connection demanded by Newtonian science. The tendency of the mind to pass beyond the limits of experience to the thought of unconditioned and self-sufficient totalities, "Ideas" of the universe, soul and God, was explained; and while cognitive validity was denied these "Ideas," they were admitted as regulative ideals which directed inquiry and interpretation. Above all, the thought of these transempirical realities left room that the postulate of free choice could fill.

In its essential framework, the Kantian scheme thus agreed marvel-ously well with the needs of the historic crisis. It gave freedom to both science and morals, with a guarantee that they could never interfere with each other. The traditional belief was that security of moral authority depends upon some source in being apart from the experiences by which values are incarnated in concrete objects and institutions. Granted this traditional belief, the Kantian scheme has such merits that it is safe to predict that as long as this belief continues to have vitality, the main elements of the Kantian position will have devoted disciples.

Thus Kant on the problem of knowledge in his *Critique of Pure Reason*. His ideas here are closely connected with the ideas which he was to put into his second *Critique*. The latter was directed toward a clarification and defense of his convic-tions in the field of ethics. Since his philosophy comprises both of these *Critiques*, together with much more, we shall return to him later on in connection with the ethical problem.

READING REFERENCES. It has been said that more books have been written on Shakespeare, Goethe, and Kant than on any three other persons. Kant is a perennially attractive figure. Anyone who is familiar with the main turns of modern philosophy can feel the tug which the man's ideas exert even when had at second hand. The accounts of Kant to be found in Will Durant's *Story of Philosophy*, in Mary Whiton Calkins's *The Persistent Problems of Philosophy*, in Royce's *Lectures on Modern Idealism* are good introductory presentations. These are for beginners. For those who desire to go a little further, Lindsay's *Kant*, Paulsen's *Immanuel Kant*, and the extended account in Volume Two of Hoffding's *History of Modern Philosophy* are recommended. Beyond that, one arrives soon at specialized and monumental treatises.

READING QUESTIONS

1. "Kant's handling of the problem of knowledge was motivated by these two considerations." Namely?
2. "During these years he was gradually awakened to the dilemmas of the modern mind." What years? What dilemmas?
3. "He looked into his own mind and found two unshakable convictions." What convictions?
4. What preliminary question is it his object to propose?
5. What is the state of metaphysics as he sees it?
6. "It is vain to assume an artificial indifference." To what? Why?
7. How does he describe the impact of Hume's work on philosophy?
8. What does he mean by *a priori* knowledge?
9. "Experience tells us what is, but not that it must necessarily be as it is." Elucidate.
10. "We have here a mystery." Elucidate.
11. "Hitherto it has been supposed . . . have come to nothing." Restate the complete passage in your own words

12. By what hypothesis does he propose to account for the *a priori?*
13. Why does he liken it to the Copernican hypothesis?
14. What is his distinction between form and content?
15. How does he propose to connect this distinction with the distinction between *a priori* and *a posteriori?*
16. State his "Copernican" hypothesis in terms of this distinction between form and content.
17. What is his thesis regarding space and time?
18. What does he mean by the *empirical reality* and *transcendental ideality* of space and time?
19. Distinguish after Kant: perception, understanding, speculation.
20. What are the formal (*a priori*) elements in each?
21. What are the three forms of speculation which Kant notes?
22. By what line of reasoning does he eliminate all three?
23. In what sense are the forms of sensibility and the categories of the understanding "constitutive" whereas the ideas of speculation are "regulative"?
24. What is his distinction between phenomena and noumena?
25. How is it derived?
26. "We only know phenomena." Meaning?
27. "The one basic fact which this elaborate theory was invoked to account for, namely, *a priori* knowledge." Elucidate.
28. "After a superficial view of this work, it may seem that its results are negative only." Elucidate.
29. "But its results are seen to be positive." How so?
30. What is his policeman analogy?
31. What bearing does he suggest his theory might have on morality?
32. "Kant's position bristles with points of internal difficulty." Can you suggest some?
33. "In its essential framework, the Kantian scheme agreed marvelously well with the needs of the historic crisis." What crisis? What needs? What essential framework?
34. Under what conditions, according to Dewey, will the main elements of the Kantian position have devoted disciples?

4. POSITIVISM — FROM AUGUSTE COMTE

FROM KANT TO COMTE.   Each century tackles the problem of knowledge in its own way.   The seventeenth century, represented most completely in Locke's essay, differs in method from the eighteenth.   The eighteenth, represented by the twin stars of Hume and Kant, differs again from the nineteenth represented in the writings of Auguste Comte. By the 1830's, it was rather unnecessary to reopen the hectic controversies which inspired and followed from earlier epistemologies.   At least, Comte appears to have felt as much.   The picture is altered.   Comte approaches the question of knowledge from the point of view of a man who is interested primarily in the range and organization of the various bodies of science.   He pins a controversial tag on himself, no doubt; for *positivism*, as will be seen, means "no more metaphysics."   But he is inclined to sweep controversy to one side and ask several new leading questions: What common method has the growth of science revealed?   What relations, if any, exist among the different sciences?   What significance, for general education, may be ascribed to the sciences as a whole?   In what fields, if any, may we look for the emergence of new sciences?   For these reasons, among others, Comte is perhaps more convincing to one who is either innocent of Hume and Kant or who has lost those peculiar sensibilities which respond to their anxieties and convictions.

BIOGRAPHICAL NOTE.   Auguste Comte was born in France in 1798, and died in 1857 at the age of fifty-nine.   He showed an early aptitude for mathematics, which he began to teach in Paris.   When he was twenty-eight, he embarked on a series of public lectures designed to offer a synoptic account of the principal sciences.   These attracted considerable attention; but after the third lecture, his brain temporarily gave way, and he tried to commit suicide.   Two years later he had sufficiently recovered to resume his lectures. In 1830 he began the publication of his great survey of the sciences. It was completed in six large volumes and served through several generations as a storehouse of fact and generalization for advanced students in France and abroad. He continued to maintain himself by teaching mathematics and serving as an examiner in that subject. Unfortunately, however, he became embroiled in controversies which caused him to lose a great part of his means of living. The English philosopher, J. S. Mill, who had been impressed by the value of Comte's work, was instrumental in securing a considerable sum of money from Comte's admirers in England. This tided him over his immediate difficulties. When this was used up, Comte faced poverty; however, aid came eventually from admirers in France who banded together to provide the lonely polymath with a small income for the rest of his life.

Comte's interest in epistemology was not direct. To get this point as clearly and, at the same time, as sympathetically as possible, we need to recall a bit of French history. Comte wrote for the first generation after Napoleon. The old regime, the epoch of the grand monarchy, formed a remote background. It had been swept away by the French Revolution. Liberal hopes had run high, only to be disappointed by the autocratic domination of Napoleon, and now, following the Congress of Vienna, France had been made over once more into a monarchy under Louis XVIII and Charles X. These drastic changes appear to have inspired Comte with the dream of a new era in which they would no longer be possible. This new era was to be built upon science and the application of science to industry. But, as Comte saw it, several obstacles blocked the path of the new age. They were remnants from the past. They were, more particularly, beliefs or mental sets which still lingered from the Middle Ages, the period of the grand monarchy, the Age of Reason, the revolution, and

Napoleon. They were beliefs about such matters as God, the soul, ultimate reality, immortality, natural laws, inalienable rights, men of destiny, and so forth. These beliefs, Comte felt, were not only groundless, they were harmful. They had been responsible for continuous tyranny, revolt, suppression, war, and they always would be. What the world needed was a riddance of such disarranging beliefs, and Comte would supply it under cover of this new term *positivism*, which was to abolish the old loyalties and controversies, to set up the ideal of scientific method and its application to nature in the interests of human welfare.

The Argument of the Citations. Comte begins by elaborating what he calls the *law of the three stages*. This enables him to dispose of metaphysics and theology. He turns then to a statement of his theory of the sciences. The citations tell their own story from that point on:

In order to understand the true value and character of positivism, we must take a brief general view of the progress of the human mind; for no conception can be understood otherwise than through its history.

From the study of the development of human understanding, in all directions and through all times, the discovery arises of a fundamental law. The law is this: that each of our leading conceptions, each branch of our knowledge, passes through three different theoretical conditions: the theological or fictitious, the metaphysical or abstract, the scientific or positive. This fundamental law should henceforth be, in my opinion, the starting point of all philosophical researches about man and society.

The human mind employs in its progress three methods of explanations, the characteristics of which are essentially different and even radically opposed: the theological, the metaphysical, and the scientific. Hence arise three philosophies, or three general systems of thought, each of which excludes the other. The first is the mind's necessary point of departure; the second is merely a state of transition; the third is the mind's fixed and definitive state.

An instance of what Comte means might be the following: In the early stages of man's study of the heavens, he accounted for their motion in terms of various deities. Later he envisaged them as controlled by the force of gravitation. Finally he repudiates explanation in terms of gods and forces and is satisfied to describe the motion in terms of formulae which enable him to locate and predict:

Different departments of our knowledge have passed through the three stages at different rates. The rate depends on the nature of the knowledge in question. Any kind of knowledge reaches the positive stage early in proportion to its generality, simplicity, and independence of other branches of knowledge. Thus astronomy, which is above all made up of facts which are general, simple, and independent of other facts, was the first science to attain the positive stage, then physics, then chemistry, and finally physiology.

In the theological stage, the human mind, seeking the essential nature of things, their first and final causes, supposes all things to be produced by the immediate action of supernatural beings. Here imagination predominates over observation.

A natural and irresistible instinct disposes the human race to adopt theological ideas as its earliest principles of explanation. The personal action exerted by man on other things is, at first, the only kind he is able to understand. He is thus led to conceive, in an analogous way, the action of external bodies on himself and on each other. This is animism. Continued observation leads him to convert this primitive hypothesis into another, less enduring one: that of a "dead" inert nature guided by invisible superhuman agents, distinct and independent of one another. This is polytheism. Continued observation and reflection disposes him gradually to reduce the number of these supernatural agencies until he is led from polytheism to monotheism. The theological system arrived at its highest perfection when it substituted the providential action of a single supreme Being for the varied operations of numerous divinities; when, that is, it passed from polytheism to monotheism.

The entire theological system is based on the supposition that the earth is made for man, and the whole universe made for the earth.

Remove this supposition, and the system crumbles.   Hence the true astronomical theory, proposed by Copernicus and proved by Kepler, Galileo, and Newton, would alone have sufficed to demolish the theological system.   In the light of the fact that our planet, one of the smallest, is in no respect different from the others, revolving like them around the sun, the hypothesis that nature is made for mankind alone so shocks good sense and contradicts fact that it must appear absurd and collapse.   With it falls the theological edifice.

In the metaphysical stage, which is only a modification of the first, the mind supposes abstract forces, personified abstractions, inherent in all things and capable of producing them, instead of supernatural beings.   What is called the *explanation* of anything is, in this stage, a reference of it to its proper force, principle, or abstraction.

To explain sleep, for example, in terms of what used to be called the *dormitive principle* is to explain observed phenomena by reference to what Comte would call a *metaphysical abstraction*.   Many such phrases are to be found strewn through the annals of science and philosophy.   Thus Hegel's *reason* or *time-spirit*, Schopenhauer's *will*, Bergson's *élan vital*, Freud's *censor*, the erstwhile *vis viva*, *vis inertia*, and *entelechy* are, I suspect, all instances of what Comte would call *metaphysical abstractions*.   His objection to them is that they are attempts to explain the known by the unknown, to postulate something which is not revealed in experience to account for what is revealed in experience.

Even today, after all our advance in positive knowledge, if we try to understand how the fact which we name a cause produces the fact which we name its effect, we should be compelled, as Hume points out, to resort to images similar to those which serve as the basis of primitive human theories.   (Cause is a metaphysical notion; regularity of succession is the positive notion.)

The metaphysical system arrived at its last stage when men substituted the one great entity — nature — as the cause of everything.

In the scientific or positive stage the mind has given over the vain search after absolute knowledge; abandoned the quest for knowledge of the origin and destination of the universe, of causes and forces; and applies itself solely to the study of laws, to the study of relations of succession and resemblance. Reasoning and observation, duly combined, are the means of this knowledge. What is now called the *explanation* of anything is the establishment of a connection between it and some general laws, the number of which continually diminishes with the progress of science.

Observation of fact is the only solid basis for human knowledge. Taking this principle in its most rigorous sense, we may say that a proposition which does not admit of being reduced to a simple enunciation of fact, particular or general, can have no real or intelligible sense.

The first characteristic of positivism is that it regards all things as subject to invariable laws. Our business — seeing how vain is any search into what are called causes, either first or final — is to pursue an accurate discovery of those laws, with a view to reducing them to the smallest possible number. The best illustration of this is in the case of the law of gravitation. We say things are explained by it, because it connects an immense variety of facts under one head.

The positive system would attain its ultimate perfection if men could represent all particular facts as instances of one general law, e.g., the law of gravitation.

There is no science, which, having attained to the positive stage, does not bear marks of having passed through the two previous stages. At some earlier period it was composed of metaphysical abstractions; and, further back in its evolution, it took its form from theological conceptions. Our most advanced sciences still bear traces of the earlier stages through which they have passed.

In mentioning just now the four principal categories of phenomena — the astronomical, the physical, the chemical, the physiological — there was an omission. Nothing was said of social phenomena. These demand a distinct classification, by reason of their importance and difficulty. They are the most complicated and the most dependent on others. Their science, therefore, will be the latest to attain positivity.

This branch of science has not hitherto entered the domain of positive knowledge. Theological and metaphysical conceptions and methods, exploded and abandoned in other departments, are still used in the treatment of social subjects, though the best minds are weary of disputes about "divine rights," "sovereignty of the people," and so on. This is the great, the only, gap to be filled to constitute solid and entire the positive philosophy. This is what men have now most need of.

This once done, the philosophical system of the moderns will be complete. There will then be no phenomena which does not enter into one of the five great categories — astronomical, physical, chemical, physiological, and sociological.

So much then, for the law of the three stages. It has a certain plausibility. But, for Comte, its principal virtue seems to reside in the fact that it eliminates, at one fell swoop, a whole army of clamorous hypotheses and controversies which constitute a large portion of modern philosophy. Comte now turns his attention to the question of the classification of the positive sciences. (It should be noted that, as Comte uses it, the term *physiology* has the broader meaning which we extend today to the term *biology*.)

We propose to classify the fundamental sciences. They are six, as we shall see. We cannot make them less; and most scientists would make them more. To classify the sciences is not so easy as may appear. It always involves something, if not arbitrary, at least artificial; and in so far, it will always involve imperfection. It is perhaps impossible to exhibit the sciences, quite rigorously, in their natural relations and mutual dependence so as to avoid, in some degree, the danger of overlapping.

What we seek to determine is the dependence of scientific studies. Does physics depend upon physiology? Does sociology depend upon chemistry? Dependence among the sciences can result only from dependence among the corresponding phenomena. For a principle in terms of which to classify the sciences, then, we must look

to the different orders of phenomena through which science discovers the laws which are her object.

All phenomena may be included within a very few natural categories, so arranged that the study of each may be grounded on the
principal laws of the preceding and serve as the basis of the next
ensuing. We have now obtained our rule. We proceed next to our
classification.

We are first struck by the clear division of all natural phenomena
into two classes: inorganic and organic. Each of these two great
halves has subdivisions. Inorganic phenomena may be divided into
two classes: celestial and terrestrial. Terrestrial inorganic phenomena may be divided into two classes according as we regard
bodies in their mechanical or chemical character. Organic phenomena may be divided into two classes: those which relate to the
individual and those which relate to groups.

Thus we have five basic sciences in successive dependence: astronomy, physics, chemistry, physiology, and sociology. The first considers the most general, simple, and remote phenomena known to
us, and those which affect all others without being affected by them.
The last considers the most particular, complex, and nearest phenomena. Between these two the degrees of speciality and complexity
are in regular proportion to the place of the respective sciences in
the scale exhibited. This we must regard as the true filiation of the
sciences.

It is proposed to consolidate the entire body of positive knowledge
into one body of homogeneous doctrine. But it must not be supposed that we are proposing to study this vast variety as proceeding
from one single law. There is something so chimerical in attempts
at explanation in terms of one single law, that it may be as well to
repudiate any such notion. Our intellectual resources are too narrow, and the universe too complex, to justify any hope that it will
ever be within our power to carry scientific perfection to this last
degree of simplicity.

This notion of all phenomena referable to a single law is by no
means necessary to the systematic formation of science. The only
necessary unity is that of method. And this is already, in great
part, attained: The scientific method of thought is the same for all

fields of knowledge, however widely they may vary and however irreducible they may be in content.

Comte's meaning is probably this: In the scientific exploration of any field, the method is the same. Initial data are collected, usually in the light of some tentatively held hypothesis; this hypothesis is then assumed to be true, and its consequences or implications deduced; facts subsequently acquired, by observation or experiment, verify the deductions made from the hypothesis. The hypothesis may be with regard to some particular fact or some general law.

The most interesting point in our hierarchical classification is its effect on education, both general and scientific. This is its direct and unquestionable result. No science can be effectually pursued without a competent knowledge of the anterior sciences upon which it depends.

Your competent physicist must have at least a general knowledge of astronomy. Chemists cannot properly understand chemistry without physics and astronomy. Physiologists require some knowledge of chemistry, physics, and astronomy. Above all, students of social science require a general knowledge of the anterior sciences. As such conditions are rarely fulfilled, there is among us, no genuinely rational scientific education. To this may be attributed, in part, the imperfection of even the most important sciences at this day.

In our enumeration of the basic sciences there is one prodigious omission. We have said nothing of mathematics. The omission was intentional, and the reason was the vast importance and unique status of mathematics. It is, however, less a constituent part of the body of positive knowledge than a basis for the whole of that knowledge. It is the most powerful instrument that the human mind can employ in the investigation of the laws of natural phenomena. It must, therefore, hold the first place in the hierarchy of the sciences and be the point of departure for all education in any of the sciences.

From the question of the classification of the sciences, Comte addresses himself to certain advantages which, he thinks, will arise from the unified view which results. It is interesting to note that these include the elimination of logic and the reduction of psychology to behaviorism.

We have now considered philosophically the articulation of the positive sciences. The order that results is this: mathematics, astronomy, physics, chemistry, physiology, and sociology. We must glance at the principal advantages to be derived from a study of them. Of these advantages, four may be pointed out.

In the first place, the study of the positive sciences affords the only rational means of exhibiting the logical laws of the human mind. Looking at all scientific theories as so many great logical facts, it is only by the observation of these facts that we can arrive at the knowledge of logical laws.

Psychology pretends to discover the laws of the human mind by contemplating the mind itself. Such an (introspective) attempt, made in defiance of the physiological study of our intellectual organs, cannot succeed. The mind may observe all phenomena but its own. There can be nothing like scientific observation of mental phenomena except from without, and by another. The observing and observed organ are here the same. In order to observe its activity, your mind must pause from activity; yet it is this very activity that you want to observe. If you cannot pause, you cannot observe; if you do pause, there is nothing to observe. The results of such a method are in proportion to its absurdity.

After two thousand years of psychology, no one proposition is established to the satisfaction of psychologists. To this day they are divided into a multitude of schools, still disputing about the very elements of their doctrine. The psychologists have done some good in keeping up the activity of our understandings when there was no better work for our minds to do.

What we have said with regard to psychology as a positive science applies yet more strikingly to logic, that is, to the "study" of scientific method. Scientific method can be judged of only in action. It cannot be studied apart from the work on which it is employed. Such a study would be dead, could produce nothing of value in the mind which loses time on it. We may talk forever about scientific method, and state it in terms very wise and learned, without knowing half so much about it as the man who has once put it into practice upon a single piece of research. Thus have logicians, by dint of reading the aphorisms of Bacon and the discourses of Descartes mistaken their own dreams for science. We cannot explain the great logical procedures apart from their applications.

In the second place, a study of positive science as here conceived will regenerate education. The best minds are agreed that our European education, still essentially theological, metaphysical, and literary, must be superseded by a scientific education conformable to our time and needs.

Everything yet done to this end is inadequate. What is required is an organic conception of the sciences such as positivism presents. The exclusive specializing tendencies of our sciences spoil our teaching. If any student desires to form a conception of science as a whole, he is compelled to go through each department as it is now taught, as if he were to be only an astronomer or only a chemist. The result, be his intellect what it may, is unsatisfactory when what he requires is a general conception of the entire range of positive knowledge.

It is such a general conception of the entire range of the sciences which must henceforth be the permanent basis of all human combinations. It will constitute the mind of future generations. But to this end it is necessary that the sciences, considered as branches from one trunk, should yield us as a whole, their chief methods and results.

In the third place, the proposed study of the organically related generalizations of the positive sciences will aid the progress of each separate science. The divisions we establish between the sciences are, though not arbitrary, essentially superficial. The subject of our researches is one; we divide it for convenience, in order to deal more easily with separate problems. But it sometimes happens that we need what we cannot obtain under the present isolation of the sciences, namely a combination of several special points of view. For want of this, important problems wait for their solution.

To go into the past for an example: Descartes' grand conception with regard to analytical geometry, a discovery which has changed the whole face of mathematics, issued from the union of two sciences which had before been separately studied and pursued.

Again, it was undecided whether azote is a simple or a compound body. Almost all chemists held that azote is a simple body. But the illustrious Berzelius, influenced by the physiological observation that animals which receive no azote in their food have as much of it in their tissue as carnivorous animals, was able to throw new light on the question. Thus must physiology unite with chemistry to inform us whether azote is simple or compound, and to institute a new series of researches upon the relation between the composition of living bodies and their mode of alimentation.

In the fourth place, philosophy based on the positive sciences offers the only solid basis for that social reorganization which must succeed the critical condition in which even the most civilized nations are now living.

It cannot be necessary to argue that ideas govern the world or throw it into chaos, that all social mechanism rests upon opinions held by the members of society. The great political and moral crisis that societies are now undergoing proceeds from intellectual anarchy. Stability in fundamental principles is the first condition of genuine social order: We witness an utter disagreement on all such matters. Till a certain number of general ideas can be acknowledged as a rallying point for social doctrine, nations will remain in a revolutionary state whatever palliatives may be advised, and their institutions only provisional and makeshift.

But when the necessary agreement on first principles can be obtained, appropriate institutions will issue from them without shock or resistance. It is in this direction that those must look who desire a natural, regular, normal state of society.

Now, the existing disorder is abundantly accounted for by the existence, all at once, of three incompatible philosophies — the theological, the metaphysical, and the positive. Any one of these might alone secure some sort of social order. But while the three coexist, it is impossible for us to understand one another upon any essential point whatever. If this is true, we have only to ascertain which of the philosophies must, in the nature of things, eventually prevail.

Comte's point here might be illustrated by controversies centering in such questions as birth control, sterilization of the subnormal and criminal, etc. Consider the case of sterilization. A sincere Catholic might oppose the measure as contrary to the will of God; a sincere democrat might oppose it as contrary to the rights of man; a social scientist disregarding both grounds of opposition, might simply argue that offspring born to such parents are likely to prove a needless burden and menace to a society which must, in the end, either support them or imprison them.

This problem, once recognized, cannot remain long unsolved; for all considerations point to a philosophy based on the positive sciences as the one destined to prevail. It alone has been advancing during the course of centuries, while others have been declining. The fact is incontestable. Some may deplore it, but none deny it or destroy it, nor neglect it save on pain of being betrayed by illusory speculations.

This general revolution of the human mind is nearly accomplished. We have only to complete the hierarchy of the positive sciences by bringing the facts and problems of society within its comprehension. The preference which almost all minds, from the highest to the commonest. accord to positive knowledge over vague and mystical conceptions, is a pledge of what this philosophy will receive when it is once completed by the addition of a positive social science. When this has been accomplished, its supremacy will be automatic and will establish order throughout society.

READING REFERENCES. Comte's influence has been very great. Most unphilosophically minded scientists are probably Comteans, in the sense that they would endorse his positivism. Further reading in Comte should be done in those writings in which he sets forth his conception of the new social sciences, the new social order, and the new religion of humanity. John Morley's essay on Comte in one of the volumes of his *Miscellanies* is worth while. John Stuart

Mill's *Auguste Comte and Positivism*, published shortly after Comte's death, is still an illuminating account and, with respect to what Mill describes as Comte's "later aberrations," a vigorous polemic. The account of Comte in Volume Two of Hoffding's *History of Modern Philosophy* is excellent. The standard work on Comte is by Lucien Lévy-Bruhl.

READING QUESTIONS

1. What are the three stages which Comte notes? *p.* 242
2. What characterizes each stage? 242 fictitious, abstract, positive
3. On what basis does Comte classify the sciences?
4. What is the resulting hierarchy?
5. "The most interesting point in our hierarchical classification is its effect on education." Namely?
6. "In our enumeration of the basic sciences there is one prodigious omission." Namely? Why?
7. On what grounds does Comte eliminate logic?
8. On what grounds does he eliminate psychology, as a separate science?
9. "A study of positive science as here conceived will regenerate education." How so?
10. "The proposed study of the . . . positive sciences will aid the progress of each separate science." How so?
11. "Philosophy based on the positive sciences offers the only solid basis for social organization." Meaning?
12. Show how Hume, Kant, and Comte reach the same antimetaphysical conclusions from different premises.

5. THE ROLE OF FICTIONS IN KNOWLEDGE — FROM HANS VAIHINGER

FROM COMTE TO VAIHINGER. We began with Locke, and have thus far read our way from him through Hume and Kant and Comte. With Comte's positivism matters seemed likely to reach a dead end. What Comte did, in effect, was to settle the problem of knowledge by definition. That is, he described the method of natural science (observation, hypothesis, deduction, verification) and the method of mathematics (postulation, definition, deduction), and then said that anything not obtained by these methods is not knowledge. Comte was then able to write off all beliefs which he could not certify in terms of these methods, as vestiges of the theological or metaphysical stages through which the mind of man has passed, but from which, here and there, some traces yet remain.

One must go back to Kant in order to make a new beginning with Vaihinger. It will be recalled that Kant conceived of his *Critique of Pure Reason* as having set limits to knowledge in order to make room for faith. There were consequences. The first was that knowledge could deal only with the world of appearances. The second was that all beliefs concerning the real world were mere speculations. It will be recalled that he describes such notions as God, the soul, and the cosmos as regulative ideas. They were regulative, in contrast to constitutive. This was a way of stating that these ideas were useful fictions, or so, at least, our next author takes it. In this concept of a useful fiction, one passes directly from Immanuel Kant to Hans Vaihinger.

Vaihinger seized upon this notion of Kant's, and elaborated it into the general theory that all knowledge rests on useful fictions. This hypothesis was stated and documented in his treatise, *The Philosophy of As-If*. By an *as-if*, the author means a useful fiction.

BIOGRAPHICAL NOTE. In place of the usual biographical facts, I am appending herewith an abridgment of Vaihinger's account of his own life. The reason for this is that his account of his life is also an account of his opinions. Anyone who has read through this volume of selections thus far is in possession of most of the names and ideas to which Vaihinger refers. This makes his autobiography both interesting and valuable to read.

I was born in a Swabian parsonage near Tübingen in 1852, and so I grew up in a very religious atmosphere. It was not exactly bigoted, but it had a limited horizon. My father, who was the author of a good many theological works, had written a pamphlet against Strauss. When I was twelve years old I was given into the charge of an excellent master and teacher. I was his favorite pupil. He used to tell me about his Sanskrit studies. He was especially interested in the great Mahabharata epic; and occasionally at the end of the lesson in religion he would tell us how this Indian epic contained the same sort of legends as the New Testament. The stories of the Old and New Testaments had already awakened doubts in my mind, so I was gradually led to the ethical value of the myth. Generally speaking, his attitude was one of rationalistic theism with a solid moral basis. I had already reached this way of thinking at the time of my confirmation in 1866. This ethical theism was a great help to me in those years, but from the time I entered grammar school it gradually evolved into pantheism, based on a deep love of nature. During this period of transition I came across Herder's book on the history of mankind. It appealed to me by its mixture of theism and pantheism. I owe a great deal to it. It gives a wide and lofty view of the whole history of mankind from the earliest origins through all kinds and varieties of civilization. The idea of evolution became one of the fundamental elements of my mental outlook. Herder draws special attention to the evolution of spiritual life out of its first animal origins; and he regards man always as linked up with that nature from which he has gradually evolved. Thus when I first heard Darwin's name, and when my school friends told me about the new theory of man's animal ancestry, it was no surprise to me.

From that time onward, one of the fundamentals in my philosophy has been this fact of man's animal ancestry. About this time I came under the influence of Plato, which acted as a counterbalancing factor. I read the usual dialogues and the *Apology*. Our professor was old, and, though very thorough, he was dull and kept us to the grammatical side. His routine teaching made nothing like the impression on me that was made by three lectures from a young man who came to replace him during an illness. This young man read us the myth on the nature of the soul, in the *Phaedrus*, and the description of the cave from the *Republic*. These opened a new world to me, and as he spoke of Plato's myths, the seed was sown of that conception which later I myself named the "World of as-if."

The introduction to philosophy which was customary at that time, with its bare outlines of logic, psychology, and ethics, played quite an insignificant part compared with the revolutionary ideas which I was discovering for myself. Philosophy should be the general principle of instruction in all subjects. It should practice the "opportunist method," which emphasizes points of philosophical significance, when the occasion arises, in other branches of study.

Last, but not least, I must mention Schiller's poems and treatises, for they too had an important influence on me at that time. Every earnest young student is inspired and fired by Schiller. His philosophic poems, in which he contrasts the ideal world of pure form with the empirical world, were easily linked up with the Platonic influences mentioned above. Many of his verses made an indelible impression on me; for instance, the words "in error only is there life, and knowledge must be death" have, in certain respects, become the foundation of my theory of fictions.

Thus equipped, I entered the University of Tübingen in the autumn of 1870, as a student at the resident theological college there. In my time the university was run on very liberal lines, and great freedom was and is given to the students to allow them to develop in their own way. In the first four terms they are given a very thorough grounding in philosophy. My first term was devoted to ancient philosophy; the second to later philosophy up to Kant; the third to the period from Kant to Hegel; and the fourth from Schleiermacher onwards. First-rate coaches gave us careful instruction. They also supervised the working out of philosophic treatises by the students, who were encouraged to think freely for themselves. No obstacles were placed in the path of my philosophical development. On the contrary, I was encouraged on all sides, especially when I started a prize essay for the faculty of philosophy on recent theories of consciousness. For this work, which took me a year, I received first prize in the autumn of 1873. This enabled me to travel in Switzerland and North Italy. This prize essay was also the decisive factor in making me abandon my theological studies. I had started them with much hesitation anyway. My transition to philosophy was made easier for me in every way. Thus I have good reason to remember the theological college of Tübingen with gratitude, particularly the open-minded and kind-hearted director at that time.

In my first term the teaching of the Greek nature philosophers made a great impression on me because of their close similarity with the modern theory of evolution. Anaximander appealed to me especially. I also worked at Aristotle very thoroughly. In my second term Spinoza absorbed me by his consistency and his dispassionate conception of the universe.

But the impression made upon me by Kant was very different from the rest. In every respect he freed my mind without fettering it. His bold theory of the ideality of space and time always liberates the mind from immediacy, from the pressure of the material world, even though one soon recognizes that in the long run it is not tenable in that form. But what impressed me most was Kant's discovery of the contradictions with which human thought is faced when it ventures into the realm of metaphysics. His theory of antinomies had a profound influence upon me. I derived permanent value from his theory of the limitation of knowledge to experience, and also from his doctrine that action, the practical, must take first place. This so-called supremacy of practical reason seemed to appeal to my innermost being.

The official plan of studies passed from Fichte, Schelling, and Hegel, direct to Schleiermacher. But I followed my own course and turned to Schopenhauer, who, until then, had been ignored, even despised, by the faculty. I had got hold of Von Hartmann's *Philosophy of the Unconscious*, and it led back to Schopenhauer. So I went straight to the source and studied Schopenhauer very thoroughly. He gave me much that was new and great and lasting: pessimism, irrationalism, and voluntarism.

1. Schopenhauer's pessimism became, with me, a fundamental and lasting state of mind; all the more so because of my own sad and difficult experiences. I have not found that this outlook tends to weaken biological and moral energy. On the contrary, I am

one of those whom only pessimism enables to endure life. Pessimism gives me the ethical strength to work and fight for myself, as well as to help others. Furthermore, I believe that pessimism has given me a more objective view of reality. For example: I have regarded the political situation of Germany, during the last thirty years, in a way quite different from the great majority. For many years I prophesied the World War and its consequences for us. I have also found that people of other nations, who have been accustomed to a more realistic philosophy than the usual German idealism and optimism, have had a far clearer view of reality. If Germany's leaders since 1871 had taken a lesson from Schopenhauer, Germany would not have fallen into her desperate condition. The development of the social question, too, might just as well have evolved toward the right as toward the left, if Schopenhauer had been the guiding influence, instead of Rousseau and Hegel. Even in Kant, as I noticed in those early days, there is a strong undercurrent of pessimism.

2. The impression which Schopenhauer made upon me was, intensively, greater than that made by Kant. To explain this I must go further afield. In all the systems of philosophy which I had hitherto met, the irrational aspect of the world and of life had not received adequate attention. The ideal of philosophy was to explain everything rationally, i.e., by logical conclusions to prove it rational, significant, fitting. The Hegelian philosophy came nearest to this ideal, and it was considered the supreme achievement in philosophy. This ideal, however, had failed to satisfy me. From my earliest days I had come across countless manifestations of the irrational in my immediate surroundings. I therefore considered it to be a lack of sincerity in most systems of philosophy that they tried more or less to hide the irrational side. Now, in Schopenhauer, I came across, for the first time, a man who recognized irrationality openly and honorably, and who attempted to explain it in his system of philosophy. Schopenhauer's love of truth was a revelation to me. I did not follow his metaphysical theories because, since I had studied Kant, the impossibility of all metaphysics had seemed to me to be obvious. But that part of Schopenhauer's teaching which can be established empirically

became my lasting possession and a source of fruitful inspiration, particularly as it could be linked up with the theory of evolution and the struggle for existence.

3. What appealed to me most in Kant was his emphasis on the practical. In Schopenhauer I found this same tendency, but much clearer, much stronger, much more comprehensive. With him "the will" was placed in the forefront. To me, much that had hitherto been inexplicable seemed suddenly to be explained, or at least capable of explanation. What struck me most was his proof of the fact that originally thought is only used by the will as a means to its own end, and that only in the course of evolution does thought free itself from the bonds of the will and become an end in itself. He pointed out that the brain of animals is quite small, yet is large enough to act as an organ for the execution of the will's purposes; whereas, in the higher animals, and particularly in man, it has grown out of all proportion. Darwin's theory of evolution, which was being worked out at this time, corroborated Schopenhauer's contention.

This theory of Schopenhauer's, that fundamentally thought is dependent on the purposes of the Life-Will, and has developed into an end in itself only as it were against all laws, became linked up in my mind with Kant's theory that human thought is bound by certain limits and that metaphysical knowledge is impossible. This limitation of human knowledge to experience, which Kant emphasizes over and over again, no longer struck me as a deplorable deficiency in the human mind. It seemed to me now to be a necessary and natural result of the fact that thought and knowledge are originally only a means to attain the life purpose. Indeed, the independence of thought signifies a breaking away from its original purpose; and by the fact of this breaking loose thought is confronted with impossible problems which are not merely insoluble to human thought but to all forms of thought as such. This conviction has become one of the most solid foundations of my conception of the universe. It has grown within me and has crystallized, with the passing of the years, into an ever clearer form.

Another powerful influence, along these same lines, was a book by Adolf Horwicz, *Psychological Analysis upon a Physiological Basis*.

In this work <u>Horwicz</u> showed that all psychology is based on the so-called scheme of reflexes: stimulation, sense impressions, ideas leading up to thought, expressive movement, and volitional action. The simplest reflexes are motor phenomena following upon stimulation. These stimuli must result in elementary feelings, which release corresponding movements, representing the most elementary beginning of volitional actions. In the interval between these impressions and the motor expression, ideas come to the surface, first in an elementary form, but growing more and more complicated so that in their highest form they may be described as thought processes. Thus <u>the idea, and later on the thought, appear as merely a bridge, an intermediary between impression on the one hand and expression on the other</u>. This theory, which Horwicz worked out most carefully and comprehensively, fitted in very well with the idea I had derived from Schopenhauer, namely, that thought is, originally, only a means for the purposes of the will. And both ideas coincided with the conviction I had gained from Kant as to the supremacy of the practical.

These comments bring Vaihinger to the year 1873. During the next three years he prosecuted his studies on a variety of fronts.

Toward the latter part of the year 1876 I wrote down my thoughts in a large manuscript to which I gave the title *Logical Studies. Part I: The Theory of Scientific Fictions*. This work is exactly the same as what was published in 1911 as *Part I: Basic Principles* of *The Philosophy of As-If*. In it I developed the whole system of scientific fictions and tried to give an exhaustive theory of this manifold as-if process.

I regarded this dissertation as only a rough outline, in need of much supplementing and correction. I made use of the next two years to work at it as much as my lectures would allow me to.

Other things intervened. His father's death obliged him to look for more remunerative work. He arranged with a publisher to write a commentary on Kant's *Critique of Pure*

Reason for the 1881 centenary. The first volume of this commentary did not appear until 1884, but it was recognized at once as perhaps the greatest work of its kind anywhere in the field of Kant studies. The author was appointed "special professor" at the University of Halle. Bad health delayed the publication of the second volume of the *Commentary* until 1892. In 1894 the author was made "regular professor" at Halle. In 1896 he founded a journal, *Kant Studien*, as a means of helping his work along. In 1904, the centenary of Kant's death, Vaihinger started a fund for the founding of a Kant Society. The drive proved a success. He was a long way from his previous 1876 essay on the theory of fictions. But events brought him back to it.

In 1906, in the midst of all these complications and crossings of my original intentions, a misfortune unexpectedly brought a happy solution and enabled me after twenty-seven years to return to my original plan which I had given up in 1879. The misfortune was the weakening of my eyesight so that it became impossible for me to continue my lectures. So I had to give up my official duties. The eyesight still remaining to me was just sufficient to allow me to publish my manuscript. I got my dissertation of 1876 copied and introduced a number of small editorial alterations. I also completed the revision I had made between 1877 and the beginning of 1879. This part took me two and a half years because of my bad eyesight. A third part took me another two and a half years. It was the spring of 1911 before the work appeared.

I called this work, *The Philosophy of As-If*, because that seemed to express more convincingly than any other possible title what I wanted to say. The point which I wished to convey was that the *as-if*, the consciously false, plays an enormous part in science, in philosophies, and in life. I wanted to give a complete enumeration of all the methods in which we operate intentionally with consciously false ideas. I wanted to reveal the secret life of these extraordinary methods. I wanted to give a complete theory of as-if.

I will end by summarizing all the conclusions which are expressed in *The Philosophy of As-If*, or which form its basis, or arise out of it:

1. From an epistemological standpoint, philosophical analysis leads to sensational contents. From a psychological standpoint it leads to sensations, feelings, and strivings or actions. Scientific analysis leads to matter and the smallest constituents and motions of matter. It is impossible for the mind to bring these two spheres of reality into a rational relation, although in intuition and experience they form a harmonious unity.

2. The strivings which probably exist in the most elementary physical processes develop in organic beings into impulses. In man, who has sprung from the animal, these higher impulses have evolved into will and action, which is expressed in movements and caused by stimuli or by the sensations arising from stimuli.

3. Ideas, judgments and conclusions, i.e., thought, act as a means in the service of the will to live and dominate. Thought is originally only a means in the struggle for existence and to this extent only a biological function.

4. It is a universal phenomenon of nature that means which serve a purpose often undergo a more complete development than is necessary for the attainment of their purpose. In this case the means, according to the completeness of its self-development, can emancipate itself partly or wholly and become established as an end in itself. This I call the law of the preponderance of the means over the end.   •

5. The preponderance of the means over the end has taken place in thought, which, in the course of time, has gradually lost sight of its original practical purpose and is finally practiced for its own sake as theoretical thought.

6. As a result, this thought, which appears to be independent and theoretical in its origins, sets itself problems which are impossible, not only to human thought, but to every form of thought. An instance of what I mean is the problem of the origin and nature of the universe. Another is the question of the relation between sensation and motion, popularly known as mind and matter.

7. These endless, and, strictly speaking, senseless questions, can-

not be answered by looking forward but only by looking backward, by showing how they arose psychologically within us.

8. If rationalism is the assumption of an original theoretical reason, as an inherent human faculty with certain problems to be determined by it, then my position must be termed *antirationalism* or even *irrationalism*.

9. From this standpoint all thought processes and thought constructs appear, *a priori*, to be not essentially rationalistic but biological phenomena.

10. In this light many thought processes and thought constructs appear to be consciously false assumptions, which either contradict reality or are even contradictory in themselves, but which are intentionally thus formed to overcome difficulties of thought by this artificial deviation and reach the goal of thought by roundabout ways and bypaths. These artificial thought constructs are called *scientific fictions* and are distinguished as conscious creations by their as-if character.

11. The as-if world, which is formed in this manner, is just as important as the so-called real or actual world (in the ordinary sense of the word). Indeed, it is far more important for ethics and aesthetics. This aesthetic and ethical world of as-if, the world of the unreal, becomes finally for us a world of values which, particularly in the form of religion, must be sharply distinguished in our mind from the world of becoming.

12. What we usually term *reality* consists of our sensational contents which press forcibly upon us with greater or less irresistibility and as "given" can generally not be avoided.

13. In these given sensational contents, which include what we call our body, there is an abundance of regularity in coexistence and succession, investigation of which forms the content of science. By means of the sensational contents which we call our body, we can exercise greater or less influence on the rich world of the other sensational contents.

14. In this world we find a great number of relations of fitness and much that is not fitting. We have to take this as we find it for there is little we can alter. It is a satisfying fiction for many to regard the world as if a more perfect Higher Spirit had created or at

least regulated it. But this implies the supplementary fiction of regarding a world of this sort as if the order created by the Higher Divine Spirit had been destroyed by some hostile force.

15. It is senseless to question the meaning of the universe. This is the idea expressed in Schiller's words "Know this, a sublime mind puts greatness into life, yet seeks it not therein." This is positive idealism.

THE ARGUMENT OF THE CITATIONS. There is no need to restate the argument of the passages quoted below. It has already been given above in Vaihinger's own words. I have introduced numbers, at irregular intervals, to indicate that the author is beginning a new line of thought at that point. The passages between any two numbers form together a more or less solid block.

I

Scientific thought is a function of the psyche. It is an active appropriation of the outer world, a useful organic elaboration of the material of sensation.

The psyche is not merely a receptacle into which foreign matter is poured. It may be compared to a machine with a chemical retort which uses foreign matter most fittingly for its own maintenance. Just as the physical organism breaks up the matter which it receives, mixes it with its own juices, so the psyche envelops the thing perceived with categories. As soon as an external stimulus reaches the psyche, it responds as though provided with delicate feelers, inner processes start, the outcome of which is the appropriation of the thing perceived for some purpose.

The procedures of the psyche are carried on, for the most part, unconsciously. Should the product finally enter consciousness, or should consciousness momentarily accompany the process, this light penetrates only to the shallows. The fundamental processes are carried on in the darkness of the unconscious. The specifically purposeful operations of the psyche are chiefly, in the beginning, wholly instinctive and unconscious, even if later they press forward into the luminous circle of consciousness.

It is the purpose of the eye to transform various waves into sensa-tions, to make reduced images of the objective world through refrac-tion and reflection of rays. It is suitably arranged to achieve this purpose and is able to carry out independent movements of accommo-dation and modification as circumstances require. In the same way, the logical or scientific function of the psyche is an activity which has a purpose and can adapt itself to circumstances and objects for the fulfillment of this purpose.

The function of the psyche is to change and elaborate perceptional material into ideas, associations of ideas and conceptual construc-tions consistent and coherent among themselves. Since, however, we do not know objective reality directly but only infer it, we are obliged to say that thought has fulfilled its purpose when it has elaborated the given sensations into valid conceptions and generali-zations and has produced such a world that objective happenings can be calculated and our behavior successfully carried out.

2

Thought must be recognized as a mechanism, as a machine, as a tool, as an instrument, in the service of life. The test of the correct-ness of a logical construct lies in practice. The purpose of thought must be sought, not in the reflection of a so-called objective world, but in rendering possible the calculation of events and of operations upon them.

The purpose of the psyche in logical procedures is to keep us in a position to deal with things so that, given certain conditions and relations, we may receive an exactly ascertainable sense impression; so that, by a certain impulse, we may produce an exactly ascertain-able effect. Sensations are the starting point of all logical activity and the terminus to which they must run.

We lay most stress on practical corroboration, on the experi-mental test of the utility of the logical constructions produced by the psyche. It is not the correspondence with an assumed objective reality (never directly accessible to us); it is not the theoretical representation of an outer world in the mirror of the mind, which, in our view, guarantees that thought has fulfilled its purpose. It is the practical test: Is it possible, with the help of the psyche's products, to calculate events and to realize our impulses?

3

To attain the purpose of its activity — namely, to deal with events and render them dependent on our will — the psyche employs the most diverse means. It undertakes ingenious operations, invents brilliant expedients, introduces complicated processes. The raw material — sensations — is remodeled, recoined, compressed . . . we emphasize the utility of the psyche's procedures because we shall be dealing with logical constructions in which this purposiveness is strikingly manifested.

It must be remembered that the purpose of the world of ideas is not to portray reality — an utterly impossible task — but to provide us with an instrument for finding our way about more easily in this world. Subjective processes of thought represent the highest and ultimate result of organic development, and the world of ideas is the fine flower of the whole process; but, for that very reason it is not a copy of reality in the ordinary sense. Its purpose is the preservation and enrichment of life. It serves as an intermediary between living beings. It is an edifice, well calculated to fulfill such purposes. But to regard it as a copy of reality is to indulge in a hasty and unjustifiable comparison.

It would indeed be strange if these concepts were actually pictures of objective reality. We need only make clear to ourselves what this term *picture* or *copy* is supposed to mean, and to ask how a logical construct could be a copy of an event in the real world. These concepts are not copies of events. They are themselves events. The world as we conceive it is only a secondary or tertiary construction, arising in our heads. This conceptual world is not a picture of the real world, but an instrument for grasping, dealing with, understanding, that world. It is only an auxiliary construct formed by the psyche in order to take its bearings. This construction can be substituted for the actual world, and in practice we all do that. But it is not a picture; it is only a sign used to deal with reality, a logical expedient devised by the psyche to enable us to act in the real world.

4

There are methods employed in scientific procedure which, up till now, have not been duly considered in logical theory. I refer to methods employed less in the natural sciences than in the mathematical and social sciences, i.e., in the most exact and the least exact sciences. The methods to which I refer may be described as irregular. In logic, a veil of secrecy has been woven about them.

5

We may distinguish between rules and artifices of thought. Rules of any function are those operations in virtue of which it is able to attain its objective directly. Artifices, on the other hand, are those operations of a somewhat mysterious character which run counter to ordinary procedure in more or less paradoxical ways. They give an onlooker the impression of magic if he be not himself initiated. They are able to overcome, indirectly, the difficulties which beset the ordinary activities. Thought has such artifices. They are strikingly purposive expressions of the organic function of thought.

Among these artifices is one which is our special concern, namely, the fiction. Fictions are mental constructions, woven by the psyche itself. It introduces these hybrid and ambiguous thought structures in order to attain its purpose indirectly where the material which it encounters resists a direct procedure.

We shall try to give an especially typical example of every variety of fiction, and to use it to study the scheme of the construct and the methodology employed.

6

A standard example is the well-known assumption of Adam Smith, according to which all human actions are dictated by egoistic motives. Human actions are excessively complicated. They present insuperable obstacles when we try to understand them and reduce them to laws. This was Smith's problem. He realized that the main cause lay in egoism. He therefore formulated the assumption that all human actions, and particularly those of an economic nature, could be looked upon as if egoism were their sole motive. Thus all other factors were neglected. By means of this as-if he succeeded in bringing the whole of economics into an ordered system. He assumed the egoism, and then deduced from it the relations in trade and commerce which followed of necessity from that assumption.

Another typical example may be found in Thünen's fiction of an imaginary city. He introduced it into economics, at the beginning of the nineteenth century, in order to explain the relations between agriculture, transportation, etc. It was this: Grant an imaginary city. Around it, in concentric zones, are arranged the different spheres of activity from which the requirements of the city are drawn. By means of this ingenious artifice agricultural and economic laws are then systematically deduced. The fictions of an isolated man, an isolated state, etc., belong to the same group.

Another instructive example of the fictional method is offered by Bentham's treatment of the problems of political science. Bentham based his general theory of the state on the assumption that men act always from self-interest. In order, then, to work up the case for constitutionalism and parliamentarism, as necessary forms of government, he reasoned as follows: If men's actions are determined by selfish interests, then the only rulers who govern in the interests of the governed are those whose selfish interests coincide with those of the governed. The interests of the rulers are brought into harmony with the interests of the ruled only by responsibility, i.e., through the dependence of the rulers upon the will of the ruled. The wish on the part of rulers to retain power and the fear of losing it are the only motives which can inspire a policy in agreement with the interests of the ruled. From this Bentham deduced representative government, responsibility of ministers, frequent elections, and so forth.

Another remarkable example of the fictional method is to be found in Condillac's statue. In his *Treatise on Sensations* he sought to show that all beliefs and conceptions could be reduced to an origin in experience. To this end he imagines a statue, similar to a human being whose mind is as yet devoid of ideas. To admit and exclude impressions at will, this imaginary man is enclosed in a marble case which prevents him from using his sense organs. In this way Condillac is able to isolate those ideas which would result from each of the senses. He limits his statue to the sense of smell, and then, in succession, to hearing, taste, sight, and touch. He then combines the various senses by opening or closing the means of access to the statue. By this means he can show the contribution of each particular sense, trace the development of consciousness, attention, memory, judgment, imagination, abstraction, reflection, and so forth.

The term *fiction* is nowhere better known than in jurisprudence. In principle the juristic fiction is identical with such others as we have considered. It consists in submitting a single case under a construct not intended for it. The basis for this is as follows: Since laws cannot include all cases, certain special examples are treated as if they belonged under them. For instance, in a recent German commercial code we find a provision that goods not returned to the sender within a specified time are to be regarded as if the recipient had definitely authorized and accepted them. Again, it is assumed, in England, that a husband is the father of a child if it can be proved that he was in the country at the time of the child's conception. This, however, is rather a *praesumptio juris* than a genuine *fictio juris*. In England in the eighteenth century every crime could be treated as if it were directed personally at the king and every plaintiff had the right to bring action under this fiction. The Code Napoléon contains a number of legal fictions, e.g., that a woman's household goods are *immobilia*, that an *enfant conçu* can under certain circumstances be regarded as an *enfant né*, etc. Elsewhere we encounter such legal fictions as that the defendant who does not put in an appearance is regarded as if he admitted the charge; an adopted son is regarded as if he were a real son; an heir who is deemed unfit to inherit is regarded as if he had died before the testator; and so forth.

In these juristic fictions the formal behavior of the psyche is identical with what we have seen it to be in other fields. Practically, the importance is great; theoretically, there is a deviation from reality. Without such deviations thought cannot attain its purposes. It is just the deviation that in the end appears to be the natural procedure, and hence the need for emphasizing the fact.

7

One of the most important fictions ever formed by man is the idea of free will. Human actions are regarded as "free," and therefore responsible, in contrast with the "necessary" course of natural events. In spite of all the contradictions which this concept contains, we use it constantly in ordinary life in making judgments, and it is the foundation of criminal law. Our judgment of our fellow men is so bound up with this construct that we can no longer do without it. Only on this basis is a high degree of culture and morality and law possible. But this does not prevent us from realizing that it is itself a logical monstrosity, a contradiction, a fiction. There is nothing in the real world corresponding to the idea of free will, but in practice it is an exceedingly necessary fiction.

Ideals are working fictions, in contradiction with reality. True morality rests upon fictions. We must act as if duty were imposed by God, as if we would be judged by Him for our conduct, as if we would be punished for immorality, etc. But as soon as we transform these as-ifs into so many "becauses," morality loses its purely ethical character and becomes merely a matter of calculating our interests. Thus, before our very eyes does a small artifice of the psyche develop into a mighty source of all the idealistic belief and behavior of mankind.

The importance of our theory for practical philosophy is obvious. Fictions enter profoundly into our practical life. Indeed, they are necessary. They are a consequence of human imperfection. But all the nobler aspects of our life are based upon fictions. A pure ethics can only be established by the recognition of its fictional basis. How closely truth and illusion thus approach one another is apparent. What we call *truth* is really only the most expedient form of error. It is an error to suppose that an absolute truth, an absolute criterion of knowledge and behavior, can be discovered. The higher aspects of life are based upon noble delusions.

8

The fundamental conceptions of mathematics are all fictions. Thus, e.g., empty space, empty time, points without extension, lines without breadth, surfaces without depth, spaces without content, are all imaginary and fictional conceptions. Upon these as foundations the psyche has constructed the entire edifice of this amazing science. Mathematicians have occasionally realized that they were dealing with fictions, but seldom have they made this the subject of any profound study. Recognition of the fictional nature of its basic concepts is, however, essential for mathematical progress. The efforts made to conceal this fact have worn thread-bare.

Another ingenious mathematical fiction is that of considering lines and surfaces as composed of elements of infinitely small extension. This fiction enables us, e.g., to subsume a curve under a straight line, to subsume an ellipse under a circle, and so forth.

The same applies to such mathematical notions as zero, negative numbers, fractions, irrational numbers, imaginary numbers, infinite series, and so forth. Their very names indicate that they are constructs. The history of mathematics is full of examples of the superstitious awe with which these number-constructs have been regarded.

9

In mechanics we are confronted with many fictions. For example, such concepts as the rigid bar, the Alpha body (the immovable central point of absolute space), the center of gravity, absolute space and time, absolute motion, *actio in distans,* and so on, are, all of them, imaginary constructs, useful in the elaboration of theoretical mechanics, but corresponding to nothing in reality.

One of the most important fictions is that notorious product of the imagination, the concept of "force." If two events are constantly conjoined, we call that peculiarity of the first event which consists in its being followed by the other event, its *force;* and we measure this force in terms of the magnitude of its effect. In reality, of course, only the sequence exists. The forces that objects are supposed to possess are nothing but a necessary consequence of succession. They are raised to the rank of real entities, placed as a permanent background, given a separate existence, all in contrast with the transitory events. What we call *force,* so far as it is thought of as the cause of motion or change is nothing but a disguised outlet for our tendency to personify.

Force is a fiction. It is nothing but a reduplication of the facts, namely, of the causal relations of succession. We interpolate this construct, and imagine we have added something. The assumption of forces that "determine" the sequence of phenomena in no way aids us in giving a theoretical explanation. As the critical, positive attitude develops, these abortive branches on the tree of knowledge wither and fall off.

All the specific forces are included here. Gravitational force, life force, sleeping force, and so on. Newton himself looked upon gravitation as a fiction. The phenomena which it correlated are, of course, real enough, but to attribute some gravitational force to them is simply a summary expression for the regularity of the correlations.

10

Such terms as *soul*, *psychic force*, *vital force*, *vis inertia*, *vis dormitiva*, etc., are names of fictions. The concept soul, for example, is a glaring fiction. We still use it. We still speak of a soul as if there were a separate, integral, simple entity, though we know there is no such reality.

What we call a *natural law* is a fiction. It is nothing but an expression for the totality of relations existing in a group of phenomena. It is a summational fiction. If by *law* we intend anything more than the regular sequence of events of which it is a summary, if we intend any "force" or "power" which determines the sequence, we are misleading ourselves by a typical fiction, comparable to abstractions and generalizations.

11

All abstractions are fictions. By an *abstraction* is meant a quality or property which, in reality, always belongs to some particular thing but may be considered in abstraction from that thing; e.g., goodness, color, smoothness, equality, etc. Abstractions get built into the language and conceal their fictional nature. We begin to apply adjectives to them, and add verbs. We say, "War destroys men." We speak of "deeds of fame," of "qualities of virtues, wisdom, justice," etc. We come thus to impart substance to what are merely abstractions. We speak of them as if they were realities existing independently of the objects with which they are always, in fact, connected. In themselves they are no more real than the square root of minus one.

All generalizations are fictions. Generalization is another favorite device of thought, closely connected with abstraction. Such words as *stone, plant, book, tree, ship* are names of general concepts, or generalizations, formed from particular instances. But the particular instance is alone real. No perception exists covering, e.g., the notion "tree." There is this tree and that tree, but not tree in general. These general concepts are psychical constructs, extracted by thought from the particulars of experience; pure fictions, for nothing real can be proved to exist corresponding to them in the external world. It would not be neccessary to waste words on this subject, were it not for the fact that in philosophy it has been held that there is something objective corresponding to these constructs.

12.

Our view gains real importance and value primarily through its application to the favorite ideas of philosophers, e.g., the ideas of God, free will, immortality, thing-in-itself, the Absolute, and so on through a long list. These gain their true significance when they are denied significance for truth, i.e., considered as fictions. The real value of our inquiry lies in the rigorous application of the notion of fictions to certain popular thoughts and famous ideas.

The German theologian, Schleiermacher, and the school which followed him made use of fictions in their interpretation of Christianity. The actual relationship, e.g., between God and the world, and between God and men, they hold to be incomprehensible. Take the relationship between God and men. For Schleiermacher, the philosopher, this is completely unknowable. But by Schleiermacher, the theologian, it is conceived of as if it were the relation of father to son. God is not the father of men, but He is to be regarded and treated as if He were. By means of this as-if Schleiermacher held thousands of people to Christianity. Such an interpretation proved to be of tremendous importance for the practice of religion and worship. Schleiermacher himself was well aware of the artificial and artistic aspect of his method, although he did not describe it quite as bluntly as we do here.

Schleiermacher further argues that prayer is a meaningful act so long as it is interpreted as if God would hearken to it. It is clear, however, that the conception of praying to an omnipotent and omniscient God contains a contradiction, i.e., is a fiction. This quite apart from the contradiction involved by the idea of prayer in relation to natural laws.

The materialistic conception of the world is a necessary and useful fiction. It proceeds as if the external world did assuredly exist outside ourselves, and as if, even without us as subjects, things would be as they appear; although, in reality, all that we experience is merely our sensations which thus have validity only in relation to us as subjects. Not only does the world of color and sound exist merely through and in our sensations, but the world of touch also. The old truth that secondary qualities are merely relative has been extended to primary qualities also.

The idea of substance or thing is a fiction. We speak of things having qualities; e.g., we speak of this tree as having the quality of hardness, smoothness, a given size, shape, etc. Now what is the *thing* which has these qualities? It is absolutely equivalent to the indefinite series of those qualities. If the qualities were all removed, there would be no thing. A thing is merely the sum of the qualities. A thing in any other sense is a mere fiction, and when we say that a thing "has" certain qualities, we are making use of a fiction if thereby we intend something outside of and beyond the qualities.

13

We must discuss one other idea, the last and greatest fiction, namely the thing-in-itself, Kant's *Ding-an-sich*. From all that has preceded, it is clear what our attitude must be: that the thing-in-itself is a fiction. In the first edition of his *Critique of Pure Reason* Kant indeed, in one place, calls it a "mere idea," i.e., a fiction. It is a device by means of which the whole world of reality can be dealt with. It is an x to which a y, our ego, corresponds. By means of these two the real world of sensations is ordered and understood. In order to explain the world of ideas Kant assumes that the real world consists of things-in-themselves, mutually interacting. On the basis of this interacting he explained the genesis of sensations. We must remember, however, that Kant had the right to say only that we must regard real existence as if things-in-themselves existed, as if they influenced us and gave rise to our idea of the world. In that case the thing-in-itself was a necessary fiction since only thus can we imagine actual reality or think and speak of it at all.

The division of the world into things-in-themselves and egos, into objects and subjects, is the primary fiction upon which all others depend. From the standpoint of a critical positivism sensations alone are real, and out of these the whole subjective world is constructed with its division into physical and psychical complexes. A critical positivism asserts that any further claim is fictional. For it, only the observed sequence and coexistence of phenomena exist, and upon these alone it takes its stand. Any explanation going beyond this can do so only by the instrumentalities of fictions. A critical positivism is the only fictionless doctrine.

14

The treatment of all ideational constructs as mere products of the psyche was originally accomplished by Hume and Kant and continued by Schopenhauer. We go further in pointing out that they are, from a logical point of view, identical with scientific fictions, i.e., with constructs that are practically useful and necessary though theoretically false, deviations from reality. This point is implicit in Hume and Kant but is not stressed by them. The view here presented we call *critical positivism*.

15

Now that we have examined various fictions it will be useful to collect the terms which have been applied, more or less appropriately, to them. They are frequently referred to by terms simply translated from the Latin: *inventions, conceits, figments of the brain.*

phantasies, *imaginary ideas*, and so on. Other terms are derived from the fact that fictions are an aid to thought: *conceptual aids*, *auxiliary words*, *makeshifts*, and so on. Others, again, arise from the ingenious character of the process: *expedients*, *devices*, *artifices*, *artificial concepts*, *stratagems*, *dodges*, *contrivances*, *short cuts*, and so on. Some terms for fictions are derived from their functional nature: *instrumental ideas*, *intermediate ideas*, *bridges*, *props*, *ladders to thought*, *crutches*, *surrogates*, *substitutes*, *suppositions*, *scaffoldings*, and so on. We also find: *chimeras*, *distorted concepts*, *auxiliary methods*, *play*, *idea*, *schema*, *deceptive idea*, *provisional concept*, *heuristic idea*, *regulative concept*, *modus dicendi*, *mere idea*, *interim idea*, *limiting concept*, *theoretical concept*, *provisional assumption*, and so on.

What is a *fiction*? What is an *as-if*? In the *if* lies the assumption of an unreal or impossible case. For example, "*If* there were infinitesimals, then the curved line could be treated as made up of them"; or, "*If* there were ultimate discrete particles, then matter could be treated as made up of them"; or, "*If* egotism were the only motive, then we ought to be able to deduce social relations from it." In the if clause something unreal or impossible is assumed. From this unreality or impossibility inferences are drawn.

16

We can now indicate the general characteristics of fictions. It is well to begin by distinguishing between semifictions and genuine fictions. The former is illustrated, e.g., in Adam Smith's assumption that all human action is selfishly motivated; the latter is illustrated, e.g., in the notion that the circumference of a circle is composed of an infinite number of infinitely short straight lines, or in Kant's notion of a thing-in-itself nowhere revealed to experience but conditioning experience. Bearing these cases in mind we can proceed to note four main characteristics of fictions.

1. The first is their deviation from reality. In the case of semifictions this deviation is partial; that is, they partially contradict reality. Thus, recurring to Adam Smith, some human action is selfishly motivated, and some is not. In the case of genuine fictions this deviation is complete; that is, they completely contradict reality. And, furthermore, they possess the added characteristic

that they contain a self-contradiction. This discloses itself, e.g.,
in the antinomies to which they give rise.

2. <u>A second main characteristic is that they disappear in the
course of history or through the operation of logic.</u> The former
holds for semifictions, the latter for genuine fictions. Those which
partially contradict reality have value only if they are used provi-
sionally until experience has become richer or methods of thought
more refined and definitive. Those which completely contradict
reality, and themselves contain a self-contradiction, are allowed for,
when recognized for what they are, because our aim is to obtain
noncontradictory results.

3. <u>The third main feature of a fiction is the awareness accompany-
ing its use that it is just a fiction.</u> This holds only of normal fictions; or rather, of fictions normally held. In the history of the
sciences this is frequently not the case. The first authors of a fiction
are not themselves clear whether they have a fiction or an hypothesis
on their hands. The realization of its fictional nature develops
later.

4. <u>The fourth characteristic of a fiction is that it is a means to a
definite end, that it is expedient, or useful, not to say necessary.</u>
Where there is no such utility the fiction is unscientific, i.e., merely
aesthetic. That fictions in scientific thought have this character of
utility is the kernel of our position, and distinguishes it fundamentally from previous positions, e.g., Hume's or (to a less extent)
Kant's. The essential element in a scientific fiction is not the mere
fact of its being a conscious deviation from reality; it is that it is a
useful or necessary deviation.

These four characteristics suffice to distinguish fictions from
hypotheses. With them as "warrant," every fiction can be at once
recognized and examined. If a survey of the whole field of science
were made today, many fictions which we have not mentioned
would certainly be discovered.

15

Fictions are very useful for scientific thought. It is quite wrong
to reject these concepts as useless as soon as their objective impossibility has been recognized. This shows the very prejudice which

dominates philosophy today; namely, that because a construct is logically contradictory, it is therefore of no value. Precisely the contrary is true. These contradictory concepts are the most valuable.

As we have seen, many of the fundamental ideas with which science operates are fictions. The problem is not how to do away with these contradictions — that would be futile — but to show that they are of utility and advantage to thought. It is an error to imagine that only what is logically noncontradictory is logically fruitful. Such an attitude, if consistently adhered to, would bring us to the conclusion that all science is valueless, since so many of the fundamental concepts are contradictory.

Our position must be sharply distinguished from this. It is, of course, true that many fundamental scientific concepts are fictional and contradictory and do not "reflect" the world of reality. But this in no way renders them valueless. They are psychical constructs which not only give rise to the illusion that the world is being comprehended but also enable us to orient ourselves in the realm of the actual.

18

It is because our conceptual world is itself a product of the real world that it cannot be a reflection of the real world. On the other hand, it can serve as an instrument within reality by means of which we can move about. It is a symbol by means of which we orient ourselves. It is in the interests of science to make this symbol more and more adequate and useful, but a symbol it will always remain.

There is no reply to the argument that the conceptual world cannot be identical with the real world because it is a product of the real world. There is no identity of thought and reality. The "world" which the psyche constructs is merely an instrument, and for that reason, the world of ideas is not the ultimate goal of thought. The ultimate purpose of thought is not thought itself, but behavior and ultimately ethical behavior. The real world, symbolized in the form of a world of ideas, is the means thereto. The world is the material of ethical behavior.

The true and final purpose of thought is action and the facilitation of action. Looked at from this point of view the world of ideas, taken as a whole, is simply a means, and its constituent elements are also merely a means. What we have in it is a system of expedients of thought which mutually help and support one another. It is just an extremely sensitive machine constructed by the psyche. It is related to a prescientific world of ideas as a modern hammer to a prehistoric stone hammer. Both are instruments and, though very different as regards delicacy and elegance, are yet identical in kind. They are instruments, products of the psyche, of the logical instinct.

The conceptual world, the world of ideas, lies between the two poles of sensation and motion, perception and action. The psyche continually adds new members between these two poles. The delicacy and elaboration of its interpolations develop with the growth of the nerve mass and the increasing isolation of the brain from the spine.

The conceptual world, the world of ideas, lies between the sensory and the motor nerves, an intermediate world, serving merely to make the interconnection between them richer and easier, more delicate and more serviceable. Science is concerned with the elaboration of this intermediate world, and with the adjustment of this instrument to the objective relations of sequence and coexistence which make themselves perceptible. But when science goes further, making of this instrument an end in itself, when it is no longer concerned merely with the perfecting of the instrument, it is to be regarded as a luxury and a passion.

It is a pardonable weakness in science to believe that its ideas are concerned with reality itself. It deals with reality only to the extent of detecting the inevitable sequence and coexistences. But the concepts, the ideas, which encompass and embrace reality are of a fictional nature, the additions of man, forming merely the frame in which man encloses the reality in order that he may thus manipulate it better.

It is this attitude alone which can free us from the pressure of the logical contradictions so constantly concealed in the basic principles of science. It is not these which really matter, for they are but a means. The psyche creates more and more delicate means of encompassing and dealing with reality. It is an error to confuse the means, the instrument, with what the instrument was created to deal with.

19

The psyche is not merely a receptacle into which foreign matter is poured. It may be compared to a machine with a chemical retort which uses foreign matter most fittingly for its own maintenance. Just as the physical organism breaks up the matter which it receives, mixes it with its own juices, so the psyche envelops the thing perceived with categories. As soon as an external stimulus reaches the psyche, it responds as though provided with delicate feelers; inner processes start, the outcome of which is the appropriation of the things perceived for some purpose.

Vaihinger has some interesting defensive comments to make on his own position. They are cited hereunder:

1. The term *skepticism* has occasionally been applied to the philosophy of as-if and its systematic doctrines. This is not a correct description. Skepticism implies a theory which raises doubting or questioning to the dignity of a principle. The as-if philosophy has never had a trace of this attitude. It claims that consciously false conceptions and judgments are applied in all sciences, and it shows that these scientific fictions are to be distinguished from hypotheses. Hypotheses are assumptions which are probable, assumptions the truth of which can be proved by further experience. They are therefore verifiable. Fictions are never verifiable, because they are assumptions which are known to be false but which are employed because of their utility. When a series of assumptions in mathematics, mechanics, physics, chemistry, ethics, or the philosophy of religion are shown in this way to be useful fictions, and so to justify themselves, this does not imply skepticism. The application of the term *skepticism* to the as-if philosophy has been made, partly, no doubt, because of the doubt with which this philosophy treats God and immortality. But, as in the case of the sciences, the above consideration applies here also. The as-if philosophy does not deny that these conceptions are fictions of ethical value.

2. Many people think they can discover not exactly skepticism

but agnosticism in the as-if philosophy. Agnosticism is the belief that human knowledge is confined within more or less narrow limits. It speaks of the Unintelligible, the Unknowable. Now, the as-if philosophy holds that knowledge has certain limits, but not in the sense that these limits bound only human knowledge but do not bound a superhuman knowledge. My opinion is that the limitations are not implicit in the specific nature of man (as compared with possible minds of a higher order) but are part of the nature of thought itself. If there are higher forms of mind, these limitations will affect them, and even the highest mind of all. For thought originally only serves the will to life as a means to an end. But when, according to the law of the preponderance of the means over the end, thought has broken loose from its original aim and has become an end in itself it sets itself problems to which it is not equal because it has not developed for this purpose, for example, such problems as the origin of the world, the formation of matter, the beginning of motion, the meaning of the world, the purpose of life, etc. If thought is regarded as a biological function, it is obvious that these are impossible problems for thought to solve, and quite beyond the natural boundaries which limit thought as such. I have no inclination to fall back on the old grievance about the limitations of human knowledge. At most, we may complain that the law of the preponderance of the means over the end has led us to ask questions that are unanswerable.

3. In the same way we can dispose of another objection which is raised against the as-if philosophy, namely that the concept of reality implied in it is not uniform. On the one hand all reality is reduced to sensations; on the other hand, to the motion of matter and the smallest constituents of matter. The question is how to unify these two notions of reality. The criticism is that the as-if philosophy does nothing to effect this union.

I am going to ask a question in return. Has *any* philosophical system ever succeeded in bringing these two spheres into a rational relation? The answer is that they have never been brought into a logically satisfactory relation by any philosopher. They never will be brought into a definitely unified association by any rational formula. We stand here at a point where an impossible problem confronts our reason. This question is just as impossible of solution by rational methods as the question of the purpose of existence. Although we, who ask this question, unite in our nature these two halves of reality, our mind is not in a position to answer it satisfactorily. He who would criticize *any* system of philosophy for not answering this question, is in the same intellectual position as a man who would reproach a mathematician for not solving the problem of squaring the circle, or an engineer for not solving the problem of a perpetual-motion machine.

Naturally, the human mind is tormented by this insoluble contradiction between the world of motion and the world of consciousness, and this torment can eventually become very oppressive. One would be well advised to remember that Kant had already pointed out that there are problems which mock us perpetually, but which we cannot get rid of. But there is one solution of this and similar torturing questions, for in intuition and in experience all this contradiction and distress fade into nothingness. Experience and intuition are higher than human reason. When I see a deer feeding in the forest, when I see a child at play, when I see a man at work or sport, but above all when I am myself working or playing, where are the problems with which my mind has been torturing itself? We do not understand the world when we are pondering over its problems, but when we are doing the world's work.

READING REFERENCES. Books and articles expounding the ideas of Hans Vaihinger are few in number, unless one is prepared to read them in German. The translation of the treatise itself, and a chapter in a book by Havelock Ellis, are all that this author has encountered: Hans Vaihinger, *The Philosophy of As-If*. Havelock Ellis, "The Art of Thinking," in *The Dance of Life*.

READING QUESTIONS

1. What is the relation between Kant and Vaihinger?
2. What does he say in favor of Schopenhauer's pessimism?
3. What in favor of Schopenhauer's irrationalism?

4. In what way did he find that Darwin corroborated Schopenhauer?
5. What notion has "grown within me, and has crystallized into an ever-clearer form"?
6. What did he learn from Adolf Horwicz?
7. Why did he call his book *The Philosophy of As-If?*
8. "Scientific thought is a function of the psyche." In what sense?
9. "Thought must be recognized as an instrument." In what sense?
10. "The purpose of the world of ideas is not to portray reality." Why not? What then?
11. About what has "a veil of secrecy been woven"?
12. What is the distinction between a rule and an artifice of thought?
13. How would you define a *fiction?*
14. Cite an example in economic thought from Adam Smith.
15. In political science from Bentham.
16. In psychology from Condillac.
17. In juristic thought.
18. In what sense is the idea of free will a fiction?
19. Why does he describe it as "one of the most important fictions ever formed by man"?
20. "True morality rests upon fictions." Explain.
21. Cite an example of a fiction in mathematical thought.
22. In mechanics.
23. "What we call a *natural law* is a fiction." In what sense?
24. "All abstractions . . . all generalizations are fictions." Explain.
25. Cite an example of a fiction in religious thought from Schleiermacher.
26. "The materialistic conception of the world is a fiction." How so?
27. "The last and greatest fiction, Kant's thing-in-itself." Elucidate.
28. What does he mean by *critical positivism?*
29. What are some synonyms for the term *fiction?*
30. Distinguish between a semifiction and a genuine fiction.

31. What are the four main characteristics of fictions?
32. Distinguish between a fiction and an hypothesis.
33. Why does he repudiate the term *skepticism* as applied to his position?
34. Why *agnosticism?*
35. What criticism does he say is made of his conception of reality?
36. How does he parry this criticism?
37. "There is one solution of this and similar torturing questions." What is this question? Wherein is it torturing? What are similar questions? What is the solution?

TOPIC FOUR. AN ETHICAL
PROBLEM

THE PROBLEM STATED

Ethics may be defined as an inquiry into the principles and problems of morality. It covers a wide field. From this total field, we shall select one problem and, as before, approach it through the writings of five modern philosophers. The problem proposed is this: Upon what principle do we discriminate between right and wrong? This principle, once formulated, we shall refer to as ''the principle of morality,'' or as ''the moral principle.''

The notion of a principle of morality is one which we use every time we pass a moral judgment on conduct, on character, on institutions, on laws, on customs. We say, of a given act, that it is right or wrong; of a type of character, that it is the right type or the wrong type; of an institution, for example, private property, that it is right or wrong; of a law, say, capital punishment, that it is right or wrong; of a custom, that it is right or wrong. Our present problem is not which particular act, or character, or institution, or law, or custom is right or wrong. Our problem is the more general one: On what principle do we judge these things right or wrong?

The sets of citations which follow present five different approaches to this question. The first set, drawn from the writings of a celebrated eighteenth-century moralist, William Paley, argues that *right* means ''according to the will of God.'' This way of grounding morality in theology is something with which we are all familiar. Paley's statement is therefore valuable as a starting point. His argment is clear and concise.

The second set of citations, drawn from the writings of Immanuel Kant, argues that *right* means "according to reason," or "what reason prescribes." Kant wrote in the Age of Reason which produced such characteristic figures as Voltaire, Rousseau, Thomas Paine, and others. His attempt to ground morality on an appeal to reason, with no reference to theological doctrine, represents one of the perennial possibilities open to the human mind. In any age which understands by *reason* what Kant intended by that term, his appeal would be instant and profound.

The third set of citations, drawn from the writings of John Stuart Mill, argues that *right* means "producing human happiness." Mill was the moralist *par excellence* of the age of the Industrial Revolution. The position in moral philosophy which he occupies was inspired by his experience of great and far-reaching changes in the social order, widespread wealth and poverty, the rise of nineteenth-century democratic governments, the emergence of new economic classes, and the rapid decay of old customs and institutions. It is in this context that we must understand his somewhat abrupt and impatient dismissal of the moral philosophies typified by Paley and Kant, and his forthright appeal to happiness as the foundation principle of human morality.

In the fourth set of citations, Friedrich Nietzsche argues that *right* means "productive of or giving expression to the superman." The notion that man has evolved from lower animals suggested at once that something higher may evolve from man. This, when it comes, will be the superman, and in this appeal to the struggle for existence, anything is right which either hastens his arrival or expresses his nature when arrived.

The fifth and last set of citations, drawn from the writings of William James, presents a curious return to the position argued for by Paley, namely, that the whole duty of man is summed up in the phrase "to know the will of God and keep it."

There are other philosophical problems in the field of ethical analysis and speculation, besides the one which is here traced from Paley's appeal to the will of God to James's appeal to the same, but this problem is central. The rest of one's moral philosophy, once this question has been settled, is largely a series of deductions from or applications of the principle adopted as fundamental.

1. MORALITY GROUNDED IN THEOLOGY — FROM WILLIAM PALEY

One of the most important questions we can direct at any human act, is this: "Was it right or wrong? Did the agent do as he ought to have done, or as he ought not to have done?" Implicit in any answer to this question is a moral principle; that is, a criterion in terms of which we distinguish between right and wrong. As long as men entertain a lively belief in the existence of God, and ascribe to Him an interest in human affairs, many are likely to base their moral judgments upon what they consider to be His will. They are going to say that *right* means "according to the will of God," and *wrong* means "contrary to the will of God." William Paley, one of the most popular and widely read moralists in the eighteenth century, was a man of precisely this turn of mind. One cannot do better than examine the essentials of the appeal to theology as these are to be found in his writings. Any virtues which reside in this view will be obvious in the simplicity and sincerity of his language. Any shortcomings can be the more readily pointed out, since his stand is clear and bold. The following passage by Sir Leslie Stephen in his *History of English Thought in the*

Eighteenth Century is worth reading before proceeding to Paley's biography and philosophy.   Says Sir Leslie:

The different religions of the world tell us, each in its own fashion, what is the plan and meaning of this universe.   Thence believers may infer what is the best method of employing our brief existence within it.   We ought to be good, say all moralists, and the question remains: What is meant by *ought* and by *goodness?*   Theology, so long as it was a vital belief in the world, afforded a complete and satisfactory answer to these questions.   Morality was, of necessity, its handmaid.   Believe in an active ruler of the universe, who reveals his will to men, who distributes rewards and punishments to the good and the evil, and we have a plain answer to most of the problems of morality.   God's will, so far as known to us, determines what is good.   We are obliged to be good, whether from love or from fear.

BIOGRAPHICAL NOTE.   William Paley was born in England in 1743 and died in 1805 at the age of sixty-two.   His father was headmaster of the school of Giggleswick in Yorkshire.   His early education was obtained under the paternal eye.   At the age of fifteen, young Paley went to the University of Cambridge.   That his father had great expectations may be gathered from a remark he made to a friend: "My son is now gone to college.   He'll turn out a great man.   Very great, indeed.   I am certain of it.   He has by far the clearest head I ever met in my life."   Paley spent four years at Cambridge, obtaining his B.A. in 1762.   The following anecdote suggests that he was a very normal young man during these years:

I spent the first two years of my undergraduate life happily, but unprofitably.   I was constantly in society, where we were not immoral, but idle and rather expensive.   At the commencement of my third year, however, after having left the usual party at a rather late hour in the evening, I was awakened at five in the morning by one of my companions, who stood at my bedside.   He said: "Paley,

I have been thinking what a fool you are. I could achieve nothing worth while, even were I to try, and anyway I can afford the idle life I lead. You could achieve anything, if you were to try, and you cannot afford to waste your time. I have had no sleep during the whole night on account of these reflections, and am now come solemnly to inform you that if you persist in your indolence, I must renounce your society." I was so struck with the visit and the visitor that I laid in bed a great part of the day, and formed my plan. I ordered my bedmaker to prepare my fire every evening, in order that it might be lighted by myself the next morning. I rose at five o'clock, read during the whole of the day, except such hours as chapel and lectures required, allotting to each portion of time its peculiar branch of study; and, just before the closing of the gates (9:00 P.M.) I went to a neighboring coffeehouse, where I constantly regaled upon a mutton chop and a dose of milk punch.

After graduating, Paley rose slowly but steadily in the ecclesiastical world. In 1785 he published his *Principles of Moral and Political Philosophy*, from which the citations below have been drawn. It passed through fifteen editions during his own lifetime. One of his contemporaries remarked of this book: "It may be said to be the only work on moral philosophy fitted to be understood by every class of readers." With his other writings, equally popular, we are not concerned.

THE ARGUMENT OF THE CITATIONS. Paley's presentation of the fundamental principle of morality is simple and clear: Right is that which agrees with the will of God; wrong is that which does not. Having stated this controlling idea, he sets himself to elaborate it. He provides first a definition of *virtue*, consistent with his basic proposition; he moves on, then, to examine the meaning of moral obligation and the distinction between prudence and duty. These matters settled, he turns to the question: if *right* means "according to the will of God," how are we to tell what is and is not the will of God? His answer here is twofold: scriptural revelation and the "light of nature." The sense in which God's will may be gathered from Scripture is then explained. But what of the light of nature; what, that is, about the morality of acts where we do not have God's express declaration? Here Paley meets a real problem, and knowing, as he did, that many occasions arise with respect to which Scripture is silent, he could not treat this matter lightly. To solve his problem he adopts the assumption that human happiness is God's primary concern. Realizing, as he says, that "this assumption is the foundation of the whole system," he sets himself to "explain the reasons upon which it rests." The explanation in question occupies the remainder of the citations. The following quotation from a seventeenth-century moralist expresses so clearly the idea which Paley proposes to develop that I give it as a kind of foreword:

That God has given a rule whereby men should govern themselves, I think there is no one so brutish as to deny. He has a right to do it. We are His creatures. He has goodness and wisdom to direct our actions to what is best, and He has power to enforce it by rewards and punishments of infinite weight and duration in another life; for nobody can take us out of His hands. This is the only touchstone of moral rectitude, and by comparing them to this law, it is that men judge of the most considerable moral good or evil of their actions; that is, whether as duty or as sins, they are like to procure them happiness or misery from the hands of the Almighty.

Now Paley. First, as to ethics in general:

Ethics is that science which teaches men their duty and the reasons of it. The use of such a study depends upon this, that, without it, the rules of life by which men are ordinarily governed, oftentimes mislead them, through a defect in either the rule or in the application.

Then, as to the meaning of *right:*

Right signifies being consistent with the will of God.
Right is a quality of persons or of actions. Of persons, as when

we say, "He has a right to his property"; of actions, as when we say, "His action was right on that occasion." Whether of persons or of actions, *right* means "consistent with, or according to, the will of God." In the one case, substituting the definition for the term, you may say, "It is consistent with or according to the will of God that he have his property"; in the other case, "His action, on that occasion, was consistent with or according to the will of God."

From this it follows that:

Virtue is doing good to mankind, in obedience to the will of God, and for the sake of everlasting happiness.

The division of virtues to which we are nowadays most accustomed is into duties: duties toward God; duties toward other men; duties toward ourselves. There are more of these distinctions, but it is not worth while to set them down.

And we are now in a position to explain what is meant by *duty* or *moral obligation*.

What are we to understand by *moral obligation*? Truthfulness, we say, is a moral obligation. What do we intend by this expression? Why am I obliged to keep my word?

When I first turned my thoughts to moral speculations, an air of mystery seemed to hang over the whole subject. This arose, I believe, from hence — that I supposed that to be obliged to do a thing was very different from being induced or urged to do it; that the obligation to practice virtue, for example, was quite another thing, and of another kind, than the obligation which a soldier is under to obey his officer, or a servant his master. Now in what does the difference consist?

I shall argue to the following effect: A man is said to be *obliged* when he is urged by a violent motive resulting from the command of another. First, the motive must be violent, strong, powerful. A person has done me some little service. Suppose, then, he asks me for my vote. From a motive of gratitude, or expectation, I may give it to him. But I should hardly say I was obliged to give it to him; because the motive, or incentive, or inducement, does not rise high enough. Second, it must result from the command of another.

Offer a man a gratuity for doing anything. He is not obliged by your offer to do it. But if a magistrate were to command it, he would then consider himself obliged to do it.

Wherever, then, the motive is violent enough and is coupled with the idea of a command, an authority, a law, a will, there, I take it, we always reckon ourselves to be obliged. Let it be remembered that to be obliged is to be urged by a violent motive resulting from the command of another.

And then let it be asked: Why am I "obliged" to keep my word? The answer will be: Because I am urged by the expectation of being rewarded after this life if I do, and punished if I do not, follow, in this respect, the command of God. This solution goes to the bottom of the subject, as no further question can reasonably be asked.

There is always understood to be a difference between an act of prudence and an act of duty. Thus, if I distrusted a man who owed me money, I should reckon it an act of prudence to get another bound with him; but I should hardly call it an act of duty. On the other hand, it would be a loose kind of language to say that, as my friend had placed a box of jewels in my hands when he went abroad, it would be prudent of me to preserve it for him until he returned.

Now, wherein does the difference consist? The difference, and the only difference, is this, that, in the one case, we consider what we shall gain or lose in the present world; in the other case, we consider also what we shall gain or lose in the world to come. Prudence has regard to the former; duty, to the latter. Those who would establish a system of morality, independent of a future state, must look out for some different idea of moral obligation.

To us, therefore, there are two great questions: Will there be, after this life, any distribution of rewards and punishments at all? If so, what actions will be rewarded and what actions will be punished? The first question comprises the credibility of the Christian religion. Proof of an affirmative answer to it, although we confess that it is the foundation upon which the whole fabric rests, must in this treatise be taken for granted. The second question comprises morality itself, and to this we shall now address ourselves.

By now the fundamental role of the will of God in Paley's moral philosophy should be clear. From it proceed all the principal terms in such a moralist's vocabulary. The question hence, begins to press: How do we determine what is and is not the will of God?

As the will of God is our rule, to inquire, in any instance, what is our duty or what we are obliged to do, is, in effect, to inquire what is the will of God in that instance. This consequently becomes the whole business of morality.

Now, there are two methods of coming at the will of God on any point: by his express declarations, when they are to be had, and which must be sought for in Scripture; by what we can discover of his designs and disposition from his works, or, as we usually call it, the light of nature. The object of both is the same — to discover the will of God; and, provided we do but discover it, it matters nothing by what means.

An ambassador may guide himself in many cases with safety by judging only from what he knows of his sovereign's disposition, by arguing from what he has observed of his conduct or what he knows of his designs. But if he have his commission and instructions in his pocket, it would be strange never to look into them. He will, naturally, conduct himself by both rules. When his instructions are clear and positive, there is an end of all further deliberation, unless, indeed, he suspect their authenticity. Where his instructions are silent or dubious, he will endeavor to supply or explain them by what he has been able to collect from other quarters of his master's general inclination or intentions.

Whoever expects to find in the Scriptures particular directions for every moral doubt that arises looks for more than he will meet with. Such a detail of particular precepts would have so enlarged the sacred volume that it would have been too bulky either to be read or circulated; or rather, as St. John says, "even the world itself could not contain the books that should be written."

Morality is taught in the Scriptures in this wise: General rules are laid down, of piety, justice, benevolence, and purity. Several of these rules are occasionally illustrated, either in fictitious examples, as in the parable of the good Samaritan; or in instances which actually presented themselves, as in Christ's reproof of his disciples or his praise of the poor widow; or, in the resolution of questions proposed to Christ, as in his answer to the young man who asked him, "What lack I yet?"

This is the way in which all practical sciences are taught, as arithmetic, grammar, navigation, and the like. Rules are laid down, and examples are subjoined, by way of explaining the principle of the rule, and as so many specimens of the method of applying it.

So far, so good. By reference to the will of God we determine what is right and wrong. By reference to Scripture we determine, in part, what is the will of God. But what of that part which is not provided for by Scripture?

The method of coming at the will of God concerning any action, where we do not have his express declaration, is to inquire into the tendency of the action to promote or diminish the general happiness. This rule proceeds on the assumption that God Almighty wills and wishes the happiness of His creatures, and, consequently, that those actions which promote that will and wish must be agreeable to Him; and the contrary.

As this assumption is the foundation of the whole system, it becomes necessary to explain the reasons upon which it rests.

When God created the human species, either He wished their happiness or He wished their misery or He was indifferent to both.

If He wished their misery, He might have made sure of His purpose, e.g., by forming our senses to be as many sores and pains to us as they are now instruments of gratification and enjoyment. He might, e.g., have made everything we tasted, bitter; everything we saw, loathsome; everything we touched, a sting; every smell, a stench; every sound, a discord.

If He had been indifferent to our happiness or misery, we must impute to our good fortune both the capacity of our senses to receive pleasure and the supply of external objects fitted to excite it. But either of these — and still more both of them — is too much to be attributed to accident, i.e., mere "good fortune." Nothing remains, therefore, than the first supposition; namely, that when God created the human species, He intended their happiness.

The same argument may be proposed in different terms, thus: The world abounds in contrivances, and all the contrivances with which we are acquainted are directed to beneficial purposes. Evil, no doubt, exists. But it is never, that we can perceive, the object of contrivance. Teeth are contrived to eat, not to ache. Their aching now and then is incidental to the contrivance, perhaps inseparable from it, perhaps even a defect in it; but it is not the object of it.

This is a distinction which well deserves to be attended to. In describing implements of husbandry, you would hardly say of a sickle that it is made to cut the reaper's fingers, though from the construction of the instrument, and the manner of using it, this mischief often happens.

On the other hand, if you had occasion to describe instruments of torture, the case would be different. This, you would say, is to stretch the sinews; this, to dislocate the joints; this, to break the bones; this, to scorch the soles of the feet; and so forth. Here pain and misery are the very objects of the contrivance.

Now, nothing of this sort is to be found in nature. We never discover a contrivance whose object is to bring about pain and misery. No anatomist ever discovered anything in the organism calculated to produce pain and disease. No anatomist, in explaining the parts of the human body, ever said, "This is to irritate, this is to inflame, this is to conduct stones to the kidneys, this is to secrete the humor which forms gout." The most he will say is that he does not understand some part or other, or that it is useless. He never suspects that it is put there to incommode, to annoy, to torment.

Since, then, God hath called forth His consummate wisdom to contrive and provide for our happiness, and the world appears to have been constituted with this design at first, then, so long as this constitution is upheld by Him, we must suppose the same design to continue.

We conclude, therefore, that God wills and wishes the happiness of His creatures. This conclusion being once established, we are at liberty to go on with the rule built upon it, namely, that the method of coming at the will of God concerning any action, where we do not have his express declaration, is to inquire into the tendency of that action to promote or diminish the general happiness.

By virtue of the two principles, that God wills the happiness of His creatures, and that God's will is the measure of right and wrong, we arrive at certain conclusions. These conclusions become rules. And soon we learn to pronounce actions right or wrong according as they agree or disagree with our rules, without looking any further.

Paley, in moral philosophy, like St. Thomas in natural theology and Descartes in metaphysics, starts from premises and arrives at conclusions that have an old and familiar ring. Like St. Thomas and Descartes, too, Paley is of interest for the difficulties which his position suggests. Stated very briefly, what he says comes to this: "_Right_ means according to God's will. God's will is to be found in the Scriptures, or discovered by the light of nature. The light of nature tells us that God intends above all to produce and promote human happiness. Where, therefore, the Scriptures are silent, we determine the rightness of an act by the fact that it produces more happiness than any other act possible at the time." This is both clear and confused. It really raises more questions than it settles. For example, does Paley mean that an act is right because it agrees with God's will, or that it agrees with God's will because it is right? These two are not the same. Then, of course, there is the problem connected with detecting God's will in the Scriptures. Why the Scriptures? Why not in Plato's dialogues? Or in the Mohammedan _Koran_? In which parts of the Scriptures? In those parts which enjoin an eye for an eye? Or in those parts which enjoin the golden rule? If in both, what about clashes? If in one, how choose which? Passing to the second half of his argument, has he proved, at all conclusively, that God's will is directed to creating and promoting human happiness? This hypothesis may account for some of the facts. But it does not account for all of them. See Hume and Schopenhauer on the misery of man's estate. Going a step further, and admitting his argument, are we justified in arguing that an act is right, if and only if, it produces more happiness than any other act possible under the circumstances? Is this not to formulate a moral principle that swings clear of the first part of Paley's argument, and could stand on its own feet, without any aid from Scripture? If so, what about cases where the "appeal to Scripture" and "the appeal to happiness" appear to clash? Finally is it or is it not the case that we are more sure of what is right and wrong than we are of God's very existence? If so, would it not be wiser to begin with what we are more sure of, than to begin with what we are less sure of? These, and other problems which suggest themselves, were engaging the attention of Immanuel Kant during the years in which Paley was writing his *Principles of Moral and Political Philosophy*. Paley published in 1785. Kant had published his *Critique of Pure Reason* in 1781, and was meanwhile engaged on a second *Critique*, directed, this time, not at the problem of knowledge but at the problem of morality. From this prosperous and rather worldly Anglican divine one turns with something like eagerness to the austere and searching professorial moralist at Königsberg.

READING REFERENCES. None are suggested.

READING QUESTIONS

1. What do you understand by the principle of morality?
2. On what sorts of things do we pass moral judgments?
3. In one sentence devoted to each, contrast the positions of Paley, Kant, Mill.
4. In what sense, according to Stephen, is morality the handmaid of religion?
5. Upon what does the use of the study of ethics depend, according to Paley?

6. In what two senses does he use the term *right?*
7. How does he define the term?
8. What "air of mystery seemed to hang over the whole subject" of moral obligation?
9. When is a man "obliged" to do something?
10. What solution goes to the bottom of what subject?
11. Wherein lies the distinction between prudence and duty?
12. Wherefore are there two great questions? What are these questions?
13. "There are two methods for coming at the will of God on any point." Namely?
14. What is the point of the ambassador analogy?
15. In what way is morality taught in the Scriptures?
16. Suppose we do not have the express declaration of God's will in the Scriptures?
17. What "rule" proceeds on what "assumption"?
18. In what sense is "this assumption the foundation of the whole system"?
19. What criticism does he make of the hypothesis "When God created the human species, He wished their misery"?
20. Of the hypothesis that God was indifferent?
21. "The same argument may be proposed in different terms." Namely?
22. Formulate one or more criticisms of Paley's position.

2. MORALITY GROUNDED IN DUTY — FROM IMMANUEL KANT

FROM PALEY TO KANT. While Paley was engaged in arguing that morality has its roots in theology, Immanuel Kant was engaged in showing that such is not the case. Paley, it will be remembered, published in 1785. Kant, who had been developing his views in lecture form since 1775, published in 1785 and again, at greater length, in 1788. The efforts made by these two moralists to formulate the principle of morality provide an excellent starting point for the study of modern analysis and speculation in these matters.

Kant lived in the Age of Reason, the age of Hume and

Rousseau and Voltaire and the revolutions in America and France. He is a firm believer in the rationality of man. He seeks to develop the notion of a rational morality, as opposed to a theological morality. He works with the conception of man as essentially a rational animal. By *rational* as applied to man I understand him to mean two things: having (1) the power to discover what is the case, and to guide conduct by such knowledge, i.e., to develop pure and applied sciences; (2) the power to discover what ought to be the case, and to guide conduct by such knowledge, i.e., to develop a moral philosophy and a morality. Just as he could speak of rational science, so he would speak of rational conduct or rational morality. Just as, by *rational science* he would mean knowledge valid and binding for all rational minds, so by *rational morality* he would mean morality valid and binding for all rational minds. To the first kind of rationality he devoted his *Critique of Pure Reason;* to the second, his *Critique of Practical Reason.*

BIOGRAPHICAL NOTE. At the end of the biographical note on Kant in the previous topic, page 220, we left him finishing his *Critique of Pure Reason* and publishing it in 1781. This treatise was the first of three, all directed to the analysis and exploration of a single theme, namely, mind and its place in nature. The first critique dealt with mind and the world order; the second is to deal with mind and the moral order; the third with mind and the aesthetic order. In other words, the relation of mind to the true, the good, and the beautiful; or to science, morality, and art. The elaboration of the ideas contained in these three studies brought Kant to a ripe old age, crowned with honors and influence. He became, and remains, one of the great formative thinkers in the history of the modern mind.

THE ARGUMENT OF THE CITATIONS. Kant's handling of the problem of morality follows from his conception of what morality is. Without a firm grip of this, one is likely to miss the point of his analysis. For that reason, it is necessary to emphasize his starting point. He begins by assuming that morality, whatever it may be in detail, is something which is universally binding on all rational minds, comparable, in this respect, to science. Thus, if it is true that two and two make four, then it is binding on all rational creatures to accept this proposition. If this is a truth, it is true for everyone, not merely true for those who care to believe it. If it is true, it is true necessarily and always. It is true, in and of itself, without any reference to why it is true, without any reference to who does or does not believe it, without any reference to consequences that follow from its being true or from its being believed. It is, to use a favorite phrase of Kant's, true categorically, without any strings or qualifications. To repeat, it is not true because God commands it, nor because it is according to nature, nor because it pays in the long run to believe it, nor because all or most people agree to it, nor for any other reason. It is simply true because it is true. Moreover, it is true of all cases of two's and two's. There are no possible exceptions. It is not something which holds for one period of time and not for another, for one pair of two's and not for another, for one stage of civilization and not for another. In this universality, necessity, objectivity, which we detect readily enough in the proposition that two and two make four, Kant finds the differential mark of rational knowledge. He has his own word for it. It is, he says, true *a priori*. It will be recalled that he began his *Critique of Pure Reason* by accepting and exploring the implications of *a priori* knowledge.

This notion of *a priori* he carries over into the field of morality. If there is such a thing as rational science, it is *a priori*. If there is such a thing as rational morality, it is *a priori*. Moreover, just as in the case of *a priori* knowledge he did not

undertake to prove that there is such a thing, but assumed its
existence as a fact, so in the case of morality he does not undertake to show that there is such a thing, but assumes its existence as a fact. His argument is after this manner: If you
admit that there is any rational knowledge, then you must
admit that it is *a priori* in character, and if you admit that
there is any rational morality, you must admit that it is *a
priori* in character. If you admit that there is any rational
knowledge, you must recognize that it is binding on all rational beings; so, by analogy, if you admit that there is any
rational morality, you must recognize that it is binding on all
rational beings. He is content to accept both rational knowledge and rational morality as facts to be recognized, not as
hypotheses to be proved.

Once the notion of a rational morality is admitted, Kant
is in a position to formulate his problem. It is this: What
must be its principle? It will be noticed that he is not seeking to justify morality, any more than one would seek to
justify arithmetic; not seeking to explain why right is right
and wrong is wrong, any more than one would seek to explain
why true is true, or false is false. He is merely saying: The
facts of morality are categorical facts, not dependent for their
moral quality upon anything beyond themselves. Such being
the case, we ask again, what principle must run through all
the cases of morality, and be absent from all the cases of
immorality?

His answer is simple: An act is moral if and only if the
principle which it embodies is capable of universalization
without self-contradiction. This notion once stated, Kant
proceeds to illustrate his meaning by some examples. His
next step is to approach this same notion of categorical rightness from two other angles, namely, duty and good will.
When these matters have been settled, he turns to consider a
question that had been hanging fire since his studies in the

problem of knowledge. I mean the problem of man's free will. Here the findings of the first *Critique* are called in to help solve the difficulty. As a moralist, his fundamental problem is, "What ought I to do?" But if, as would appear from the "scientific" view of the world, everything happens "of necessity," what sense is there to claiming that some things "ought" or "ought not" to be done? Here Kant is at once clarifying and baffling. Clarifying because he has the insight and tenacity to hold on to the "ought" as being every bit as much a reality as the "is," baffling because he concludes by admitting his inability to solve the paradox involved in their joint acceptance. His treatment of this question would require too much space to be summarized here. From freedom he passes on to God and immortality. As in the case of Kant's handling of the problem of knowledge, it will be necessary to state a few of his claims in the form of a condensed summary. His own language is too involved to permit direct citation. Wherever possible, however, his own words will be introduced.

Morality, the rightness and wrongness of actions, is categorical (not dependent upon anything) and *a priori* (valid for all persons and all times and all cases). In this it resembles rational knowledge. To quote: "The morality of an action is quite a peculiar thing. When we are considering the goodness of an action, we are concerned with what constitutes the goodness in and of itself."

If morality is of this categorical and *a priori* nature, then we can rule out several misleading attempts to formulate its principle. For example, the morality of an act is said, by some, to reside in the "feeling" which one has about the act. But this could not be for two reasons: (1) If morality is a matter of someone's feelings, then it is not categorical; that is, an act would depend, for its morality, upon the fact (external to the act itself) that it was or was not felt about in some way or other by some person or other. (2) If morality is a matter of feeling, then it is not anything universally binding and valid for all men, because feelings vary notoriously from time to time and from person to person; that is, one and the same act could be both right and wrong provided merely that two persons had opposite feelings about it. But this is to rob morality of its categorical nature, to give as the defining characteristic of morality a quality in virtue of which it would fail to be categorical and *a priori*.

Much the same line of reasoning is adduced by Kant against those who seek to locate the rightness of an act in its agreement with God's will. He says:

There are those who argue that we must first have God and then morality — a very convenient principle. But ethics and theology are neither of them a principle of the other. We are not discussing, here, the fact that theology is a motive for ethics — which it is — but we are asking whether the principle of ethical discrimination is theological — and it cannot be that.

Were it so, then before a nation could have any conception of duties it would first have to know God. Nations which had no right conception of God would have no duties, and this is not the case. Nations had a right idea of their duties, e.g., were aware that lies were detestable, without having the proper notion of God. Duties must therefore be derived from some other source.

If we do as God commanded, because He has commanded, and because He is so mighty that He can force us to, or punish us if we do not, we act under orders from fear and fright, not appreciating the propriety of our actions and knowing why we should do as God has commanded. Might cannot constitute a *vis obligandi*. Threats do not impose a (moral) obligation; they extort. Such conduct does not make the heart better.

Moral laws can be right without any commander, promulgator, obligator. How do we know the divine will? None of us feels it in his heart. We cannot know the moral law from any revelation, for if we did so, then those who had no revelation would be wholly ignorant of it.

We imagine God as possessing the most holy and most perfect will. But what then is the most perfect will? The moral law shows us what it is. We say the divine will accords with the moral law and is, therefore, holiest and most perfect. Thus we recognize the perfection of the divine will from the moral law. God wills all that is morally good and proper, and His will is, therefore, holy and perfect. But what is it that is morally good? Ethics supplies the answer to this question.

These strictures may be summarized. To locate the rightness of an act in its agreement with God's will is to deny its categorical nature, i.e., to make it depend, for its rightness, upon something other than or outside of itself. It is, too, to render morality an impossibility for all who do not know what God's will is, or who have a wrong notion of that will, or (it may be) deny His existence. There is, Kant would say, such a thing as morality apart from God's existence or our knowledge of the same. Finally, the view fails to take into account that when we say, "God is good," we are making goodness prior to and independent of God. He is good because His will or His action corresponds to the good; not vice versa.

There remains for consideration what Kant calls the *pragmatic* view of morality. The pragmatic view of morality is that an act is right because of the nature of its consequences; not right in itself, but because of the results that do or do not follow from it. Kant does not need to concern himself with the question of the nature of the results. He has two objections to doing so: (1) To locate the rightness of an act in the nature of its consequences is to deny the categorical nature of morality. It is to make its morality depend upon something other than the act. (2) To find the morality of an act in its consequences is to deprive morality of its *a priori* nature, because we can never know the consequences of an act until after the act is done, and even then never know them completely. This would reduce morality to a matter of probability; make it, as Kant says, *a posteriori*, instead of *a priori*. At this point, direct citations from Kant may be resumed.

Having examined what the principle of morality is not, we must now examine what it is.

What is the one principle of morality, the criterion by which to judge everything and in which lies the distinction between moral goodness and all other goodness? What is the principle upon which we establish morality, and through which we are able to discriminate between what is moral and what immoral?

In this connection we must first notice that there are two points to be considered: the principle upon which we discriminate, and the mainspring or motive of performance. We must distinguish between the measuring rod and the mainspring. The measuring rod is the principle of discriminating; the mainspring is the motive of the performance of our obligation. If we ask, "What is morally good and what is not?" it is the principle of discrimination that is in question; but if we ask, "What is it that leads me to be moral?" it is the motive that is in question. We must guard against confusing the principle of morality with the motive to morality. The first is the norm. The second is the incentive.

The essence of morality is that our actions are motivated by a general rule. If we make it the foundation of our conduct that our actions shall be consistent with a universal rule, valid at all times and for everyone, then our actions exemplify the principle of morality.

In all moral judgments the idea which we frame is this: What is the character of the action taken by itself? If the principle of the action can, without self-contradiction, be universalized, it is moral; if it cannot be so universalized without contradicting itself, it is immoral. That action is immoral whose principle cancels and destroys itself when it is made a universal rule.

From this wholly general statement of the nature of rightness Kant turns to some concrete illustrations. He considers the case of lying and suicide. These, being instances of wrongness, illustrate his notion of rightness only indirectly.

May I, when in distress, make a promise with the intention not to keep it? Considerations of prudence aside, would such an act be moral? The shortest way to answer this question is to ask, "Would I be content that the principle (getting out of difficulties by making false promises) should hold good as a universal law, for myself and all others?"

If I ask, "Can the principle of making deceitful promises to get out of difficulties be universalized?" I realize that it cannot. For with such a law there would be no promises at all. With such a principle made universal, it would be in vain to allege my intentions in regard to future actions. As soon as it were made a universal law, the principle would necessarily destroy itself, necessarily defeat its own end.

A man finds himself forced to borrow money. He knows that he will not be able to repay it, but he sees also that nothing will be lent to him unless he promises to repay it. Would it be right to promise? The principle of his action would be: When in need, to borrow and promise to repay, knowing that I cannot do so. Could this principle become a universal law? I see at once that it could not. As a universal law, it would contradict itself. For if this principle were a universal law, such promises would become impossible. For no one would consider such promises as binding, and all would ridicule them as vain pretenses.

A man reduced to despair by a series of misfortunes feels wearied of life. Would it be right to take his own life? Could the principle of his action become a universal law of nature? The principle would be: To shorten life when its longer duration is likely to bring more evil than satisfaction. Could this principle become a universal law of nature? Clearly not. A system of nature in which it was a law to destroy life by means of the very feeling whose special office it is to impel to the improvement of life, would contradict itself, and therefore could not exist as a system of nature. Hence that principle could not possibly exist as a universal law of nature. Hence it would be wholly inconsistent with the supreme principle of all duty.

If we attend to ourselves, on occasion of any transgression of duty, we shall find that we do not will that the principle of our action should become a universal law. On the contrary, we will that the opposite should remain a universal law, only we assume the liberty of making an exception in our own favor — just for this time only, it may be.   This cannot be justified to our own impartial judgment, and it proves that we do recognize the validity of the moral principle I have formulated, even while we allow ourselves a few exceptions which we think important and forced upon us.

Thus far Kant has been developing the notion of a rational morality as something categorical and *a priori*. He has used this conception of morality to eliminate certain other theories which are incompatible with it, e.g., the theory that morality is a matter of feeling or emotion. He has disentangled what he takes to be the underlying principle of morality so conceived and advanced a few illustrations of his thesis. He returns again and again throughout his ethical writings to these basic claims. One example of such a reworking is contained in his distinction between hypothetical and categorical imperatives. The statement of this is given below. But a word first on Kant's use of these terms. The term *imperative*, used as a noun, means "a command." Kant inclines to use it in this sense. We shall, I think, come closer to his real meaning if we construe it by our word *ought*. We do, as a matter of everyday usage, employ the term *ought* in precisely the sense Kant would appear to have in mind. We say, for example, "If you wish to be there on time, you *ought* to leave early." Here the force of the *ought* is hypothetical; that is, it depends on whether you do or do not wish to get there on time. But there are times, Kant would claim, when we do not so use the term; when, for instance, we are pointing out what we take to be a duty. Thus, "you *ought* to be honest," "you *ought* to respect the rights of others." Here, we might feel, the *ought* is not dependent upon any *if*. It is not an hypothetical *ought*. It is, Kant would say, a categorical *ought*. The same idea could also be expressed in the distinction between an hypothetical obligation and a categorical obligation. Kant says:

All imperatives command either hypothetically or categorically. The former represent the practical necessity of a possible action as means to something else that is willed or might be willed. The latter would be that which represented an action as obligatory of itself without reference to some other end.

If an action is good only as a means to something else, then the imperative which commands it is hypothetical only; but if it is conceived to be good in itself, that is, without reference to any further end, the imperative which commands it is categorical.

The hypothetical imperative only says that the action is good for some purpose, actual or possible. The categorical imperative declares an action to be binding in itself, without reference to any purpose or end beyond itself.

All sciences have a practical part, consisting of problems connected with ends or purposes possible for us, and of imperatives directing how these may be attained. Here there is no question whether the end is good or rational, but only what one must do in order to attain it. The precepts for the physician to make his patient healthy and for a poisoner to insure his victim's death, are of equal value in this respect, namely that each serves to effect its purpose.

There is one imperative which commands certain conduct immediately, without having as its condition any other purpose to be attained by it. This imperative is categorical. It concerns not the matter of the action, nor its intended result, but its form and principle. This imperative may be called the imperative of morality.

There is but one categorical imperative, namely, "Act only on that principle which thou canst will should become a universal law."

This imperative of duty may be expressed, by analogy with natural laws, as follows: "Act as if the principle of thy action were to become by thy will a universal law of nature."

If there is a supreme practical principle or categorical imperative.

it must be one which constitutes an objective principle, and can therefore serve as a universal practical law. From this, as a supreme practical law, all laws of the will must be capable of being deduced. Accordingly the categorical imperative may be stated in a third way: "So act as to treat humanity, whether in thine own person or in the person of another, as an end withal, never as a means only."

If all the imperatives of duty can be deduced from this one imperative, as from it as their principle, then, although it should remain undecided whether what is called *duty* is not merely a vain notion, yet at least we shall be able to show what we understand by it; be able, that is, to show what the notion means.

To act out of respect for this principle constitutes duty. To this every other motive must give place, because it is the condition of a will being good in itself, good absolutely, good without qualification; and the worth of such a will is above everything.

The direct opposite of acting on the principle of morality is acting on the principle of private happiness. This would ruin morality altogether, were not the voice of reason so clear, so irrepressible, so distinctly audible even to the commonest men. That action should be based on the principle of private happiness can only be maintained by such as are bold enough to shut their ears against that heavenly voice in order to support a theory that costs no trouble.

Two things fill the mind with ever new and increasing admiration and awe, the oftener and more steadily we reflect on them: the starry heavens above and the moral law within. I have not to search for them and conjecture them as though they were veiled in darkness or in a region transcending my horizon. I see them before me and connect them directly with the consciousness of my existence.

Duty! Thou sublime and mighty name! Thou seekest not to move the will by threatening nor by charming. Thou merely holdest forth a law which finds entrance into the mind, a law before which all inclinations and desires are dumb. What origin is worthy of thee? Where is to be found the root of thy noble descent?

I do not, therefore, need any far-reaching penetration to discern what I have to do in order that my will may be morally good. Inexperienced in the course of the world, incapable of being prepared for all its contingencies, I need only ask, "Can I will that the principle of my action should become a universal law?" If not, then it must be rejected.

A second reworking of his fundamental insight is contained in his remarks on the intrinsic goodness of a good will. This thought requires a few words of explanation. Kant has spoken thus far of the morality of acts and wherein it resides. He has, also, restated the same notion in terms of *ought* and *ought not*. But, he is quite aware, there is no such thing as an act apart from someone who does the act. We may analyze and define the morality of an act, but we must end by addressing our remarks, not to acts, but to persons who act. There can be right acts only insofar as persons act rightly; hence the need to restate the matter in terms of will or intention. Every moralist, no matter what his principle of morality, is brought around at last to this point; hence Kant's genuine concern over a good will, i.e., a will inspired and controlled by the principle he has defined.

Nothing can be called *good*, without qualifications, except a good will. We now proceed to examine what exactly constitutes that will, simply good in itself, on which moral goodness depends.

Intelligence, wit, judgment, courage, resolution, perseverance, and so on, are no doubt good and desirable in many respects. But these gifts of nature may also be bad and mischievous if the will which is to make use of them is not good.

It is the same with gifts of fortune. Power, riches, honor, even health and happiness, inspire pride and often presumption if there is not a good will to check their influence.

A good will is good, not because of what it performs or accomplishes, not because of its usefulness or fruitfulness, but is simply good in itself. Even if it should happen that, owing to a special disfavor of fortune or the niggardly provision of a stepmotherly nature, a good will should wholly lack power to achieve its purpose, should by its greatest efforts achieve nothing, yet, like a jewel it would shine by its own light as a thing which has its whole value in itself.

We have, then, to develop the notion of a will good in itself and without reference to anything further. This notion already exists in the sound natural understanding, and requires rather to be clarified than taught or proved. In order to define more closely the notion of a good will, we will consider the wider notion of duty which includes the notion of a good will.

To have moral worth an act must be done from a sense of duty alone. We must distinguish between acts which accord with what duty requires, and acts done because duty requires. The latter alone have moral worth. We must distinguish between doing what duty requires, and doing because duty requires. Only the latter possesses moral worth.

If I do a thing because it is commanded, or because it brings advantage, my action is not moral. But if I do a thing because it is absolutely right in itself, my disposition is a moral one. We ought to do a thing, not because God wills it, but because it is righteous and good in itself.

Thus, it is a matter of duty that a dealer should not overcharge an inexperienced customer. Refraining from so doing for any other motive than that duty requires it, has no moral worth. It is one's duty to maintain life and happiness. Doing so for any other reason than that duty requires it, has no moral worth. It is one's duty to be generous, kind, honest, and so on. Being so for any reason except that duty requires it, has no moral worth. An action done from a sense of duty must wholly exclude the influence of inclination. An action, to be wholly moral, must exclude wholly the influence of inclination.

Take for instance a man who pays his debts. He may be swayed by the fear of being punished if he defaults, or he may pay because it is right that he should. In the first case his conduct is legally right, but it is only in the latter case that it is morally right.

It is a very beautiful thing to do good to men out of love for them or to be just from love of order. But this is not the true moral principle, suitable to our position among rational beings as men. To pretend it were, would be to set ourselves, with fanciful pride, above the thought of duty, like volunteers independent of command;

to want to do, of our own pleasure, what we think we need no command to do.

An action done from a sense of duty derives its moral worth, not from the purpose which is to be attained by it, but from the principle upon which it is done. . . . The moral worth of an action does not lie in the results expected from it, but from the principle which it embodies.

What sort of principle, or moral law, can that be, the conception of which must determine the will, without regard to expected consequences, in order that the will may be called *good* absolutely and without qualifications?

It is this: "So act that the principle of your action might become a universal law." Canst thou will that the principle of thy action should become a universal law? If not, then it must be rejected.

Kant has now declared himself on the fundamental problem of moral philosophy. One other large problem remains. It grows out of his remarks on the nature and importance of a good will. A *good* will may be defined, after Kant, as a will to do what ought to be done. Here the crucial term is *ought*. And it is crucial because it implies that the will in question is a free will. There would be no point to the remark that a man ought to do so-and-so if, as a matter of fact, he has no free will. Furthermore, we hold a man responsible for his action, but only on the hypothesis that his action expresses his free will in the matter. The moralist in all of us is brought up short by any denial of man's free will. Such a denial would deprive our everyday ethical language of all meaning. If you doubt this, try some time to be a moralist about your own or other people's conduct, and resolutely refrain from using such words as *ought*, *ought not*, *obligation*, *responsible*, *accountable*, *answerable*, *deserved*, *undeserved*, etc. I know of no experiment better calculated to give point to Kant's far-reaching concern over the question of man's free will.

Without freedom of the will, no moral law and no moral responsibility are possible.

A man commits a theft. By the physical law of causality this deed is a necessary result of the causes preceding it in time; it was impossible that it could not have happened. How then can the moral judgment make any difference, and suppose it could have been omitted? The moral judgment says it ought to have been omitted. How can this be? How can a man be called free, at the same moment and with respect to the same act in which he is subject to an inevitable physical necessity?

Actions which are not free, and do not involve one's personality, do not give rise to obligations. Thus no man can be placed under an obligation to give up swallowing for the very reason that it would not be within his powers. Obligation, therefore, presupposes the use of freedom.

That is the difficulty. No free will, no morality. This dilemma cannot be stated too starkly. It is as unblinkable as "no eyes, no vision," or "no light, no vision." Deny freedom of will, and at one stroke you annihilate morality, and I do not mean that by denying freedom of will you "discourage" people, so that they will "give up trying to do what is right." I mean that you make the term *morality* a meaningless term. So concerned was Kant over this matter that he spent some eleven years thinking out a theory of knowledge which would legitimate the notion of free will. In this sense his *Critique of Pure Reason* was thought out with an eye to the *Critique of Practical Reason* which followed it. In the very next sentence, we are back once more in the ideas of the first *Critique:*

If we take things in time as things-in-themselves, as is commonly done, then it is impossible to reconcile the necessity of the causal relation with freedom. They are contradictory. From the former, it follows that every event, every action, is a necessary result of what existed in time preceding. So, since time past is no longer in my power, it would follow that every action I perform is the necessary result of causes which are not in my power. That is, it would follow that at the moment in which I act, I am never free.

Obligation expresses a sort of necessity which occurs nowhere else in nature except in man. It is impossible that anything in nature *ought to be* other than in fact it is. In truth, obligation, if one has before one's eyes only the succession in nature, has simply and solely no meaning. We can as little ask what ought to happen in nature as what attributes a circle ought to have.

If existence in time, that is, existence as phenomena, were the only kind we could ascribe to things-in-themselves, freedom would have to be rejected as a vain and impossible suggestion.

Consequently, if we would save freedom, no other way remains but to consider that the existence of a thing in time and therefore according to the law of physical necessity, is appearance only. Freedom we must attribute to the thing as a reality, as a thing-in-itself. This is inevitable, if we would retain both these contradictory conceptions of necessity and freedom. However, when we try to explain their combination in one and the same action, great difficulties present themselves.

Now, in order to remove the apparent contradition between freedom and mechanism in one and the same action, we must recall what was said in the *Critique of Pure Reason*, or what follows from what was said there. It was said there that the necessity of nature — which cannot coexist with the freedom of the will — pertains only to things as phenomena. The category of causation, it was argued, extends to phenomena or appearances only. The possibility of freedom was thus left open, although its reality was not thereby proved.

Kant's words are important. He says, "The possibility of freedom was thus left open." That is all the help he claims from his theory of knowledge. It is sufficient, however. As his discourse shows, he proposes to use the undeniable *ought*. That we ought to do some things and ought not to do others is a point upon which all moralists would agree. They might differ as to what we ought or ought not to do That is a mere detail. The essential point is that they would all use the notions of "oughtness" and "ought-notness." It is necessary to give Kant credit here for proposing to cut a Gordian knot which no person dare leave tied. Picking up the argument where we broke in, the only point is to change this "may be free," which Kant's theory of knowledge permits, into an "is free" which his moral insight demands.

The only point is to change this "may be free" into "is free." That is, to show, in an actual case, that certain actions do imply freedom. Now, it is a duty to realize the moral law in our acts. Therefore it must be possible. ("I ought" implies "I can.") Therefore every rational being must assume whatever is implied by this possibility. Freedom of the will, independence of causal necessity, is implied by this possibility. The assumption is as necessary as the moral law, in connection with which alone it is valid.

Freedom and duty reciprocally imply each other. It is the moral law, of which we become directly conscious, that leads directly to the conception of freedom. It is morality that first discovers to us the notion of freedom. The moral law — "I ought" — which itself does not require any proof, proves the actuality of freedom in those who recognize it as binding on themselves. A man judges he can do, or refrain from doing, a certain act because he is conscious that he ought to. No one would ever have been so rash as to introduce freedom into science had not the moral law forced it upon us.

Morality requires us only to be able to think freedom without self-contradiction, not to understand it. It is enough that our notion of the act as free puts no obstacle in the way of the notion of it as mechanically necessary. Our notion is that the act stands in quite a different relation to freedom from that in which it stands to the mechanism of nature. From the point of view of my *Critique of Pure Reason* this is possible; the doctrine of nature and necessity and the doctrine of morality and freedom may each be true in its own sphere.

How freedom of the will is possible, how we are to conceive it theoretically and positively, how man is a member of two worlds, how man's moral actions must always appear necessitated while they are nonetheless free — all this is not discoverable. Only that there is such a freedom, is postulated by the moral law. How free-dom is possible no human intelligence will ever fully fathom. That freedom is possible, on the other hand, no sophistry will ever wrest from the conviction of even the commonest man.

It will be said that the solution here proposed to the problem of freedom involves great difficulty. But is any other solution easier and more intelligible?

Thus far one is inclined to let Kant have things pretty much his own way. Grant him his initial hypothesis of a rational morality, and it is difficult to challenge his argument. He gives a clarifying and convincing presentation of what is implied in this conception, but he was not satisfied to be simply a moralist; he must also say his word as a theologian. In this sense he might have anticipated the cry of Goethe's *Faust*, "*Zwei Seelen wohnen ach in meiner Brüst.*" His transition from moral philosophy to theology comes about in connection with his doctrine of the postulates of morality. One of these postulates we have already seen, namely, free will. But there are two more to come, namely, immortality and God. It is perhaps as well to let Kant tell his own story. First, immortality:

The immortality of the soul is also a postulate of the moral law. By a *postulate* I mean a theoretical proposition, not demonstrable as such, but which is an inseparable result of an unconditional, *a priori*, practical (i.e., moral) law.

The connection is this. The moral law commands the perfect accordance of the will with it. This must be possible, since it is commanded. But perfect accordance of the will with the moral law is a perfection of which no rational being of the sensible world is capable at any moment of his existence. Since, nevertheless, it is commanded, it can only be realized in an infinite progression toward that perfect accordance. Now, this endless progress is only possible on the supposition of an endless duration of the exis-tence and personality of the same rational being. This is called the *immortality of the soul*. The highest good for man, the perfect accord of his will with the moral law, is only possible on the supposition of the immortality of the soul. Consequently, this immortality, being inseparably connected with the moral law, is a postulate of pure practical reason.

For a rational but finite being, the only thing possible is an endless progress from the lower to higher degrees of perfection. . . . And thus he may hope, not indeed here nor at any imaginable point of his future existence, but only in the endlessness of his duration, to be perfectly adequate in his will.

This principle of the moral destination of our nature, namely, that it is only in an endless progress that we can attain perfect accordance with the moral law, is of the greatest use, not merely for supplementing the impotence of speculative reason, but also with respect to religion.

It is interesting to note that Kant has here reversed the usual order of things. Paley, it will be recalled, deduced morality from theology. Kant is deducing theology from morality. Some amends, one must suppose, were required in order to square accounts: From his theory of knowledge he had deduced an agnosticism with respect to speculative theology; in his analysis of the conception of a rational morality he had demonstrated its independence of theology. The argument continues:

The existence of God is also a postulate of the moral law. We proceed to exhibit this connection in a convincing manner.

Happiness is the condition of a rational being in the world with whom everything goes according to his wish and will. It rests, thus, on the harmony of physical nature with his ends and purposes. But the rational being in the world is not the cause of the world and of physical nature. There is, therefore, not the least ground in the moral law for any necessary connection between morality (i.e., virtue) and proportionate happiness.

To repeat: In a being that belongs to the world as part of it, is therefore dependent on it, and for that reason cannot by his will be a cause of nature nor by his own power make it completely har-

monize, as far as his happiness is concerned, with his practical (i.e.,
moral) principles, in such a being there is not the least ground for
any connection between morality and proportionate happiness.

Therefore, the _summum bonum, the union of virtue and happiness_,
is possible in the world only on the supposition of a Supreme Being
having a causality corresponding to moral character.

Accordingly, the existence of a cause of nature, distinct from nature itself, and containing the principle of this connection, this
exact harmony of happiness with morality, is postulated.

Now, a being that is capable of acting on the conception of laws
is an intelligence, and the causality of such a being according to
this conception of laws, is his will. Therefore, the supreme cause
of nature, which must be presupposed as a condition of the _summum
bonum_ (the union of virtue and happiness) is a being who is the cause
of nature by intelligence and will, that is, its author; that is, God.

Now, in as much as it is a duty for us to promote the _summum
bonum_, it is not merely allowable but a duty to presuppose the possibility of this _summum bonum_. And so, as this is possible only on
condition of the existence of God, it is morally necessary, it is a
matter of duty, to assume the existence of God.

These postulates of immortality, freedom, and the existence of
God, all proceed from the principle of morality which is itself not a
postulate but a law, an imperative. . . . These postulates are not
theoretical dogmas, but suppositions practically necessary, i.e., required in the interests of practice. While they do not extend our
speculative knowledge, they do give objective reality to the ideas
of speculative reason in general, do give it a right to conceptions
the possibility of which it could not otherwise venture to affirm. . . .
Thus respect for the moral law leads, through these postulates, to
conceptions which speculation might indeed present as problems
but could never solve.

By way of conclusion it might be well to repeat the main
turns of Kant's argument. He begins by assuming that a
rational morality is the only morality. He shows that this
means categorical and _a priori_. This enables him to eliminate
three misleading conceptions — that it is a matter of feelings,

that it is a matter of consequences, that it is a matter of agreeing with God's will, since on these counts it would be neither categorical nor *a priori*. He returns again to the conception of rational morality as categorical and *a priori*, and formulates its principle. This central thesis he then works over in terms of the notion of *ought* or *duty*, and in terms of the *good will*. These considerations raise the problem of free will. He sharpens the point of this problem. He then reaches back into his theory of knowledge for justification of the claim that free will "may be so." He returns, finally, to the conception of morality as necessitating free will as a postulate. There his moral philosophy proper stops, and his theology begins. Kant's moral philosophy, I think, contains some of the soundest and most clarifying analyses to be found anywhere in the history of human thought.

It is customary, among historians of these matters, to distinguish between the morality of principles and the morality of consequences. This distinction cannot be pressed very far, but it serves to set Kant off from those who attempt to determine the morality of actions in terms of the consequences which follow from those actions. Of moralists who have developed the latter approach, one stands out pre-eminent among the rest, and forms an instructive contrast to Immanuel Kant. I mean John Stuart Mill, who is the subject of the next chapter.

READING REFERENCES. The references given under the Kant section, in the third topic, are valuable here also. A few titles are here added which have special reference to Kant as a moralist, e.g., J. W. Scott's *Kant on the Moral Life;* A. K. Rogers' *Morals in Review*, chapter on Kant; discussion of Kant in Paulsen's *System of Ethics;* discussion of Kant in Rashdall's *Theory of Good and Evil.*

READING QUESTIONS

1. Distinguish Kant's use of *a priori* in epistemology and in ethics.
2. To what did he ascribe the *a priori* element in knowledge?
3. To what, by parity of reasoning, might he ascribe the *a priori* element in morality?
4. What is his criticism of the claim that the morality of an act resides in one's feelings about the act?
5. Show how his claim regarding the *a priori* nature of morality is the basis of this criticism; and of the next two, as you come to them.
6. What criticisms would Kant have directed at Paley?
7. Wherein does Kant find "the essence of morality"?
8. What illustrations does he offer of his general idea?
9. What is his distinction between hypothetical and categorical imperatives?
10. "There is but one categorical imperative." Namely?
11. "Two things fill the mind with ever new and increasing admiration and awe." Namely?
12. Distinguish "what duty requires" and "because duty requires."
13. "We have to develop the notion of a will good in itself." Develop it.
14. How does Kant define a *moral* act?
15. A will is good if it is motivated by what principle?
16. "Without freedom of will no moral law and no moral responsibility are possible." Elucidate.
17. How does Kant use his theory of knowledge in this connection?
18. "To change this 'may be free' into 'is free.'" Explain.
19. What does he mean when he describes freedom as a postulate of morality?
20. What is Kant's argument for immortality?
21. For the existence of God?
22. "Kant reversed the usual relation between morality and religion." Elucidate.
23. Indicate the relation between the *Critique of Pure Reason* and the *Critique of Practical Reason*.

3. *MORALITY GROUNDED IN HAPPINESS — FROM JOHN STUART MILL*

FROM KANT TO MILL.   Our subject is still the principle of morality.   Our quest began with Paley's attempt to ground morality in theology.   Paley, we found, distinguished between right and wrong by reference to God's will; that is right which agrees, and wrong which disagrees with God's will.   He supplemented this principle by another, designed to help out when God's will was not known.   This principle was that *right* means "producing human happiness," and *wrong* means "producing human unhappiness."   Difficulties latent in Paley's position were noted and need not be repeated here.   In Kant's attempt to argue that morality is categorical, that it is not grounded in anything, but "stands on its own feet," we met a complete antithesis to the position represented by Paley.   Kant's effort to disengage morality from theology, as well as from happiness, repudiating both terms of Paley's argument, stands alone.   The trend of moral philosophizing has been for the most part away from Kant. In J. S. Mill one meets a moralist who is prepared to argue in support of the latter half of Paley's position: that an act is right if, and only if, it produces more happiness than any other act possible under the circumstances.

BIOGRAPHICAL NOTE.   John Stuart Mill was born in England in 1806 and died in 1873 at the age of sixty-seven.   He was educated privately by his father.   He grew up in the group which included Jeremy Bentham, James Mill (father of J. S.), T. R. Malthus, David Ricardo, George Grote, and others.   These men were interested primarily in political, economic, and social reform.   They were the driving force behind the first Reform Bill, the early Factory Acts, and so on. They were known, in their own day, as the Utilitarians and as the Philosophical Radicals.   Each term tells their story. They were utilitarians because they enquired of any law, custom, or institution, "What is its utility?   Of what use is it?"

If no answer were forthcoming, beyond some vague statement about its prestige or its long standing, they proposed to
scrap it. They were philosophical radicals because they
aimed to go to the roots of things, the word *root* being English
for the Latin word *radix*. The root to which these men proposed to go was human happiness. That, for them, was the
"root question" to be addressed to any law, custom, or institution. For the most part they did not spend time seeking to
justify this principle. This task J. S. Mill undertook to do.
They applied the principle that *right* means "producing human
happiness." He undertook to clarify and defend the principle, undertook, that is, a philosophical exposition of the
principle. Most of his other writings stem from the celebrated little book in which this defense is set forth. Thus, in
his *Essay on Liberty*, written a few years before his *Utilitarianism*, but based on the principles subsequently given in the
later book, he argued that the greatest happiness of the
greatest number is more likely to be achieved by allowing as
much freedom of thought and action as possible. In his
treatise, *Considerations on Representative Government*, he argued
that government by elected representatives would offer a
better guarantee of human happiness than government by
monarchs or aristocrats. In his monograph *On the Subjection
of Women* he argued that the purpose of representative government was, in part, frustrated by refusing votes to women.
The range and sincerity of his writings have combined to
make him one of the greatest single influences throughout
the past hundred years. The heart of his work is contained
in his statement of the case for human happiness as the ultimate test of right and wrong. For other biogra phical notes,
see page 58.

THE ARGUMENT OF THE CITATIONS. Mill's exposition and
defense of the appeal to happiness as the basis of morality
moves through five turns. He first states the problem:

What is the basis or principle of morality?   He then explores
two "false leads," and shows grounds for rejecting them.
He then states his own position at some length.   He then
asks the question: Is this belief open to any kind of proof or
disproof? and answers as best he can.   He turns then to review
a long series of objections and misunderstandings which, he
knows, will be brought against his claim.   These he seeks to
answer, one by one.   With this accomplished, he is in a position to say, "I have posed an age-long problem.   I have criticized two widely held theories.   I have advanced my own
answer.   I have shown what sort of proof it is amenable to.
I have stated and removed as many objections as I can think
of.   The defense rests."

The *Utilitarianism* begins as follows:

There are few circumstances more significant of the backward
state of speculation than the little progress which has been made in
the controversy respecting the criterion of right and wrong.

From the dawn of philosophy the question concerning the foundation of morality has been accounted the main problem in speculative
thought, has occupied the most gifted intellects, and divided them
into sects and schools carrying on a vigorous warfare against one
another.

After more than two thousand years the same discussions continue.
Philosophers are still ranged under the same contending banners.
Neither thinkers nor mankind at large seem nearer to agreement
than when the youthful Socrates listened to the old Protagoras.

The problem is now before us: What is the foundation of
morality?   He proposes to examine two familiar answers.
The first of these is the observation that this is a matter of
personal opinion.   Thus one reads the remarks, "There's
nothing right or wrong, but thinking makes it so."   "Right
you are, if you think you are."   That is, an act is right if you,
or the community, or all mankind, think it is; right and
wrong are mere matters of opinion, are merely subjective.

There are many different ways of stating this notion. Of all moralists, who hold this view Mill says:

> They all, in one phrase or another, place the test of right and wrong in a feeling of approval or disapproval . . . they find certain feelings of approval and disapproval in themselves . . . a great part of all the ethical reasoning in books and in the world is of this sort.

His criticism of this appeal to moral feeling to settle the matter is short and pointed:

> All experience shows that "moral feelings" are eminently artificial, and the product of culture; that the most senseless and pernicious "feelings" can be raised to the utmost intensity by inculcation, as hemlock and thistles could be reared to luxuriant growth by sowing them instead of wheat.
>
> Things which have been really believed by all mankind have been proved to be false, as that the sun rises and sets. Can immunity for similar error be claimed for the "moral feelings"?
>
> I do not found the morality of actions upon anybody's opinion or feeling of them. I found it upon facts.

What facts, we ask. Wait a moment, is the answer, till I glance at another doctrine. This time it is the appeal to nature. A thing is right, it will be said, if it is according to nature, if it is natural; wrong, if it is contrary to nature, if it is unnatural.

> We will inquire into the truth of the doctrines which make nature a test of right and wrong, good and evil, or which in any mode or degree attach merit or approval to following, imitating, or obeying nature. A reference to that supposed standard is the predominant ingredient in the vein of thought and feeling which was opened by Rousseau, and which has infiltrated itself most widely into the modern mind.
>
> That any mode of thinking, feeling, or acting is "according to nature" is usually accepted as a strong argument for its goodness. If it can be said, with any plausibility, that "nature enjoins" any-

thing, the propriety of obeying the injunction is considered to be made out.   And, conversely, the imputation of being "contrary to nature" is thought to bar the thing so designated from being tolerated or excused.   It is thought that nature affords some criterion of what we ought to do.

Mill's handling of the appeal to nature is a masterpiece of condensed refutation.   He first points out that the term *nature*, or *according to nature*, is ambiguous.   He states the two senses in which it might be used.   He then shows that, given the first sense, the appeal to nature is meaningless; and, given the second sense, it is irrational and immoral.

The word *nature* has two principal meanings: it either denotes the entire system of things, with the aggregate of all their properties, or it denotes things as they would be, apart from human intervention.

Such being the two principal senses of the word *nature*, in which of these is it taken when the word and its derivatives are used to convey ideas of commendation, approval, and even moral obligation?

In the first of these senses, the doctrine that man ought to follow nature is unmeaning, since man has no power to do anything else than follow nature; all his actions are done through, and in obedience to, some one or many of nature's physical or mental laws.

In the other sense of the term, the doctrine that man ought to follow nature, or in other words, ought to make the spontaneous course of things the model of his voluntary actions, is equally irrational and immoral.

Irrational, because all human action whatever, consists in altering, and all useful action in improving the spontaneous course of nature. Immoral, because the course of natural phenomena being replete with everything which when committed by human beings is most worthy of abhorrence, any one who endeavored in his actions to imitate the natural course of things would be universally seen and acknowledged to be the wickedest of men.

The doctrine that the existing order of things is the natural order, and that, being natural, all innovation upon it is criminal, is vicious.

Conformity to nature has no connection whatever with right and wrong. The idea can never be fitly introduced into ethical discussions at all. That a thing is unnatural is no argument for it being blamable.

At this point we may cite Mill's own position. We have now two alternatives with which to compare it. He says:

All action is for the sake of some end, and rules of action must take their whole character and color from the end to which they are subservient.

The creed which accepts the greatest happiness principle as the foundation of morals holds that actions are right in proportion as they tend to promote happiness, wrong as they tend to produce the reverse of happiness. By happiness is intended pleasure, and the absence of pain; by unhappiness, pain, and the privation of pleasure. This theory I propose to expound and defend.

The standard is not the agent's own greatest happiness, but the greatest amount of happiness altogether. As between his own happiness and that of others, utilitarianism requires him to be as strictly impartial as a disinterested and benevolent spectator.

The test of morality is not the greatest happiness of the agent himself. Utilitarianism does not dream of defining morality to be the self-interest of the agent. The greatest happiness principle is the greatest happiness of mankind and of all sentient creatures.

He who does anything for any other purpose than to increase the amount of happiness in the world is no more deserving of admiration than the ascetic mounted on his pillar. He may be an inspiring proof of what men can do, but assuredly not an example of what they should do.

Pleasure and freedom from pain are the only things desirable as ends, and all desirable things are desirable either for the pleasure inherent in them or as means to the promotion of pleasure and the prevention of pain.

Mill has stated that morality is a matter of consequences. An act is right or wrong, according to its consequences, not because it agrees with someone's opinion, or with universal

opinion, or with nature, or (by implication) with God's will.
He pauses a moment to elaborate this point:

By "calculating the consequences" is meant, generally, calculating
the consequences of classes of actions. There are, as we shall note,
exceptions to this, but over all we must look at actions as though
multiplied, and in large masses. Take murder for example. There
are many persons, to kill whom would be to remove men who are a
cause of no good to any human being, who are a cause of cruel
physical and moral suffering to several, and whose whole influence
tends to increase the mass of unhappiness and vice. Were such a
man to be murdered, the balance of traceable consequences would be
greatly in favor of the act. But, the counter consideration, still
on the principle of utility, is that unless persons were punished for
killing, and taught not to kill, nobody's life would be safe.

We say, "generally," not "universally." For the admission of
exceptions to rules is a necessity equally felt in all systems of morality. To take an obvious instance: The rule against homicide,
the rule against deceiving, the rule against taking advantage of
superior strength, are suspended against enemies in the field and
partially against malefactors in private life. In each case, the rule
is suspended as far as is required by the peculiar nature of the case.
That the moralities arising from special circumstances of the action
may be so important as to over-rule those arising from the class of
acts to which it belongs, is a liability common to all ethical systems.
The existence of exceptions to moral rules is no stumbling block
peculiar to the principle of utility. The essential is that the exception should itself be a general rule; so that, being definite, and not
left to the partial judgment of the individual, it might not shake
the stability of the wider rule in the cases to which the reason of the
exception does not extend. This is an ample foundation for "the
construction of a scheme of morality."

With respect to the means of inducing people to conform in their
actions to the scheme so formed, the utilitarian system depends,
like all other schemes of morality, on the external motives supplied
by law and opinion and the internal motives produced by education
or reason.

The greatest happiness principle is now before us. Two things remain. The first is the question of whether the principle is open to any kind of proof. Mill's answer to this question should be carefully considered. It amounts to a denial that any such principle can be proved. The rationale of this denial is as follows:

Of what sort of proof is this principle of the greatest happiness susceptible?

It is evident that it cannot be proof in the ordinary and popular meaning of the term. Questions of ultimate ends are not amenable to direct proof. Whatever can be proved to be good must be shown to be a means to something admitted to be good without proof.

The medical art is proved to be good by its conducing to health. But how is it possible to prove that health is good? The art of music is good, for the reason among others, that it produces pleasure. But what proof is it possible to give that pleasure is good?

No comprehensive formula, including all things good in themselves and not as means to things good in themselves, is a subject of what is commonly meant by *proof*. It may be accepted or rejected, but not proved in the usual sense of that term.

There is a larger meaning of the word *proof* in which this question of ultimate principles is as amenable to proof as any other of the disputed questions of philosophy. The subject is within the cognizance of the rational faculty. Its acceptance or rejection does not depend on blind impulse or arbitrary choice.

The problem has been stated. False solutions have been exposed. His own solution has been given. The meaning of *proof* in these matters has been made clear. He turns to that inevitable job — seeking to formulate objections that may be raised. A careful study of these objections and replies will do a great deal to clarify and fix the doctrine in one's mind.

It may not be superfluous to notice a few of the common misapprehensions of utilitarian ethics, even those which are so obvious and

gross that it might appear impossible for any person of candor and *objections*
intelligence to fall into them.

The first objection is that such a moral philosophy is a
godless doctrine:

Utilitarianism is a godless doctrine: The appeal to happiness,
instead of the appeal to the will of God, is a godless, i.e., irreligious,
principle of morality.

Mill's answer is to carry the war into the enemy's camp:

The question [whether the appeal to happiness is a godless ethic]
depends upon what idea we have formed of the moral character of
the Deity.   If it be a true belief that God desires above all things the
happiness of His creatures, and that this was His purpose in their
creation, then utilitarianism is not only not a godless doctrine, but
more profoundly religious than any other.

Although the existence of God as a wise and just lawgiver is not
a necessary part of the feelings of morality, it may still be maintained
that those feelings make His existence eminently desirable.   No
doubt they do, and that is the great reason why we find that good
men and women cling to the belief and are pained by its being
questioned.

If the objection [that utilitarianism is a godless doctrine] means
that utilitarianism does not recognize the revealed will of God as
the supreme law of morals, I answer: An utilitarian who believes
in the perfect goodness and wisdom of God, necessarily believes that
whatever God has thought fit to reveal on the subject of morals must
fulfill the requirements of utilitarianism in a supreme degree.

A second objection:

To suppose that life has no higher end than pleasure, no better *2*
and nobler object of desire and pursuit, is utterly mean and groveling;
a doctrine worthy only of swine.

Mill's answer:

This supposes that human beings are capable of no pleasures
except those of which swine are capable.   If this supposition were

true, the charge could not be denied; but it would then be no charge, for if the sources of pleasure were precisely the same for human beings and for swine, then the rule of life which is good enough for the one would be good enough for the other.

The comparison is felt to be degrading precisely because a beast's pleasures do not satisfy a human being's conception of happiness. Human beings have faculties more elevated than the animal appetites, and do not regard anything as happiness which does not include their gratification.

A third objection:

Utilitarianism [the appeal to the pleasure-pain consequences of action] renders men cold and unsympathizing; that it chills their moral feelings toward individuals; that it makes them regard only the consequences of actions, not taking into account the personal qualities from which those actions emanate.

Mill's answer:

If this means that utilitarians do not allow their judgment concerning the rightness or wrongness of an act to be influenced by their opinion of the quality of the person who does it, then it is a complaint not against utilitarianism but against having any standard of morality at all. For certainly no known ethical standard decides an action to be good or bad because it is done by a good or bad man; still less because it is done by an amiable, brave, or benevolent man, or the contrary. These considerations are relevant, not to the estimation of actions, but of persons; and there is nothing in utilitarianism inconsistent with the fact that there are other things which interest us in persons besides the rightness or wrongness of their actions.

The stoic moralists, indeed, were fond of saying that he who has virtue has everything. But no claim of this description is made for the virtuous man by the utilitarian moralist. There are other desirable possessions and qualities besides virtue. A right action does not necessarily indicate a virtuous character. Actions that are blamable often proceed from qualities entitled to praise. When this is so in any particular case, it modifies one's moral estimation of the agent, but not of the act.

A fourth objection is that the morality of an action, depends upon the motive, not upon the consequences. Mill answers:

As to motive, the utilitarian position is this: Motive has nothing to do with the morality of the action, though much with the worth of the agent. He who saves a fellow creature from drowning does what is morally right, whether his motive be duty or the hope of being paid for his trouble.

A fifth objection:

A stock argument against utilitarianism consists in saying that an utilitarian will be apt to make his own particular case an exception to moral rules, and when under temptation, will see an utility in the breach of a rule, greater than he will see in its observance.

Mill's answer:

But is utilitarianism the only creed which is able to furnish us with excuses for evil doing and means of cheating our own conscience? They are afforded in abundance by all doctrines which recognize as a fact in morals the existence of conflicting considerations; which all doctrines do that have been believed by sane persons.

It is not the fault of any creed, but of the complicated nature of human affairs, that rules of conduct cannot be so framed as to require no exceptions, and that hardly any kind of action can safely be laid down as either always obligatory or always condemnable.

There is no ethical creed which does not temper its laws by giving a certain latitude, under the moral responsibility of the agent, for accommodation to peculiarities of circumstances. At the opening thus made, self-deception and dishonest casuistry get in.

There exists no moral system under which cases of conflicting obligation do not arise. These are the real difficulties, the knotty points, both in a theory of ethics and in the conscientious guidance of personal conduct. But is any one less qualified to deal with cases of conflicting obligations by reason of the fact that he possesses an ultimate standard to which such cases can be referred?

A sixth objection:

Utilitarianism is only an appeal to expedience, and an appeal to expedience is not as high morally as an appeal to principle.

Mill's answer:

This objection rests on a loose use of the term *expedience*. Generally, the *expedient* means that which is expedient for the particular interests of the agent himself; as when a minister of state sacrifices the interests of his country to keep himself in place. The expedient in this sense is a branch of the hurtful; and to claim that utilitarianism is an appeal to the expedient, in this sense, is simply to misunderstand or misrepresent its meaning.

Utilitarianism does recognize in human beings the power of sacrificing their own greatest good for the good of others. I must repeat again, what critics seldom have the justice to acknowledge, that the happiness which forms the standard of what is right in conduct, is not the agent's own happiness but the happiness of all concerned.

Utilitarianism does, however, refuse to admit that sacrifice of one's own good is itself a good. A sacrifice which does not increase the sum of happiness is wasted. The only sacrifice which utilitarianism applauds is that which is made in the interests of the happiness either of mankind or of individuals within the limits imposed by the interests of mankind.

A seventh objection:

Happiness cannot be the rational purpose of life, because it is unattainable.

Mill's answer:

This objection, were it well founded, would go to the root of the matter; for if no happiness is to be had at all by human beings, the attainment of it cannot be the end of morality. However, the assertion that it is impossible that human life be happy is an exaggeration.

If by *happiness* be meant a continuity of highly pleasurable excitement, it is evident that this is impossible.   A state of exalted pleasure lasts only for a few moments, or in some cases for somewhat longer periods.   If this kind of intense rapture be meant by *happiness*, then happiness is unattainable.

But this is not what philosophers have meant by *happiness* when they taught that happiness was the end of life.   The happiness which they meant was not a life of rapture, but moments of such in an existence made up of few and transitory pains, many and various pleasures, with a decided predominance of the active over the passive, and having as the foundation not to expect more from life than it is capable of bestowing.   A life thus composed, to those who have been fortunate enough to obtain it, has always appeared worthy of the name of happiness.   And such an existence is even now the lot of many.

An eighth objection:

We cannot calculate all the consequences of any action and thus cannot estimate the degree in which it promotes human happiness.

Mill's answer:

Is there any department of human affairs in which we can do all that is desirable?   Because we cannot foresee everything, is there no such thing as foresight?   Can no estimate be formed of consequences, which would be any guide for our conduct, unless we can calculate all consequences?   Because we cannot predict every effect which may follow from a person's death, are we to say that we cannot know that murder would be destructive to human happiness?   Whether morality is or is not a question of consequences, it cannot be denied that prudence is a question of consequences, and if there is such a thing as prudence, it is because the consequences of actions can be calculated.

A ninth objection:

There is not time, previous to action, for calculating and weighing the effects of any line of conduct on the general happiness.

Mill's answer:

This is exactly as if any one were to say that it is impossible to guide our conduct by Christianity, because there is not time, on every occasion on which everything has to be done, to read through the Old and New Testaments.

The answer to the objection is that there has been ample time, namely, the whole past duration of the human species. During all that time mankind have been learning by experience the tendencies of actions; on which experience all the prudence, as well as all the morality, of life is dependent.

Nobody argues that the art of navigation is not founded on astronomy, because sailors cannot wait to calculate the nautical almanac. Being rational creatures, they go to sea with it ready calculated, and all rational creatures go out upon the sea of life with their minds made up on the common questions of right and wrong.

There is no difficulty in proving any ethical standard whatever to work ill, if we suppose universal idiocy to be conjoined with it, but on any hypothesis short of that, mankind must by this time have acquired positive beliefs as to the effects of some actions on their happiness. To inform a traveler respecting the place of his ultimate destination is not to forbid the use of landmarks and direction posts on the way.

A tenth objection:

If happiness is made the ultimate standard by which other things are judged to be good or bad, then we are not in a position to distinguish among kinds of happiness with respect to their goodness or badness.

Mill's answer:

It is quite compatible with the principle of utility to recognize the fact that some kinds of pleasure are more desirable and more valuable than others. It would be absurd that while, in estimating all other things, quality is considered as well as quantity, the estimation of pleasures should be supposed to depend on quantity alone.

Of two pleasures, if there be one to which all or almost all who have experience of both give a decided preference, irrespective of any feeling of moral obligation to prefer it, that is the more desirable pleasure.

Now it is an unquestionable fact that those who are equally acquainted with, and equally capable of appreciating and enjoying, both, do give a most marked preference to the manner of existence which employs their higher faculties. It is better to be a human being dissatisfied than a pig satisfied; better to be Socrates dissatisfied than a fool satisfied. And if the fool, or the pig, is of a different opinion, it is because they only know their side of the question. The other party to the comparison knows both sides.

Few human creatures would consent to be changed into any of the lower animals for a promise of the fullest allowance of an animal's pleasures. No intelligent human being would consent to be a fool, no instructed person would consent to be an ignoramus, no person of feeling and conscience would consent to be selfish and base, even though they should be persuaded that the fool, the dunce or the rascal is better satisfied with his lot than they are with theirs.

From this verdict of the only competent judges, I apprehend there can be no appeal. On the question of which of two pleasures is the best worth having, which of two modes of existence is the most grateful to the feelings, the judgment of those who are qualified by knowledge of both must be admitted as final. . . . There is no other tribunal to be referred to.

READING REFERENCES. It is not easy to find a sympathetic account of Mill as a moralist. In a little book by George Santayana, *Some Turns of Thought in Modern Philosophy*, there is a passage, beginning on page 55, "With this dissolution always in prospect . . .," which is an exception to this rule. The trouble arose, even in Mill's own day, over his somewhat unsatisfactory handling of the tenth objection: The appeal *to* happiness does not permit criticism *of* happiness. Nor does it. In F. H. Bradley's *Ethical Studies*, chapter 3, "Pleasure for Pleasure's Sake" will be found a severely critical examination of Mill's argument. Mill's *Autobiography* is splendid reading. It gives one a picture of the man who made a bold stand for happiness in moral philosophy. There is no really first-class book on Mill. The nearest approaches are Courtney's *Life of Mill* and the third volume of Stephen's *English Utilitarians*. The subsequent elaboration and defense and modification of Mill's position is to be traced in Henry Sidgwick's *Method of Ethics* and G. E. Moore's *Principia Ethica*.

READING QUESTIONS

1. What connection exists between Paley and Mill?
2. Who were the Utilitarians? By what other name were they known? What do these names signify?
3. What is Mill's criticism of the appeal to "feeling"?
4. "The appeal to nature is unmeaning in one sense of the term *nature*." What sense? Wherein unmeaning?
5. " . . . or irrational and immoral, in the other sense." Explain.
6. What principle does Mill formulate?
7. Whose happiness is not referred to in the principle?
8. What about "exceptions"? Exceptions to what?
9. "Of what sort of proof is this principle susceptible?"
10. "Such a philosophy is a godless doctrine." Wherein? Mill's answer?
11. "It is a doctrine worthy of swine." How so? Mill's answer?
12. "Such a doctrine renders men cold and unsympathizing." Mill's answer?
13. How does Mill deal with the question of motive?
14. "The principle of utility may serve as a cloak for selfishness." Mill's answer?
15. "An appeal to expedience is not as high morally as an appeal to principle." What does that statement mean? How does Mill deal with it?
16. "Happiness cannot be the rational purpose of life." Why not? Mill's answer?
17. "We cannot calculate all the consequences." Mill's answer?

18. "There is not time, previous to action, for calculating the effects." Mill's answer?
19. Formulate the tenth objection carefully, in your own words.
20. What is Mill's answer?
21. Is it an answer?

4. MORALITY GROUNDED IN POWER — FROM FRIEDRICH NIETZSCHE

FROM MILL TO NIETZSCHE. We have examined three attempts to formulate the principle of morality. Paley found the rightness of an act to depend upon its agreement with the will of God. Kant denied that the rightness of an act depended upon anything, asserting that an act, if right, is so categorically, without reference to anything outside of itself. Mill found the rightness of an act to depend upon its consequences, these consequences being the amount of happiness which it brought about. We have now to examine the claim of a fourth moralist whose findings differ radically from any of the other three. The difference is so great that it is rather difficult to institute a comparison. The point may be approached in terms of an example. Consider honesty, the habit of telling the truth and being "square" in one's dealings. Let us suppose each of our moralists to be asked, "Why is it right to be honest and wrong to be dishonest?" "Because it agrees with God's will," Paley would say. "There is no reason why honesty is right," Kant would say, "It is right simply because it is right." "Because it makes for the greatest amount of happiness in the long run and for the most people," Mill would say. Now our fourth moralist would be inclined to answer the question by asking another: "Who said that honesty is right, and dishonesty wrong?" That is, he would ask whether the very wording of the question doesn't beg the question. You first accept certain things as right and wrong, he would argue, then you ask what principle is involved in thus distinguishing them. That is to beg the question. In other words, you can only ask this question by first assuming, without inquiry, that some things are right and others wrong, but if you query *that* fact, then where are you?

BIOGRAPHICAL NOTE. Friedrich Nietzsche was born in Germany in 1844 and died in 1900 at the age of fifty-six. His biography may be epitomized in terms of three periods: years of preparation, years of production, and years of insanity. (1) He was born into a puritanical, religious family and was intended by his parents to enter the church. To this end he was educated privately and at a denominational school. In the University at Bonn he broke completely with his family in matters doctrinal. He moved on to the University at Leipzig. There he met Wagner, the German composer, and became a fervent Wagnerite. He discovered Schopenhauer's writings in a second-hand bookshop and became a convinced Schopenhaurian. He met Erwin Rhode, the historian of Greek culture, and became engrossed in the problems and perspectives of the cultural history of mankind. He did military service for a year in a war with Austria, returning to the University at Leipzig to complete his studies. The following year he was appointed to the chair of classical philology in the university at Bâle, received his Ph.D., and began work on his important book, *The Birth of Tragedy*. The next year he was called once more into military service in the Franco-Prussian War which had just begun, 1870. He was head of an ambulance corps, but did only three weeks' service. Diphtheria ended his military career. He returned to the university at Bâle and resumed lectures. For eight years he remained at this work. During this period he was arriving at conclusions which formed the basis of his future writings. He published *The Birth of Tragedy*. It met with a chilly reception. His prestige began to decline. His next book, *Thoughts Out of Season*, contained four essays in which he criticized Strauss, Schopenhauer, German historians, and others. Two years later for reasons of poor health he retired on a small pension from the university.

(2) It should never be forgotten that Nietzsche was, first and last, a cultural historian; that is, he was interested in, and drew his inspiration from, the study of the cultures achieved by various peoples, ancient and modern. He wrote a series of books which develop really one theme. His investigations into mankind's cultural history, understanding by the term *culture* such things as art, religion, science, morality, government, etc., left him profoundly impressed, in the first place, by the enormous diversity which has obtained in these things at different times and places. But that was not all. He was equally impressed with the fact that cultural values are local and transitory affairs. He expressed this in the notion of the relativity of cultural values. By this he meant that cultural values are relative to time and place and relative to the needs peculiar to the peoples among whom they flourish. In other words, there is nothing eternal or absolute or immutable about them, and this, he felt, holds for values of all descriptions: religious, artistic, social, moral, scientific, and so on. On the rebound from his earlier orthodox training, he dismissed them with a flourish of his pen in his book, *Human, All Too Human*. That was his "great discovery." Values, one and all, are "human-all-too-human." The rest of his work may be described as a series of studies in the natural history of human values. *Human, All Too Human*, was followed by *Dawn of Day*, and it, in turn, by *Joyful Wisdom*. Clearly, a new note was being struck. What idea was Nietzsche working out in these books?

It was something like this: The cultural history of mankind shows that those aristocratic qualities flourish in the early stages of a culture and disappear gradually as that culture becomes old. In Homer's time, the Greeks were "heroes"; by the time of Pericles and the Spartan war, they had become mere "sophists" and "philosophers" and "scientists." In early Roman history there were great kings who founded a race which conquered the ancient world, but centuries later, in the days of imperial decline, this nation of "strong, silent men" had become helpless victims of their own weakening civilization and the new races of barbarians as yet "untouched" by such things. These newcomers swept over Europe, and another page in cultural history was begun, but with the same result. By the nineteenth century these "Germanic" peoples who had made over the civilization of ancient Rome had become democratic, even socialistic; they cultivated "science," "art," "morality" or (in some instances) decadent forms of "immorality," wealth, ease, the "emancipation of women," optimism, pessimism, philosophy, and so on.

There is no quarreling with Nietzsche's likes and dislikes in these matters. The sight of Achilles sulking in his tent was simply something he admired more than the sight of Karl Marx sulking in the library of the British Museum. A Greek athlete or a Roman warrior was simply not in the same degenerate class with J. S. Mill pleading for representative government and the political enfranchisement of women, or Schopenhauer brooding over the misery and folly of human affairs. Hence, the titles of his books. To "see through" modern degeneration was "the dawn of day"; to realize that "real virtues" belong in the context of fresh and vigorous young cultures was the first step in "joyful wisdom." Nietzsche was carried away on the wings of this sort of thing. Lonely, poor, sickly, unpopular, a bachelor *malgré lui*, he nevertheless lived on in the private world of "transvalued values," heaping scorn on "art" and "science" and "morality" and "religion" and "emancipation" and "democracy" and "socialism" and "humanitarianism." He poured his soul into the mold of one beautiful book, *Thus Spake Zara-*

thustra. This was the fine flower of his genius. Through the mouth of Zarathustra, the prophet of his doctrine, he preached and exhorted and satirized in pages of marvelous beauty and suggestiveness. But the nineteenth century passed Zarathustra by on the other side. Only a handful took the trouble to read him, and even these few were puzzled and disturbed. For their enlightenment, Nietzsche wrote two more books, *Beyond Good and Evil* and *The Genealogy of Morals.* They were intended as commentaries on the *Zarathustra.* The substance of their argument is given in the citations which follow. The balance of Nietzsche's writings carry further the ideas presented already. The Zarathustra group was followed by *The Twilight of the Idols, Antichrist, The Will to Power* (unfinished), and his own autobiography bearing the significant title *Ecce Homo.*

(3) In 1889, now forty-five, Nietzsche began to lose the use of his mind. For the next eleven years he was caught in the toils of a steadily increasing insanity. The picture brings to mind Schopenhauer's gloomy hypothesis and leaves one impatient with the century which had allowed the man's genius to flicker out alone and unheeded.

THE ARGUMENT OF THE CITATIONS. The following passages, chosen principally from Nietzsche's *Beyond Good and Evil* and *The Genealogy of Morals,* exhibit six turns of thought. He begins by repudiating the whole notion of trying to formulate any principle of morality, in the sense that moralists have traditionally sought to do this. He insists that there is no such thing as morality having one fundamental principle running through it; that, on the contrary, there have been and are many moralities; and that any attempt to think philosophically about morality must begin by recognizing its diversity and the fact of its having had a history like any other phase of human culture. He propounds then a tentative natural history or genealogy of morals. From this he undertakes to draw some far-reaching conclusions. These he calls collectively his *immoralism, or transvaluation of values*. One fundamental distinction, arising out of his account of the natural history of morals and forming the foundation of his immoralism, is that between master morality and slave morality. The characteristics of each he then describes at some length. The doctrine is now substantially complete. However, to illustrate it more concretely, he applies it in a critical way to two phenomena of modern morality, namely, the emancipation of woman, and the close connection between modern morality and Christianity. He closes with a few reflections on his own significance.

The opening citations are fundamental. In these Nietzsche draws the searching distinction between accepting morality and trying to formulate its principle, and making moralities the subject of impartial investigation. It is the historian of humanity's manifold cultures and cultural values who speaks:

Hitherto all moralists, with a pedantic and ridiculous seriousness, have wanted to give a "basis" to morality, and each has believed that he has given this "basis" to morality. Morality itself, however, has been regarded as something "given."

That which moralists have called "giving a basis to morality," has proved merely a learned form of good faith in prevailing morality, a new means of expressing prevailing morality, consequently just a phenomenon within one definite morality, a sort of denial that it is lawful for this particular morality to be called in question. In no case has the attempt to "provide a basis for morality" ever involved a testing, analyzing, doubting, and vivisecting of the prevailing moral faith.

The philosophical workers, after the pattern of Kant and Hegel, have to fix and systematize some existing body of valuations, that is to say, creations of value which have become prevalent and are for a time called "the truth." It is for these thinkers to make conspicuous, conceivable, intelligible, manageable what has happened and been esteemed hitherto.

Apart from the value of such assertions as "there is a categorical imperative in us," we can always ask: "What does such an assertion indicate about him who makes it?"

Because moralists have known the moral facts imperfectly, in an arbitrary epitome, perhaps the morality of their environment, their position, their church, their *Zeitgeist*, their climate; because they have been badly instructed with regard to nations, eras, and past ages, and were by no means eager to know about these matters; precisely because of this fact, they did not even come in sight of the real problems of morality, problems which disclose themselves only to a comparison of many kinds of morality.

There are systems of morals which are meant to justify their author in the eyes of other people; systems which are meant to tranquilize him and make him self-satisfied; systems which are meant to enable him to crucify and humble himself. By means of one system of morals, he wishes to take revenge; by means of another, to conceal himself; by means of another, to glorify himself and gain superiority and distinction. In short, systems of morals are only sign languages of the emotions.

What is still necessary is the collection of material, the comprehensive survey and classification of sentiments of worth, distinctions of worth, which live, grow, propagate, and perish; and the attempt, perhaps, to give a clear idea of the recurring and more common forms of these living crystallizations. This is necessary as preparation for a theory of types of morality.

So much as a start. The primary problem is not to formulate the principle of morality, but to recognize the existence and study the natural history of many moralities. An acquaintance with these matters, Nietzsche feels, will reveal the fact that genuine moralities arise from the presence in any group of an aristocratic or ruling-class element. He offers an hypothetical reconstruction of the natural history or genealogy of morals.

Every elevation of the type "man" has hitherto been the work of an aristocratic society, and so it will always be: a society believing in a long gradation of rank and differences of worth among human beings, and requiring slavery in some form or other.

Without the pathos of distance, such as grows out of the difference of classes, out of the constant outlooking and downlooking of the ruling class on subordinates and instruments, out of the constant practice of obeying and commanding, out of the keeping down and keeping at a distance, without these, that other more mysterious pathos could never have arisen: the longing for the continued self-surmounting of man.

To be sure, one must cherish no humanitarian illusions about the origin of aristocratic societies. The truth is hard. Every higher civilization has originated in barbarism. Men, barbarians in every respect, men of prey, still in possession of unbroken strength of will and desire for power, threw themselves upon weaker, more moral, more peaceful races, upon old mellow civilizations in which the final vital force was flickering out in brilliant fireworks of wit and depravity. In the beginnings, the noble caste was always the barbarian caste.

The essential thing in a good and healthy aristocracy is that it should regard itself not as a function of the king or the people but as the significance and highest justification thereof; that it should accept with a clear conscience the sacrifice of a legion of individuals, who, for its sake, must be suppressed and reduced to imperfect men, to slaves and instruments. Its fundamental belief must be that society is not allowed to exist for its own sake, but only as a foundation and scaffolding by which a select class may be able to elevate themselves to their higher duties: like those climbing, sun-seeking plants in Java which encircle a tree till, high above it but supported by it, they can unfold their tops in the open light and exhibit their happiness.

Consider an aristocratic commonwealth, e.g., an ancient Greek city state, as a voluntary or involuntary contrivance for rearing human beings. There men are beside one another, thrown on their own resources, who want to make their species prevail, chiefly because they must prevail or be in danger of extermination. The favor, the abundance, the protection, are lacking under which variations are fostered. The species needs itself as species; as something which by its hardness, its uniformity, its simplicity of structure, can prevail in the struggle against neighbors or rebellious vassals. Experience teaches it what are the qualities to which it owes its continued existence in spite of gods and men. These qualities it calls *virtues*, and these virtues alone it develops to maturity.

These virtues it develops with severity. Every aristocratic morality is intolerant in the education of its youth, in the control of its women, in the customs which control marriage, in the relations between old and young, in the penal laws (which have an eye only for the degenerating). It counts intolerance itself among the virtues.

Thus is established a type, with few but very marked features. The constant struggle with unfavorable conditions is the cause of the type becoming stable and hard.

Finally, however, a happy state of security results, and the enormous tension is relaxed. Perhaps there are no more enemies among neighboring peoples; perhaps the means of life and enjoyment are present in abundance. With one stroke the bond and constraint of the old discipline snaps. It is no longer regarded as a necessary condition of existence and survival. If it would continue, it can do so only as an archaizing "taste." Variations appear suddenly in the greatest exuberance and splendor. The individual dares to be individual and detach himself.

At this turning point of history there manifest themselves a magnificent manifold growth and an extraordinary decay, owing to the savagely opposed and seemingly exploding egoisms which strive for "light and sun" and can no longer assign any limit or restraint to themselves by the hitherto existing morality. It was this morality itself which piled up the enormous strength, which bent the bow in so threatening a manner, but it is now out of date, or getting out of date.

The dangerous and disquieting point has now been reached. The greater, more manifold, more comprehensive life now coming into existence is lived beyond the old morality. The "individual" stands out and is obliged to have recourse to his own law giving, his own arts and artifices for self-preservation, self-elevation, self-deliverance. Nothing but new "whys"; nothing but new "hows." No longer any common formulae; misunderstanding and disregard in league together; decay, deterioration, lofty desire, frightfully entangled; the genius of the race overflowing from all the cornucopias of good and bad; new charms and mysteries peculiar to the still inexhausted, still unwearied, corruption.

Danger, the mother of morality, is present once more. This time the danger point has shifted, into the individual, the neighbor, the friend; into the street, into their own child, into all the most personal and secret recesses of their desires and volitions.

After the fabric of a society seems established and secure against external dangers, it is the fear of our neighbor which creates new perspectives of moral evaluation.

It is by the loftiest and strongest instincts, when they break out and carry the individual above and beyond the average, above and beyond the low level of the herd conscience, that the self-reliance of the community is destroyed. Its belief in itself breaks. Consequently these instincts will be most branded and most defamed.

Strong and dangerous instincts, e.g., the love of enterprise, foolhardiness, revengefulness, astuteness, rapacity, love of power, which, up till then had to be honored and fostered and cultivated because required in the common dangers against common enemies, are now felt to be themselves dangerous, are gradually branded as immoral and given over to calumny. The opposite instincts and inclinations now attain to moral honor. The herd instinct gradually draws its conclusions.

How much danger to the community or its equality is contained in an opinion, a condition, an emotion, a character, a disposition? That is now the moral perspective. Here again fear is the mother of morals.

The lofty, independent spirit, the will to stand alone, are felt to be dangers. Everything that elevates the individual above the herd, and is a source of fear to the neighbor, is henceforth called evil. The tolerant, unassuming, self-adapting, self-equalizing disposition, the middle-of-the road desires, attain to moral distinction and honor.

Under peaceful circumstances there is always less opportunity and less need for training the feelings to severity and rigor. Now every form of severity, even severity in justice, begins to disturb the conscience. A lofty and rigorous nobleness and self-responsibility becomes now almost an offense.

The man of an age of dissolution, of an age which mixes the races with one another; who has the inheritance of a diversified descent in his body, contrary instincts and standards of value which struggle among themselves and are seldom at peace; such a man, of late culture and broken lights, will, as a rule, be a weak man.

His fundamental desire is that the war which is in him should come to an end. Happiness appears to him in the character of a soothing medicine and mode of thought; it is above all things the happiness of repose, of undisturbedness, of repletion, of final unity.

All systems of morals which address themselves to "happiness" are only suggestions for behavior adapted to the degree of danger from themselves in which the individuals live. They are thus recipes for their passions, their good and bad propensities, insofar as the individuals would like to play the master. They are all so many small and great expediences, permeated with the musty odor of old family medicines and old wives' wisdom; all grotesque and absurd because they are generalizations where generalization is not justified.

The rank-and-file man assumes an air of being the only kind of man that is allowable. He glorifies, as the peculiarly human virtues, his qualities, such as public spirit, kindness, deference, industry, temperance, modesty, indulgence, sympathy (by virtue of which he is gentle, endurable, and useful to the herd).

In cases where it is believed that a leader cannot be dispensed with, attempt after attempt is made to replace rulers by summing together clever herd-minded men. All representative constitutions, for example, are of this origin.

There arises what I call the moral hypocrisy of the ruling class. They know no other way to protect themselves from bad conscience than to play the role of executors of older and higher orders. (These "older and higher orders" may be predecessors, the constitution, justice, the law, or God himself.) Or they even justify themselves by maxims drawn from the current opinions of the herd, as, for example, "the first servants of their people," or "instruments of public weal."

The end is quickly approaching; everything decays and produces decay; nothing will endure until the day after tomorrow; nothing, that is, except one species of man, the incurably mediocre. The mediocre alone have a prospect of continuing, of propagating themselves. They will be the men of the future, the sole survivors. "Be like them! Be mediocre!" is now the only morality which has still a significance or obtains a hearing. But it is difficult to preach this morality of mediocrity. It can never avow what it is and what it desires. It has to talk of "moderation," and "dignity," and "duty," and "brotherly love." It will have difficulty in concealing its irony!

But this herding-animal morality is only one kind of morality, beside which, before which, and after which, many other moralities, above all, higher moralities, are or should be possible. Against such a possibility, this herd morality defends itself with all its strength. It says obstinately and inexorably: "I am morality and nothing else is morality."

The first corollary which follows from Nietzsche's conception of the genealogy of morals is what he calls his *immoralism*, or his proposed *transvaluation of values*. Thus:

What will the moralists who appear at this time have to preach? What shall be the message of these sharp on-lookers, these unhurried ones?

What is essential and invaluable in every system of morals, is that it is a long constraint.

A species originates, a type becomes established and strong in the long struggle with essentially unfavorable conditions. On the other hand, species which receive abundant nourishment, a surplus of protection and care, tend to develop variations, become fertile in prodigies and monstrosities.

The essential thing, to repeat, is that there should be a long obedience in the same direction. Thereby results something which makes life worth living; for instance, virtue, art, music, dancing, reason, spirituality; whatever, in short, is transfiguring, refined, or divine.

One may look at every system of morals in this light. It teaches us to hate the lax, the too great freedom. It implants the need for limited horizons, for immediate duties, for narrow perspectives. "Thou must obey some one, and for a long time; otherwise thou wilt come to grief, and lose all respect for thyself."

The tension of soul in misfortune, its shuddering in view of rack and ruin, its inventiveness and heroism in enduring and exploiting misfortune, its depth, mystery, greatness; have these not been bestowed through the discipline of great suffering?

Up to now man has been in the worst hands, has been ruled by the misfits, the physiologically botched, the cunning and revengeful, the so-called *saints* — slanderers of the world, traducers of humanity. The morality of decadence, the will to nothingness, passes as morality *par excellence*. Proof of this: Altruism is considered an absolute value, while egoism meets with hostility everywhere. He who disagrees with me on this point I regard as infected.

For a physiologist, such an opposition of altruism and egoism would leave no room for doubt. If the smallest organ in the body neglects its self-preservation, its recuperative powers, its "egoism," the whole organism will degenerate. The physiologist insists that such decayed parts be cut out. He pities them not at all. But the priest wants precisely the degeneration of mankind; hence he strives to preserve the decayed elements in humanity. This is the price of his rule. This is the "harm that good men do."

When one is no longer serious about self-preservation and the increase of bodily energy, when anemia is made an ideal and contempt of the body is construed as "salvation of the soul," what can all this be, if not a recipe for decadence? Loss of ballast, resistance to natural instincts, "selflessness," these have hitherto been called *morality*.

You want, if possible, to do away with suffering. There is not a more foolish "if possible." We would rather have it increased and made worse. Well-being, as you understand it, is certainly not a goal. The discipline of great suffering is the only discipline that has produced all the elevations of humanity hitherto.

To consider distress as something to be destroyed is sheer idiocy. Generally, it is actually harmful in its consequences, a fatal stupidity, almost as mad as the desire to abolish bad weather out of pity for the poor. In the great economy of the universe the terrors of reality, e.g., the passions, the desires, the will to power, are incalculably more essential than that petty happiness, so-called *goodness*.

It is only among decadents that pity is called a virtue. They are too ready to forget modesty, reverence, and that delicacy of feeling which knows how to keep at a distance. They forget that this sentimental emotion stinks of the mob; that pity is only one step removed from bad manners; that pitying hands may be thrust with destructive results into a great destiny, into a wounded isolation. . . . The overcoming of pity I reckon among the noble virtues.

There is nowadays a sickly irritability and sensitiveness to pain, a repulsive complaining, an effeminizing, which, with the aid of religious and philosophical nonsense, seeks to deck itself out as something superior. There is a regular cult of suffering. The unmanliness of what such groups of visionaries call *sympathy* is, I believe, the first thing that strikes the eye. One must resolutely taboo this latest form of bad taste.

There is a point of diseased mellowness and effeminacy in the history of society, at which society itself takes the part of him who injures it, the part of the criminal. To punish now appears to be somehow "unfair." Is it not sufficient, it is asked, if the criminal be rendered harmless? Why should we still punish? Punishment is barbarous! And so on. With these questions, the herd morality, the morality of fear, draws its ultimate conclusion.

On no point is the ordinary mind of Europe more unwilling to be corrected, than on this matter. People rave nowadays, even under the guise of "science," about coming social conditions in which the "exploiting character" of human relations is to be absent. Particularly is this true of socialistic shallowpates and howling anarchistic dogs. Their words sound to me as if they were promising a mode of life which should refrain from all organic functions. "Exploitation" is not the mark of a depraved or primitive society; it belongs to the nature of the living, as a primary organic function; it is a consequence of the will to power which is precisely the will to life.

You may note that I do not care to see rudeness undervalued. It is by far the most humane form of contradiction, and amid modern effeminacy, it is one of our first virtues.

To be able to be an enemy, to be an enemy, presupposes a strong nature. Strong natures need resistance, accordingly they seek it. The pathos of aggression belongs to strength as much as feelings of revenge and rancor belong to weakness. The strength of the aggressor is determined by the opposition he needs; every increase of strength betrays itself by a search for a more formidable opponent.

To refrain from mutual injury, from violence, from exploitation, to put one's will on a par with others' may result in a kind of good conduct among individuals; but only when the necessary conditions are given, namely, an equality of the individuals in force and worth, and their correlation within one organization.

To take this principle more generally, however, to use it as the fundamental principle of society, would immediately reveal what it actually amounts to, namely, a principle of dissolution and decay. Here one must think profoundly and resist all sentimentality; life itself is essentially appropriation, injury, exploitation, conquest. suppression, severity, obtrusion, incorporation.

Even the organization within which the members treat each other as equal, must, itself, do that toward other organizations which its members refrain from doing to each other; if, that is, it be a living, growing, and not a dying organization. It will endeavor to grow, to gain ground, to attract to itself, to acquire ascendency; not owing to any morality or immorality, but simply because it lives, and because life is precisely will to power.

Fortunately, the world is not built merely on those instincts in which the good-natured herd animal would find his paltry happiness. To demand that everyone become a "good man," a gregarious animal, a blue-eyed benevolent "beautiful soul," or (as Herbert Spencer wished) an altruist, would mean robbing existence of its greatest character, emasculating mankind. And this has been attempted. It is just this that men call *morality*.

The "good" man is the most harmful kind of man. He secures his existence at the cost of truth. He cannot create. He crucifies the man who writeth new values on new tables. He crucifies the whole future of humanity. Whatever harm the slanderers of the world may do, the harm which good men do is the most calamitous of all harm.

Let me say again what I have already said a hundred times. In all our principal moral judgments, that which is sure of itself, that which glorifies itself with praise and blame, that which calls itself good, is the instinct of the herding human animal: the instinct which is coming more and more to the front, coming more and more to dominate other instincts. Morality at present is herding-animal morality.

All questions of politics, of the social order, of education, have been falsified from top to bottom, because the most harmful men have been taken for great men, and because people were taught to despise the fundamentals of life.

Nietzsche's characteristic doctrines have their basis in these conceptions of the genealogy of morals and the transvaluation of values. His distinction between man and superman, between master morality and slave morality, his reiterated criticisms of the softer, more humanitarian virtues and customs, follow reasonably enough. Perhaps the most famous of all Nietzsche's teachings is in his distinction between master morality and slave morality. Its point is this:

Moral systems must be compelled to bow before the gradations of rank. Their presumption must be driven home, until they thoroughly understand that it is immoral to say that "what is right and proper for one is right and proper for another."

In a tour through the many finer and coarser moralities which have hitherto prevailed, or still prevail, on the earth, I have found certain traits recurring regularly together, until finally two primary types revealed themselves to me: There are master morality and slave morality.

Moral valuations have originated, either in a ruling class pleasantly conscious of being different from the ruled, or in a ruled class, among slaves and dependents of all sorts.

In the master morality, when it is the rulers who determine the notion of "goodness," it is the exalted, proud type of character which is regarded as the distinguishing feature, as that which determines the order of rank. The noble man separates from himself the persons in whom these characteristics are absent; them he despises.

They say: "Thus shall it be." They determine the whither and the why of mankind. They grasp at the future with a creative hand. Whatever is and was becomes for them a means, an instrument, a hammer. Their knowing is creating. Their creating is law-giving. Their will to truth is will to power.

In master morality the antithesis is between "noble" and "despicable." The cowardly, the timid, the no-accounts, the narrowly utilitarian, the distrustful, the self-abasing, the doglike who submit to abuse, the mendicant flatterers, and above all the liars, are despised.

A man who says, "I like that, I take it for my own, I mean to guard it and protect it"; a man who can carry out a resolution, keep hold of a woman, punish and overthrow insolence; a man who has his indignation and his sword; a man whom the weak, the suffering, even the animals, willingly submit to and naturally belong to; such a man is a master by nature.

The noble type of man regards himself as the determiner of values; he does not require to be approved of; he passes the judgment: "What is injurious to me is injurious in itself"; he knows that it is he himself only who confers honor on things; he is a creator of values. He honors whatever he recognizes in himself: such morality is self-glorification. In the foreground there is the feeling of plenitude, of power which seeks to overflow, the consciousness of a wealth which would fain give and bestow.

The noble man honors in himself the powerful one, him who has power over himself, who knows how to speak and how to keep silent, who takes pleasure in subjecting himself to severity and hardness and has reverence for all that is severe and hard. "Wotan placed a hard heart in my breast," says an old Scandinavian saga: it is thus rightly expressed from the soul of a proud Viking.

The noble man is furthest removed from the morality which sees the essence of the moral in sympathy, or in "acting for the good of others." Faith in oneself, pride in oneself, a radical irony and enmity toward "selflessness," belong as definitely to master morality as do scorn and precaution in the presence of sympathy and the "warm heart."

A man of this sort is carved from a single block, which is hard, sweet, fragrant. He enjoys only what is good for him. His desire ceases when the limits of what is good for him are overstepped. . . . Whatever does not kill him makes him stronger. He gathers his material from all he sees, hears, and experiences. He is a selective principle: he rejects much. . . . He reacts slowly to all kinds of stimuli, with that slowness which long caution and pride have bred in him. . . . He is always in his own company, whether mingling with men or books or nature. . . . He honors the thing he chooses.

There is an instinct for rank, which, more than anything else, is the sign of a high rank. The refinement, the goodness, the loftiness of a soul are put to a real test when something of the highest rank passes by but is not yet protected with the awe of authority; something that goes its way like a living touchstone, undistinguished, undiscovered, tentative, perhaps veiled and disguised.

The noble and powerful know how to honor; it is their art, their domain for invention. The profound reverence for age and tradition, the belief and prejudice in favor of ancestors and against newcomers, is typical of master morality. If, contrariwise, men of "modern ideas" believe in "progress" and the "future," and are increasingly lacking in respect for the past, the ignoble origin of these "ideas" is thereby betrayed.

He whose task is to investigate souls will avail himself of many varieties of this very art to determine the ultimate value of a soul, the innate order of rank to which it belongs. He will test it by its instinct for reverence. The vulgarity of many a soul spurts up like dirty water when any holy vessel, any jewel from closed shrines, any book bearing the marks of great destiny, is brought before it. Contrariwise, there is an involuntary silence, a hesitation, a cessation, by which is indicated that a soul feels the nearness of what is worthy of respect.

In the so-called *cultured* classes today, the dealers in "modern ideas," nothing is perhaps so repulsive as their lack of shame, their lack of reverence, the easy insolence of hand and eye with which they touch, finger, and examine everything. It is possible that more tact for reverence exists among the lower classes and peasants than among the newspaper-reading demimonde of "intellect" and "culture."

Much has been achieved when the sentiment of reverence has been finally instilled into the masses, i.e., the shallowpates and nitwits of every kind; when they realize that they are not allowed to touch everything, that there are some experiences before which they must take off their shoes and restrain their hand.

The master morality is especially foreign and irritating to present-day taste. It is disliked and distrusted for the sternness of its principle that one has duties only to one's equals; that one may act toward persons of a lower rank, toward all that is foreign, just as one pleases; that its values are "beyond good and evil."

It is typical of the master morality to be able and obliged to exercise prolonged gratitude and prolonged revenge, but both only within the circle of one's equals; artfulness in retaliation; a need for enemies as outlets for emotions of envy, quarrelsomeness, arrogance. This, of course, is not "modern morality," and is therefore difficult to realize, to discover.

In contrast to the master morality stands the slave morality:

It is otherwise with the second type of morality; what I have named slave morality. If the abused, the oppressed, the suffering, the unemancipated, the weary, the uncertain-of-themselves, should moralize, what will be the common element in their moral evaluations?

The slave has an unfavorable eye for the virtues of the powerful. He has a skepticism and distrust of everything which they honor. He would fain persuade himself that their happiness is not genuine.

On the other hand, those qualities which serve to alleviate the existence of sufferers are brought into prominence and flooded with light. It is here that sympathy, the kind helping hand, the warm heart, patience, diligence, humility, friendliness, attain to honor. For here these are the most useful equalities, almost the only means of supporting the burden of existence.

Slave morality is essentially the morality of utility. It is oriented

around the idea of the "useful." Here is the seat of the origin of
the famous antithesis of "good" and "evil," which I have distinguished from the antithesis of "good" and "bad." According to
slave morality, the "evil" man rouses fear. According to master
morality, the "good" man rouses fear, and seeks to rouse it, while the
"bad" man is regarded as the despicable being.

According to slave morality, the good man must be the "safe"
man: he must be good-natured, easily hoodwinked, perhaps a little
stupid. Wherever slave morality gains the ascendency, language
shows a tendency to approximate the significations of the words
good and *stupid*.

A last fundamental difference: the desire for freedom, the enthusiasm for "liberty" the instinct of being "happy" belong as in-
herently to slave morality as artifice in reverence and enthusiasm in
devotion belong to master morality. Hence, we can understand,
love as a passion, romantic love, with its ardors and endurances and
binding ties, is a phenomenon of master morality.

Nietzsche never wearied of criticizing those phases of modern morality which smacked of "degeneration" and "slaves."
Among the topics singled out for castigation was the nineteenth-century enthusiasm for the emancipation of women.
Says Nietzsche:

To be mistaken in the fundamental problem of "man and woman"
is the typical sign of a shallow mind. To deny here the profoundest
antagonism, the need for hostile tension; to dream here of "equal
rights," equal training, equal claims and obligations; to prove
oneself shallow at this dangerous spot, may be regarded as suspicious,
nay more, as betrayed. Such an one may probably prove "too
short" for all the fundamental issues of life, unable to descend into
any of the depths.

In no previous age have women been treated with so much respect
by men as at present. This belongs to the tendency and fundamental taste of democracy. Is it any wonder that abuse should be
made of this respect? Women want more; they learn to make
claims; they become rivals for rights. In a word, they lose their
modesty. And, let me add, they also lose their taste.

They unlearn their fear of men. But the woman who "unlearns" her fear of men, sacrifices her most womanly instincts. That woman should venture forward when man has ceased to inspire fear, is reasonable enough, and intelligible enough. But what is more difficult to grasp is that precisely thereby woman deteriorates. That is happening these days: let us not deceive ourselves about it.

Wherever the industrial spirit has triumphed over the military and aristocratic spirit, woman strives for the economic and legal independence of a clerk. "Woman as clerk" is inscribed on the portal of that modern society which is in course of formation.

While she thus appropriates new rights, aspires to be master, and inscribes the "progress" of woman on her flags and banners, the very opposite realizes itself with terrible obviousness — woman retrogrades.

There is stupidity in this movement, an almost masculine stupidity, of which a well-bred sensible woman might be heartily ashamed. To lose the ground on which she can most surely achieve victory; to neglect her proper weapons; to let herself go before man where formerly she kept herself in control in artful humility; to neutralize man's faith in a fundamentally different ideal in woman, something eternally feminine; to emphatically and loquaciously dissuade man from the idea that woman must be preserved, protected, and indulged like some delicate, strangely wild, and often pleasant domestic animal; what does all this betoken, if not a disintegration of womanly instincts?

There are, to be sure, enough of idiotic friends and corrupters of woman amongst the learned asses of the male sex, who advise woman to defeminize herself in this manner, and to imitate all the stupidities from which man suffers, who would like to lower woman to "general culture," indeed, even to newspaper reading and meddling with politics.

In their efforts to rise to the ideal woman, to the higher woman, they have really wished to lower the general level of women, and there are no more certain means to this end than university education, trousers, and the rights of voting like cattle. Fundamentally, the "emancipated" and the "emancipators" (for example, that typical old maid, Henrik Ibsen) are anarchists, misbegotten souls whose most deep-rooted instinct is revenge.

Almost everywhere her nerves are being ruined, and she is daily being made more hysterical and more incapable of fulfilling her first and last function, namely, the rearing of robust children. These "friends of woman" wish to "cultivate" her, to make the weaker sex strong by "culture," as if history did not teach that the "cultivating" of mankind and the weakening of mankind have always kept pace with one another.

That which inspires respect in woman, and often also fear, is her real nature, her genuine, carnivora-like cunning and flexibility, her tiger claws beneath the glove, her naïveté in egoism, her untrainableness, her innate wildness, her incomprehensibleness, the extent and deviation of her virtues.

That which, in spite of fear, excites one's sympathy for the dangerous and beautiful in woman, is that she seems more afflicted, more vulnerable, more needful of love and more condemned to disillusion, than any other creature. Fear and sympathy — it is with these feelings that man has hitherto stood in the presence of woman, always with one foot in tragedy which rends while it delights. And all that is now to be at an end? The disenchantment of women is in progress? The tediousness of woman is slowly evolving?

Another object of Nietzsche's criticism was what he describes as "Christian morality." He never tires of railing at it. From among pages and pages, the following citations may be taken as representative:

All the things men have valued heretofore are not even realities. They are mere fantasies; more strictly speaking, they are lies. All the concepts, "God," "soul," "virtue," "sin," "Beyond," "truth," "eternal life," are lies arising from the evil instincts of diseased and harmful natures.

I am the first immoralist. Basically, there are two denials included in this term. First, I deny the type of man who formerly passed as the highest, the "good" man, the "benevolent" man, the "charitable" man. Second, I deny that kind of morality which

has become recognized and dominant, namely Christian morality.
. . . The second of these denials is the more decisive.

No one before me has felt Christian morality beneath him. To
do that one must have height, far vision, depth. Up to now,
Christian morality has been the Circe of all thinkers; they stood at
her service. What man before me has descended into the caves
from which the poisonous fumes of this ideal burst forth? Who
before me ever dared to suspect they were caves? What philosopher
before me was a real moralist and not a superior swindler, an idealist?

Have you understood me? What defines me is the fact that I un-
masked Christian morality. For this reason I needed a word which
would contain the idea of a universal challenge: immoralist. Blindness in the face of Christian morality is the essential crime. It is the
great uncleanliness.

Christian morality is the most pernicious form of the will to falsehood, the denial of life. It is not error as error which infuriates me
here. It is not the age-long lack of "good will," of discipline, of
decency, of spiritual courage, which betrays itself in the triumph of
Christian morality. It is the ghastly fact that what was unnatural
received the highest honors as morality, and remained suspended
over man as the law of the categorical imperative. This is the great
blundering. To teach contempt of the primal life instincts; to set
up a "soul," a spirit, in order to overthrow the body; to teach man
to find impurity in sex; to look for the principle of evil in the need
for expansion; to see a "higher moral value" in "selflessness," in
"objectivity," in "neighbor love"; these things are the will to
nothingness, the denial of life, the great nay-saying.

The Jews performed the miracle of the inversion of valuations, by
means of which life on earth obtained a new and dangerous charm
for a couple of thousand years. Their prophets fused the expressions
rich, godless, wicked, violent, sensual, into one expression, and for the
first time coined the word *world* as a term of reproach. In this inversion of values (which included the use of *poor* as synonymous with
saint and *friend*) the significance of the Jewish people is to be found.
It is with them that slave morality begins.

From the beginning, Christian morality was essentially the surfeit
of life which disguised itself under the belief in "another" and

"better" life. The hatred of the world, the condemnation of emotion, the fear of beauty, the distrust of sensuality, all these have always appeared to me as the most dangerous forms of the "will to perish," symptoms of the deepest weariness, exhaustion, anemia.

The teachers and preachers and leaders of mankind, including the theologians, have been decadents. Hence their inversion of values into a hostility to life; hence "morality." Here is a definition of _morality:_ _the idiosyncrasy of decadents actuated by a desire to_ _avenge themselves successfully upon life._ I attach great value to this definition.

Have you understood me? The unmasking of Christian morality is a unique event. It breaks the history of mankind in two. Man lives either before or after that. Everything which was until then called the _truth_, is now recognized as the most harmful, spiteful, and concealed falsehood. The sacred pretext, the "improvement of man," is recognized as a ruse to drain life of its blood. This morality is vampirism.

He who unmasks Christian morality unmasks the worthlessness of the values in which men believe. He sees in them only the most fatal kind of abortions; fatal, because they fascinate. The notion of "God" was invented as the counternotion to life. The notion of a "Beyond" was invented to depreciate the only world that exists. The notion of an "immortal soul" was invented to despise the body. The notion of "sin" was invented to mislead our instincts. Finally, the notion of a "good man" has come to mean everything that is weak, ill, misshapen, everything which should be obliterated. The law of selection is thwarted. And all this was believed in as morality! _Ecrasez l'infâme!_

We who hold a different view, we who regard Christian morality and democratic politics to be a degenerating form of organization, where have we to fix our hopes?

In new moralists and a new morality. There is no other alternative. In minds strong enough and original enough to initiate a transvaluation of values, to invert "eternal valuations," lies our only hope. In forerunners, in men of the future, who shall fix the constraints and fasten the knots which will compel millenniums to take new paths; make preparations for vast hazardous enterprises and collective attempts in rearing and educating; put an end to the frightful rule of folly and chance which has hitherto gone by the name of *history;* in such do we fix our hopes.

For these purposes a new type of moralist and ruler will some time be needed, at the very idea of which everything that has existed might look pale and dwarfed. The image of such leaders hovers before our eyes.

But their image fills our hearts with anxiety and gloom. How are they to be born? How are they to be bred? How nurtured to that elevation and power which will feel the present needs as their tasks? Of them is demanded a transvaluation of values. In them is needed a new conscience of steel, a new heart of brass, to bear the weight of such responsibility. There is always the danger that they may be lacking, or miscarry and degenerate. These are our real anxieties and glooms. These are the heavy thoughts and storms which sweep across our skies.

There are few pains so grievous as to have seen an exceptional man miss his way and deteriorate. But he who has the rare eye to see the danger of mankind itself missing its way and deteriorating; he who has recognized the element of wild chance in human affairs; he who has detected the fate that is hidden under the idiotic unwariness and blind confidence of "modern ideas," and still more of Christian morality and democratic politics; suffers from an anguish beyond comparison.

The universal degeneracy of mankind to the level of the ideals of socialistic fools and humanitarian shallowpates, the dwarfing of man to an absolutely gregarious animal, the brutalizing of man into pigmy with equal "rights" and "claims" — this is undoubtedly possible. He who has foreseen this possibility knows another loathing unknown to the rest of mankind.

From these themes, Nietzsche turns to the question of his own significance for the modern mind. Nietzsche on the genealogy of morals is interesting. Nietzsche on the distinction between master morality and slave morality is suggestive. Nietzsche on woman and Christianity is challenging. But Nietzsche on himself is unique:

Idealism is alien to me. Where you see ideal things I see human things, alas all-too-human.

He who would be a creator in good and evil must first be a destroyer, and break values into pieces. I am the most terrible man that has ever existed. But I shall be the most beneficent. I know the joy of annihilation. I am the first immoralist. I am thus the essential destroyer.

I know my destiny. I am not a man. I am a fatality. I am dynamite. Some day my name will be bound up with the recollection of something terrific, a crisis, a profound clash of consciences, a decisive condemnation of all that before me had been believed, required, hallowed.

I am the voice of truth. But my truth is terrible, for hitherto lies have been called truth. "The transvaluation of all values" is my formula for mankind's act of highest self-recognition. I contradict as no one has contradicted before. For when truth engages in a struggle with the falsehoods of ages, we must expect shocks, earthquakes, rearrangements of hills and valleys, such as never yet have been dreamt of. All the mighty forms of the old social structure I blow into space, for they rest on falsehoods. Politics on a grand scale will date from me.

My life task is to prepare humanity for a moment of supreme self-consciousness, a great noontide, a transvaluation of all values, an emancipation from all moral values, a yea-saying, a confidence in all that has formerly been forbidden, despised, and damned; when it will gaze both backwards and forwards, emerge from the tyranny of accident and priesthood, and, for the first time, pose the question of the why and wherefore of humanity as a whole.

But with all this there is nothing in me to suggest the founder of a "religion." Religions are the business of the mob. After coming in contact with a religious man, I have always to wash my hands. I want no "believers." I never address myself to the masses. I do not wish to be a saint: I would rather be a clown. Perhaps I am a clown.

READING REFERENCES. The best thing to do with Nietzsche, having read carefully the selections given here, is to try his

Thus Spake Zarathustra. This is at first a somewhat difficult book, but it has a strange, exotic charm.

It may be supplemented by chapters from *Beyond Good and Evil* and *The Genealogy of Morals.* Among items that may be consulted with profit, for a beginning, is Will Durant's chapter in his *Story of Philosophy.* The best single book on Nietzsche is George A Morgan's *What Nietzsche Means.* The author of the Philo Vance detective novels was a student of Nietzsche's works. His real name was W. H. Wright, and his book *What Nietzsche Taught* is a good introduction. The same goes for H. L. Mencken's *The Philosophy of Friedrich Nietzsche.* Among books of a more academic character may be mentioned W. K. Salter's *Nietzsche the Thinker.*

READING QUESTIONS

1. What quarrel does Nietzsche have with all previous moral philosophies?
2. What is necessary as a preparation for what?
3. Through what stages does he trace the genealogy of morality?
4. What do you understand by these phrases: "the pathos of distance," "sun-seeking plants in Java," "Danger, the mother of morality," "herd-minded," "the moral hypocrisy of the ruling class," "morality of mediocrity," "herding-animal morality," "a long constraint"?
5. What do you understand by "immoralism"? What by "the transvaluation of values"?
6. Elucidate these phrases: "the discipline of great suffering," "pity as a vice," "socialistic shallowpates," "the pathos of aggression," "the harm that good men do"?
7. How does he characterize master morality?
8. How slave morality?
9. "Slave morality is essentially the morality of utility." Meaning?
10. What are his views on the emancipation of women?
11. What are his views on what he conceives as Christian morality?
12. Formulate two or more criticisms you would make of his position.

5. MORALITY GROUNDED IN DEMANDS — FROM WILLIAM JAMES

FROM NIETZSCHE TO JAMES. The moral philosophy of
Nietzsche assumed, on its negative side, the form of a critique
of traditional morality, especially of such portions as derived
from historical Christianity. Naturally, matters were not
left at that. Among the many who rallied to the cause of
religion, against its critics, none was more colorful and engaging than William James. We have seen him at work already, in two earlier chapters. In the present chapter we
meet him once more, this time in the role of moralist. I
think it would be instructive, having read this chapter carefully, to recall what the author had to say on the questions
of natural theology and metaphysics. There is a general consistency among the different parts of his philosophy which
endeared him to those who shared that philosophy.

BIOGRAPHICAL NOTE. See under "A Theological Problem,"
page 73.

THE ARGUMENT OF THE CITATIONS. James begins by calling
attention to the fact that ethical skepticism is not one among
other possible moral philosophies. It is the denial or the
bankruptcy of moral philosophy. If it is, in essential part at
least, the aim of a moral philosophy to explain what is
meant by *right*, *good*, *obligation*, and other such ethical terms,
and to indicate what things or classes of things are right,
good, obligatory, etc. then ethical skepticism would be the
admission that we do not or cannot know the answers to
questions formulated in these terms. For example: "What
does it mean to say of an act that it is right?" Answer: "I
don't know." "What acts are right?" Answer: "I don't
know." "Is this particular act right?" "I don't know."
"Is any act whatever right?" Answer: "I don't know."
Ethical skepticism is the belief that the answer to all ethical
questions is "I don't know." Thus James:

What is the position of him who seeks an ethical philosophy? To begin with he must be distinguished from all those who are satisfied to be ethical skeptics. He *will* not be skeptic. Therefore, so far from ethical skepticism being one possible fruit of ethical philosophizing it can only be regarded as that residual alternative to all philosophy which from the outset menaces every would-be philosopher who may give up the quest discouraged and renounce his original aim.

From this provisional warning that he will pay any price within limits to avoid ethical skepticism, James settles down to formulate his questions. What do we mean by such words as *good* and *ill?* He begins by noting that there are some things, or classes of things, to which these words are inapplicable.

First of all, such words as *good* and *ill* can have no application or relevancy in a world in which no sentient life exists. Imagine a world containing only physical and chemical facts, without a God, without even an interested spectator. Would there be any sense in saying of that world that one of its states is better than another? If there were two such worlds, would there be any rhyme or reason in calling one good and the other bad?

I am asking whether goods and evils exist in physical facts, *per se.* There is, it seems to me, no status for goods and evils to exist in, in a purely insentient world. How can one physical fact, considered simply as a physical fact, be "better" than another? A physical fact, in its mere material capacity, can no more be good or bad than it can be pleasant or painful. Physical facts simply are, or are not. No world composed of merely physical facts can possibly be a world to which ethical propositions apply.

To sharpen his initial claim that ethical terms can have no application in a world where no sentient life exists, James suggests, by way of minimum contrast, a world in which only one person exists.

Let us suppose a universe containing one person. Let us call the supposed universe which he inhabits a *moral solitude.* There is a chance now for goods and evils to exist. They have their status in that being's consciousness. So far as he feels anything to be good, he makes it good. It is good, for him, and being good for him, is absolutely good, for he is the sole creator of values in that universe, and outside of his opinion things have no moral character at all.

In such a universe as we have supposed, it would be absurd to ask whether the solitary thinker's judgments of good and evil are true or false. Truth supposes a standard outside of the thinker to which he must conform. But here the thinker is subject to no higher judge.

What happens to the argument if we add one more person to our universe?

If now we introduce a second thinker, with his likes and dislikes, into the universe, the ethical situation becomes more complex, and several possibilities are seen to obtain.

The two thinkers may ignore each other's attitude about good and evil altogether, and indulge each his own preferences, indifferent to what the other may feel or do. In such a case we have twice as much of the ethical quality in our world as we had in our moral solitude, only it is without ethical unity. The same object is good or bad, in such a universe, according as you measure it by the view which this one or the other one of the thinkers takes.

In such a universe as we are now supposing, if the two persons ignore each other, you cannot find any possible ground for saying that the opinion of one is more correct than the opinion of the other, or that one of the two has a truer moral sense than the other. There is no single point of view within it from which the values of things can be judged, since the two thinkers are supposed to be indifferent to each other.

Multiply the thinkers into a pluralism, and the result remains the same. Individual minds are the measures. No one "objective" truth can be found for moral judgments; only a multitude of "subjective" opinions.

The argument has reached an impasse. In a world of many persons, each recognizing only his private ideals, we could not give any general answer to the question, what does *good* mean? Or what things are good? There would be no single answer to such questions. This is veering around to skepticism, and as we know, James wishes to avoid that possibility.

But this is the kind of a world with which the philosopher will not put up. Among the various ideals represented, there must be, he thinks, some which have more truth or authority, and to these the others *ought* to yield.

The outcome of the discussion so far has been to show that nothing can be good or right except so far as some consciousness feels it to be good or right. Of these qualities we may say that their *esse* is *percipi*. Therefore, the moralist who seeks to know which ideal ought to have supreme weight must trace the *ought* itself to some existing consciousness. This consciousness must make the one ideal right by feeling it to be right, the other wrong by feeling it to be wrong. Now, what particular consciousness in the universe *can* enjoy this prerogative of obliging others to conform to a rule which it lays down? All one's slumbering revolutionary instincts waken at the thought of any single moralist wielding such power. Better chaos forever than an order based on any philosopher's rule, even though he were the most enlightened member of his tribe.

We can't allow skepticism. We can't allow subjectivism. We can't admit the arbitrary. How then can we say, or get into a position to say, of any particular account of the nature of the good, that all persons ought to accept it? How can any ideal impose any moral obligation upon any one to accept it?

Before we can address ourselves to this question we must deal first with the question, what is the *ground* of an ought, an obligation?

When we first try to answer this question, what is the *ground* of an obligation?, there is a tendency to imagine an abstract moral order in which the objective truth resides, and to try to prove that this pre-existing moral order is more accurately reflected in our own ideas than in the ideas held by some one else. Backed by this overarching abstract order, we think that others should submit. This attitude of regarding ourselves as subject to an overarching system of moral relations true in themselves is, taken as it stands, an out-and-out superstition.

We want an account of good and ill which will be binding upon all persons, which will be obligatory upon all persons to accept. To this end we enquire concerning the grounds upon which anything can be obligatory upon anyone. We note that such grounds are not to be discovered "in any abstract moral order which antedates and overarches the mere facts." Where then? What does set up obligations?

We cannot find the *ground* of an obligation in any such abstract moral order which antedates and overarches the mere facts, and makes it right that we should conform to it. Where then? The moment we take a steady look at the question, what is the *ground* of an obligation?, we see that it is *always* a claim actually made by some concrete person.

Claim and *obligation* are, in fact, coextensive terms. They cover each other exactly. Without a claim, actually made by some concrete person, there can be no obligation. Wherever there is a claim, there is some obligation. It is hard for those who are accustomed to what I have called the *superstitious* view, to realize that *every* claim creates, in so far forth, an obligation. We inveterately think that something which we call the *validity* of the claim gives to it its obligatory character; and that this validity is something outside of the claim's mere existence as a claim. Its validity, we think, rains down upon the claim, much as the influence of the pole rains down upon the steel of the compass needle.

Take any claim, however slight, which any creature, however weak, may make. Ought it not to be satisfied? If not, prove why not. The only possible kind of proof you could adduce would be a claim, made by some other creature, that ran the other way. The only reason why any claim ought to be satisfied is that it is made. It makes itself valid by the fact that it exists at all.

Any claim is imperative to the extent of its amount. Some claims are small claims. They are put forward by insignificant persons. We customarily make light of the obligations which they bring. But the fact that small claims impose small obligations does not keep the largest obligations from having their ground in personal claims.

Wherever persons exist and value things, wherever they make claims upon one another, there good, evil, and obligation exist, and there is an ethical world in its essential features. Were there but one rock, with two loving souls upon it, that rock would have as thoroughly moral a constitution as any possible world which the eternities and immensities could harbor. There would be real goods and real evils. There would be claims and obligations. In short, there would be a moral life whose active energy would have no limit but the intensity of interest in each other with which the two souls were endowed.

If we, on this earth of ours, are like the inhabitants of such a rock, we constitute an ethical republic. Ethics would have as genuine and real a foothold as in any possible universe. Whether this conception of an ethical republic, in which the valuers and claimants are only human beings, in which no higher consciousness exists, can gratify the moral philosopher's demands of a unified moral world, is a different question.

James is meeting his old difficulty in a new form. He didn't wish to accept skepticism or relativism or subjectivism. To avoid them, he turned from "good" to "obligation," and finds now that the ground of any obligation is the fact of a claim issued by some person or persons. But we can all make claims and have, therefore, the power to set up obligations. Whose claims shall take precedence? Whose claims are to be the grounds for the obligation that is to be binding on all persons? Hence James's puzzlement: "What can the philosopher do, then, except fall back on skepticism and thus give up the notion of being a philosopher at all?"

The controls of James's argument have been these: We cannot admit ethical skepticism, relativism, subjectivism, but if the good is only some person's good, we cannot avoid these.

Nor can we avoid them by means of the notion of obligation, if we admit that the ground of an obligation is a claim made by some one. What then?

It would seem that the stable and systematic moral universe for which the moral philosopher asks is fully possible only in a world where there is a divine thinker with all-enveloping demands. If such a thinker existed, his way of subordinating the demands to one another would be the finally valid one. His claim would be the most appealing. His ideal would be the most inclusive. In his thought would be that ethical philosophy which we ask as the pattern. In the interests of our own ideal of systematically unified moral truth, therefore, we, as would-be philosophers must postulate a divine thinker. Exactly what the thought of the infinite thinker may be, is hidden from us, even were we sure of his existence.

God, then, is the necessary answer to the problem of avoiding the confusions of ethical skepticism and relativism. If God's conception of the good is admitted, we have something objective and independent of any individual. If God's claim is made the ground of obligation, we have an obligation that is objective, independent of any individual, and binding upon all individuals. What is God's conception of the good? Either James doesn't know, or he feels that that is another question to be dealt with elsewhere. The same holds for the claims made by God and the obligations which they set up for men. Those two questions would seem to be paramount. Otherwise, of course, we are brought around again to ethical skepticism. I presume that James knew this. The fact remains that he does nothing about it. His line of defense, at this point, is a curious one. It begins by drawing attention to a psychological distinction, that, namely, between the easygoing and the strenuous mood.

The deepest difference, in the moral life of man, is the difference between the easygoing and the strenuous mood. The easygoing mood makes us shrink from present ill. The strenuous, on the contrary, makes us indifferent to present ill, if only the greater ideal be attained.

The capacity for the strenuous mood probably lies slumbering in every man. But it has more difficulty in some than in others in waking up. It needs the wilder passions to arouse it, the big fears, loves and indignations; or else the deeply penetrating appeal of some one of the higher fidelities, like justice, truth, or freedom. Strong relief is a necessity of its vision. A world where all the mountains are brought down and all the valleys are exalted is no congenial place for its habitation.

In a solitary thinker the strenuous mood might slumber on forever without waking. In a merely human world, composed of many finite thinkers, the appeal to our moral energy would be greater, but it would still fall short of its maximal stimulating power. To be sure, in such a world, life would be a genuine ethical symphony played in a couple of poor octaves. The infinite scale of values would fail to open up. It would lack the note of infinitude and mystery. There would be no need of agonizing ourselves or making others agonize. It could all be dealt with in the easygoing mood.

The case for the strenuous mood is that when it is on, things get done. But the relativities of goods private to individuals, and obligations private to individuals, cannot set up the strenuous mood. If the good is God's good, and obligation is grounded in God's claims, then the strenuous mood will descend upon us.

When, however, we believe that a God is there, and that he is one of the claimants, the infinite perspective opens out. The scale of the symphony is incalculably prolonged. The more imperative ideals now begin to speak with an altogether new objectivity and significance, and to utter the penetrating, shattering, tragically challenging note of appeal.

The strenuous mood awakens at the sound. It saith among the trumpets, "Ha, ha!" It smelleth the battle afar off, the thunder of the captains and the shouting. Its blood is up. Cruelty to the lesser claims, so far from being a deterrent, does but add to the stern joy with which it leaps to answer the greater.

James appeals to history to document his claim that a moral philosophy which does generate the strenuous mood will always triumph over a moral philosophy which does not.

All through history, in the periodical conflicts of puritanism with the don't-care temper, we see the antagonism of the strenuous and the genial mood, and the contrast between the ethics of infinite and mysterious obligation from on high, and those of prudence and the satisfaction of merely finite need.

The capacity for the strenuous mood lies so deep down among our natural possibilities that even if there were no metaphysical or traditional grounds for believing in a God, men would postulate one simply as a pretext for living hard, and getting out of the game of existence its keenest possibilities of zest.

Our attitude toward concrete evils is entirely different in a world where we believe there are none but finite demanders, from what it is in one where we joyously face tragedy for an infinite demander's sake.   Every sort of energy and endurance, of courage and capacity for handling life's evils, is set free in those who have religious faith. For this reason the strenuous type of character will always outwear the easygoing type, on the battlefield of human history, and religion will drive irreligion to the wall.

That is the defense James offers for his main argument. Morality grounded in the will of God will generate the strenuous mood, whereas others will not.   He now turns, by way of conclusion, to a defense of this defense.

To some readers, such advocacy will seem a sad misuse of one's professional position.   Mankind, they will say, is only too prone to follow faith unreasoningly, and needs no preaching or encouragement in that direction.

I quite agree.   What mankind at large most lacks is criticism and caution, not faith.   Its cardinal weakness is to let belief follow recklessly upon lively conception.   Were I addressing the Salvation

Army, or a miscellaneous popular crowd, it would be a misuse of opportunity to preach as I have preached. What such audiences most need is that their faiths should be broken up and ventilated, that the northwest wind of science should get into them and blow their sickliness and barbarism away.

But I am speaking to an academic audience, and academic audiences, fed already on science, have a very different need. Paralysis of their native capacity for faith is *their* special form of mental weakness, brought about by the notion, carefully instilled, that there is something called "scientific evidence," by waiting upon which they shall escape all danger of shipwreck in regard to truth.

But there is no method, scientific or other, by which men can steer safely between believing too little and believing too much. To face such dangers is apparently our duty, and to hit the right channel between them is the measure of our' wisdom as men. It does not follow that, because recklessness may be a vice in soldiers, courage ought never to be preached to them.

READING REFERENCES. James wrote several topical essays which can be read to supplement the material in this chapter: "Is Life Worth Living?" "The Moral Equivalent of War," "The Dilemma of Determinism," "The Energies of Men," are a few. Perry's *The Life and Thought of William James*, already mentioned in an earlier chapter, is valuable here, too. Consult the table of contents of Perry's book.

READING QUESTIONS

1. What do you understand by *ethical skepticism?*
2. What is James's objection to it?
3. To what have ethical terms no application?
4. What is the point of his parable of a universe containing only one person?
5. What happens to the argument if we add another person?
6. How is he brought near to skepticism and relativism again?
7. What raises the question of the nature of an *ought?*
8. What does he mean by the *ground* of an obligation?
9. Wherein can it not be found? Why?

10. Wherein can it be found?
11. How is he brought near to skepticism and relativism again?
12. How does he use God to enable him to deal with the problem?
13. What new problem does this create?
14. How does he defend his appeal to God in moral philosophy?
15. What does he appeal to history to substantiate?
16. How does he defend his defense?
17. Formulate two or more criticisms of James's position.

TOPIC FIVE. A POLITICAL PROBLEM

The fact that men have religions, and that most religions include beliefs about God, provided us with the subject matter of our first topic. The fact that men distinguish between appearance and reality, and entertain beliefs about the nature of reality, provided us with the subject matter of our second topic. The fact that men distinguish between knowledge and speculation, and formulate theories to clarify and sharpen this distinction, provided us with the subject matter of our third topic. The fact that men distinguish between right and wrong, and formulate theories to clarify and sharpen this distinction, provided us with the subject matter of our fourth topic. The fact that men live in political organizations, and that political organization involves rights and duties of an imperative nature, provides us with the subject matter of our present topic.

Our subject is the state. Our problem is the justification of its claim to possess sovereign power over the wills of its subjects. Before elaborating upon this problem, we must note three terms, namely, *society*, *state*, *government*. The term *society* is not easily defined with any precision. We could perhaps say "Any group of people held together by actual or potential common interests." There seems to be intended some such meaning when we say, "Society insists that criminals be punished," or "The interests of society require a certain amount of fair dealing in business." The term *society* should not be confused with the term *state*. By the term *state* is meant a "society organized to make law possible."

'The state, again, is not the government. Statehood is a kind of organization which a society can exhibit. Government is an organization, within society, whose function is to make and administer the laws. A government may be elective or hereditary; again, it may be by one man or many men. These distinctions do not apply to the state.

The government of a state differs from the government of a church or university or industrial corporation in the amount of power which it sometimes possesses and always claims over the wills of individuals who compose the society of which it is the government. Thus, the government of a church may claim and sometimes possess the power to stipulate the conditions under which an individual may belong to the church. But it does not usually claim the power to prevent an individual from leaving the church, if he chooses to do so, nor the power to inflict physical punishment upon its members, to dispossess them of their property, to imprison them, to conscript them, or to execute them.

The unique characteristic of the government of a state is that under some circumstances it does claim power to deal in these and other ways with individuals without their consent, even against their wills. This is the claim to possess and exercise sovereignty. There are several interesting things about such a claim. It may be made, but it may be disputed. It may be challenged from within, in which case there is revolt. It may be challenged from without, in which case there is conquest. Or it may be merely evaded, in which case there is crime. The criminal, the invader, the rebel are differently related to the central claim which defines the government of a state.

We have distinguished between making and making good the claim to possess sovereign power. We need, also, to distinguish between both of these and justifying the claim. It is one thing to make a claim. It is another to enforce it. It is still another to justify it. The problem of the present topic arises out of this distinction between *de facto* and *de jure* claim to possess absolute sovereignty. Upon what is this claim based? If the question of justification be raised, to what shall appeal be made? The authors included in this topic have written with this or a closely related problem in mind. The issue is clearer in some than it is in others, but if, at any time, you have a sense of having lost this point of connection, you can always restate the matter in very simple terms, thus: The government of a state claims absolute sovereignty over its subjects. Upon what grounds can this claim be justified? Then ask yourself what light the author in point is shedding or attempting to shed on this problem.

The first author, James I of Great Britain, sets himself to answer the question of what are "the true grounds of the mutual duty and allegiance betwixt an absolute monarch and his people." This is our question, somewhat differently worded. The second author, Thomas Hobbes, says that he "will consider what are the rights and just power of a sovereign, and what it is that preserveth and dissolveth it." This, too, is our question, somewhat differently worded. The third author, Jean Jacques Rousseau, begins, "Man is born free, and is everywhere in chains. . . . How does this change come about? I do not know. What can make it legitimate? That question I think I can answer." This is again our problem, somewhat differently worded. The fourth author, Edmund Burke, after denying the notion of popular sovereignty, advances the claim that the foundation of the state, meaning its principle of justification, is to be sought among the needs of human nature, and specifically in the need to be coerced and restrained in things that are our duties when we might choose to violate these in the name of supposed rights. This again is our problem. The fifth author, John Stuart Mill, argues the case for vesting the absolute power claimed by the state in a government of representatives chosen by the people.

1. THE DIVINE RIGHT OF KINGS — FROM JAMES I

There is little to say by way of introduction to the argument which follows. Many persons have doubtless heard of the doctrine of the divine right of kings; few have had an opportunity to examine a somewhat detailed statement of it. For that reason, it is included here. The author, as will be seen from the biographical note which follows, was king of Scotland at the time this argument was written. Five years later, he became king of Scotland and England, that is, Great Britain. He is aware of the threefold distinction between claiming sovereignty, making good the claim to sovereignty, and justifying the claim to sovereignty. He would justify the claim to sovereignty by an appeal to the will of God, as revealed in the Scriptures and manifested in the order of nature.

BIOGRAPHICAL NOTE. James Stuart, subsequently James VI of Scotland and James I of Britain, was born in Edinburgh in 1566 and died in England in 1625 at the age of fifty-nine. He was the son of Mary, Queen of Scots. His life may be divided into three periods. (1) Until 1583 he was growing up, getting an education in the classics, the Bible, and Protestant theology, and discovering the vast difference between claiming and exercising supreme power. The question of justifying did not come until later. His mother was forced to abdicate in 1567. Scotland carried on under a regency until 1583, at which time James took matters into his own hands. (2) From 1583 to 1603 his energies were absorbed by a prolonged struggle with the still feudal nobility of Scotland. By the end of twenty years, he had reduced the anarchical baronage of sixteenth-century Scotland to obedience, and had replaced the divided sovereignty which was the essence of feudalism by a strong centralized authority. In fact, he did for Scotland what the Tudors had done for England, what

Louis XI had done for France, what Ferdinand and Isabella had done for Spain. During this period, in 1598, he wrote *The True Law of Free Monarchies*, which contains his argument for the divine right of kings. A year later, 1599, he published a treatise, *Demonologie*, denouncing witchcraft and exhorting the civil power to the strongest measures of suppression. (3) In 1603, Queen Elizabeth died closing the Tudor line in England. James VI of Scotland was invited to become James I of Britain, uniting Scotland and England under one throne. His career in England was less successful than it had been in Scotland. By disposition and conviction he was unfitted to succeed to the throne of the Henrys and Elizabeth. The Tudors had been strong monarchs, but they had not written books or made speeches in which they drew on the Bible to justify their absoluteness. They had claimed supremacy and, for the most part, made good their claim; they had not cast about for any subtle or elaborate justification.

THE ARGUMENT OF THE CITATIONS. James's argument may be divided into four parts. There is, first, a preamble in which he explains why and how he proposes to expound the doctrine of the divine right of kings. There is, second, a consideration of the duties of a king to his subject. These are explained, and the explanations documented by arguments drawn from the Scriptures and from the order of nature. There is, third, a consideration of the duties of a subject to his king. These are explained, and the explanations documented by arguments drawn from the Scriptures and the order of nature. This third portion of the total argument, "the duty that the lieges owe to their king, and the ground thereof" is the main thing. James's efforts to prove his case reach here a maximum. The whole doctrine of the divine right of kings is at stake. There is, finally, a consideration of objections to the doctrine. These objections are stated and refuted by arguments drawn from the Scriptures or the order of nature.   They will bear careful watching, because, in disclosing what James considers a relevant objection and a relevant reply, these passages reveal quite clearly the level at which the entire argument moves.   He begins:

My dear countrymen: Accept, I pray you, as thankfully this pamphlet that I offer unto you, as lovingly it is written for your weal.   It may be ye miss many things that ye look for in it.   But, for excuse thereof, consider rightly that I only lay down herein the true grounds, to teach you the right way, without wasting time upon refuting the adversaries.

My intention is to instruct, not to irritate.   The profit I would wish you to make of it, is, to frame all your actions according to these grounds, as may confirm you in the course of honest and obedient subjects to your king in all times coming, as also, when ye shall fall in with any that shall praise or excuse the by-past rebellions that brake forth either in this country, or in any other, ye shall herewith be armed against their siren songs.   Whereby ye shall soundly keep the course of righteous judgment, discerning wisely of every action only according to the quality thereof, and not according to your prejudged conceits of the committers.   So shall ye, by reaping profit to yourselves, turn my pain into pleasure.

As there is nothing so necessary to be known by the people of any land, next to their knowledge of God, as the right knowledge of their allegiance, according to the form of government established among them, especially in a monarchy, so hath the ignorance and seduced opinion of the multitude (blinded by them who think themselves able to teach and instruct) procured the wreck and overthrow of sundry flourishing commonwealths, and heaped heavy calamities, threatening utter destruction, upon others.

And among others, no commonwealth that ever hath been since the beginning hath had greater need of the true knowledge of this ground, than this our so long disordered and distracted common-wealth.   The misknowledge hereof is the only spring from whence hath flowed so many endless calamities, miseries, and confusions; as is better felt by many than the cause thereof well known and deeply considered.

The natural zeal, therefore, that I bear to this my native country, with the great pity I have to see the so-long disturbance thereof, hath compelled me to break silence, to discharge my conscience to you, my dear countrymen, so that, knowing the ground from whence these your many endless troubles have proceeded, ye may, by knowledge and eschewing of the cause, escape and divert the lamentable effects that ever necessarily follow thereupon.

I have chosen, then, only to set down in this short treatise, the true grounds of the mutual duty and allegiance betwixt a free and absolute monarch and his people.

First, I will set down the true grounds, whereupon I am to build, out of the Scriptures, since monarchy is the true pattern of divinity; next, from the law of nature, by divers similitudes drawn out of the same; and will end by answering the most weighty and apparent incommodities that can be objected.

From a statement of his aims and method, he turns to the first part of the argument. What have the Scriptures to say concerning the king's duties to his subjects? He begins:

The king's duty to his subjects is so clearly set down in many places of the Scriptures, and so openly confessed by all good princes, that it needeth not that I be long therein.

Kings are called Gods by the prophetical King David, in the sixth verse of the eighty-second Psalm, because they sit upon God His throne in the earth, and have the count of their administration to give unto Him. Their office is "to minister justice and judgment to the people," as the same David saith; "to advance the good and punish the evil," as he likewise saith; "to establish good laws to his people, and procure obedience to the same," as divers good kings of Judah did; "to procure the peace of the people," as the same David saith; "to decide all controversies that arise among them," as Solomon did; "to be the minister of God for the weal of them that do well, and to take vengeance upon them that do evil," as Saint Paul saith; "to go out and in before his people, as a good pastor," as is said in first Samuel; "that through the prince's prosperity, the people's peace may be procured," as Jeremiah saith.

And therefore, in the coronation of every Christian monarch,

they give their oath: first, to maintain the religion presently professed within their country, according to their laws whereby it is
established, and to punish all those who should seek to alter or
disturb the profession thereof; next, to maintain all the lowable
and good laws made by their predecessors, to see them put into
execution and the breakers and violators thereof punished according
to the tenor of the same; and lastly, to maintain the whole country,
and every state therein, in all their ancient privileges and liberties,
as well against all foreign enemies as among themselves.

In short, they take each his oath to procure the weal and flourishing of the people, not only by maintaining and executing the old
lowable laws of the country, by establishing new laws (as necessity
and evil manners will require), but by all other means possible to
foresee and prevent all dangers that are likely to fall upon them;
and to maintain concord, wealth, and civility among them as a
loving father and careful watchman, caring for them more than for
himself, knowing himself to be ordained for them, and not they for
him, accountable therefore to that great God who placed him as His
lieutenant over them, upon the peril of his soul to procure the weal
of both souls and bodies as far as in him lieth.

From the Scriptures he turns to the order of nature. What
does the order of nature show regarding a king's duties to
his subjects? He continues:

By the law of nature the king becomes a natural father to all his
lieges. As the father is bound to care for the nourishing, education, and virtuous government of his children, even so is the king
bound to care for all his subjects. As all the toil and pain that
the father can take for his children will be thought light and well
bestowed by him, so the effect thereof redounds to their profit
and weal; so ought the king to do toward his people. As the
kindly father ought to foresee all the inconveniences and dangers
that may arise toward his children, and with the hazard of his own
person to press to prevent the same; so ought the king toward his
people. As the father's wrath and correction upon any of his
children that offendeth ought, by a fatherly chastisement to be
seasoned with pity, as long as there is any hope of amendment in

them; so ought the king towards any of his lieges that offend in that measure.

In short, as a father's chief joy ought to be in procuring his children's welfare, rejoicing at their weal, sorrowing and pitying at their woe, hazarding for their safety, traveling for their rest, waking for their sleep, thinking (in a word) that his earthly felicity and life standeth and lieth more in them than in himself; so ought a good prince to think of his people.

Having dealt with the question of the king's duties to his subject, he turns to the much more controversial question of the subject's duties to the king. What do the Scriptures say regarding "the other branch of this tie"? He begins:

The other branch of this mutual and reciprocal tie is the duty and allegiance that the lieges owe to their king. The ground hereof I take out of the words of Samuel, dited by God's spirit, when God had commanded him to hear the people's voice in choosing and anointing them a king. Because that place of Scripture is so pertinent for our purpose, I insert herein the very words of the text.

That these words and discourses of Samuel were dited by God's spirit, it needs no further probation than that it is in the Scripture; since the whole Scripture is dited by that inspiration, as Paul saith; which ground no good Christian will or dare deny.

And it came to pass, when Samuel was old, that he made his sons judges over Israel. And his sons walked not in his ways, but turned aside after lucre, and took bribes, and perverted judgment. Then all the elders of Israel gathered themselves together, and came to Samuel unto Ramah, and said unto him: "Behold, thou art old, and thy sons walk not in thy ways: now make us a king to judge us like all the nations." But the thing displeased Samuel, when they said: "Give us a king to judge us." And Samuel prayed unto the Lord. And the Lord said unto Samuel: "Hearken unto the voice of the people in all that they say unto thee: for they have not rejected thee, but they have rejected Me, that I should not reign over them. According to all the works which they have done since the day that I brought them up out of Egypt even unto this day, wherewith they have forsaken Me, and served other gods, so do they also unto thee. Now therefore hearken unto their voice: howbeit yet protest solemnly unto them, and shew them the manner of the king that shall reign over them."

And Samuel told all the words of the Lord unto the people that asked of him a king. And he said: "This will be the manner of the king that shall reign over you: he will take your sons, and appoint them for himself, for his chariots, and to be his horsemen; and some shall run before his chariots. And he will appoint him captains over thousands, and captains over fifties; and will set them to ear his ground, and to reap his harvest, and to make his instruments of war, and instruments of his chariots. And he will take your daughters to be confectionaries, and to be cooks, and to be bakers. And he will take your fields, and your vineyards, and your oliveyards, even the best of them, and give them to his servants. And he will take the tenth of your seed, and of your vineyards, and give to his officers, to his servants. And he will take your menservants, and your maidservants, and your goodliest young men, and your asses, and put them to his work. He will take the tenth of your sheep: and ye shall be his servants. And ye shall cry out in that day because of your king which ye shall have chosen you; and the Lord will not hear you in that day." Nevertheless the people refused to obey the voice of Samuel; and they said: "Nay; but we will have a king over us; that we also may be like all the nations; and that our king may judge us, and go out before us, and fight our battles." And Samuel heard all the words of the people, and he rehearsed them in the ears of the Lord. And the Lord said to Samuel: "Hearken unto their voice, and make them a king."

If ye will consider the very words of the text, as they are set down, it shall plainly declare the obedience that the people owe to their king in all respects.

First, God commanded Samuel to grant the people a king. Then, He commanded Samuel to forewarn them of what some kings will do unto them, that they may not thereafter say, "We would never have had a king of God, had He let us know how we would have been used by him."

Next, Samuel declares unto them what points of justice and equity their king will break in his behavior unto them; and putteth them out of hope that they shall have leave to shake off that yoke which God, through their importunity, hath laid upon them.

Now, the erection of this kingdom and monarchy among the Jews, and the law thereof, may and ought to be a pattern to all Christian and well-founded monarchies, as being founded by God Himself. What liberty, then, can broiling spirits and rebellious minds justly claim against any Christian monarchy? They can claim no greater liberty, on their part, than the people of God might have done. They can point to no greater tyranny than was here forewarned to the people of God; and yet all rebellion was countermanded unto them.

That this proposition, grounded upon the Scripture, may the more clearly appear to be true, we never read that ever the prophets persuaded the people to rebel against the king, howsoever wicked he was.

There never was a more monstrous persecutor and tyrant nor Ahab was. Yet all the rebellion that Elias ever raised against him was to flee to the wilderness, where, for fault of sustentation, he was fed with the corbies.

I think no man will doubt but Samuel, David, Elias, had as great power to persuade the people, had they liked to employ their credit to uproars and rebellions against wicked kings, as had any of our seditious preachers in these days of whatsoever religion, either in this country or in France. (Only love of verity, I protest, has moved me this far to be somewhat satiric.)

I could cite further. Jeremiah threatened the people of God with utter destruction for rebellion against Nebuchadnezzar, the king of Babel, although he was an idolatrous persecutor, a foreign king, a tyrant and usurper of their liberties. Yet, in respect they had once received and acknowledged him for their king, Jeremiah not only commanded them to obey him but even to pray for his prosperity, adjoining the reason to it: because in his prosperity stood their peace.

To end the grounds of my proposition as taken out of the Scripture, let a notable example from the New Testament be considered. That king, whom Paul bids the Romans obey and serve for conscience' sake, was Nero — that bloody tyrant, that infamy to his age, that monster to the world, being also an idolatrous persecutor. If then, idolatry and defection from God, tyranny and the persecution of the Saints, hindered not the spirit of God to command his people under highest pain to give all due and hearty obedience for conscience, sake, giving to Caesar what was Caesar's and to God what was God's, what shameless presumption, I say, is it in any Christian people nowadays to claim that unlawful liberty which God refused to his own peculiar and chosen people?

In short, to take up in two or three sentences, grounded upon all these arguments out of the law of God, the duty and allegiance of the people to their lawful king, I say: Their obedience ought to be to him, as to God's lieutenant on earth answerable to God alone, obeying his commands in all things as the commands of God's minister; acknowledging him as a judge set by God over them and having power to judge them; fearing him and loving him; praying for him as their protector, for his continuance if he be good, for his amendment if he be wicked; following his lawful commands and fleeing his fury in his unlawful commands; offering no resistance, but by sobs and tears to God.

Thus the Scriptures. They are clearly on the king's side. What about the order of nature? Does it, too, support the king's claim to possess absolute sovereignty? He continues:

The agreement of the law of nature with the laws and constitutions of God will by two similitudes easily appear.

The king toward his people is rightly compared (1) to a father of children, and (2) to a head of a body composed of divers members.

As fathers, the good princes and magistrates of the people of God acknowledged themselves to their subjects. And for all other well-ruled commonwealths the style of *pater patriae* was ever used of kings.

Now, for the father's part, consider, I pray you, what duty his children owe to him, and whether, upon any pretext whatsoever, it will not be thought monstrous and unnatural in his sons to rise up against him, to control him, to slay him when they think good, or to cut him off and adopt to themselves any other they please in his room.

Can any pretense of wickedness or rigor on his part be a just excuse for his children to put a hand to him? Even suppose the father hated and wronged the children never so much, will any man, endowed with the least spark of reason, think it lawful for them to meet him with the line? Yea, suppose the father were furiously following his sons with a drawn sword, is it lawful for them to turn and strike back, or to make any resistance but by flight?

I think surely, if there were no more but the example of brute beasts, it may serve well enough to qualify and prove this my argument. For instance, we read often of the pity that storks have to their old and decayed parents. And generally, we know, there are many sorts of beasts and fowls that with violence and many bloody strokes will beat and banish their young ones from them as soon as they perceive them able to fend for themselves; but we never read or hear of any resistance on the part of the young, except among the vipers. This proves such persons as unnaturally follow this example to be endowed with a viperous nature.

As for the similitude of the head and the body, the proper office of a king toward his subjects agrees very well with the office of the head toward the body. For, from the head, being the seat of judgment, proceedeth the care and foresight of guiding, and preventing all evil that may come to the body or any part thereof. The head careth for the body; so doeth the king for his people. Discourse and directions flow from the head, execution according thereunto belongs to the rest of the members every one according to his office; so it is betwixt a wise prince and his people. Judgment, coming from the head, may employ the members every one in their own office as long as they are able for it; in case any one of them be affected with any infirmity, it must care and provide for their remedy, so it be curable, and if otherwise, cut them off for fear of infecting the rest. Even so it is betwixt the prince and his people. There is always hope of curing any diseased member by the direction of the head, as long as it is whole; but, by the contrary, if the head be troubled, all the members are partakers of that pain. So it is betwixt the prince and his people.

Now, it may very well fall out that the head will be forced to cut off some rotten members to keep the rest of the body in its integrity:

but what state the body can be in, if the head, for any infirmity that can befall it, be cut off, I leave to the reader's judgment.

To conclude these similitudes: If the children may upon any pretext lawfully rise up against their father, cut him off and choose any other they please in his room; if the body may for any infirmity that can be in the head, strike it off — then I cannot deny that the people may rebel, control, displace, or cut off their king.

The case is complete. Both God and nature are on the side of the king who claims absolute sovereignty. "In case any doubts might arise," however, he proposes four possible objections to his argument:

In case any doubts might arise in any part of this treatise, I will conclude with the solution of the principal and most weighty objections.

First, it is cast up by divers who employ their pens upon apologies for rebellions and treasons: every man is born to carry such a natural zeal and duty to his commonwealth that, seeing it so rent and deadly wounded, as whiles it will be by wicked kings, good citizens will be forced, out of said zeal and duty, to put their hand to work for freeing their commonwealth from such a pest.

Whereunto I give two answers: (1) It is a sure axiom in theology that evil should not be done in order that good may come of it. The wickedness, therefore, of the king can never make them that are ordained to be judged by him, to become his judges. If it be not lawful to a private man to revenge his private injury upon a private adversary, how much less is it lawful to the people, or any part of them, to take upon them the use of the sword against the public magistrate?

(2) In place of relieving the commonwealth out of distress, they shall keep double distress and trouble upon it; and so their rebellion shall procure the contrary effects that they pretend for it. For a king cannot be imagined to be so unruly and tyrannous but the commonwealth will be kept in better order by him than it can by his way-taking. For all sudden mutations are perilous in commonwealths, hope being thereby given to all bare men to set themselves up and fly with other men's feathers, the reins being loosed to all the

insolencies that disordered people can commit by hope of impunity because of the looseness of all things.

Second, it is objected: A curse hangeth over the commonwealth where a wicked king reigneth, and, say they, there cannot be a more acceptable deed in the sight of God than to free the country of such a curse.

Whereunto for answer: I grant indeed that a wicked king is sent by God for a curse to his people, and a plague for their sins. But, that it is lawful to them to shake off that curse by their own hand, which God hath laid upon them, that I deny, and may so do justly. Will any deny that the king of Babylon was a curse to the people of God, as was plainly forespoken and threatened unto them in the prophecy of their captivity? What else was Nero to the Christian church in his time? And yet, Jeremiah and Paul commanded the people not only to obey them, but heartily to pray for their welfare. It is certain then, that patience, earnest prayers to God, and amendment of their lives, are the only lawful means to move God to relieve them of that heavy curse.

The third objection: They say that the fortunate success which God hath so often given to enterprises of rebellion proveth plainly that God favored the justness of these quarrels.

To which I answer: It is true indeed that all the success of battles lieth only in God's hands. But, to conclude on that principle that He always gives victory to the just quarrel would prove that the Philistines, and divers other enemies of the people of God, had, in respect to the many victories they obtained over the people of God, justice on their side. It hath been so in many other instances. Therefore, I say, it is oft times a very deceivable argument to judge of the cause by the event.

The last objection is grounded upon the mutual pact and adstipulation betwixt the king and his people at the time of his coronation. For there, they say, was a mutual pact whereupon it followeth that if the contract be broken upon the king's side, the people are no longer bound to keep their part of it, but are thereby freed of their oath.

My answer: I confess that a king at his coronation oath promiseth to discharge honorably and truly the office given him by God over his people. But, presuming that thereafter he breaks his promise unto them never so inexcusably, the question is: Who should be judge? A contract cannot be broken by one party and so free the other party except first a lawful trial and cognition be had by the ordinary judge of the breakers thereof. Otherwise every man may be both party and judge in his own cause: which is absurd once to be thought.

Now (I say) in this contract betwixt the king and his people, God is the only judge, because to Him only the king must make count of his administration. For in His presence, as only judge of oaths, and therefore of coronation oaths, all oaths ought to be made. Since, then, God is the only judge betwixt the two contracting parties, the trial and revenge must only appertain to Him. It follows therefore that God must first give sentence upon the king before the people can think themselves freed of their oath.

The argument stated, the objections met, he concludes:

And as ye see it manifest: the king is overlord of the whole land. . . . In the parliament (which is nothing else but the head court of the king and his vassals) the laws are but craved by his subjects. For, although the king make daily statutes and ordinances, enjoining such pains thereto as he thinks fit, yet it lies in the power of no parliament to make any kind of law or statute without his scepter be to it giving it the force of law. He is master over every person that inhabiteth the land, having power over the life and death of every one of them. For, although a just king will not take the life of any of his subjects without a clear law, yet the laws whereby he taketh them are made by him; so the power flows always from him. . . . Likewise, although a good king will frame his actions to be according to the law, yet he is not bound thereto but of his good will and for good example-giving to his subjects.

READING REFERENCES. Other items by James I will be found in *The Political Works of James I* edited by C. H. McIlwain. To this volume Professor McIlwain has contributed a long and enlightening introduction. A history of Great Britain, especially if it included a chapter on the history of

Scotland during the period of James VI, would provide good background reading.

READING QUESTIONS

1. From whence have so many calamities flowed?
2. What has he chosen "to set down in this short treatise"?
3. Specify two or three duties enjoined upon kings by the Scriptures.
4. What analogy from the order of nature does he use to indicate the duties of kings to their subjects?
5. Give the story which he reads from the book of Samuel?
6. What was his point in referring to it?
7. What is the point of his reference to Ahab? To Nebuchadnezzar? To Nero?
8. Do you detect a cumulative effect in these three references?
9. What follows from his "king as father" argument?
10. What from his "king as head" argument?
11. What moral does he draw from what brute beasts?
12. How does he meet the objection: "It is the duty of a good citizen to free the commonwealth from a wicked king"?
13. What is the second objection which he considers?
14. How does he meet the objection: "The success which God hath given to rebellion proveth the justness of these quarrels"?
15. How does he deal with the objection: "If the contract be broken upon the king's side, the people are no longer bound to keep their part of it"?
16. Quote two or three sentences which indicate that James was seeking to justify absolute sovereignty in the monarch.

2. THE GREAT LEVIATHAN — FROM THOMAS HOBBES

FROM JAMES I TO HOBBES. King James had published *The True Law of Free Monarchy*, stating the case for the divine right of kings, in 1598. In 1603 he had become king of Great Britain. Throughout his reign, he sought to act upon the assumption that he possessed an absolute sovereignty delegated to him by God. His parliaments resented this notion, but bided their time. In 1625 James I was succeeded by Charles I, who also believed strongly in the doctrine of divine rights and tried to live up to it. Indeed, for eleven years, he ruled without parliament. But in 1640, needing extra money to finance some military operations, he convoked his parliament. This parliament continued in session for twenty years. It began by passing the Triennial Act, which required its convocation every three years, and presented, in the Grand Remonstrance, a summary of its objections to Stuart absolutism. In 1642, it conducted a civil war under the leadership of Cromwell. In 1649 it executed Charles I and set up a Commonwealth which lasted eleven years. During the early years of this Commonwealth period, in 1651, Thomas Hobbes published his book, *The Leviathan*.

The Leviathan contains a restatement of the case for absolute sovereignty. But this time the argument is not carried out in theological terms. It is not made to rest upon the claim that absolute sovereignty is something delegated to governments by God. It is a statement in naturalistic instead of supernaturalistic terms. It represents, therefore, a step toward the wholly secular statement of the claim that sovereignty is delegated to the government by a people organized as a state.

BIOGRAPHICAL NOTE. In Topic Two, "A Metaphysical Problem," we encountered Hobbes in the role of a propounder of materialism. In the present topic we are to meet him in the role of propounder of what he conceived to be the implications in political theory of his position in metaphysical theory. It will be remembered, from the previous biographical note, that Hobbes was born in 1588 and died in 1679. His political theory acquires considerable persuasiveness when one recalls the tumultuous period which it reflects. Hobbes was born ten years before James published the defense of the divine right of kings. He lived to see James I antagonize parliament by those claims, to see Charles I executed by his parliament, to see Cromwell become an absolute dictator under the Commonwealth, to see Charles II (restored to the throne in 1660) gradually alienate his parliament by absolutist claims. When Hobbes died, the reign of Charles II was six years from its close, and the reign of the House of Stuarts was but nine years from its close, for in 1688 the parliament deposed James II, thus putting an end to the Stuart dynasty and the political theory which it had exemplified. All this being so, it would seem that the argument of Hobbes's *Leviathan* reflected two elements in his own experience. He saw clearly that the divine-rights doctrine was a bankrupt trouble-maker, but he saw, equally clearly, that some person or persons not only do claim sovereignty, but must needs do so if society is not to disintegrate amid stresses and strains such as had been set up by James I, Charles I, the Civil War, and the Commonwealth, to mention only matters within the society in question.

THE ARGUMENT OF THE CITATIONS. There are two thoughts running through Hobbes's argument. Both refer to absolute sovereignty considered as a fact. The first thought is: On what hypothesis can the occurrence of this fact be accounted for? The second thought is: On what principle can this fact be morally justified? Hobbes does not always keep these matters distinct. We must do so. He begins with a pretty conceit, in which the body politic is likened to the body physical. From this he passes to an explanation of the formation of states. Out of this he derives a justification of the same. From this he passes to a description of the institution of sovereignty within any state; from this to an inventory of the rights and powers possessed by the person or persons in whom sovereignty is vested; from this to an inventory of the rights and powers reserved by individuals despite the absolute sovereignty supposed to exist in the government. And he ends with the thought that the universities of England would do well to propagate his views. He begins:

Two chief kinds of bodies offer themselves to such as search after their generation and properties: One is called a *natural body;* the other is called a *commonwealth* and is made by the wills and agreement of men.

Nature is imitated by the art of man in many ways; but especially in this, that it can make an artificial animal. For by art is created that great Leviathan called a *commonwealth* or *state,* which is but an artificial man, though of greater stature and strength than the natural man. The sovereignty is an artificial soul, as giving life and motion to the whole body; the magistrates and other officers of judicative and executive are artificial joints; rewards and punishments, by which every joint and member is moved to perform his duty, are the nerves; the wealth and riches of all the particular members are the strength; the people's safety is its business; councilors, by whom all things needful for it to know are suggested unto it, are the memory; equity and laws are its reason and will; concord is its health; sedition is its sickness; and civil war its death.

How and why does it come to pass that men make this "artificial animal" of which Hobbes here speaks? Why do men set up the state, limiting thereby their own liberties by the will of the person or persons in whom an absolute sovereignty is vested? Because of such facts as the following:

Nature hath made men so equal, in the faculties of the body and mind, as that though there be found one man sometimes manifestly stronger in body or of quicker mind than another, yet when all is reckoned together, the difference between man and man is not so considerable as that one man can thereupon claim to himself any benefit, to which another may not pretend as well as he. For as to strength of body, the weakest hath strength enough to kill the strongest, either by secret machinations or by confederacy with others that are in the same danger with himself.

From this equality of ability ariseth equality of hope in the attaining of our ends. And therefore, if any two men desire the same thing, which nevertheless they cannot both enjoy, they become enemies; and in the way to their end, which is principally their own conservation and sometimes their own pleasure only, endeavor to destroy or subdue one another.

So that in the first place, I put for a general inclination of all mankind a perpetual and restless desire of power after power that ceaseth only in death. And the cause of this that no man can assure the power and means to live well, which he hath at present, without the acquisition of more.

It may seem strange to some, who have not well weighed these things, that nature should thus dissociate and render men apt to invade and destroy one another. Such persons, not trusting to this inference made from the passions, may therefore desire to have the same confirmed by experience.

Let him therefore consider within himself. When taking a journey, he arms himself. When going to sleep, he locks his doors. Even in his own home, he locks his chests. What opinion has he of his fellow subjects, when he rides armed? Of his fellow citizens, when he locks his doors? Of his children and servants, when he locks his chest? Does he not there as much accuse mankind by his actions, as I do by my words?

Hereby it is manifest, that during the time men live without a common power to keep them all in awe, they are in that condition which is called war; and such a war as is of every man against every man. For war consisteth not in battle only, but in a tract of time wherein the will to contend by battle is sufficiently known.

Whatsoever therefore is consequent to a time of war, where every man is enemy to every man; the same is consequent to the time wherein men live without other security than what their own strength and their own invention shall furnish them withal.

In such condition, there is no place for industry because the fruit thereof is uncertain, and consequently no culture of the earth, no ←WAR navigation, no use of commodities that may be imported by sea, no commodious buildings, no instruments of moving and removing, no knowledge of the face of the earth, no account of time, no arts, no letters, no society; and, which is worst of all, continual fear of

<u>violent death</u>; and the life of man, solitary, poor, nasty, brutish, and short.

To this war of every man against every man this also is consequent, that nothing can be unjust. The notions of right and wrong, justice and injustice have there no place. <u>Where there is no common power, there is no law; where there is no law, there is no injustice.</u> Justice and injustice are faculties of neither the body nor the mind, differing herein from both the senses and the passions. They are <u>qualities that relate to men in society, not in solitude.</u> It is consequent also to the same condition that there be no propriety, no dominion, no mine and thine distinct, but only that to be every man's that he can get, and for so long as he can keep. Thus much for the ill condition which man by mere nature is actually placed in.

It may peradventure be thought that there never was such a time, nor condition of war such as this. And I believe it was never generally so, over all the world. But there are many places where they live so now. However, it may be perceived what manner of life there would be, where there were no common power to fear, by the manner of life that men degenerate into in a civil war.

The state, when it comes, is to be a union of wills to the end that law and order may be possible. The intolerable nature of the alternative — "the life of man, solitary, poor, nasty, brutish, and short" — is the justification. The state, man's answer to the threat of chaos, is founded upon a contract. What are the terms of this contract? Who are the parties to this contract? Hobbes continues:

Without the terror of some common power to cause them to be observed, justice, equity, modesty, mercy, doing to others as we would be done to, are contrary to our natural passions that carry us to partiality, pride, revenge, and the like. Covenants without the sword are but words, and of no strength to secure a man at all. <u>The only way to erect such a common power is for men to confer all their power and strength upon one man or one assembly of men that may reduce their wills unto one will</u>: which is as much as to say, for all to appoint one man or one assembly of men to bear their person, for all to acknowledge themselves to be the authors of whatsoever he shall do or cause to be done, in those things which concern the common peace and safety, for all to submit their wills to his will, and their judgments to his judgment.

This is more than consent or concord. It is a real unity of all in one person or one assembly of persons, made by covenant of every man with every man, as if every man should say to every man, "I give up my right of governing myself to this man or assembly of men on condition that thou give up thy right in like manner." This done, the multitude so united in one person or one assembly of persons is called a *commonwealth*. This is the generation of that great Leviathan, of that mortal god to which we owe (under the immortal God) our peace and defense.

He that carrieth this power is called *sovereign*, and is said to have sovereign power. Everyone besides is said to be his *subject*. In him consisteth the essence of the commonwealth; which, to define it, is "one person of whose acts a great multitude, by mutual covenants one with another, have made themselves everyone the author to the end that he may use the strength and means of all for their peace and defense."

The difference of commonwealth consisteth in the difference of the sovereign. When the representative is one man, then is the commonwealth a monarchy; when an assembly of all, then is the commonwealth a democracy; when an assembly of part only, then is the commonwealth an aristocracy. Other kind of commonwealth there can be none, for either one, or some, or all must have the sovereign power. The difference between these three kinds of commonwealth consisteth not in the difference of power, but in the difference of convenience or aptitude to produce the peace and security of the people; which end they were instituted to. [Hobbes then argues that on six counts of efficiency an absolute monarchy is to be preferred to any other form of sovereignty.]

We have, by now, seen why men set up a state. We have seen the nature of that contract upon which it rests. We have seen the peculiar relation of the sovereignty to this contract. He is a beneficiary of it but not a party to it. What follows, if this be so? Hobbes proceeds:

From this institution of a commonwealth are derived all the rights and powers of him or them on whom sovereign power is conferred by the consent of the people.

First, because they covenant, they cannot lawfully make a new covenant among themselves to be obedient to any other, in anything whatsoever, without his permission. They that are subject to a sovereign cannot, without his leave, cast him off and return to the confusion of a disunited multitude, nor transfer to another man or assembly of men; for they are bound every man to every man.

Second, because sovereignty is given by covenant only of one to another and not him to any of them, there can be no breach of covenant on the part of the sovereign. He that is made sovereign maketh no covenant with his subject beforehand. The opinion that any sovereign receiveth his power by covenant, that is on condition, proceedeth from want of understanding this easy truth that covenants, being but words and breath, have no force to oblige any man but what it has from the public sword, that is from the untied hands of that man or assembly of men that hath the sovereignty.

Third, because every subject is by this institution the author of all the actions of the sovereign, it follows that whatsoever the sovereign doth can be no injury to any of his subjects; nor ought he to be accused of injustice by any of them. For he that doth anything by authority of another, doth no injury to him by whose authority he acteth. He that complaineth of injury from his sovereign, complaineth of that whereof he himself is the author, and therefore ought not to accuse any man but himself; nor even himself, since to do injury to oneself is impossible.

Fourth, it follows from what was said last that no sovereign can justly be put to death or otherwise punished in any manner by his subjects. For seeing every subject is the author of the actions of his sovereign, he but punisheth another for the actions committed by himself.

Fifth, it is annexed to sovereignty to be judge of what opinions and doctrines are averse and what are conducive to peace; and, consequently, on what occasions, how far, and what men are to be trusted in speaking to multitudes, and who shall examine the doctrines of all books before they be published.   For the actions of men proceed from their opinions; and in all the well-governing of opinions consisteth the well-governing of men's actions in order to their peace and concord.   And, though in matter of doctrine, nothing ought to be regarded but the truth, yet this is not repugnant to regulating the same by reference to peace.   For doctrine repugnant to peace cannot be true.   For those men that are so remissly governed that they dare take up arms to defend or introduce an opinion, are still in a state of war.   Their condition is not peace, but only a cessation of arms for fear of one another, and they live as it were in the precincts of battle continually.   It belongeth therefore to sovereignty to be judge, or to appoint all judges, of opinions and doctrines, as a thing necessary to peace, and to prevent discord and civil war.

Sixth, the whole power of prescribing rules whereby every man may know what goods he may enjoy and what actions he may do without being molested by any of his fellow men, is annexed to sovereignty.   For before the constitution of sovereignty, as hath been shown, all men had right to all things, which necessarily causeth war.   And therefore, these rules of property and conduct, being necessary to peace and depending on sovereignty, are the act of that power in order to preserve the public peace.

Seventh, the right of hearing and deciding all controversies which may arise concerning law or concerning fact, is annexed to sovereignty.   For without such decision of controversies there is no protection of one subject against another, the laws concerning mine and thine are in vain, and to every man remaineth the right to protect himself by his private strength, which is the condition of war and contrary to the end for which commonwealth is instituted.

Eighth, the right of making war and peace, of judging when it is for the public good, of levying money upon the subjects to defray expenses thereof, is annexed to the sovereignty.

Lastly, to sovereignty is committed the power of rewarding every subject with riches or honor or dignity or titles; of punishing every subject by fine, by imprisonment, by corporal punishment, by ignominy, according to the law that sovereignty hath formerly made.

These are the rights which make the essence of sovereignty, and which are the marks whereby one may discern in what man or assembly of men the sovereign power is placed. For these are incommunicable and inseparable. And as the power, so also the honor of the sovereign ought to be greater than that of any or all of the subjects. Though his subjects shine, some more and some less when they are out of his sight, yet in his presence they shine no more than the stars in the presence of the sun.

Such are the rights and powers invested in government by men who form a state. Is this sovereignty absolute? Hobbes is evasive here. He seems to say, "In a sense, yes"; but, equally clearly, he means also, "In a sense, no." It appears that there are limits which define sovereignty. These take the form of rights reserved by men in case the sovereign should overreach itself. Thus:

As men, for the attaining of peace and conservation of themselves thereby, have made an artificial man which we have called a *commonwealth*, so also have they made artificial chains called *civil laws*, which they themselves by mutual covenants, have fastened at one end to the lips of that man or assembly of men to whom they have given sovereign power, and at the other end to their own ears. These bonds, in their own nature but weak, may nevertheless be made to hold, by the danger though not by the difficulty of breaking them. In relation to these bonds only it is that I am to speak now, of the liberty of subjects. What are the things which, though commanded by the sovereign, the subject may nevertheless justly refuse to do?

If the sovereign (i.e., the government) command a man, though justly condemned, to kill, to wound, or to maim himself; not to resist those that assault him; to refrain from anything without which he cannot live; that man hath the liberty to disobey.

If the sovereign interrogate a man concerning a crime done by himself, he is not bounden, without assurance of pardon, to confess it.

If a man be held in prison, he is not bounden by covenant to subjection. If he can, he may make his escape by any means whatsoever.

If the sovereign command a man to execute any dangerous or dishonorable office, and refusal to obey frustrates the end for which the sovereignty was ordained, there is no liberty to refuse; otherwise there is.

To resist the sword of the commonwealth, in defense of another man, guilty or innocent, no man hath liberty; because such liberty takes away from the sovereign the means of protecting us, and is therefore destructive of the very essence of government. But in case a great many men together have already resisted the sovereign power unjustly, or committed some capital crime, for which every one of them expecteth death, have they not the liberty to join together, and assist and defend one another?

They have, for they but defend their lives, which the guilty as well as the innocent may do. But the offer of pardon taketh from them the plea of self-defense and maketh their perseverance unlawful.

If a subject have a controversy with his sovereign, he hath the same liberty to sue for his rights as if it were against a subject.

If the sovereign, either monarch or assembly, grant any liberty to all or any subject, by virtue whereof he is disabled to provide for their safety, the grant is void.

The obligation of subject to sovereign lasts no longer than the power by which he is able to protect them. For the right men have by nature to protect themselves when none else can protect them, can by no covenant be relinquished.

If a subject be taken prisoner in war, and hath his life and liberty given him on condition he be subject to the victor, he hath liberty to accept the conditions.

If the sovereign shall relinquish the sovereignty without appointing successor, his subjects thereby return to the absolute state of nature.

If the sovereign banish the subject, during banishment he is not subject.

If the sovereign be subdued by war, subjects are delivered from their obligation and become obligated to the victor.

As for other liberties, they depend on the silence of the law. In cases where the sovereign has prescribed no rule, the subject hath the liberty to do or foredo according to his own discretion. And therefore, such liberty is in some places more and in some less, in some times more and in some times less, according as they that have the sovereignty shall think most convenient.

The argument closes with a few observations upon the wisdom of spreading these ideas among the students at the universities, and with the hope that the author may hereafter be left in that peace of mind required for the prosecution of his other studies.

I think what I have writ may be profitably printed, and more profitably taught at the universities, in case they also think so. For, seeing the universities are the fountains of civil and moral doctrine from whence the preachers and gentry, drawing such water as they find, sprinkle the same (both from the pulpit and in their conversation) upon the people, there ought to be great care taken to have it pure, both from the venom of heathen politicians and from the incantations of heathen spirits.

And thus I have brought to an end my discourse on government, occasioned by the disorders of the present time, without partiality, without application, without other design than to set before men's eyes the mutual relation between protection and obedience of which the condition of human nature and the laws both natural and positive, require an inviolable observation.

In the revolution of states there can be no very good constellation for truth of this nature to be born under. Yet I cannot think it will be condemned at this time, either by the public judge of doctrine, or by any that desire the continuance of public peace. And in this hope I return to my uninterrupted speculation of bodies natural, wherein I hope the novelty will as much please as, in the doctrine of this artificial body, it useth to offend.

READING REFERENCES. More by Hobbes is the best commentary on anything by Hobbes. Despite his somewhat archaic English, he is thoroughly readable and exceedingly suggestive. There is a refreshing cynicism about the man.

Further reading in *The Leviathan*, particularly that portion in which Hobbes describes the "kingdom of Darkness" is in order. Sir Leslie Stephen's book, *Hobbes*, in the *English Men of Letters* series, is good. So is Sir G. P. Gooch's book, *Political Thought in England: Bacon to Halifax*, in the *Home University Library* series. An older commentary will be found in the first two chapters of William Graham's *English Political Philosophy: Hobbes to Maine*.

READING QUESTIONS

1. Through what important events in English history did Hobbes live?
2. What light do these cast upon the argument of his *Leviathan?*
3. Wherein does he differ from James I?
4. To what sort of facts does he direct attention to explain the formation of states?
5. Pick out three or four apt or vivid phrases from his paragraph.
6. Who are parties to the contract upon which the state is founded?
7. What is the relation of the sovereign to this contract? Is he a contracting party? If not, why not?
8. "The difference of commonwealth consisteth in the difference of the sovereign." Explain.
9. What rights and powers comprise sovereignty?
10. What rights and powers are reserved?
11. Why does he recommend the teaching of his doctrines at th: universities?
12. "Artificial chains, fastened at one end to the lips of the sovereign and at the other to their own ears." Elucidate this image.
13. Are there any inconsistencies between the rights and powers of the sovereign and those reserved by the citizens?
14. How far would a believer in democracy go along with Hobbes? A believer in fascism?

3. THE SOCIAL CONTRACT AND THE GENERAL WILL — FROM JEAN JACQUES ROUSSEAU

FROM HOBBES TO ROUSSEAU. Hobbes published his account of the state, in his *Leviathan*, in 1651. It had been written with reference to the Puritan revolution in England in 1649. The intention of the author had been to explain to all parties what issues had been at stake in that upheaval. Between the *Leviathan* in 1651 and Rousseau's *Social Contract* in 1762, there came a second English revolution in 1688. This is referred to, sometimes, as the "bloodless" revolution, because of the fact that James II was deposed, the Stuart line closed, a new monarch invited to come to England from Holland, with little or no actual fighting. This revolution of 1688 was celebrated in the annals of political theory by John Locke in his *Two Treatises of Government*. This book defended the revolution on the ground that government rests upon the consent of the governed, and that what the governed consent to is a satisfactory definition and protection of their natural rights. There is, between sovereign and subject, a contractual relation. If the sovereign violates this contract, revolution is justified. This doctrinal claim that government *is* founded — in contrast to the historical claim that it *was* founded — on a contract was made the central theme of Jean Jacques Rousseau's important and influential little book, *The Social Contract*. Locke and Rousseau together provided the theory upon which the revolutionary movements at the end of the eighteenth century professed to rest. | Americans in 1776 and French in 1789 were convinced that their actions were susceptible of justification in terms of the *Two Treatises of Government* and the *Social Contract*. The essence of these books is perhaps expressed in the claims that an ideal government is one which permits self-government by the people; and that true self-government is the imposition by each man on himself of rules and limitations demanded by him of all others.

BIOGRAPHICAL NOTE. Jean Jacques Rousseau was born in Switzerland in 1712, and died in 1778 at the age of sixty-six. His life falls into three periods. (1) During the period from

1712 to 1748 he was acquiring the elements of a formal education and a great deal more than the elements of a worldly education. These matters are set down in his *Confessions*. As might be expected from the haphazard and undisciplined way in which he conducted himself during these years, Rousseau arrived at a state of thorough maladjustment. The times looked out of joint. The mores looked cramped and artificial. Civilization looked decadent.

(2) During the period from 1749 to 1762 he formulated his criticisms of the then modern world in a series of tracts which have given him his place in the scheme of things. The first of these (1749) was addressed to the question: Have the sciences and arts contributed to purify morals? Rousseau's answer was No. The second (1755) *On the Origin of Inequality Among Men*, argued that the root of inequality is the division of labor within society which permits the strong and wealthy to subject the mass of mankind to toil and poverty. The third (1760), *The New Heloise*, was a protest against the artificialities of marriage and the family. The fourth (1762), *Émile*, was an elaborate indictment of education conceived as discipline and restraint. It stated the case for education, conceived as expression and development. The fifth (1762), *The Social Contract*, was addressed to the problem: Man is born free, and is everywhere in chains. How can this be justified? In these writings, Rousseau managed to touch on practically every phase of eighteenth-century civilization. His pronouncements were usually in terms of such words as *artificial, unnatural, narrow, selfish, ignoble, crass*. Art, science, society, education, religion, the family, the state — all gave evidence that mankind was paying too great a price for the fruits of "civilized" living.

(3) During the period from 1763 to 1778 he was again a wanderer. He had said "Wasteland" to his generation. The authorities ordered him out of France. He moved to

Switzerland. The authorities ordered him out of Switzerland. He moved, at the invitation of David Hume, to England. This proved no better. He returned to France. During the last years of his life his mind became unbalanced. He died suddenly in 1778, two years after the American Revolution and eleven years before the French Revolution, for both of which in *The Social Contract* he had formulated the principles of justification.

THE ARGUMENT OF THE CITATIONS. The problem which Rousseau set himself to explore has been stated several times already. It was this: "Man is born free, and is everywhere in chains. How did this come about? I do not know. What can make it legitimate? That question I think I can answer." It is clear, from his manner of stating it, that Rousseau does not propose to account for the fact that man is everywhere in chains. That is, he is not proposing a piece of historical research into origins. Nor is he proposing to remove the chains in question. That is, he is not proposing an argument for anarchism. His question is the more searching one: Granted that men must live in chains (i.e., under laws) what considerations will justify the fact? He begins by rejecting the notion that the right of this condition is to be found in the might that enforces it. Might does not make right. What does, then? His answer is common need, common confrontation with conditions which no individual could handle if left to himself. This idea is contained in the notion of the social contract. The terms of the contract are noted. The attributes of the sovereignty created and sustained by the contract are noted. The role of lawmaker is noted. The nature of law is noted. The separation of powers within government is argued for. The alternative forms of government (monarchy, aristocracy, democracy) are noted, together with their defining virtues and vices. He notes, finally, "the unavoidable and inherent defect which

tends ceaselessly to destroy" any form of political organization in any society.   The argument begins as follows:

Man is born free, and is everywhere in chains.   One thinks himself the master of others, and still remains a greater slave than they.
How did this come about?   I do not know.   What can make it
legitimate?   That question I think I can answer.

The first thing to be clear about is that the restrictions
which law imposes cannot be justified by any appeal to the
fact of force which lies back of them.   Might does not make
right.   Thus:

Suppose that "force" creates "right."   The result is a mass of
nonsense.   For, if force creates right, then every force that is greater
than the first succeeds to its right.   As soon as it were possible to
disobey with impunity, disobedience would become legitimate;
and, the strongest being always in the right, the only thing that
would matter (so far as concerns "justification") would be to act
so as to become the strongest.

But what kind of "right" is it that perishes when force fails?
If we "must" obey, there is no question that we "ought" to obey.
And, on the principle that force makes right, if we are not forced to
obey, we are under no obligation to do so.   A brigand surprises me
at the edge of a wood.   The pistol he holds gives him power.   Does
it also give him right?   Even if I could withhold my purse, am I in
conscience bound to give it up?   Does his "might" create a "right"?

Force is a physical power, and I fail to see what moral effect it
can have.   To yield to force is an act of necessity, not of will;   at
most, an act of prudence.   In what sense can it be a duty?

"Obey the powers that be."   If this means "yield to force," it is a
good precept;   but superfluous: I can answer for its never being
violated.   If it means "yield, because all power comes from God,"
the case is no better.   All power comes from God, I admit;   but so
does sickness.   Does that mean that we are forbidden to call in a
doctor?

Let us admit then that force does not create right, and that we are
obligated to obey only legitimate powers.   In that case my original
question recurs: What is the basis of political obligation?

If might does not make right, if the "chains" cannot be justified by noting the fact that we are forced to wear them, what can we say? Rousseau shifts from the force which is admittedly necessary to the existence of law, to the conditions which justify law backed by force. Thus:

Suppose men to have reached the point at which the obstacles in the way of their preservation in the state of nature are greater than the resources at the disposal of each individual. That primitive condition can then subsist no longer, and the human race would perish unless it changed its manner of existence.

The problem is to find a form of association which will protect the person and goods of each individual with the whole common force of all; and in which each, uniting himself with all, may still obey himself alone and remain as free as before. This is the fundamental problem of which the "social compact" provides the solution.

If we disregard what is not of the essence of the social compact we shall find that it reduces itself to the following terms: "Each of us puts his person and his power in common under the supreme direction of the general will; and, in our corporate capacity, we receive each member as a part of the whole."

At one stroke, in place of the individual personality of each contracting party, this act of association creates a collective body, receiving from this act its unity, its common identity, its life, and its will. This public person, so formed by the union of all other persons, takes the name of *body politic*. It is called *state* when passive, *sovereign* when active, and *power* when compared with others like itself. Those who are associated in it take collectively the name of *people*, are severally called *citizens* as sharing in the sovereign power, and *subjects* as being under the laws of the state.

As soon as this multitude is united in one body politic, it becomes impossible to offend against one of the members without attacking the body politic, and still more to offend against the body politic. Duty and interest, therefore, equally obligate the two contracting parties to give each other help.

The social contract creates the state. It thereby creates the "chains" he had referred to. But it does more than that. The chains are seen to be, in principle, self-imposed restrictions; and they bring with them compensating advantages. Thus:

In the social compact there is no real "renunciation" on the part of the individuals. The position in which they find themselves, as a result of the compact, is really preferable to that in which they were before. Instead of a "renunciation," they have made an advantageous exchange; instead of an uncertain and precarious way of living, they have got one that is better and more secure; instead of natural independence, they have got liberty; instead of the power to harm others, they have got security for themselves; instead of their strength, which others might overcome, they have got a right which social union makes invincible.

What a man loses by the social compact is his natural liberty, and an unlimited right to everything he tries to get and succeeds in getting. What he gains is civil liberty and the proprietorship of all he possesses. If we are to avoid mistake in weighing one against the other, we must distinguish natural liberty, bounded only by the strength of the individual, from civil liberty, limited by the general will; and we must distinguish possession, the effect of force, from property, founded only on a positive title.

For such physical inequalities as nature may have set up between men, the social compact substitutes an equality that is moral and legitimate: by it, men who may be unequal in strength or intelligence, become every one equal by convention and legal right.

Under bad governments, this equality is only apparent and illusory: it serves only to keep the pauper in his poverty and the rich man in the position he has usurped. In fact, laws are always of use to those who possess, and harmful to those who have nothing: from which it follows that the social state is advantageous to men only when all have something and none have too much.

The general will alone can direct the state according to the object for which it was instituted, i.e., the common good: for, if the clashing of particular interests made the establishing of societies necessary, the agreement of these interests made it possible. The common element in these different interests is what forms the social tie; and, were there no point of agreement between them all, no society could exist. It is solely on the basis of this common interest that every society should be governed.

There is often a great difference between the "will of all" and the "general will." The latter considers only the common interest; the former takes private interest into account, and is no more than a sum of particular wills. But deduct from the sum of particular wills the plusses and minuses that cancel one another, and the general will remains.

Each individual may have a particular will contrary or dissimilar to the general will which he has as a citizen. His particular interest may speak to him quite different from the common interest; may make him look upon what he owes to the common cause as a gratuitous contribution, the loss of which will do less harm to others than the payment of it is burdensome to himself. He may come to regard the moral person which constitutes the state as a *persona ficta*, because not a man; and, as a result, may wish to enjoy the rights of citizenship without being ready to fulfill the duties of a subject. This, continued, would prove the undoing of the body politic.

The social contract creates sovereignty, i.e., a society organized to define and enforce its laws. This sovereignty inheres in the people. Rousseau proceeds to note several of its defining properties:

In order that the social compact may not be an empty formula, it includes the undertaking, that whoever refuses to obey the general will shall be compelled to do so. In this lies the key to the working of the body politic. This alone legitimizes civil undertakings which, without it, would be absurd, tyrannical and liable to the most frightful abuses. The social compact gives the body politic absolute power over all its members. It is this power, under the direction of the general will, which bears the name of *sovereignty*.

The sovereign, being formed wholly of the individuals who compose it, neither has nor can have any interest contrary to theirs. The sovereign, therefore, need give no guarantee to its subjects.

Merely by virtue of what it is, the sovereign is always what it should be.

Sovereignty, being nothing less than the exercise of the general will, is inalienable, and the sovereign, who is no less than a collective being, cannot be represented except by himself. The power may be delegated, but not the general will from which it derives. To be "general," the will need not be unanimous, but every vote must count; any exclusion is a breach of generality. For the same reason that it is inalienable, sovereignty is indivisible.

The social compact sets up among the citizens an equality of such a kind that they all bind themselves to observe the same conditions and should therefore all enjoy the same rights. Thus, from the very nature of the compact, every act of sovereignty binds or favors all the citizens equally; so that the sovereign recognizes only the body of the nation and draws no distinctions between those of whom it is made up.

What, then, is an act of sovereignty? It is not a convention between a superior and an inferior, but a convention between the body politic and each of its members. It is legitimate, because based on the social contract; equitable, because common to all; useful, because it can have no other object than the general good; and stable, because guaranteed by the public force and the supreme power.

The people are sovereign. Granted. But what can they do about it? They can delegate their sovereignty to a legislature and an administration. Of themselves the sovereign people cannot draw up good law nor can they administer it.

But how are the people to "regulate the conditions of society"? By a common agreement? By a sudden inspiration? Has the body politic an organ to declare its will? Who can give it the foresight to formulate and announce its acts in advance? How is it to announce them in the hour of need? How can a blind multitude, who often does not know what is good for it and hence what it wills, carry out for itself so great and difficult an enterprise as a system of legislation?

Of itself, the people always wills the good, but of itself it by no means always sees it. The general will is always in the right, but the judgment which guides it is not always enlightened. It must be got to see things as they are, and, sometimes, as they ought to appear to it. It must be shown the good road it is in search of, secured against the seductive influences of individual wills. It must be taught to see times and places, made to weigh the attractions of present and sensible advantages against the dangers of distant and hidden evils.

All stand equally in need of guidance. Individuals must be compelled to bring their wills into conformity with their reason. The public must be taught to know what is the good which it wills. If that is done, there is a union of understanding and will in the social body. The parts work together, and the whole is raised to its highest power. This makes a legislator necessary.

The function of lawmaker needs to be considered. The unique qualifications are noted. The "legislator" is a paradoxical ideal.

To discover the rules of society best suited to nations, a superior intelligence beholding all the passions of men without experiencing any of them, would be needed. This intelligence would have to be wholly unrelated to our nature, while knowing it through and through. Its happiness would have to be independent of our happiness and yet ready to occupy itself with it. It would have to look forward and, working in one century, to be able to enjoy the next. It would take gods to give men laws.

He who dares undertake the making of a people's institutions ought to feel himself capable of changing human nature, of transforming each individual into part of a greater whole, of altering men's constitution for the purpose of strengthening it, of substituting a shared and moral existence for the independent and natural existence which nature has conferred on us all. In a word, he must take away from man his own resources and give him in their stead new ones incapable of being used without the help of other men. The more completely these "natural" resources are annihilated, the greater and more lasting are those which supplant them, and the more stable and perfect are the new institutions.

The office of legislator, which gives form to the state, nowhere enters into its constitution. He who holds command over men (the government), ought not to hold command over the laws. He who holds command over the laws (the legislator) ought not to hold command over men. Else would his laws be the ministers of his passions serving to perpetuate his injustices, and his private aims mar the sanctity of his work.

When Lycurgus gave laws to Sparta, he began by resigning his throne. Most Greek towns entrusted the establishment of their laws to foreigners.

The republics of modern Italy in many cases followed this example. Geneva did the same and profited by it. Rome suffered a revival of tyranny and was brought to the verge of destruction, because it put legislative authority and sovereign power into the same hands.

Thus in the task of legislation we find two things which appear to be incompatible: an enterprise too difficult for human powers, and, for its execution, an authority that is no authority.

The great soul of the legislator is the only miracle that can prove his mission. Any man may engrave on tables, buy an oracle, feign secret intercourse with the gods, train a bird to whisper into his ear, or find some other trumpery way to impose on the people. He whose knowledge goes no further may perhaps gather round him a band of fools, but he will never found an empire, and his extravagances will perish with him. Idle tricks form a passing tie; only wisdom can make it lasting.

Provided the miracle of a good law can be performed, what does society have at its disposal? An instrument, essentially, for dealing with general conditions. The particulars must be seen to fall under the law by the wisdom of the executive.

What is a law? When the whole people declares for the whole people, this is what I call a *law*.

The matter about which such decree is made is, like the decreeing will, general. When I say that the matter is "general," I mean that law considers subjects *en masse* and actions in the abstract, never a particular person or action. Thus law may declare that there shall be privileges; but it cannot confer them on any one by name. It may set up classes of citizens. It may specify qualifications for membership of these classes. But, as law, it cannot nominate such and such persons as belonging to these classes. Law may, e.g., establish a monarchical form of government and an hereditary succession. It cannot choose a king or nominate a royal family. In a word, no function which has a particular object in view can be a matter of law.

On this view, we see at once that it can no longer be asked whose business it is to make laws, since they are acts of the general will; nor whether "government is above the law," since governors are part of the state; nor whether laws can be unjust, since no one is unjust to himself; nor how we can be both "free" and at the same time subject to laws, since they are but registers of our wills.

The law unites universality of will with universality of object. What any man commands of his own motion cannot be law. Even what sovereignty commands with regard to some particular matter cannot be law; it is then merely a decree of the government.

Laws are, strictly speaking, the conditions of civil association. The people, being subject to the laws, ought to be their author: the conditions of the society ought to be regulated by those who unite to give it form.

Thus far we have had society, the contract, the sovereign people, the legislator, and laws. We come now to government, what we would call the executive arm of government. It is not to be confused with any of the other terms:

I have argued that the power to make laws belongs to the sovereign people, and can belong to it alone. On the other hand, the power to execute these laws cannot belong to the generality, because such power consists wholly of particular acts which fall outside the competency of lawmaking as such.

The body politic, therefore, needs an agent of its own to bind it together, to set it to work under the direction of the general will, to serve as a means of communication between the (people as) state and the (people as) sovereign. Here we have the basis of government, something which is often confused with the sovereign whose minister it is.

What then is government? It is an intermediate body, set up

between the (people as) subjects and the (people as) sovereign, to secure their mutual correspondence, to execute the laws and to maintain liberty. The members of this body are called governors.

Government is hence simply and solely a commission, in which the governors, mere officials of the sovereign people, exercise in their own name the power which is invested in them by the people. This delegated power the sovereign people can limit, modify, or recover at pleasure.

The government gets from the (people as) sovereign the orders which it gives to the (people as) subjects. For the state to be properly balanced there must be an equality between the power of the government and the power of the citizens, for the latter are, on the one hand, sovereign, and, on the other hand, subject.

None of these three terms — *sovereign, subjects, government* — can be altered without the equality being instantly destroyed. If the sovereign tries to govern, if the government tries to give laws, or if the subjects refuse to obey, disorder replaces order, force and will no longer act together, and the state is dissolved into despotism or anarchy.

Government, then, is distinct from such matters as society, sovereignty, legislator, etc. Its function is to administer the laws. What form should it have?

There has been at all times much dispute concerning the best form of government. Is it democratic? Aristocratic? Or monarchical? This question, "What, absolutely, is the best form of government?" is unanswerable and indeterminate. The fact is that each is in some cases the best, and in others the worst.

Let us see. Consider first the notion of democracy:

The sovereign people may commit the charge of the government to the whole people or to a majority of the people. The result would be that more citizens would be actual governors than mere private subjects. This form of government is called *democracy*.

If we take the term in the strict sense, there never has been a real democracy, and there never will be. It is unimaginable that the people should remain continually assembled to devote their time to public affairs.

Besides, how many conditions, difficult to unite, would such a form of government presuppose! First, a very small state, where the people can readily be got together and where each citizen can with ease know all the rest. Second, great simplicity of manners, to prevent business from multiplying and raising thorny problems. Third, a large measure of equality in rank and fortune, without which equality of rights and authority cannot long subsist. Fourth, little or no luxury, for luxury either comes of riches or makes them necessary.

Moreover, it is a certainty that promptitude in execution diminishes as more people are put in charge of it. Where prudence is made too much of, not enough is made of fortune; opportunity is let slip, and deliberation results in the loss of its object.

It may be added that no form of government is so subject to civil wars and intestinal agitations as democracy, because there is none which has so strong and persistent a tendency to change to another form, or which demands more vigilance and courage for its maintenance. Were there a people of gods, their government would be democratic. So perfect a government is not for men.

Obviously, pure democracy is unsuited to the needs of the modern state. Another possibility is an elected aristocracy. It holds more promise:

The sovereign people may restrict the government to a small number, so that there are more private citizens than magistrates. This is named *aristocracy*.

There are three sorts of aristocracy: natural, elective, and hereditary. The first is only for simple peoples; the second is the best, and is aristocracy properly so-called; the third is the worst of all governments.

There is much to be said for an elective aristocracy. It has the advantage of keeping clear the distinction between the two powers, sovereignty and government. Besides this, its members are chosen to be governors, not born to this office, as in the case of a pure democracy or an hereditary aristocracy. By this means uprightness, understanding, experience, and all other claims to pre-eminence become so many guarantees of wise government.

It is more efficient. Assemblies are more easily held; affairs are better discussed and carried out with more order and diligence; the credit of the state is better sustained abroad.

It is more economical. There is no need to multiply instruments, or get twenty thousand men to do what a hundred picked men can do better.

However, if an elective aristocracy does not demand all the virtues needed by popular government, it demands others which are peculiar to itself; for instance, moderation on the side of the rich, and contentment on the side of the poor. If this form of government carries with it a certain inequality of fortune, this is justifiable on the grounds that the administration of public affairs may be entrusted to those who are most able to give them their whole time.

In Rousseau's day the commonest form of government was hereditary monarchy. It has its good points and its bad points. Thus:

The sovereign people may concentrate the whole government in the hands of a single person from whom all others hold their power. This form of government is the most usual, and is called *monarchy*.

No form of government is more vigorous than this. All answer to a single motive power. All the springs of the machine are in the same hands. The whole moves toward the same end. There are no conflicting movements to cancel one another. In no constitution does a smaller amount of effort produce a greater amount of action. Archimedes seated quietly on the bank of a river, easily drawing a great floating vessel, stands in my mind for a skillful monarch governing vast estates from his study, moving everything while he seems himself unmoved.

For a monarchical state to have a chance of being well governed, its population and extent must be proportionate to the abilities of its governor. It is easier to conquer than to rule. With a lever long enough, the world could be moved with a single finger; to sustain it requires the shoulders of Hercules.

Everything conspires to take away from a man who is set in authority the sense of justice and reason.

Kings desire to be absolute, and men are always crying out to them from afar that the best means is to get themselves loved by their people. This is all very well, and true enough in some respects. Unfortunately, it will always be derided at court. The power that comes of a people's love is no doubt the greatest; but it is precarious and conditional, and princes will never rest content with it. The best of kings desire to be in a position to be wicked, if they so please, without forfeiting thereby their mastery. Political sermonizers may tell them, to their hearts' content, that the people should be prosperous, numerous, and formidable. Kings know this to be untrue. Their personal interest is that the people should be weak, wretched, and unable to resist them.

There is an essential and inevitable defect which will always rank a monarchy below a republic. It is this. In a republic the people hardly ever raises men who are unenlightened and incapable to the highest positions; whereas, under a monarch, those who rise to power are most often petty blunderers, petty swindlers, petty intriguers, men whose petty talents cause them to get into stations of the greatest eminence at court. The people is far less often mistaken in its choice than the monarch. A man of real worth among the king's ministers is almost as rare as a fool at the head of a republic.

Another disadvantage in monarchical government is the lack of any continuous succession. When one king dies, another is needed. In the case of an elective monarchy, dangerous interregnums occur, and are full of storms; unless, that is, the citizens are upright and disinterested to a degree which seldom goes with this kind of government.

What has been done to prevent these evils? Succession has been made hereditary in certain families. That is to say, men have chosen rather to be ruled by children, monstrosities, or imbeciles than to endure disputes over the choice of good kings. Apparent tranquillity has been preferred to wise administration.

These difficulties have not escaped our political writers. But they are not troubled by them. The remedy, they say, is to obey without a murmur: God sends bad kings in His wrath, and they are to be borne as the scourges of heaven. Such talk is doubtless edifying, but it would be more in place in a pulpit than in a political book. What are we to say of a doctor whose whole art is to exhort the sufferer to patience?

By way of conclusion we may note the fundamental fact from which political instability continually proceeds:

All forms of government contain within them the seeds of destruction and dissolution. As the particular will acts constantly in opposition to the general will, the government continually exerts itself against the sovereign. The greater this exertion becomes, the more the constitution changes. This is the unavoidable and inherent defect which, from the very birth of the body politic, tends ceaselessly to destroy it, as age and death end by destroying the human body.

Such is the natural and inevitable tendency of the best constituted governments. If Sparta and Rome perished, what state can hope to endure for ever? We desire a long-lived form of government? Let us not dream of making it eternal. If we are to succeed, we must not attempt the impossible; nor must we flatter ourselves that we are endowing the work of man with a stability which human conditions do not permit.

The body politic begins to die as soon as it is born, and carries in itself the causes of its own destruction. The state is a work of art, not of nature. It is for men to prolong its life as much as possible, by giving it the best possible constitution. But even the best will have an end.

The life principle of the body politic lies in the sovereign authority. The legislative power is the heart of the state; the executive power is its brain. The brain may become paralyzed, and the body still live. But as soon as the heart ceases to perform its function, the organism is dead. Wherever the laws grow weak as they become old, there is no longer a legislative power, and the state is dead.

READING REFERENCES. The number of books written on Rousseau is exceedingly large. Each generation has found it necessary to take stock of his ideas. Lord Morley's *Rousseau* is good reading for those who continue to share Lord Morley's typically nineteenth-century rationalism and liberalism. A most provocative chapter on *The Social Contract* is to be found in Bernard Bosanquet's *Philosophical Theory of the State*. The author stresses the fact that Rousseau's self-imposed problem was *not* how to justify revolution, but how to justify restraint of the individual by the state. A good biography is to be found in Matthew Josephson's *Jean Jacques Rousseau*. The best comprehensive accounts of Rousseau's ideas are to be found, so far as books written in English are concerned, in C. W. Hendel's two volumes, *Rousseau as Moralist*, and in Matthew Josephson's *Jean-Jacques Rousseau*.

READING QUESTIONS

1. What is Rousseau's problem?
2. What does he say is *not* his problem?
3. On what grounds does he deny that force or might makes right?
4. What is the fundamental problem of which the social compact provides the solution?
5. What compensations attend the adoption of the social compact?
6. What "continued, would prove the undoing of the body politic"?
7. "Sovereignty is inalienable." Explain.
8. "And indivisible." Explain.
9. "It would take gods to give men laws." Why?
10. "The office of legislator nowhere enters into the constitution." Meaning? Why not?
11. "Law must deal with general considerations." Meaning? Reason?
12. Explain the status of government in Rousseau's argument?
13. What is his case against a democratic government?
14. What are the virtues and requirements of an elective aristocratic government?

15. "There is an essential and inevitable defect which will always rank a monarchy below a republic." Namely?

16. "The unavoidable and inherent defect which tends ceaselessly to destroy the body politic." Namely?

4. PRINCIPLES OF CONSERVATISM — FROM EDMUND BURKE

FROM ROUSSEAU TO BURKE. Rousseau published *The Social Contract* in 1762. The American Revolution began in 1775. It was scarcely over when the French Revolution began, in 1789. This political restlessness in the colonies and in Europe was accompanied by a sharp demand for parliamentary reform in England. The revolutionary Society for Constitutional Information was organized in 1780. Prime Minister Pitt tried three times, and each time in vain, to persuade a reluctant House of Commons to consider the case for parliamentary reform. During these years, Tom Paine was gaining his reputation as spokesman for liberal and revolutionary movements in America and Europe. Jeremy Bentham published in 1789 his epoch-making treatise on liberal social reform, *Principles of Morals and Legislation*, in which he argued that customs, laws, institutions, and constitutions should be evaluated in terms of one standard, namely, the greatest happiness of the greatest number.

Such was the climate of opinion in which Edmund Burke wrote his exposition and defense of political conservatism. On all hands he saw, or thought he saw, signs that the old regimes of monarchies and aristocracies were weakening before popular demand for democratic politics. Wherever he looked, he detected "factions now busy amongst us who endeavor to propagate an opinion that the people, in forming their commonwealth, have by no means parted with their power over it." He set himself to stem this tide. He might as well have bade the sun stand still. These democratizing tendencies swept on and left the memory of his plea stranded

amid the welter of wars, revolutions, reforms, and changes.
If this were all, there would be little need to include Burke
among spokesmen of political philosophy. But there is more
to Burke than a neglected warning against democratic politics. In his words may be found a careful account of the
principles of political conservatism. It is an expression of
one of man's perennial needs.

BIOGRAPHICAL NOTE. Edmund Burke was born in Ireland
in 1729 and died in England in 1797 at the age of sixty-eight.
He received his academic education at Trinity College, Dublin. He spent some time acquiring the rudiments of a legal
training in London in the Middle Temple. He entered
Parliament in the 1760's and rose there to a position of great
prestige. In 1775 he delivered his famous speech, "Concilia-
tion with America." In 1785 he opened his attack on Warren
Hastings' India administration with his equally famous
speech "The Nabob of Arcot's Debts." In 1790 he published
his *Reflections on the French Revolution*. The ideas advanced in
this tract were subsequently elaborated in his *Appeal from the
New to the Old Whigs*, his *Letter to a Noble Lord* and his *Letter on a
Regicide Peace*. The citations in this chapter are, for the most
part, from the *Reflections* and the *Appeal* and the *Letters*.

THE ARGUMENT OF THE CITATIONS. Burke begins by noting
that there are certain "factions now busy amongst us who
endeavor to propagate an opinion that 'the people' in forming
their commonwealth have by no means parted with their
power over it." In other words, the notion of popular
sovereignty is being argued for. The substance of such claims
is noted. A general criticism is passed upon them. The
concept of "the people," upon which the whole argument
turns, is then proposed for analysis. What does one mean by
the people? If by *the people* one means a numerical majority,
then certain criticisms may be advanced. At this point the
argument is suspended while Burke makes two long excur-

sions into recent French history with a view to documenting
his critique of the concept of the people as sovereign. The
first aside is addressed to a Frenchman, pointing out the extent to which, in Burke's mind, alternative steps had been
possible in France at the time the revolution was launched.
Various excesses are noted. "Were all these dreadful
things necessary?" he demands. The second aside recounts
the fate of the French king and queen and laments the absence
of wisdom and decency exhibited by those who put them to
death. "Alas, the age of chivalry is gone." From these
historical asides, he returns to his criticism of the "barbarous
philosophy" which has led to this havoc.

At this point Burke's arguments become positive. He
sketches the foundation in which government is laid. From
this, there results a more austere conception of the state than
is held by those who launch and defend revolution in the
name of the "rights of man." Does this commit Burke to a
repudiation of the notion of the rights of man? "I am far
from denying the real rights of man," he protests. The notion of "real" rights, in contrast to spurious rights, is outlined. This involves a clarification of "real" liberties in
contrast to spurious liberties. The "real" rights and liberties, which Burke is prepared to ascribe to "the people" presuppose government by a natural aristocracy. This notion
is outlined. It is then contrasted with a sham aristocracy
of mere lords and dukes.

The fundamental claim is disclosed at this point: Burke
will entertain the notion of rights only in terms of the notion
of duties. We have rights because we have duties, and, within limits, we do not choose our duties. They await us in the
society into which we are born and in which we grow up.
This idea may involve difficult problems and nice distinctions.
In all such cases, it is wiser to keep an eye on duties than on
rights. The burden of proof rests with those who violate

obligations in the name of their rights. This, however, is not to be taken as a categorical denial of all change and reform, merely an insistence that wisdom ordinarily lies with custom and tradition, and that an individual should address himself to the problem of extracting the wisdom which these contain. It is folly to "trade each on his own private stock of reason." This conservative political philosophy rests upon a recognition of the fact that wise politics has, in the last analysis, a religious basis. "On religion all our laws and institutions stand." "The awful author of our being has disposed and marshaled us by a divine tactic." The argument concludes with several eloquent paragraphs setting forth the great wisdom which attends the policy, arising out of these views, of regarding "liberties as an entailed inheritance" to be held as a sacred trust and passed on intact to one's posterity.

Factions now busy amongst us, in order to divest men of all love for their country, and remove from their minds all duty with regard to the state, endeavor to propagate an opinion that the "people," in forming their commonwealth, have by no means parted with their power over it. Discuss any of their schemes, and their answer is, It is the act of the people and that is sufficient.

These theorists hold, that sovereignty, whether exercised by one or many, did not only originate from the people, but that in the people the same sovereignty constantly and unalienably resides; that the people may lawfully depose kings; not only for misconduct, but without any misconduct at all; that they may set up any new fashion of government for themselves, or continue without any government at their pleasure; that the people are essentially their own rule, and their will the measure of their conduct; that the tenure of rulers is not a proper subject of contracts, because rulers have duties, but no rights; and that if a contract *de facto* is made with them in one age, allowing that it binds at all, it binds only those who are immediately concerned in it, but does not pass to posterity.

They hold that to a majority of the people belongs the right of altering the whole frame of their society, if such should be their pleasure. They may change it, say they, from a monarchy to a republic today and tomorrow back again from a republic to a monarchy, and so backward and forward as often as they like. They are masters of the commonwealth, because in substance they are themselves the commonwealth.

The ceremony of cashiering kings, of which these gentlemen talk so much, can rarely, if ever, be performed without force. It then becomes a case of war, and not of constitution. Laws are commanded to hold their tongues amongst arms, and tribunals fall to the ground with the peace they are no longer able to uphold.

Whilst they are possessed by these notions, it is vain to talk to them of the practice of their ancestors, the fundamental laws of their country, the fixed form of a constitution, whose merits are confirmed by the solid test of long experience, and an increasing public strength and national prosperity. They despise experience as the wisdom of unlettered men, and as for the rest, they have wrought underground a mine that will blow up, at one grand explosion, all examples of antiquity, precedents, charters, and acts of parliament.

Burke now has the political heresy stated. It is the claim that the people are sovereign and need acknowledge no masters save of their own choosing. Those who hold this view are, Burke feels, beyond the reach of argument. Nevertheless, over against the time when experience shall have disclosed to them the folly of their ways, he proposes to analyze and evaluate their claim:

These doctrines concerning "the people" tend, in my opinion, to the utter subversion, not only of all government, in all modes, but all stable securities to rational freedom, and all the rules and principles of morality itself.

On such principles every individual would have a right to originate what afterwards is to become the act of the majority. Whatever he may lawfully originate, he may lawfully endeavor to accomplish. He has a right therefore to break the ties and engagements which bind him to the country in which he lives, and he has a right to make as many converts to his opinions, and to obtain as many associates in his designs, as he can procure: <u>for how can you know the dispositions of the majority to destroy their government, but by tampering with some part of the body?</u> You must begin by a secret conspiracy, that you may end with a national confederation.

The mere pleasure of the beginning must be the sole guide, since the mere pleasure of others must be the sole ultimate sanction, as well as the sole actuating principle in every part of the progress. Thus, arbitrary will (the last corruption of ruling power) step by step poisons the heart of every citizen.

No sense of duty can prevent any man from being a leader or a follower in such enterprises. Nothing restrains the tempter; nothing guards the tempted. Nor is the new state, fabricated by such arts, safer than the old. What can prevent the mere will of any person, who hopes to unite the wills of others to his own, from an attempt wholly to overturn it? It wants nothing but a disposition to trouble the established order, to give a title to the enterprise.

By such doctrines, all love to our country, all pious veneration and attachment to its laws and customs, are obliterated from our minds; and <u>nothing can result from this opinion,</u> when grown into a principle, and animated by discontent, ambition, or enthusiasm, <u>but a series of conspiracies and seditions, sometimes ruinous to their authors, always noxious to the state.</u>

There is, it appears, much to be said against this popular doctrine. A few obvious things have already been noted. But nothing fundamental has been offered as yet. Burke moves, accordingly, to the essential point. Everything turns upon the meaning of this phrase, *the people*. So he proceeds:

Believing it a question at least arduous in theory, and in practice very critical, it would become us to ascertain what our incantations are about to call up from darkness and the sleep of ages when the supreme authority of "the people" is in question. Before we attempt to extend or to confine, we ought to fix in our minds, with some degree of distinctness, an idea of what it is we mean, when we say *the people*.

We are so little affected by things which are habitual, that we consider this idea of the decision of a majority as if it were a law of our original nature, but such constructive whole, residing in a part only, is one of the most violent fictions that ever has been or can be made on the principles of artificial incorporation. Out of civil society nature knows nothing of it; nor are men, even when arranged according to civil order, otherwise than by very long training, brought at all to submit to it.

In a state of rude nature there is no such thing as "a people." A number of men in themselves have no collective capacity. The idea of a people is the idea of a corporation. It is wholly artificial, and made like all other legal fictions, by common agreement. What the particular nature of that agreement was, is collected from the form into which the particular society has been cast. Any other is not their covenant.

When men, therefore, break up the agreement which gives its corporate form and capacity to a state, they are no longer a people; they have no longer a corporate existence; they have no longer a legal, coactive force to bind within, nor a claim to be recognized abroad. They are a number of vague, loose individuals and nothing more. With them all is to begin again. Alas! They little know how many a weary step is to be taken before they can form themselves into a mass, which has a true, political personality.

The phrase *the people* cannot be identified with a mere voting majority. Such an idea, namely that a voting majority shall be "the people" is a product of late political experience. Men must have learned much from long trial and error before they can act on that notion. It expresses an agreement or consensus that political experience alone makes possible. If this meaning of the phrase is a product of group experience of state organization, then it cannot be argued to be prior to and more fundamental than state organization. To overlook or to deny this fact is to court much trouble. Thus:

I see as little of policy or utility, as there is of right, in laying down a principle that a majority of men, told by the head are to be considered as "the people," and that as such their will is to be law. What policy can there be in arrangements made in defiance of every political principle? To enable men to act with the weight and character of a people, and to answer the ends for which they are incorporated into that capacity, we must suppose them to be in that state of habitual social discipline, in which the wiser, the more expert, and the more opulent conduct, and by conducting enlighten and protect the weaker, the less knowing, and the less provided with the goods of fortune. When the multitude are not under this discipline, they can scarcely be said to be in civil society.

It is not necessary to teach men to thirst after power. But it is very expedient that by moral instruction, they should be taught, and by their civil constitutions they should be compelled, to put many restrictions upon the immoderate exercise of it, and the inordinate desire for it. The best method of obtaining these great points forms the important, but at the same time the difficult problem to the true statesman. No legislator, at any period of the world, has willingly placed the seat of active power in the hands of the multitude: because there it admits of no control, no regulation, no steady direction whatsoever.

The people are not to be taught to think lightly of their engagements to their governors; else they teach their governors to think lightly of their engagements toward them. In that kind of game in the end the people are sure to be the losers. To flatter them into a contempt of faith, truth, and justice, is to ruin them; for in those virtues consists their whole safety. To flatter any man, or any part of mankind, in any description, by asserting that in engagements he or they are free whilst any other human creature is bound, is ultimately to vest the rule of morality in the pleasure of those who ought to be rigidly submitted to it, to subject the sovereign reason of the world to the caprices of weak and giddy men.

The democratic commonwealth is the foodful nurse of ambition.

Under other forms of government it meets with many restraints. Whenever, in states which have a democratic basis, the legislators have endeavored to put restraints upon ambition, their methods were as violent, as in the end they were ineffectual: as violent indeed as any the most jealous despotism could invent. The caution could not very long save the state which it was meant to guard, from the attempts of ambition, one of the natural, inbred, incurable distempers of a powerful democracy.

I am well aware that men love to hear of their power, but have an extreme disrelish to be told of their duty. This is a matter of course; because every duty is a limitation of some power. Indeed arbitrary power is so much to the depraved taste of the vulgar of every description, that almost all dissensions, which lacerate the commonwealth, are not concerning the manner in which it is to be exercised, but concerning the hands in which it is to be placed.

The people are, to a far less extent than are princes and other persons of exalted station, under responsibility to one of the greatest controlling powers on earth, the sense of fame and estimation. The share of infamy that is likely to fall to the lot of each individual in public acts is small indeed; the operation of opinion being in the inverse ratio to the number of those who abuse power. Their own approbation of their own facts has to them the appearance of a public judgment in their favor. A perfect democracy is therefore the most shameless thing in the world. As it is the most shameless, it is also the most fearless.

At this point Burke turns from his criticism of the notion of "the people" to some of the facts in recent French history. These facts, he feels, will amply bear out what he claims.

We hear much from men, who have not acquired their hardiness of assertion from the profundity of their thinking, about the omnipotence of a majority, in such a dissolution of an ancient society as hath taken place in France.

It appears to me as if I were in a great crisis, not of the affairs of France alone, but, of all Europe, perhaps of more than Europe. All circumstances taken together, the French Revolution is the most astonishing that has hitherto happened in the world. The most wonderful things are brought about in many instances by means the most absurd and ridiculous; in the most ridiculous modes; and apparently, by the most contemptible instruments. Everything seems out of nature in this strange chaos of levity and ferocity, and of all sorts of crimes jumbled together with all sorts of follies. In viewing this monstrous tragicomic scene, the most opposite passions necessarily succeed, and sometimes mix with each other in the mind; alternate contempt and indignation; alternate laughter and tears; alternate scorn and horror.

His estimate at this point is addressed to a citizen of France under the new regime. Hence his use of the second person:

Your constitution was suspended before it was perfected, but you had the elements of a constitution very nearly as good as could be wished. In your old estates you possessed that variety of parts corresponding with the various descriptions of which your community was happily composed; you had all that combination, and all that opposition of interests; you had that action and counter-action which, in the natural and in the political world, from the reciprocal struggle of discordant powers, draws out the harmony of the universe.

You had all these advantages in your ancient states, but you choose to act as if you had never been molded into civil society, and had everything to begin anew. You began ill, because you began by despising everything that belonged to you. You set up your trade without a capital. If the last generations of your country appeared without much luster in your eyes, you might have passed them by, and derived your claims from a more early race of ancestors. Under a pious predilection for those ancestors, your imaginations would have realized in them a standard of virtue and wisdom, beyond the vulgar practice of the hour, and you would have risen with the example whose imitation you aspired. Respecting your forefathers, you would have been taught to respect yourselves. You would not have chosen to reconsider the French people as a people of yesterday, as a nation of low-born servile wretches until the emancipating year of 1789.

You might, if you pleased, have given to your recovered freedom a dignity. Your privileges, though discontinued, were not lost to memory. Your constitution, it is true, whilst you were out of possession, suffered waste and dilapidation, but you possessed in some parts the walls, and, in all, the foundations of a noble and venerable castle. You might have repaired those walls; you might have built on those old foundations.

You would have rendered the cause of liberty venerable in the eyes of every worthy mind in the nation. You would have shamed despotism from the earth, by showing that freedom was not only reconcilable, but, as when well disciplined, it is auxiliary to law. You would have had an unoppressive but a productive revenue. You would have had a flourishing commerce to feed it. You would have had a free constitution; a potent monarchy; a disciplined army; a reformed and venerated clergy; a mitigated but spirited nobility, to lead your virtue, not to overlay it; you would have had a liberal order of commons, to emulate and to recruit that nobility; you would have had a protected, satisfied, laborious, and obedient people, taught to seek and to recognize the happiness that is to be found by virtue in all conditions; in which consists the true moral equality of mankind, and not in that monstrous fiction, which, by inspiring false ideas and vain expectations into men destined to travel in the obscure walk of laborious life, serves only to aggravate and embitter that real inequality, which it never can remove; and which the order of civil life establishes as much for the benefit of those whom it is able to exalt to a condition more splendid, but not more happy.

From a consideration of what the citizens might have done, Burke turns to note some of the things they have done. Thus:

Who that had not lost every trace of humanity could think of casting down men of exalted rank and sacred function, some of them of an age to call at once for reverence and compassion; casting them down from the highest situation in the commonwealth, wherein they were maintained by their own landed property; casting them down to a state of indigence, depression, and contempt.

Who but a tyrant could think of seizing on the property of men, unaccused, unheard, untried, by wholesale descriptions, by hundreds and thousands together? I hope we shall never be so totally lost to all sense of the duties imposed upon us by the law of social union, as, upon any pretext of "public service," to confiscate the goods of a single unoffending citizen.

That a man should rejoice and triumph in the destruction of an absolute monarchy; that in such an event he should overlook the captivity, disgrace, and degradation of an unfortunate prince, and the continual danger to a life which exists only to be endangered; that he should overlook the utter ruin of whole orders and classes of men, extending itself directly, or in its nearest consequences, to at least a million of our kind, and to at least the temporary wretchedness of a whole community, I do not deny to be in some sort natural: when people see a political object, which they ardently desire, they are apt extremely to underrate the evils which may arise in obtaining it. This is no reflection upon the humanity of those persons. Their good nature I am the last man in the world to dispute. It only shows that they are not sufficiently informed or sufficiently considerate. When they come to reflect seriously on the transaction, they will think themselves bound to examine what the object is that has been acquired by all this havoc.

This was unnatural. The rest is in order. They have found their punishment in their success. Laws overturned; tribunals subverted; industry without vigor; commerce expiring; the revenue unpaid, yet the people impoverished; a church pillaged, and a state not relieved; civil and military anarchy made the constitution of the kingdom; everything human and divine sacrificed to the idol of public credit, and national bankruptcy the consequence; and, to crown all, the paper securities of new, precarious, tottering power, the discredited paper securities of impoverished fraud, and beggared rapine, held out as a currency for the support of the empire, in lieu of the two great recognized species that represent the lasting, conventional credit of mankind, which disappeared and hid themselves in the earth from whence they came, when the principle of property, whose creatures and representatives they are, was systematically subverted.

Compute your gains; see what is got by those extravagant and presumptuous speculations which have taught your leaders to despise all their predecessors, and all their contemporaries, and even to despise themselves, until the moment in which they became truly despicable. By following those false lights, France has bought undisguised calamities at a higher price than any nation has purchased the most unequivocal blessings! France has bought poverty by crime! France has abandoned her interest, that she might prostitute her virtue. All other nations have begun the fabric of a new government, or the reformation of an old, by establishing originally, or by enforcing with greater exactness, some rights or other of religion. All other people have laid the foundations of civil freedom in severer manners and a system of more austere and masculine morality. France, when she let loose the reins of regal authority, doubled the license of a ferocious dissoluteness in manners, and of an insolent irreligion in opinions and practices; and has extended through all ranks of life, as if she were communicating some privilege, or laying open some secluded benefit, all the unhappy corruptions that usually were the disease of wealth and power. This is one of the new principles of equality in France.

Were all these dreadful things necessary? Were they the inevitable results of the desperate struggle of determined patriots, compelled to wade through blood and tumult, to the quiet shore of a tranquil and prosperous liberty? No! nothing like it. The fresh ruins of France, which shock our feelings wherever we can turn our eyes, are not the devastation of civil war; they are the sad but instructive monuments of rash and ignorant counsel in time of profound peace. They are the display of inconsiderate and presumptuous, because unresisted and irresistible authority. The persons who have thus squandered away the precious treasure of their crimes, the persons who have made this prodigal and wild waste of public evils, have met in their progress with little, or rather with no opposition at all. Their whole march was more like a triumphal procession, than the progress of a war. Their pioneers have gone before them, and demolished and laid everything level at their feet. Not one drop of their blood have they shed in the cause of the country they have ruined. They have made no sacrifices to their projects of greater consequence than their shoe buckles, whilst they were imprisoning their king, murdering their fellow citizens, and

bathing in tears, and plunging in poverty and distress, thousands of
worthy men and worthy families. Their cruelty has not even been
the base result of fear. It has been the effect of their sense of perfect
safety, in authorizing treasons, robberies, rapes, assassinations,
slaughters, and burnings, throughout their harassed land.

So far his indictment has been in terms of rather large
general issues. He moves to consider more specific outrages,
particularly the case of the king and queen. Burke's prose
here should be read aloud.

Let those who have the trust of political or of natural authority
ever keep watch against the desperate enterprises of innovation; let
even their benevolence be fortified and armed. They have before
their eyes the example of a monarch, insulted, degraded, confined,
deposed; his family dispersed, scattered, imprisoned; his wife insulted to his face like the vilest of the sex, by the vilest of all populace; himself three times dragged by these wretches in an infamous
triumph; his children torn from him, in violation of the first right
of nature, and given into the tuition of the most desperate and impious of the leaders of desperate and impious clubs; his revenues
dilapidated and plundered; his magistrates murdered; his clergy
proscribed, persecuted, famished; his nobility degraded in their
rank, undone in their fortunes, fugitives in their persons; his armies
corrupted and ruined; his whole people impoverished, disunited,
dissolved; whilst through the bars of his prison, and amidst the
bayonets of his keepers, he hears the tumult of two conflicting
factions.

All this accumulation of calamity, the greatest that ever fell upon
one man, has fallen upon his head, because he had left his virtues
unguarded by caution; because he was not taught that, where power
is concerned, he who will confer benefits must take security against
ingratitude.

It is now sixteen or seventeen years since I saw the queen of France,
then the dauphiness, at Versailles; and surely never lighted on this
orb a more delightful vision. I saw her just above the horizon,
glittering like the morning star, full of life and splendor and joy.

Oh! what a revolution, and what a heart must I have, to contemplate without emotion that elevation and that fall. Little did I dream, when she added titles of veneration to those of enthusiastic, distant, respectful love, that she should ever be obliged to carry the sharp antidote against disgrace concealed in that bosom. Little did I dream that I should have lived to see such disasters fallen upon her in a nation of gallant gentlemen, a nation of men of honor and of cavaliers. I thought ten thousand swords must have leaped from their scabbards to avenge even a look that threatened her with insult!

But alas, the age of chivalry is gone. The age of sophisters, economists, and calculators has succeeded, and the glory of Europe is extinguished for ever. Never, never more shall we behold that generous loyalty to rank and sex, that proud submission, that dignified obedience, that subordination of the heart, which kept alive, even in servitude itself, the spirit of an exalted freedom. The unbought grace of life, the cheap defense of nations, the nurse of manly sentiment and heroic enterprise, is gone. That sensibility of principle, that chastity of honor, which felt a stain like a wound, which inspired courage while it mitigated ferocity, which ennobled whatever it touched, under which vice lost half its evil by losing all its grossness, is gone.

Now all is changed. All the pleasing illusions, which made power gentle and obedience liberal, which harmonized the different shades of life, which by a bland assimilation incorporated into politics the sentiments which beautify and soften private society, are to be dissolved by this new conquering empire of "light and reason." All the decent drapery of life is to be torn off. All the superadded ideas, furnished from the wardrobe of a moral imagination, which the heart owns and the understanding ratifies as necessary to cover the defects of our naked shivering nature and raise it to dignity in our own estimation, are to be exploded as ridiculous, absurd, and antiquated fashion.

Back of all this chaos and cruelty and injustice and folly lies the doctrine of popular sovereignty. That was what

Burke set out to criticize. His asides have been intended merely to document his claims:

The pretended "rights of man," which have made this havoc, cannot be the rights of the people. For to be a people, and to have these rights, are things incompatible. The one supposes the presence, the other the absence of a state of civil society. The very foundation of the French commonwealth is false and self-destructive; nor can its principles be adopted in any country, without the certainty of bringing it to the very same condition in which France is found.

On the scheme of this barbarous philosophy, which is the offspring of cold hearts and muddy understandings, which is void of solid wisdom, which is destitute of all taste and elegance, laws are to be supported only by their own tenors and by the concern which each individual may find in them from his own private speculations or can spare to them from his own private interests. In the groves of their academy, at the end of every vista, you see nothing but the gallows.

On the principles of this philosophy institutions can never be embodied in persons. That sort of "reason" which banishes the affections is incapable of filling their place. These public affections, combined with manners, are required, sometimes as supplements, sometimes as correctives, always as aids, to law.

At this point he returns to his original argument. "The people" cannot be the foundation of government, it seems, or he has misread French history of late. What then? If the foundation of coercive government is not to be found in the doctrine of the "rights of man," where then? He settles down to this more positive question:

The dislike I feel to revolutions, the signals for which have so often been given from pulpits; the spirit of change that is gone abroad; the total contempt which prevails of all ancient institutions, when set in opposition to a present sense of convenience, or to the bent of a present inclination — all these considerations make it not unadvisable, in my opinion, to call back our attention to the true principle of laws.

The foundation of government is laid, not in imaginary rights of men, but in political convenience, and in human nature; either as that nature is universal, or as it is modified by local habits and social aptitudes. The foundation of government is laid in a provision for our wants, and in a conformity to our duties; it is to purvey for the one; it is to enforce the other.

Among men's wants is to be reckoned the want of a sufficient restraint upon their passions. Society requires not only that the passions of individuals should be subjected, but that even in the mass and body, as well as in the individuals, the inclinations of men should frequently be thwarted, their will controlled, and their passions brought into subjection. This can only be done by a power out of themselves; not subject to that will and those passions which it is its office to bridle and subdue.

In this sense the restraints on men, as well as their liberties, are to be reckoned among their rights. But as the liberties and the restrictions vary with times and circumstances, and admit of infinite modifications, they cannot be settled upon any abstract rule; and nothing is so foolish as to discuss them upon that principle.

The state ought to be considered as something better than a partnership agreement in a trade of pepper and coffee, calico or tobacco, to be taken up for a little temporary interest, and to be dissolved by the fancy of the parties. It is to be looked on with reverence, because it is not a partnership in things subservient only to the gross animal existence of a temporary and perishable nature.

The state is a partnership in all science, a partnership in all art, a partnership in every virtue and in all perfection. As the ends of such a partnership cannot be attained in many generations, it becomes a partnership not only between those who are living, but between those who are living, those who are dead, and those who are to be born. People will not look forward to posterity who never look backward to their ancestors.

Each contract of each particular state is but a clause in the great primeval contract of eternal society, linking the lower with the higher natures, connecting the visible and the invisible world.

according to a fixed compact sanctioned by the inviolable oath which holds all physical and all moral natures each to their appointed places.

The "rights of man" are not the foundation of the state. They are not "prior" to the state. Indeed, they are made possible by the state; and the foundation of anything is not to be sought in that which the things in question makes possible. What then does he think about the "real" rights of men which *proceed* from political organization?

I am far from denying the real rights of men. In denying their false claims of right, I do not mean to injure those which are real, and are such as their pretended rights would totally destroy. If civil society be made for the advantage of man, all the advantages for which it is made become his right.

Men have right to the fruits of their industry, and to the means of making their industry fruitful. They have a right to the acquisitions of their parents; to the nourishment and improvement of their offspring; to instruction in life, and to consolation in death. Whatever each man can separately do, without trespassing upon others, he has a right to do for himself, and he has a right to a fair portion of all which society, with all its combination of skill and force, can do in his favor.

In this partnership all men have equal rights, but not to equal things. He that has but five shilling in the partnership, has as good a right to it as he that has five hundred pounds has to his larger proportion. But he has not a right to an equal dividend in the product in the joint stock, and as to the share of power, authority, and direction which each individual ought to have in the management of the state, that I must deny to be amongst the direct original rights of man in civil society; for I have in my contemplation the civil social man, and no other. It is a thing to be settled by convention.

Circumstances (which with some gentlemen pass for nothing) give in reality to every political principle its distinguishing color and discriminating effect. The circumstances are what render every civil and political scheme beneficial or noxious to mankind.

I must be tolerably sure, before I venture publicly to congratulate men upon a blessing, that they have really received one. Flattery corrupts both the receiver and the giver, and adulation is not of more service to people than to kings. I should therefore suspend my congratulations on the acquisition of liberties, until I was informed how it had been combined with government; with public force; with the discipline and obedience of armies; with the collection of an effective and well-distributed revenue; with morality and religion; with solidity and property; with peace and order; with civil and social manners.

All these (in their way) are good things too, and, without them, liberty is not a benefit whilst it lasts, and it is not likely to continue long. The effect of liberty to individuals is that they may do what they please; we ought to see what it will please them to do, before we risk congratulations, which may be soon turned into complaints. Prudence would dictate this in the case of separate, insulated, private men; but liberty, when men act in bodies, is power. Considerate people, before they declare themselves, will observe the use which is made of power, and particularly of so trying a thing as new power in new persons, of whose principles, tempers, and dispositions, they have little or no experience, and in situations where those who appear the most stirring in the scene may possibly not be the real movers.

I flatter myself that I love a manly, moral, regulated liberty as well as any gentleman, be he who he will; and perhaps I have given as good proofs of my attachments to that cause, in the whole course of my public conduct. I think I envy liberty as little as they do, to any other nation. But I cannot stand forward, and give praise or blame to anything which relates to human actions, and human concerns, on a simple view of the object, as it stands stripped of every relation, in all the nakedness and solitude of abstraction.

Is it because liberty in the abstract may be classed amongst the blessings of mankind, that I am seriously to felicitate a madman, who has escaped from the protecting restraint and wholesome darkness of his cell, on his restoration to the enjoyment of life and liberty? Am I to congratulate a highwayman and murderer, who has broke prison, upon the recovery of his natural rights?

If true rights and liberties presuppose government, and therefore, coercion, the question, as in Rousseau, presents itself: What is the best form of government? Again as in Rousseau, the answer is an aristocracy. But where Rousseau had suggested an elective, Burke suggests a natural aristocracy. Thus:

Believe me, those who attempt to level never equalize. In all societies, consisting of various descriptions of citizens, some description must be uppermost. The levelers therefore only change and pervert the natural order of things; they load the edifice of society, by setting up in the air what the solidity of the structure requires to be on the ground. Tailors and carpenters cannot be equal to the situation, into which, by the worst of usurpations, an usurpation on the prerogatives of nature, you attempt to force them.

You will hear it said that all occupations are honorable. If this means only that no honest employment was disgraceful, it does not go beyond the truth. But in asserting that anything is honorable, we imply some distinction in its favor. The occupation of a hairdresser, or of a working tallow chandler, cannot be a matter of honor to any person — to say nothing of a number of other more servile employments. Such men ought not to suffer oppression from the state, but the state suffers oppression, if such as they, either individually or collectively, are permitted to rule. In this you think you are combatting prejudice, but you are at war with nature.

A true natural aristocracy is not a separate interest in the state, or separable from it. It is an essential integrant part of any large body rightly constituted. It is formed out of a class of legitimate presumptions, which, taken as generalities, must be admitted for actual truths. To be bred in a place of estimation; to see nothing low and sordid from one's infancy; to be taught to respect oneself; to be habituated to the censorial inspection of the public eye; to look early to public opinion; to stand upon such elevated ground as to be enabled to take a large view of the widespread and infinitely diversified combinations of men and affairs in a large society; to have leisure to read, to reflect, to converse; to be enabled to draw the court and attention of the wise and learned wherever they are to be found; to be habituated to command and to obey; to be taught to despise danger in the pursuit of honor and duty; to be formed to the greatest degree of vigilance, foresight, and circumspection, in a state of things in which no fault is committed with impunity, and the slightest mistakes draw on the most ruinous consequences; to be led to a guarded and regulated conduct, from a sense that you are considered as an instructor of your fellow citizens in their highest concerns, and that you act as a reconciler between God and man; to be employed as an administrator of law and justice, and to be thereby amongst the first benefactors to mankind; to be a professor of high science, or of liberal and ingenuous art; to be amongst rich traders, who from their success are presumed to have sharp and vigorous understandings, and to possess the virtues of diligence, order, constancy, and regularity, and to have cultivated an habitual regard to commutative justice — these are the circumstances of men that form what I should call a *natural* aristocracy, without which there is no nation.

Men, qualified in the manner I have just described, form in nature, as she operates in the common modification of society, the leading, guiding, and governing part. It is the soul to the body, without which the man does not exist. To give therefore no more importance, in the social order, to such men, than that of so many units, is a horrible usurpation.

When great multitudes act together, under that discipline of nature, I recognize the people. I acknowledge something that perhaps equals, and ought always to guide the sovereignty of convention. In all things the voice of this grand chorus of national harmony ought to have a mighty and decisive influence.

But when you disturb this harmony; when you break up this beautiful order, this array of truth and nature, as well as of habit and prejudice; when you separate the common sort of men from their proper chieftains so as to form them into an adverse army, I no longer know that venerable object called *the people* in such a disbanded race of deserters and vagabonds. For a while they may be terrible indeed, but in such a manner as wild beasts are terrible. The mind owes to them no sort of submission. They are, as they have been reputed, rebels.

Woe to the country which would madly and impiously reject the service of the talents and virtues, civil, military, or religious, that are given to grace and serve it, and would condemn to obscurity everything formed to diffuse luster and glory around a state. Woe to that country too that, passing into the opposite extreme, considers a low education, a mean contracted view of things, a sordid, mercenary occupation, as a preferable title to command.

He wishes to be clear about one point. His doctrine of a natural aristocracy does not commit him to a theory of government by lords and dukes. Thus:

I am accused of being a man of aristocratic principles. If by *aristocracy* they mean the peers, I have no vulgar admiration, nor any vulgar antipathy, toward them; I hold their order in cold and decent respect. I hold them to be of absolute necessity in the constitution, but I think they are only good when kept within their proper bounds.

I am no friend to aristocracy, in the sense at least in which that word is usually understood. If it were not a bad habit to moot cases on the supposed ruin of the constitution, I should be free to declare that, if it must perish, I would rather by far see it resolved in any other form than lost in that austere and insolent domination.

Do not imagine that I wish to confine power, authority, and distinction to blood and names and titles. There is no qualification for government but virtue and wisdom, actual or presumptive. Wherever they are actually found, they have, in whatever state, condition, profession or trade, the passport of Heaven to human place and honor.

From the notion of a natural aristocracy, Burke returns to his earlier theme that government is justified by reason of the fact that men have duties which they need to have enforced. He desires to point out that "duties" is a basic notion, and that duties are seldom a matter of choice:

Look through the whole of life, and the whole system of duties. Much the strongest moral obligations are such as were never the result of our option.

<u>I cannot too often recommend it to the serious consideration of</u> <u>all men, who think civil society to be within the province of moral</u> <u>jurisdiction, that if we owe to it any duty, it is not subject to our</u> <u>will.   Duties are not voluntary.   *Duty* and *will* are even contra-</u> <u>dictory terms.</u>

Men without their choice derive benefits from association; without their choice they are subjected to duties in consequence of these benefits; and without their choice they enter into a virtual obligation as binding as any that is actual.   Look through the whole of life and the whole system of duties.   Much the strongest moral obligations are such as were never the result of our option.

When we marry, the choice is voluntary, but the duties are not matter of choice.   They are dictated by the nature of the situation. Dark and inscrutable are the ways by which we come into the world. The instincts which give rise to this mysterious process of nature are not of our making.   But out of physical causes, unknown to us, perhaps unknowable, arise moral duties, which as we are able per- fectly to comprehend, we are bound indispensably to perform.

Parents may not be consenting to their moral relation; but con- senting or not, they are bound to a long train of burdensome duties toward those with whom they have never made a convention of any sort.   Children are not consenting to their relation, but their rela- tion, without their actual consent, binds them to its duties, or rather it implies their consent, because the presumed consent of every rational creature is in unison with the predisposed order of things.

Nor are we left without powerful instincts to make this duty as grateful to us, as it is awful and coercive.   Our country is not a thing of mere physical locality.   It consists, in a great measure, in the ancient order into which we are born.   We may have the same geographical situation, but another country; as we may have the same country, in another soil.   The place that determines our duty to our country is a social civil relation.

Obviously, the notion of duties contains problems.   There is always the problem of a clash between duties and rights. There is, too, the more difficult problem of a clash between one duty and another, and of deciding when, precisely, one is

confronted with a duty. Burke acknowledges all this, but
would not emphasize it:

> I admit, indeed, that in morals, as in all things else, difficulties
> will sometimes occur. Duties will sometimes cross one another.
> Then questions will arise: Which of them is to be placed in subordi-
> nation? Which of them may be entirely superseded? These doubts
> give rise to that part of moral science called *casuistry*. It requires a
> very solid and discriminating judgment, great modesty and caution,
> and much sobriety of mind in the handling; else there is a danger
> that it may totally subvert those offices which is its object only to
> methodize and reconcile.
>
> Duties, at their extreme bounds, are drawn very fine, so as to be-
> come almost evanescent. In that state some shade of doubt will
> always rest upon these questions, when they are pursued with
> subtlety. But the very habit of stating these extreme cases is not
> very laudable or safe, because, in general, it is not right to turn our
> duties into doubts. They are imposed to govern our conduct, not
> to exercise our ingenuity; and therefore, our opinions about them
> ought not to be in a state of fluctuation, but steady, sure, and re-
> solved.

> Amongst these nice, and therefore, dangerous points of casuistry,
> may be reckoned the question so much agitated at the present hour —
> whether, after the people have discharged themselves of their orig-
> inal power by an habitual delegation, no occasion can possibly occur
> which may justify the resumption of it. This question, in this lati-
> tude, is very hard to affirm or deny, but I am satisfied that no occasion
> can justify such a resumption, which would not equally authorize
> a dispensation with any other moral duty, perhaps with all of them
> together.
>
> However, if, in general, it be not easy to determine concerning the
> lawfulness of such devious proceedings, which must be ever on the
> edge of crimes, it is far from difficult to see the perilous consequences
> of the resuscitation of such a power in the people. The practical
> consequences of any political tenet go a great way in deciding upon
> its value. Political problems do not primarily concern truth or
> falsehood. They relate to good or evil. What in the result is

likely to produce evil, is politically false; that which is productive of good politically true.

The natural conservative in him has the floor by now. He cannot abide the thought of all the nice problems in casuistry which he sees rising before him:

I confess, I never liked this continual talk of resistance and revolution, or the practice of making the extreme medicine of the constitution its daily bread. It renders the habit of society dangerously valetudinarian; it is taking periodical doses of mercury sublimate, and swallowing down repeated provocatives of cantharides to our love of liberty.

As it was not made for common abuses, so it is not to be agitated by common minds. The speculative line of demarcation, where obedience ought to end, and resistance must begin, is faint, obscure, and not easily definable. It is not a single act, or a single event, which determines it. Governments must be abused and deranged indeed, before it can be thought of, and the prospect of the future must be as bad as the experience of the past.

The subversion of a government, to deserve any praise, must be considered but as a step preparatory to the formation of something better, either in the scheme of the government itself, or in the persons who administer it, or in both. These events cannot in reason be separated.

This, I think, may be safely affirmed: that a sore and pressing evil is to be removed, and a good, great in its amount and unequivocal in its nature, must be probable almost to certainty, before the inestimable price of our own morals, and the well-being of a number of our fellow citizens, is paid for a revolution. If ever we ought to be economists even to parsimony, it is in the voluntary production of evil. Every revolution contains in it something of evil.

The burden of proof lies heavily on those who tear to pieces the whole frame and contexture of their country, that they could find no other way of settling a government fit to obtain its rational ends, except that which they have pursued by means unfavorable to all the present happiness of millions of people, and to the utter ruin of several hundreds of thousands.

It is not worth our while to discuss, like sophisters, whether, in no case, some evil, for the sake of some benefit, is to be tolerated. Nothing universal can be rationally affirmed on any moral, or any political subject. Pure abstraction does not belong to these matters. The lines of morality are not like ideal lines of mathematics. They are broad and deep as well as long. They admit of exceptions; they demand modifications. These exceptions and modifications are not made by the process of logic, but by the rules of prudence.

This line of argument against emancipation by citing hard cases reaches its high point in the paragraphs which follow:

I would not exclude alteration, but even when I changed, it should be to preserve, not to destroy. I should be led to my remedy by a great grievance. In what I did, I should follow the example of our ancestors. I would make the reparation as nearly as possible in the style of the building.

We know that we have made no discoveries, and we think that no discoveries are to be made, in morality; nor many in the great principles of government; nor in the ideas of liberty, which were understood long before we were born, altogether as well as they will be after the grave has heaped its mold upon our presumption, and the silent tomb shall have imposed its law on our pert loquacity.

Prejudice is of ready application in the emergency; it previously engages the mind in a steady course of wisdom and virtue, and does not leave the man hesitating in the moment of decision, sceptical, puzzled, and unresolved. Prejudice renders a man's virtue his habit, and not a series of unconnected acts. Through just prejudice, his duty becomes a part of his nature.

Prescription [i.e., tradition] is the most solid of all titles, not only to property, but, which is to secure that property, to government. All titles terminate in prescription. Nor is prescription of government formed upon blind unmeaning prejudices for man is a most unwise and most wise being. The individual is foolish . . . but the species is wise, and when time is given to it, as a species it almost always acts right.

If you apprehend that on a concession you shall be pushed by metaphysical process to the extreme lines, and argued out of your whole authority, my advice is this: When you have recovered your old, your strong, your tenable position, then face about — stop short — do nothing more — reason not at all — oppose the ancient policy and practice of the empire as a rampart against the speculations of innovators on both sides of the question, and you will stand on great, manly, and sure ground.

We are afraid to put men to live and trade each on his own private stock of reason . . . individuals would do better to avail themselves of the general bank and capital of nations and of ages. Thanks to our sullen resistance to innovation, thanks to the cold sluggishness of our national character, we still bear the stamp of our forefathers.

Burke has one last point to make. It is that politics, like morals, is based ultimately on religion. This is for him the taproot of his conservatism. It brings him rather close to James I whom we have already read. He begins:

Nothing is more certain than that manners, civilization, and all good things connected with manners and civilization, have, in this European world of ours, depended for ages upon two principles, and were indeed the result of both combined: I mean, the spirit of a gentleman and the spirit of religion.

We know, and what is better, we feel inwardly that religion is the basis of civil society, and the source of all good and all comfort; that on religion, according to our mode, all our laws and institutions stand as upon their base.

The religious sense of mankind, like a wise architect, hath built up the august fabric of states; like a provident proprietor, to preserve the structure from profanation and ruin, as a sacred temple purged from all the impurities of fraud and violence and injustice and tyranny, it hath solemnly and forever consecrated the commonwealth and all that officiate therein.

This consecration is made that all who administer in the government of men should have high and worthy notions of their function and destination; that their hope should be full of immortality; that they should not look to the paltry pelf of the moment, nor to the temporary and transient praise of the vulgar, but to a solid, permanent existence, in the permanent part of their nature, and to a permanent fame and glory, in the example they leave as a rich inheritance to the world.

This principle ought to be impressed, even more strongly, upon the minds of those who compose the collective sovereignty. For the people at large can never become the subject of punishment by any human hand. They ought therefore to be persuaded that they are fully as little entitled and far less qualified, with safety to themselves, to use any arbitrary power whatsoever; that they are not, under a false show of "liberty," tyranically to exact, from those who officiate in the state, an abject submission to their occasional will.

When the people have emptied themselves of all the lust of selfish will, which without religion it is utterly impossible they ever should; when they are conscious that they exercise a power, which to be legitimate must be according to that eternal and immutable law in which will and reason are the same, they will be more capable how they place power in base and incapable hands.

In their nomination to office they will not appoint to the exercise of authority as to a pitiful job, but as to a holy function; not according to their sordid selfish interest, nor to their wanton caprice, nor to their arbitrary will. They will confer that power, which any man may well tremble to give or to receive, on those only in whom they discern a predominant portion of active virtue and wisdom.

Those who believe that God willed the state think some part of the wealth of the country is as usefully employed in maintaining a church and a clergy as in fomenting the luxury of individuals. It is the public ornament. It is the public consolation. It nourishes the public hope. The poorest man finds his own importance and dignity in it. It is for the man in humble life — to raise his nature, to put him in mind of a state in which the privileges of opulence will cease, when he will be equal by nature, and may be more than equal by virtue — that his portion of the general wealth of the country is thus employed and sanctified.

The awful author of our being is the author of our place in the order of existence. Having disposed and marshalled us by a divine tactic, not according to our will, but according to His, He has, in and by that disposition, virtually subjected us to act the part which belongs to the place assigned us. We have obligations to mankind at large, which are not in consequence of any special voluntary pact. They arise from the relation of man to man, and the relation of man to God, which relations are not matters of choice.

An "alliance" between church and state in a Christian commonwealth is, in my opinion an idle and a fanciful speculation. An alliance is between two things that are in their nature distinct and independent, such as between two sovereign states. But in a Christian commonwealth, the church and state are one and the same thing, being different integral parts of the same whole.

Religion is so far, in my opinion, from being out of the province or duty of a Christian magistrate that it is, and ought to be, not only his care, but the principal thing in his care; because it is one of the great bonds of human society.

Against infidels [i.e., unbelievers] I would have the laws rise in all their terrors. . . . I would cut up the very root of atheism. The infidels are outlaws of the constitution; not of this country, but of the human race. They are never to be supported, never to be tolerated.

The concluding paragraphs sum up the argument. Rights and liberties are products of the political organization of society. In the political organization of society one is confronted, largely, with matters of tradition — *prescription* is his word — matters of slow growth and gradual change:

From Magna Charta to the Declaration of Right, it has been the uniform policy of our constitution to claim and assert our liberties as an entailed inheritance from our forefathers and to be transmitted to our posterity; as an estate, specially belonging to the people of this realm without any reference whatever to any other more general or prior right.

By thus regarding our liberties as an entailed inheritance, our constitution preserves a unity in the great multiplicity of its parts. We have an inheritable crown; an inheritable peerage; and a house of commons and a people inheriting privileges, franchises, and liberties, from a long line of ancestors.

This policy appears to me to be the result of profound reflection; or rather, the happy effect of following nature, which is wisdom without reflection, and above it. The idea of inherited liberties, rights, and privileges furnishes a sure principle of conservation and transmission, without at all excluding a principle of improvement. It leaves acquisition free, but it secures what it acquires. Whatever advantages are obtained, are locked fast as in a sort of family settlement, grasped as in a kind of mortmain forever.

We receive, we hold, we transmit our government and our privileges, in the same manner in which we enjoy and transmit our property and our lives. The institutions of policy, the goods of fortune, the gifts of Providence, are handed down to us and from us in the same course and order. Our political system is placed in a just correspondence and symmetry with that mode of existence decreed to a permanent body composed of transitory parts, by the disposition of a stupendous wisdom, molding together the great mysterious incorporation of the human race, the whole at one time, is never old or middle-aged or young, but in a condition of unchangeable constancy moves on through the varied tenor of perpetual decay, fall, renovation, and progression.

By preserving thus the method of nature in the conduct of the state, in what we improve we are never wholly new; in what we retain, we are never wholly obsolete. By adhering in this manner and on those principles to our forefathers, we are guided, not by the superstition of antiquarians but by the spirit of philosophic analogy. In this choice of entailment, inheritance, we have given to our frame of polity the image of a relation in blood; binding up the constitution of our country with our dearest domestic ties; adopting our fundamental laws into the bosom of our family affections; keeping inseparable, and cherishing with the warmth of all their combined and mutually reflected charities, our state, our hearths, our sepulchers, and our altars.

We procure reverence to our civil institutions on the principle upon which nature teaches us to revere individual men, on account of their age, and on account of those from whom they are descended. All your sophisters cannot produce anything better adapted to preserve a rational and manly liberty than the course we have pursued, who have chosen our nature rather than our speculations, our breasts rather than our inventions, for the great conservatories and magazines of our rights and privileges.

A politic caution, a guarded circumspection, a moral timidity, were among the ruling principles of our forefathers in their most decided conduct. They were not illuminated with that "light of reason," of which the gentlemen of France tell us they have got so abundant a share. They acted under a strong sense of the ignorance and fallibility of mankind. He that made them thus fallible, rewarded them for having in their conduct attended to their nature. Let us imitate their caution, if we wish to deserve their fortune or retain their bequests. Let us add, if we please; but let us preserve what they have left; let us be satisfied to admire, rather than attempt to follow in their desperate flights the aeronauts of France.

READING REFERENCES. John Maccun has a good book, *The Political Philosophy of Burke*. It is not easy reading. Lord Morley has done the Burke volume in the *English Men of Letters* series. It is easier reading. Chapter six in Volume One and Chapter one in Volume Two of C. E. Vaughan's *Studies in the History of Political Philosophy* are good. Chapters eight, ten, and eleven in Sir Leslie Stephen's *English Thought in the Eighteenth Century* are also good. An interesting contrast between author and subject will be found in Harold Laski's pages on Burke in *Political Thought in England from Locke to Bentham*. A good recent biography will be found in R. H. Murray's *Edmund Burke*. But better than any of these would be a careful reading of Burke's *Letter to a Noble Lord*, *Appeal from the New to the Old Whigs*, or any hundred pages from his *Reflections*.

READING QUESTIONS

1. What doctrine does Burke propose to criticize?
2. Cite one of Burke's criticisms.
3. What does he make of the notion of "the people"?

4. Cite one warning from Burke of what may well befall a country which entertains the false idea of "the people."

5. Why does he turn to French history?

6. Cite any two things the French might have done.

7. What did they do?

8. "Compute your gains." Elucidate.

9. "Were all these dreadful things necessary?" What things?

10. "To be a people and to have these rights are things incompatible." What rights? Wherein incompatible?

11. "The foundation of government is laid. . . ." Where?

12. "Among these wants is to be reckoned. . . ." What?

13. "In this sense restraints are to be reckoned among rights." Meaning?

14. In what sort of thing is the state to be considered a partnership?

15. What "real" rights will he recognize?

16. What must he know about a liberty before he will congratulate its possessor?

17. "When great multitudes act together under that discipline of nature I recognize the people." What discipline of nature?

18. "I am accused of being a man of aristocratic principles." Why? What does he say?

19. "*Duty* and *will* are ever contradictory terms." How so?

20. "Difficulties will sometimes occur . . . some shade of doubt will always rest upon these questions. . . . Among these nice points of casuistry may be reckoned. . . ."

21. What is his advice, in view of the things noted in question 20?

22. What does he mean by *prescription*?

23. Why does he urge it on men?

24. In what sense is religion the base of "all our laws and institutions"?

25. "This principle ought to be impressed even more strongly upon. . . ." Whom? Why? What principle?

26. What about state appropriation of funds to pay for the church?

27. What is the "divine tactic" of which he speaks?

28. What about infidels?

29. "Liberties as an entailed inheritance." Elucidate.

5. *THE CASE FOR REPRESENTATIVE GOVERNMENT — FROM JOHN STUART MILL*

FROM BURKE TO MILL. Burke, it will be remembered, published his *Reflections on the French Revolution* in 1790, one year after the outbreak of the revolution in France. His book attained to an immediate and widespread prestige. It was read with approval in the chancelleries of Europe. Here, it was felt, was the answer to radical political philosophy. A year later, in 1791, Thomas Paine, newly returned from the revolutionary war in America, and now settled in revolutionary Paris, published his celebrated reply to Burke's *Reflections*. He called his book *The Rights of Man*, thus drawing attention to the root of the matter which, he felt, Burke had misunderstood. With the argument of this eighteenth-century defense of the democratic idea, we are not concerned. Its importance lay in its readability and vigor and consequent great popularity. It contributed vastly to clarifying and fixing in the public mind the case for the democratic idea. This was timely, since agitation for parliamentary reform in England was brought to a standstill two years later, in 1793, when the British Government declared war on France with a view to checking the spread of revolutionary politics in Europe. By that time, Napoleon Bonaparte was beginning to emerge in French politics. His power continued to grow, in France and then over Europe. The war dragged on for twenty-two years, until 1815, at which time Napoleon was exiled and the monarchy restored in France. It was then feasible to reopen the question of a democratic reform of British politics. The idea met with considerable opposition from entrenched interests. The task of breaking down this inertia was undertaken by the Philosophical Radicals. Among these was James Mill, who was invited to contribute articles on government and related topics to the supplement to the fifth edition of the *Encyclopedia Britannica*. These articles were subsequently published in volume form in 1825. They contained the clearest and most persuasive statement of the aims of the reform party. They circulated widely. They performed, during the years 1825 to 1832, somewhat the same function which Tom Paine's *Common Sense* had performed in the American colonies in 1776. The movement to which they gave written articulation culminated in 1832 with the passage of the first Reform Act.

By this time, James Mill's son, John Stuart Mill, a young man of twenty-six, was engrossed in the questions which were involved in the democratizing of British politics. He watched the reform experiment with close interest. In 1859 he published *Thoughts on Parliamentary Reform* and *On Liberty*. Both were seasoned comments upon the experiment of 1832. Two years later, in 1861, he published *Considerations on Representative Government*. This became at once the best single statement and defense of the claim that representative government is the method of democracy in politics. In 1865 Mill himself was elected to Parliament. In 1867, during Mill's term of office, the House of Commons passed the second Reform Act which carried further the democratizing process begun in 1832. Mill's book *Considerations on Representative Government* (1861) stood to the second Reform Act (1867) much as his father's *Essay on Government* (1825) stood to the first Reform Act (1832).

BIOGRAPHICAL NOTE. The main facts of Mill's life have been stated already in connection with the reading from Mill under Topics One and Four (see pages 58 and 321).

ARGUMENT OF THE CITATIONS. The form of government is open, in some degree, to choice. By what test should society's choice be directed? The test is twofold: To what extent does a proposed form of government make for the moral and intellectual development of the people? To what extent does it make use of the present moral and intellectual resources at its command? On these grounds the ideal form of

government would be a complete democracy. Reasons for
this. But a complete democracy is not practicable. Reasons
for this. The device of governing by elected representatives
is as close as a modern state can come to straight democracy.
Three fundamental conditions which representative government must fulfill. The proper functions of representative
government.

The argument of the following citations is so simple and
direct that it seems superfluous to add any comment. I have,
accordingly, left the Mill citations to speak for themselves,
grouping paragraphs by a number when they state or develop
some single thought. He begins:

I

The form of government for any given country being within
limits amenable to choice, it is pertinent to ask by what test the
choice should be directed. What are the distinctive characteristics of the form of government best fitted to promote the interests
of any given society?

If we ask ourselves on what conditions good government depends,
we find that the principal of them is the qualities of the human
beings composing the society over which the government is
exercised.

The first question in respect to any political institution is, how
far it tends to foster in the members of the community various
desirable qualities, moral and intellectual. The government which
does this the best has every likelihood of being the best in all other
respects, since it is on these qualities, so far as they exist in the
people, that all possibility of goodness in the practical operations
of the government depends.

The other constituent element of the merit of a government is the
degree in which it is adapted to take advantage of the amount of
good qualities which may at any time exist, and make them instrumental to the right purposes.

2

There is no difficulty in showing, if the above considerations be granted, that the ideally best form of government is that in which the sovereignty, or supreme controlling power is vested, in the last resort, in the entire aggregate of the community; every citizen not only having a voice in the exercise of that ultimate sovereignty, but being, at least occasionally, called on to take an actual part in the government, by the personal discharge of public function, local or general.

To test this proposition, it has to be examined in reference to the two branches into which, as pointed out, the inquiry into the goodness of a government conveniently divides itself; namely, how far it promotes the good management of the affairs of society by means of the existing faculties, moral, intellectual, and active, of its various members; and what is its effect in improving or deteriorating those faculties.

3

The superiority of popular government in reference to present well-being rests upon two principles. The first is that the rights and interests of every or any person are only secure from being disregarded when the person interested is himself able, and habitually disposed to stand up for them. The second is, that the general prosperity attains a greater height, and is more widely diffused, in proportion to the amount and varieties of the personal energies enlisted in promoting it.

Human beings are only secure from evil at the hands of others in proportion as they have the power of being, and are self-protecting; and they only achieve a high degree of success in their struggle with nature in proportion as they are self-dependent, relying on what they themselves can do, either separately or in concert, rather than on what others do for them.

Thus stands the case as regards present well-being, the good management of the affairs of the existing generation. If we now pass to the influence of the form of government upon character, we shall find the superiority of popular government over every other to be, if possible, still more decided and indisputable.

4

This question really depends upon a still more fundamental one, viz., which of two common types of character, for the general good of humanity, it is most desirable should predominate — the active, or the passive type; that which struggles against evils, or that which endures them; that which bends to circumstances, or that which endeavors to make circumstances bend to itself.

The commonplaces of moralists, and the general sympathies of mankind, are in favor of the passive type. Energetic characters may be admired, but the acquiescent and submissive are those which most men personally prefer. The passiveness of our neighbors increases our sense of security, and plays into the hands of our willfulness. Passive characters, if we do not happen to need their activity, seem an obstruction the less in our own path. A contented character is not a dangerous rival.

Yet nothing is more certain than that improvement in human affairs is wholly the work of the uncontented characters; and, moreover, that it is much easier for an active mind to acquire the virtues of patience than for a passive one to assume those of energy.

The striving, go-ahead character is only a fit subject of disapproving criticism on account of the very secondary objects on which it commonly expends its strength. In itself it is the foundation of the best hopes for the general improvement of mankind.

Inactivity, unaspiringness, absence of desire, are a more fatal hindrance to improvement than any misdirection of energy, and are that through which alone, when existing in the mass, any very formidable misdirection by an energetic few becomes possible.

5

Now there can be no kind of doubt that the passive type of character is favored by the government of one or a few, and the active, self-helping type by that of the many. Irresponsible rulers need the quiescence of the ruled more than they need any activity but that which they can compel. Submissiveness to the prescriptions of men as necessities of nature is the lesson inculcated by all governments upon those who are wholly without participation in them.

The will of superiors, and the law as the will of superiors, must be passively yielded to.

Very different is the state of the human faculties where a human being feels himself under no other external restraint than the necessities of nature, or mandates of society which he has his share in imposing, and which it is open to him, if he thinks them wrong, publicly to dissent from, and exert himself actively to get altered.

What is still more important than even this matter of feeling is the practical discipline which the character obtains from the occasional demand made upon the citizens to exercise, for a time and in their turn, some social function.

It is not sufficiently considered how little there is in most men's ordinary life to give any largeness either to their conceptions or to their sentiments. Their work is a routine; not a labor of love, but of self-interest in the most elementary form, the satisfaction of daily wants; neither the thing done, nor the process of doing it, introduces the mind to thoughts or feelings extending beyond individuals; if instructive books are within their reach, there is no stimulus to read them; and in most cases the individual has no access to any person of cultivation much superior to his own. Giving him something to do for the public, supplies, in a measure, all these deficiencies. If circumstances allow the amount of public duties assigned him to be considerable, it makes him an educated man.

Still more salutary is the moral part of the instruction afforded by the participation of the private citizen, if even rarely, in public functions. He is called upon, while so engaged, to weigh interests not his own; to be guided, in case of conflicting claims, by another rule than his private partialities; to apply, at every turn, principles and maxims which have for their reason of existence the common good: and he usually finds associated with him in the same work minds more familiarized than his own with these ideas and operations, whose study it will be to supply reasons to his understanding and stimulation to his feeling for the general interest.

Where this school of public spirit does not exist, scarcely any sense is entertained that private persons, in no eminent social situation, owe any duties to society, except to obey the laws and submit to the government. There is no unselfish sentiment of identification with the public. Every thought or feeling, either of interest or of duty, is absorbed in the individual and in the family. The man never thinks of any collective interest, of any objects to be pursued jointly with others, but only in competition with them, and in some measure, at their expense.

From these accumulated considerations it is evident that the only government that can fully satisfy all the exigencies of the social state is one in which the people participate: that any participation, even in the smallest public function, is useful; that the participation should everywhere be as great as the general degree of improvement in the community will allow; and that nothing less can be ultimately desirable than the admission of all to a share in the sovereign power of the state.

6

But, in a community exceeding a single small town, all cannot participate personally in any but some very minor portions of the public business. It follows that the ideal type of a perfect government must be representative.

The meaning of representative government is that the whole people, or some numerous portion of them, exercise through deputies periodically elected by themselves, the ultimate controlling power, which, in every constitution, must reside somewhere. This ultimate power they must possess in all completeness. They must be masters, whenever they please, of all the operations of government.

7

We have recognized in representative government the ideal type of the most perfect polity, for which, in consequence, any portion of mankind are better adapted in proportion to their degree of general improvement. As they range lower and lower in development, that form of government will be, generally speaking, less suitable to them. Let us examine at what point in the descending series representative government ceases altogether to be admissible, either through its own unfitness, or through the superior fitness of some other regimen.

Representative government must fulfill three fundamental conditions. 1. The people should be willing to receive it. 2. They should be willing and able to do what is necessary for its preservation. 3. They should be willing and able to fulfill the duties and discharge the functions which it imposes on them.

8

The willingness of the people to accept representative government only becomes a practical question when an enlightened ruler, or a foreign nation or nations who have gained power over the country, are disposed to offer it. To individual reformers the question is almost irrelevant, since, if no other objection can be made to their enterprise than that the opinion of the nation is not yet on their side, they have the ready and proper answer, that to bring it over to their side is the very end they aim at. When opinion is really adverse, its hostility is usually to the fact of change, rather than to representative government in itself.

When a people have no sufficient value for, and attachment to, a representative constitution, they have next to no chance of retaining it. Representative institutions necessarily depend for permanence upon the readiness of the people to fight for them in case of their being endangered. If too little valued for this, they are almost sure to be overthrown, as soon as the head of the government, or any party leader who can muster a force for a *coup de main*, is willing to run some small risk for absolute power.

These considerations relate to the first two causes of failure in a representative government. The third is, when the people lack either the will or the capacity to fulfill the part which belongs to them in a representative constitution.

When nobody, or only some small fraction, feels the degree of interest in the general affairs of the state necessary to the formation of a public opinion, the electors will seldom make any use of the right of suffrage but to serve their private interest, or the interest of their locality, or of some one with whom they are connected as adherents or dependents. The small class who, in this state of public feeling, gain the command of the representative body, for the most part use it solely as a means of seeking their fortune.

9

The preceding are the cases in which representative government cannot permanently exist. There are others in which it possibly might exist, but in which some other form of government would be preferable. These are principally when the people, in order to advance in civilization, have some lesson to learn, some habit not yet acquired, to the acquisition of which representative government is likely to be an impediment.

The most obvious of these cases is the one in which the people have still to learn the first lesson of civilization, that of obedience. A race who have been trained in energy and courage by struggles with nature and their neighbors, but who have not yet settled down into permanent obedience to any common superior, would be little likely to acquire this habit under the collective government of their own body. A representative assembly drawn from among themselves would simply reflect their own turbulent insubordination. It would refuse its authority to all proceedings, which would impose, on their savage independence, any improving restraint.

Another of the strongest hindrances to improvement, up to a rather advanced stage, is an inveterate spirit of locality. Portions of mankind, in many other respects capable of, and prepared for, freedom, may be unqualified for amalgamating into even the smallest nation. They may not yet have acquired any of the feelings or habits which would make the union real, supposing it to be nominally accomplished. They may have had considerable practice in exercising their faculties on village or town interests, and have even realized a tolerably effective popular government on that restricted scale, and may yet have but slender sympathies with anything beyond, and no habit or capacity of dealing with interests common to many such communities.

A people are no less unfitted for representative government by the contrary fault to that last specified; by extreme passiveness, and ready submission to tyranny. If a people thus prostrated by character and circumstances could obtain representative institutions, they would inevitably choose their tyrants as their representatives, and the yoke would be made heavier on them by the contrivance which *prima facie* might be expected to lighten it.

Among these tendencies which, without rendering a people absolutely unfit for representative government, seriously incapacitate them from reaping the full benefit of it, another deserves particular notice.

There are nations in whom the passion for governing others is so much stronger than the desire for personal independence, that for the mere shadow of the one they are found ready to sacrifice the whole of the other. An average individual among them prefers the chance, however distant or improbable, of wielding some share of power over his fellow citizens, above the certainty, to himself and others, of having no unnecessary power exercised over them.

These are the elements of a people of place hunters; in whom the course of politics is mainly determined by place hunting; where equality alone is cared for, but not liberty; where the contests of political parties are but struggles to decide whether the power of meddling in everything shall belong to one class or another; where the idea entertained of democracy is merely that of opening offices to the competition of all instead of a few; where the more popular the institutions, the more innumerable are the places created, and the more monstrous the overgovernment exercised by all over each, and by the executive over all.

10

We have examined, thus far, several questions fundamental to the philosophy of government. We began by a consideration of the general question: What is the criterion of a good form of government? We argued that the ideally best form of government is representative government. We turned aside, at that point, to consider what conditions render such government inapplicable. It remains to consider what are the proper functions of representative bodies.

While it is essential to representative government that the practical supremacy in the state should reside in the representatives of the people, it is an open question what actual functions shall be directly and personally discharged by the representative body. Great varieties in this respect are compatible with the essence of representative government, provided the functions are such as secure to the representative body the control of everything in the last resort.

There is a radical distinction between controlling the business of government and actually doing it. The same person or body may be able to control everything, but cannot possibly do everything; and in many cases its control over everything will be more perfect the less it personally attempts to do.

Some things cannot be done except by bodies; other things cannot be well done by them. It is one question, therefore, what a popular assembly should control, another what it should itself do.

It should, as we have already seen, control all the operations of government. But in order to determine what portion of the business of government the representative assembly should hold in its own hands, it is necessary to consider what kinds of business a numerous body is competent to perform properly. That alone which it can do well it ought to take personally upon itself. With regard to the rest, its proper province is not to do it, but to take means for having it well done by others.

The principles which are involved and recognized in this constitutional doctrine, if followed as far as they will go, are a guide to the limitation and definition of the general functions of representative assemblies.

II

In the first place, bodies ought not to administer. The maxim is grounded not only on the most essential principles of good government, but on those of the successful conduct of business of any description. No body of men, unless organized and under command, is fit for action in the proper sense.

What can be done better by a body than by an individual is deliberation. When it is necessary or important to secure hearing and consideration to many conflicting opinions, a deliberative body is indispensable. Those bodies, therefore, are useful in general only as advisers.

A popular assembly is still less fitted to dictate in detail to those who have charge of administration. Even when honestly meant, the interference is almost always injurious. Every branch of public administration is a skilled business, which has its own peculiar principles and traditional rules, many of them not even known, in any effectual way, except to those who have at some time had a hand in carrying on the business, and none of them likely to be duly appreciated by persons not practically acquainted with the department. I do not mean that the transaction of public business has esoteric mysteries, only to be understood by the initiated. Its principles are all intelligible to any person of good sense, who has in his mind a true picture of the circumstances and conditions to be dealt with: but to have this he must know those circumstances and conditions; and the knowledge does not come by intuition.

Difficulties are sure to be ignored by a representative assembly which attempts to decide on special acts of administration. At its best it is inexperience sitting in judgment on experience: ignorance on knowledge; ignorance which never suspecting the existence of what it does not know, is equally careless and supercilious, making light of, if not resenting, all pretensions to have a judgment better worth attending to than its own. . . . Thus it is when no interested motives intervene; but when they do, the result is jobbery more unblushing and audacious than the worst corruption which takes place in a public office under a government of publicity.

It is not necessary that the interested bias should extend to the majority of the assembly. In any particular case it is often enough that it affects two or three of their number. Those two or three will have a greater interest in misleading the body, than any other of its members will have in putting it right. The bulk of the assembly may keep their hands clean, but they cannot keep their minds vigilant or their judgment discerning in matters they know nothing about; and an indolent majority, like an indolent individual, belongs to the person who takes most pains with it.

To a minister, or the head of an office, it is of more importance what will be thought of his proceedings some time hence than what is thought of them at the instant; but an assembly, if the cry of the moment goes with it, however hastily raised or artificially stirred up, thinks itself and is thought by everybody to be completely exculpated however disastrous may be the consequences. Besides, an assembly never personally experiences the inconveniences of its bad measures until they have reached the dimensions of national evils.

The proper duty of a representative assembly in regard to matters of administration is not to decide them by its own vote, but to take care that the persons who have to decide them shall be the proper persons. Even this they cannot advantageously do by nominating the individuals. There is no act which more imperatively requires to be performed under a strong sense of individual responsibility than the nomination to employments. The experience of every person conversant with public affairs bears out the assertion, that there is scarcely any act respecting which the conscience of an average man is less sensitive; scarcely any case in which less consideration is paid to qualifications, partly because men do not know, and partly because they do not care for, the difference in qualifications between one man and another.

The qualifications which fit special individuals for special duties can only be recognized by those who know the individuals, or who make it their business to examine and judge of persons from what they have done, or from the evidence of those who are in a position to judge.

Numerous bodies never regard special qualifications at all. Unless a man is fit for the gallows, he is thought to be about as fit as other people for almost anything for which he can offer himself as candidate. When appointments made by a public body are not decided, as they almost always are, by party connection or private jobbing, a man is appointed either because he has a reputation, often quite undeserved, for *general* ability, or frequently for no better reason than that he is personally popular.

12

It is equally true, though only of late and slowly beginning to be acknowledged, that a numerous assembly is as little fitted for the direct business of legislation as for that of administration.

There is hardly any kind of intellectual work which so much needs to be done, not only by experienced and exercised minds, but by minds trained to the task through long and laborious study, as the business of making laws. This is a sufficient reason, were there no other, why they can never be well made but by a committee of very few persons. A reason no less conclusive is that every provision of a law requires to be framed with the most accurate and long-sighted perception of its effect on all the other provisions, and the law when made should be capable of fitting into a consistent whole with the previous existing laws.

It is impossible that these conditions should be in any degree fulfilled when laws are voted clause by clause in a miscellaneous assembly. The incongruity of such a mode of legislating would strike all minds, were it not that our laws are already, as to form and construction, such a chaos, that the confusion and contradiction seem incapable of being made greater by any addition to the mass.

If that as yet considerable majority of the House of Commons who never desire to move an amendment or make a speech would no longer leave the whole regulation of business to those who do; if they would bethink themselves that better qualifications for legislation exist, and may be found if sought for, than a fluent tongue and the faculty of getting elected by a constituency; it would soon be recognized that, in legislation as well as administration, the only task to which a representative assembly can possibly be competent is not that of doing the work, but of causing it to be done; of determining to whom or to what sort of people it shall be confided, and giving or withholding the national sanction to it when performed.

Any government fit for a high state of civilization would have as one of its fundamental elements a small body, not exceeding in number the members of a cabinet, who should act as a commission of legislation, having for its appointed office to make the laws, to watch over the work, protect it from deterioration, and make further improvements as often as required.

No one would wish that this body should of itself have any power of enacting laws: The commission would only embody the element of intelligence in their construction; Parliament would represent that of will. No measure would become a law until expressly sanctioned by Parliament: and Parliament would have the power not only of rejecting but of sending back a bill to the commission for reconsideration or improvement.

By such arrangements as these, legislation would assume its

proper place as a work of skilled labor and special study and experience; while the most important liberty of the nation, that of being governed only by laws assented to by its elected representatives, would be fully preserved, and made more valuable by being detached from the serious, but by no means unavoidable, drawbacks which now accompany it in the form of ignorant and ill-considered legislation.

13

Instead of the function of governing, for which it is radically unfit, the proper office of a representative assembly is to watch and control the government; to throw the light of publicity on its acts; to compel a full exposition and justification of all of them which any one considers questionable; to censure them if found condemnable; and, if the men who compose the government abuse their trust, or fulfill it in a manner which conflicts with the deliberate sense of the nation, to expel them from office, and either expressly or virtually appoint their successor. This is surely ample power, and security enough for the liberty of the nation.

14

Representative assemblies are often taunted by their enemies with being places of mere talk. There has seldom been more misplaced derision. I know not how a representative assembly can more usefully employ itself than in talk, when the subject of talk is the great public interest of the country, and every sentence of it represents the opinion either of some important body of persons in the nation, or of an individual in whom some such body have reposed their confidence. A place where every interest and shade of opinion in the country can have its cause even passionately pleaded, in the face of the government and of all other interests and opinions, can compel them to listen, and either comply, or state clearly why they do not, is in itself, if it answered no other purpose, one of the most important political institutions that can exist anywhere, and one of the foremost benefits of free government.

Such "talking" would never be looked upon with disparagement if it were not allowed to stop "doing"; which it never would, if assemblies knew and acknowledged that talking and discussion are their proper business, while doing, as the result of discussion, is the task not of a miscellaneous body, but of individuals specially trained to it; that the fit office of an assembly is to see that those individuals are honestly and intelligently chosen, and to interfere no further with them, except by unlimited latitude of suggestion and criticism, and by applying or withholding the final seal of national assent.

Their part is to indicate wants, to be an organ for popular demands, and a place of adverse discussion for all opinions relating to public matters, both great and small; and, along with this, to check by criticism, and eventually by withdrawing their support, those high public officers who really conduct the public business, or who appoint those by whom it is conducted. Nothing but the restriction of the function of the representative bodies within these rational limits will enable the benefits of popular control to be enjoyed in conjunction with the not less important requisites (growing ever more important as human affairs increase in scale and in complexity) of skilled legislation and administration. There are no means of combining these benefits except by separating the functions which guarantee the one from those which essentially require the other; by disjoining the office of control and criticism from the actual conduct of affairs, and devolving the former on the representatives of the many, while securing for the latter, under strict responsibility to the nation, the acquired knowledge and practiced intelligence of a specially trained and experienced few.

Parliament is at once the nation's committee of grievances, and its congress of opinions; an arena in which not only the general opinion of the nation, but that of every section of it, and as far as possible of every eminent individual whom it contains, can produce itself in full light and challenge discussion; where every person in the country may count upon finding somebody who speaks his mind as well or better than he could speak it himself — not to friends and partisans exclusively, but in the face of opponents, to be tested by adverse controversy; where those whose opinion is overruled, feel satisfied that it is heard, and set aside not by a mere act of will, but for what are thought superior reasons, and commend themselves as such to the representatives of the majority of the nation; where

every party or opinion in the country can muster its strength, and
be cured of any illusion concerning the number or power of its
adherents; where the opinion which prevails in the nation makes
itself manifest as prevailing, and marshals its hosts in the presence
of the government, which is thus enabled and compelled to give
way to it on the mere manifestation, without the actual employment, of its strength; where statesmen can assure themselves, far
more certainly than by any other signs, what elements of opinion
and power are growing, and what declining, and are enabled to
shape their measures with some regard not solely to present exigencies, but to tendencies in progress.

READING REFERENCES. The above citations are taken from
J. S. Mill's *Considerations on Representative Government*. The
entire book, which is not long, should be read. It is an excellent example of the author's ability to deal with the whole
question of democratic politics. It can, with profit, be read
along with his *On Liberty*. The third volume of Sir Leslie
Stephen's *English Utilitarians* gives an account of Mill's
views. Emery Neff's *Carlyle and Mill: An Introduction to Victorian Thought* is also well worth consulting, although it is
more favorable to Carlyle than to Mill. Perhaps the best
short account is to be found in W. L. Davidson's *Political
Thought in England: The Utilitarians*. There does not, however, exist in English any good single book devoted to the life
and philosophy of J. S. Mill. In the second volume of
Hoffding's *History of Modern Philosophy* will be found sixty or
seventy pages which, if expanded to two or three hundred,
would fill the bill. The Danish historian, apparently alone
among historians of modern philosophy, had a sense for the
many-sidedness and vitality of Mill's ideas.

READING QUESTIONS

1. What twofold test does Mill propose by which a form of government would be chosen?
2. On this test, which form of government would be ideally best?

3. Show this for each of the two elements in his proposed test.
4. Why does he shift from this form of government to representative government?
5. "Representative government must fulfill three fundamental conditions." What conditions?
6. What are the proper functions of representative governments?
7. What are not the proper functions? Why?
8. The nature and function of the commission of legislation?
9. "Representative governments . . . are mere places of talk." Elucidate.
10. Be prepared to trace the main turns of the argument from James I to John Stuart Mill.

TOPIC SIX. AN HISTORICAL PROBLEM

Our first problem arose out of the distinction between nature and God; our second, out of the distinction between appearance and reality; our third, out of the distinction between speculation and knowledge; our fourth, out of the distinction between moral and immoral; our fifth, out of the distinction between society and state. In each case, we have been concerned with the justification for these distinctions, and with the justification for beliefs about the second member of each set. Thus, for example, we distinguish between appearance and reality. With what justification? We proceed to assert beliefs about reality. Upon what grounds can such beliefs be justified?

Our sixth, and final, problem arises out of the distinction between event and history. We make this distinction readily enough. We distinguish between the death of Caesar and the history of Rome, between the taking of the Bastille and the history of the French Revolution, between the production of *Hamlet* and the history of Elizabethan drama, between the invention of the steam engine and the history of the Industrial Revolution. We "stumble upon" events in the context of a history. We "understand" events in terms of a history. We "isolate" events within a history. We "abstract" events from a history. We "locate" events by referring them to a history.

What is a *history*? It is not easy to say. We cannot say that a history is "nothing but" the events which "make it up," because an event, in turn, is soon seen to be "nothing but" a moment in its history. These terms are correlative. Each is useless without the other.

If we cannot define *history* in terms of events, except on pain of involving ourselves in a circular definition, can we describe *history* by means of a metaphor? Can we say, that a history is a pattern, a plot, a theme, a motif, a frame, a structure, a plan, a *schema*, an outline? The term *pattern* is perhaps the most neutral of these metaphors. The idea which it is intended to convey is illustrated in the familiar newspaper drawing containing scattered numbers which the reader is invited to connect up by means of lines. The result is a "picture," perhaps of a horse or a man's head. The scattered numbers occur in a pattern. When we first look at them, we do not detect the pattern. Gradually, as we fill in the lines from number to number, we begin to "see" the pattern. It was "there" all the time.

Now, suppose we liken a history to the pattern which is implicit or latent in the scattered numbers in the cartoon. The scattered numbers would be the events. Drawing lines between them would be tracing connections between the events. Seeing the picture which gradually emerges would be grasping the history within which the events occur.

Granted the legitimacy of this pattern metaphor, we can pose the problem of the present topic: What is the pattern which holds the events of history together, which gradually emerges as we fill in the events, which is merely latent in the events considered in their bare particularity. Is there one such pattern which takes in all events? Or many limited patterns? If there are many limited patterns, do they themselves form parts of a more inclusive pattern? If there are many limited patterns, do single events occur in more than one of these? Do they belong equally fundamentally to each of the patterns in which they occur?

We could use this pattern metaphor to avail ourselves of

some terminology. The claim that there is "patternedness" we could call historical *rationalism*. The claim that there is one overarching and all-inclusive pattern we could call historical *monism*. The claim that there is more than one pattern, each equally fundamental and irreducible, we could call historical *pluralism*. The claim that there is no pattern, we could call historical *nihilism* or historical *irrationalism*. The claim that we do not know whether there is a pattern we could call historical *skepticism*. The claim that a pattern is something which we arbitrarily impose, one pattern being no more there than any other, we could call historical *subjectivism*.

When we think about events, we use a pattern as an hypothesis. How many facts does it enable us to account for? Does it do this better than any alternative hypothesis? Are there any facts which it ought to account for, but will not? This is not to suggest that historical patterns are merely in our heads. Unless, of course, we would be prepared to admit that the pattern marked out by the planets around the sun, is also merely in our heads; because this pattern we also use as an hypothesis to account for the facts, the observed or recorded positions and changes of the planets.

There are three fundamental types of philosophy of history. The first, historical rationalism, is the claim that there is "patternedness." The second, historical nihilism, is the claim that there is no "patternedness." The third, historical skepticism, is the claim that we do not know whether or not there is "patternedness." What was referred to above as historical subjectivism is a form of historical nihilism. It asserts that the "patternedness" is not there in history, but merely in our heads.

There are accordingly two fundamentally distinct sorts of controversy possible within the field of philosophy of history. (1) The first sort of controversy would be whether historical rationalism, historical nihilism, or historical skepticism can be justified. An extension of this controversy, which would be possible only after historical rationalism had been proved or postulated, would be whether historical monism or historical pluralism has truth on its side. (2) The second sort of controversy, possible only after historical monism or historical pluralism had been proved or postulated, would be over what the pattern is, or what the patterns are, which events hold implicit in their apparent particularity.

The first sort of controversy is not illustrated by any of the authors assembled in this topic. Each of the five is, in his own way, a rationalist. That is, he believes there is a rationale, or pattern, to history. Each differs from the other in respect to what the precise pattern is. Each offers a different interpretation of history. Each reads a different meaning out of the events. The first, St. Augustine (presented by George Santayana) sees in history the realization of God's plan for man's salvation. The second, Kant, sees in history the story of rationality in the social order. The third, Hegel, sees in history the self-realization of the world spirit in the self-realization of individual spirits and nations. The fourth, Karl Marx, sees in history the struggle between economic classes, and the eventual triumph of the proletariat class. The fifth, Oswald Spengler, sees in history the recurrence of a cyclical movement which begins in a culture and ends in a civilization.

1. THE MEDIEVAL INTERPRETATION OF HISTORY — FROM GEORGE SANTAYANA

Not many persons hold a philosophy of history. The reason may be that they do not know enough history to be able to catch at the notion of a vast pattern detectable amid its manifold particulars. Or it may be that they know too much history, with the result that they are skeptical about any single theme amid so great a welter of particulars. Time was when a majority of persons with any pretensions to historical knowledge would have expressed themselves in no uncertain terms. They would have begun with Creation. They would have continued with the Fall. They would have concluded with the Incarnation, the Crucifixion, the Ascension, the Redemption, the Last Judgment, and the Life to Come. This "golden thread" they would have detected amid the myriad beads. This inclusive "meaning" they would have read into or out of the story of the past.

If we should ask who proposed this interpretation of history, in the sense that we might ask who proposed the idea of evolution, the answer would perhaps be: St. Augustine, fifth-century Bishop of Hippo, in his book, *City of God*. We would not intend thereby to suggest that Augustine invented the idea, any more than we would say that Darwin invented the idea of evolution. Others had held it before him, but he gave it something like definitive expression. It is hence sometimes referred to as the Augustinian interpretation. In its essentials it has probably been held in the Western world by more people and over a longer period than any other single interpretation of history. It seems fitting, therefore, to go back to Augustine for a point of departure, despite the fact that he flourished so many centuries before the Renaissance and that we are concerned with philosophy since the Renaissance.

BIOGRAPHICAL NOTE. St. Augustine was born in the middle of the fourth century A.D., and died in the year 430. He was made Bishop of Hippo, a town in North Africa, in 395. These were times that tried men's souls. The "barbarian tribes" were "invading" the Roman Empire. In 410, for example, the West Goths under Alaric captured and sacked the city of Rome. A few years later, the Vandals under Genseric moved into Roman territory in North Africa, thus bringing matters close to home for Augustine. The presence of these wandering peoples within the confines of the Roman Empire, and their destructive activities raised a large problem for the Christian world of Augustine's day. What were they doing here? Why were they allowed to come? Had not Emperor Constantine accepted the Christian religion? What more did God want? Where, in His plan of things, did all these misfortunes belong? Was Rome to be the Eternal City no longer? What had the civilized world done to deserve such calamitous treatment?

Augustine set himself to straighten out this tangle. He wrote the *City of God* to account for the decline of Rome. His argument, very briefly, was this: The eternal city is not Rome, but the congregation of all who shall be saved through the death of Christ, and shall pass their eternity in Paradise. To lament the possible destruction of Rome or the Empire is to admit only temporal and human values. Of what significance is Rome or the Empire in that great sweep of events between Creation and the Life to Come? Only from the perspective of that world is it possible to place a proper evaluation upon the affairs of this world.

THE ARGUMENT OF THE CITATIONS. The selection which follows is not taken from Augustine's *City of God*. It is from George Santayana's *Reason in Religion*. It is a paraphrase of Augustine's argument. The justification for having recourse to a second-hand account is twofold: The original is exceedingly difficult to quote from, by reason of its enormous length and prolixity, and the passage from Santayana is an example of such fine prose that one welcomes almost any excuse for making use of it. It requires no comment or summary.

There was in the beginning, so runs the Christian story, a great celestial King, wise and good, surrounded by a court of winged musicians and messengers. He had existed from all eternity, but had always intended, when the right moment should come, to create temporal beings, imperfect copies of himself in various degrees. These, of which man was the chief, began their career in the year 4004 B.C., and they would live on an indefinite time, possibly, that chronological symmetry might not be violated, until A.D. 4004. The opening and close of this drama were marked by two magnificent tableaux.

In the first, in obedience to the word of God, sun, moon, and stars, and earth with all her plants and animals, assumed their appropriate places, and nature sprang into being with all her laws. The first man was made out of clay, by a special act of God, and the first woman was fashioned from one of his ribs, extracted while he lay in a deep sleep. They were placed in an orchard where they often could see God, its owner, walking in the cool of the evening. He suffered them to range at will and eat of all the fruits he had planted save that of one tree only. But they, incited by a devil, transgressed this single prohibition, and were banished from that paradise with a curse upon their head, the man to live by the sweat of his brow and the woman to bear children in labor. These children possessed from the moment of conception the inordinate natures which their parents had acquired. They were born to sin and to find disorder and death everywhere within and without them.

At the same time God, lest the work of his hands should wholly perish, promised to redeem in his good season some of Adam's children and restore them to a natural life. This redemption was to come ultimately through a descendant of Eve, whose foot should bruise the head of the serpent. But it was to be prefigured by many partial and special redemptions. Thus, Noah was to be saved from the deluge, Lot from Sodom, Isaac from the sacrifice, Moses from Egypt, the captive Jews from Babylon, and all faithful souls from heathen forgetfulness and idolatry. For a certain tribe had been set apart from the beginning to keep alive the memory of God's judgments and promises, while the rest of mankind, abandoned to its natural depravity, sank deeper and deeper into crimes and vanities.

The deluge that came to punish these evils did not avail to cure them. "The world was renewed and the earth rose again above the bosom of the waters, but in this renovation there remained eternally some trace of divine vengeance. Until the deluge all nature had been exceedingly hardy and vigorous, but by that vast flood of water which God had spread out over the earth, and by its long abiding there, all saps were diluted; the air, charged with too dense and heavy a moisture, bred ranker principles of corruption. The early constitution of the universe was weakened, and human life, from stretching as it had formerly done to near a thousand years, grew gradually briefer. Herbs and roots lost their primitive potency, and stronger food had to be furnished to man by the flesh of other animals. . . . Death gained upon life, and men felt themselves overtaken by a speedier chastisement. As day by day they sank deeper in their wickedness, it was but right they should daily, as it were, stick faster in their woe. The very change in nourishment made manifest their decline and degradation, since as they became feebler they became also more voracious and bloodthirsty."

Henceforth there were two spirits, two parties, or, as St. Augustine called them, two cities in the world. The City of Satan, whatever its artifices in art, war, or philosophy, was essentially corrupt and impious. Its joy was but a comic mask and its beauty the whitening of a sepulcher. It stood condemned before God and before man's better conscience by its vanity, cruelty, and secret misery, by its ignorance of all that it truly behooved a man to know who was destined to immortality. Lost, as it seemed, within this Babylon, or visible only in its obscure and forgotten purlieus, lived on at the same time the City of God, the society of all the souls predestined to salvation; a city which, however humble and inconspicuous it might seem on earth, counted its myriad transfigured citizens in heaven, and had its destinies, like its foundations, in eternity.

To this City of God belonged, in the first place, the patriarchs and the prophets who, throughout their plaintive and ardent lives, were faithful to what echoes still remained of a primeval revelation, and waited patiently for the greater revelation to come. To the same city belonged the magi who followed a star till it halted over the stable in Bethlehem; Simeon, who divined the present salvation of Israel; John the Baptist, who bore witness to the same and made straight its path; and Peter, to whom not flesh and blood, but the spirit of the Father in Heaven, revealed the Lord's divinity. For salvation had indeed come with the fullness of time, not, as the carnal Jews had imagined it, in the form of an earthly restoration, but through the incarnation of the Son of God in the Virgin Mary, His death upon a cross, His descent into hell, and His resurrection at the third day according to the Scriptures. To the same city belonged finally all those who, believing in the reality and efficacy of Christ's mission, relied on His merits and followed His commandment of unearthly love.

All history was henceforth essentially nothing but the conflict between these two cities; two moralities, one natural, the other supernatural; two philosophies, one rational, the other revealed; two beauties, one corporeal, the other spiritual; two glories, one temporal, the other eternal; two institutions, one the world, the other the church. These, whatever their momentary alliances or compromises, were radically opposed and fundamentally alien to one another. Their conflict was to fill the ages until, when wheat and tares had long flourished together and exhausted between them the earth for whose substance they struggled, the harvest should come; the terrible day of reckoning when those who had believed the things of religion to be imaginary would behold with dismay the Lord visibly coming down through the clouds of heaven, the angels blowing their alarming trumpets, all generations of the dead rising from their graves, and judgment without appeal passed on every man, to the edification of the universal company and his own unspeakable joy or confusion. Whereupon the blessed would enter eternal bliss with God their master and the wicked everlasting torments with the devil whom they served.

The drama of history was thus to close upon a second tableau: long-robed and beatified cohorts passing above, amid various psalmodies, into an infinite luminous space, while below the damned, howling, writhing, and half transformed into loathsome beasts, should be engulfed in a fiery furnace. The two cities, always opposite in essence, should thus be finally divided in existence, each bearing its natural fruits and manifesting its true nature.

Let the reader fill out this outline for himself with its thousand details; let him remember the endless mysteries, arguments, martyrdoms, consecrations that carried out the sense and made vital the beauty of the whole. Let him pause before the phenomenon; he can ill afford, if he wishes to understand history or the human mind, to let the apparition float by unchallenged without delivering up its secret. What shall we say of this Christian dream?

Those who are still troubled by the fact that this dream is by many taken for a reality, and who are consequently obliged to defend themselves against it, as against some dangerous error in science or in philosophy, may be allowed to marshal arguments in its disproof. Such, however, is not my intention. Do we marshal arguments against the miraculous birth of Buddha, or the story of Cronos devouring his children? We seek rather to honor the piety and to understand the poetry embodied in those fables. If it be said that those fables are believed by no one, I reply that those fables are or have been believed just as unhesitatingly as the Christian theology, and by men no less reasonable or learned than the unhappy apologists of our own ancestral creeds. Matters of religion should never be matters of controversy. We neither argue with a lover about his taste, nor condemn him, if we are just, for knowing so human a passion. That he harbors it is no indication of a want of sanity on his part in other matters. But while we acquiesce in his experience, and are glad he has it, we need no arguments to dissuade us from sharing it. Each man may have his own loves, but the object in each case is different. And so it is, or should be, in religion. Before the rise of those strange and fraudulent Hebraic pretensions there was no question among men about the national, personal, and poetic character of religious allegiance. It could never have been a duty to adopt a religion not one's own any more than a language, a coinage, or a costume not current in one's own country. The idea that religion contains a literal, not a symbolic representation of truth and life is simply an impossible idea. Whoever entertains it has not come within the region of profitable philosophizing on that subject. His science is not wide enough to cover all existence. He has not discovered that there can be no moral allegiance except to the ideal. His certitude and his arguments are no more pertinent to the religious question than would be the insults, blows, and murders to which, if he could, he would appeal in the next instance. Philosophy may describe unreason, as it may describe force; it cannot hope to refute them.

The eclectic Christian philosophy thus engendered constitutes one of the most complete, elaborate, and impressive products of the human mind. The ruins of more than one civilization and of more than one philosophy were ransacked to furnish materials for this heavenly Byzantium. It was a myth circumstantial and sober enough in tone to pass for an account of facts, and yet loaded with enough miracle, poetry, and submerged wisdom to take the place of a moral philosophy and present what seemed at the time an adequate ideal to the heart. Many a mortal, in all subsequent ages, perplexed and abandoned in this ungovernable world, has set sail resolutely for that enchanted island and found there a semblance of happiness, its narrow limits give so much room for the soul and its penitential soil breeds so many consolations. True, the brief time and narrow argument into which Christian imagination squeezes the world must seem to a speculative pantheist childish and poor, involving, as it does, a fatuous perversion of nature and history and a ridiculous emphasis laid on local events and partial interests. Yet just this violent reduction of things to a human stature, this half-innocent, half-arrogant assumption that what is important for a man must control the whole universe, is what made Christian philosophy originally appealing and what still arouses, in certain quarters, enthusiastic belief in its beneficence and finality.

Nor should we wonder at this enduring illusion. Man is still in his childhood; for he cannot respect an ideal which is not imposed on him against his will, nor can he find satisfaction in a good created by his own action. He is afraid of a universe that leaves him alone. Freedom appals him; he can apprehend in it nothing but tedium and desolation, so immature is he and so barren does he think himself to be. He has to imagine what the angels would say, so that his own good impulses (which create those angels) may gain in authority, and none of the dangers that surround his poor life make the least impression upon him until he hears that there are hobgoblins hiding in the wood. His moral life, to take shape at all, must appear to him in fantastic symbols. The history of these symbols is therefore the history of his soul.

READING REFERENCES. A good essay on Augustine's *City of God* is contained in the volume of King's College lectures edited by F. J. C. Hearnshaw, *The Social and Political Ideas of Some Great Medieval Thinkers*. The lecture in question occurs in two parts. The first part is by A. J. Carlyle. The second part is by Hearnshaw; it should be read. Professor Hearnshaw's lecture may be supplemented by J. N. Figgis' *The Political Aspects of Saint Augustine's "City of God."*

READING QUESTIONS

1. When did men begin their career?
2. Why might their career close in 4004 A.D.?
3. "The opening and close of this drama were marked by two magnificent tableaux." What drama? What tableaux?
4. "They transgressed this single prohibition." Who did? What prohibition? With what result? How is this episode described in theological or biblical language?
5. "It was to be prefigured with many partial and special redemptions." What was? By whom?
6. Why was the deluge sent? What results did it produce?
7. Contrast the City of Satan and the City of God.
8. "Two moralities." Namely?
9. "Two philosophies." Namely?
10. "Two beauties." Namely?
11. "Two glories." Namely?
12. "Two institutions." Namely?
13. Who will behold what with dismay?
14. "Matters of religion should never be matters of controversy." Why?
15. What is the point of Santayana's reference to Buddha and Cronos?
16. "And so it is, or should be, in religion." What is? Agreed?
17. "The idea . . . is an impossible idea." What idea? Why impossible?
18. Who has not come within the region of profitable philosophizing on what subject?
19. What must seem childish and poor to whom?

20. What made the Christian philosophy of history originally appealing?

21. "The history of these symbols is therefore the history of his soul." What symbols? Why "therefore"?

2. HISTORY AS THE EVOLUTION OF A RATIONAL SOCIAL ORDER — FROM IMMANUEL KANT

FROM AUGUSTINE TO KANT. The overview that Augustine proposed for history was the drama of salvation; man's creation, fall, redemption, and destiny in heaven. This overview died hard; indeed, it may be an exaggeration to say that it is dead yet. But from Augustine to Kant is a shift from an "age of faith" to an "age of reason." Kant wrote toward the end of the eighteenth century, in the period following the rise of modern science, and itself crowded with the American Revolution, the French Revolution, the Encyclopedists, Hume, Voltaire, Condorcet, Rousseau, Tom Paine. These men repudiated the whole Augustinian standpoint. What philosophy of history could a man propose that would command their belief and support? That is the problem which Immanuel Kant tackled in his *Idea of a Universal History*, published in 1784, just three years after his *Critique of Pure Reason*.

BIOGRAPHICAL NOTE. See under "An Epistemological Problem," page 220, and under "An Ethical Problem," page 299.

THE ARGUMENT OF THE CITATIONS. Can we find a clue to any plan implicit in human history? Kant answers yes, and outlines his idea as follows: If creatures are predisposed by nature to develop any latent tendencies, they will do so. Men are predisposed by nature to develop tendencies which will involve the use of their reason. This development will take place in the species as a whole, not in any individual. Nature intends that man should owe to himself alone the development of his rational powers and the sort of happiness that attends their exercise and growth. To this end she has so created man that his distinctively human tendencies can develop only in the antagonism, conflict, give-and-take of life in a society. <u>The highest problem she has set man is, therefore, the formation of a social order in which the fruitfulness of conflict will not be destroyed by conflict.</u> This problem is not only the highest, it is also the hardest and the last. <u>The problem requires for its final solution the formation of a world state.</u> History is the unraveling of nature's plan for establishing this perfect political order.

Whatever difference there may be in our notions of the freedom of the will, it is evident that the manifestations of this will,viz., human actions, are as much under the control of universal laws of nature as any other physical phenomena. It is the province of history to narrate these manifestations; and let their causes be ever so secret, we know that history, simply by taking its station at a distance and contemplating the agency of the human will upon a large scale, aims at unfolding to our view a regular stream of tendency in the great succession of events; so that the very same course of incidents, which taken separately and individually would have seemed incoherent and lawless, yet viewed in their connection never fail to discover a steady and continuous though slow development of certain great predispositions in our nature. Thus for instance deaths, births, and marriages, considering how much they are separately dependent on the freedom of the human will, should seem to be subject to no law according to which any calculation could be made beforehand of their amount; and yet the yearly registers of these events in great countries prove that they go on with as much conformity to the laws of nature as the oscillations of the weather; the latter again are events which in detail are so far irregular that we cannot predict them individually, and yet taken as a whole series we find that they never fail to support the growth of plants, the currents of rivers, and other arrangements of nature in a uniform and uninterrupted course. Individual men, and even nations, are little aware that, whilst they are severally pursuing their own peculiar and often contradictory purposes, they are unconsciously following the guidance of a natural purpose which is wholly unnoticed by themselves, and are thus promoting and making efforts for a process which, even if they perceived it, they would little regard.

Considering that men, taken collectively as a body, do not proceed like animals under the law of an instinct, nor yet like wholly rational beings under the law of a preconcerted plan, one might imagine that no systematic history of their actions (such, for instance, as the history of bees or beavers) could be possible. At the sight of the actions of man displayed on the great stage of the world, it is impossible to escape a certain degree of disgust; with all the occasional indications of wisdom scattered here and there, we cannot but perceive the whole sum of these actions to be a web of folly, childish vanity, and often even of the idlest wickedness and spirit of destruction. Hence at last one is puzzled to know what judgment to form of our species so conceited of its high advantages. In this perplexity there is no resource for the philosopher but this: that, finding it impossible to presume in the human race any rational purpose of its own, he must endeavor to detect some natural purpose in such a senseless current of human actions, by means of which a history of creatures that pursue no plan of their own may yet admit a systematic form as the history of creatures that are blindly pursuing a plan of nature. Let us now see whether we can succeed in finding out a clue to such a history, leaving it to nature to produce a man capable of executing it.

Proposition the First. All tendencies of any creature, to which it is predisposed by nature, are destined in the end to develop themselves perfectly and agreeably to their final purpose.

External as well as internal (or anatomical) examination confirms this remark in all animals. An organ which is not to be used, a natural arrangement that misses its purpose, would be a contradiction in physics. Once departing from this fundamental proposition, we have a nature no longer tied to laws, but objectless and working at random; and a cheerless reign of chance steps into the place of reason.

Proposition the Second. In man, those tendencies which have the use of his reason for their object are destined to obtain their perfect development in the species only and not in the individual.

Reason in a creature is a faculty for extending the rules and purposes of the exercise of all its powers far beyond natural instinct, and it is illimitable in its plans.   It works however not instinctively, but stands in need of trials, of practice, and of instruction in order to ascend gradually from one degree of illumination to another.   On this account either it would be necessary for each man to live an inordinate length of time in order to learn how to make a perfect use of his natural tendencies;   or else, supposing the actual case that nature has limited his term of life, she must then require an incalculable series of generations (each delivering its quota of knowledge to its immediate successor) in order to ripen the germs which she has laid in our species to that degree of development which corresponds with her final purpose.   Otherwise man's own natural predispositions must of necessity be regarded as objectless; and this would at once take away all practical principles, and would expose nature — the wisdom of whose arrangements must in all other cases be assumed as a fundamental postulate — to the suspicion of capricious dealing in the case of man only.

PROPOSITION THE THIRD.   It is the will of nature that man should owe to himself alone everything which transcends the mere mechanical constitution of his animal existence, and that he should be susceptible of no other happiness or perfection than what he has created for himself, instinct apart, through his own reason.

Nature does nothing superfluously, and in the use of means to her ends does not play the prodigal.   Having given to man reason, and freedom of the will grounded upon reason, she had hereby sufficiently made known the purpose which governed her in the choice of the furniture and appointments, intellectual and physical, with which she has accoutered him.   Thus provided, he had no need for the guidance of instinct, or for knowledge and forethought created to his hand;   for these he was to be indebted to himself.   The means of providing for his own shelter from the elements — for his own security, and the whole superstructure of delights which add comfort and embellishment to life — were to be the work of his own hands.   So far indeed has she pushed this principle, that she seems to have been frugal even to niggardliness in the dispensation of her animal endowments to man, and to have calculated her allowance

to the nicest rigor of the demand in the very earliest stage of existence: as if it had been her intention hereby to proclaim that the
highest degree of power — of intellectual perfection — and of
happiness to which he should ever toil upwards from a condition
utterly savage, must all be wrung and extorted from the difficulties
and thwartings of his situation — and the merit therefore be exclusively his own, thus implying that she had at heart his own rational
self-estimation rather than his convenience or comfort. She has
indeed beset man with difficulties; and in no way could she have so
clearly made known that her purpose with man was not that he
might live in pleasure; but that by a strenuous wrestling with those
difficulties he might make himself worthy of living in pleasure.
Undoubtedly it seems surprising on this view of the case that the
earlier generations appear to exist only for the sake of the latter —
viz., for the sake of forwarding that edifice of man's grandeur in
which only the latest generations are to dwell, though all have
undesignedly taken part in raising it. Mysterious as this appears,
it is however at the same time necessary, if we once assume a race of
rational animals, as destined by means of this characteristic reason
to a perfect development of their tendencies, and subject to mor-
tality in the individual but immortal in the species.

PROPOSITION THE FOURTH. The means, which nature employs to
bring about the development of all the tendencies she has laid in
man, is the antagonism of these tendencies in the social state — no
farther however than to that point at which this antagonism becomes the cause of social arrangements founded in law.

By antagonism of this kind I mean the unsocial sociality of man;
that is, a tendency to enter the social state combined with a perpetual resistance to that tendency which is continually threatening
to dissolve it. Man has gregarious inclinations, feeling himself, in
the social state, more than man by means of the development thus
given to his natural tendencies. But he has also strong antigregari-
ous inclinations prompting him to insulate himself, which arise out
of the unsocial desire (existing concurrently with his social propensities) to force all things into compliance with his own humor;
a propensity to which he naturally anticipates resistance from his
consciousness of a similar spirit of resistance to others existing in
himself. Now this resistance it is which awakens all the powers of

man. It drives him to master his propensity to indolence, and, in the shape of ambition or avarice, impels him to procure distinction for himself amongst his fellows. In this way arise the first steps from the savage state to the state of culture, which consists peculiarly in the social worth of man: Talents of every kind are now unfolded, taste formed, and by gradual increase of light a preparation is made for such a mode of thinking as is capable of converting the rude natural tendency to moral distinctions into determinate practical principles, and finally of exalting a social concert that had been extorted from the mere necessities of the situation into a moral union founded on reasonable choice. But for these antisocial propensities, so unamiable in themselves, which give birth to that resistance which every man meets with in his own self-interested pretensions, an Arcadian life would arise of perfect harmony and mutual love such as must suffocate and stifle all talents in their very germs. Men, as gentle as the sheep they fed, would communicate to their existence no higher value than belongs to mere animal life, and would leave the vacuum which exists in reference to the final purpose of man's nature, as a rational being, unfilled. Thanks be, therefore, to nature for the enmity, for the jealous spirit of envious competition, for the insatiable thirst after wealth and power! These wanting, all the admirable tendencies in man's nature would remain for ever undeveloped. Man, for his own sake as an individual, wishes for concord; but nature knows better what is good for man as a species, and she ordains discord. He would live in ease and passive content; but nature wills that he shall precipitate himself out of his luxury of indolence into labors and hardships, in order that he may devise remedies against them and thus raise himself above them by an intellectual conquest — not sink below them by an unambitious evasion. The impulses, which she has laid in his moral constitution, the sources of that antisociality and universal antagonism from which so many evils arise, but which again stimulate a fresh reaction of the faculties and by consequence more and more aid the development of the primitive tendencies — all tend to betray the adjusting hand of a wise creator, not that of an evil spirit that has bungled in the execution of his own designs, or has malevolently sought to perplex them with evil.

PROPOSITION THE FIFTH. The highest problem for the human species, to the solution of which it is irresistibly urged by natural impulses, is the establishment of a universal civil society founded on political justice.

Since it is only in the social state that the development of all man's tendencies can be accomplished; since such a social state must combine with the utmost possible freedom, and consequent antagonism of its members, the most rigorous determination of the boundaries of this freedom in order that the freedom of such individual may coexist with the freedom of others; and since this as well as all other objects of man's destination should be the work of men's own efforts, on these accounts a society in which freedom under laws is united with the greatest possible degree of irresistible power is the highest problem nature sets for man; because it is only by the solution of this problem that nature can accomplish the rest of her purpose with our species. Into this state of restraint man, who is otherwise so much enamored of lawless freedom, is compelled to enter by necessity, his natural inclinations making it impossible for man to preserve a state of perfect liberty for any length of time in the neighborhood of his fellows. But, under the restraint of a civil community, these very inclinations lead to the best effects — just as trees in a forest, for the very reason that each endeavors to rob the other of air and sun, compel each other to shoot upwards in quest of both; and thus attain a fine erect growth; whereas those which stand aloof from each other under no mutual restraint, and throw out their boughs at pleasure, become crippled and distorted. All the gifts of art and cultivation which adorn the human race — in short, the most beautiful forms of social order — are the fruits of the antisocial principle — which is compelled to discipline itself, and by means won from the very resistance of man's situation in this world to give perfect development to all the germs of nature.

PROPOSITION THE SIXTH. This problem is at the same time the most difficult of all, and the one which is latest solved by man.

The difficulty, which is involved in the bare idea of such a problem, is this: Man is an animal that, so long as he lives amongst others of his species, stands in need of a master. For he inevitably abuses his freedom in regard to his equals; and, although as a reasonable creature he wishes for a law that may set bounds to the liberty of all, yet do his self-interested animal propensities seduce him into making an exception in his own favor whensoever he dares. He requires a master therefore to curb his will, and to compel him into submission to a universal will which may secure the possibility of universal freedom. Now where is he to find this master? Of necessity amongst the human species. But, as a human being, this master will also be an animal that requires a master. Lodged in one or many, it is impossible that the supreme and irresponsible power can be certainly prevented from abusing its authority. Hence it is that this problem is the most difficult of any; nay, its perfect solution is impossible; out of wood so crooked and perverse as that which man is made of, nothing absolutely straight can ever be wrought. An approximation to this idea is therefore all which nature enjoins. That it is also the last of all problems, to which the human species addresses itself, is clear from this — that it presupposes just notions of the nature of a good constitution, great experience, and a will favorably disposed to the adoption of such a constitution; three elements that can hardly, and not until after many fruitless trials, be expected to concur.

PROPOSITION THE SEVENTH. The problem of the establishment of a perfect constitution of society depends upon the problem of a system of international relations adjusted to law; and, apart from this latter problem, cannot be solved.

To what purpose is labor bestowed upon a civil constitution. adjusted to law for individual men, i.e., upon the creation of a commonwealth? The same antisocial impulses, which first drove men to such a creation, is again the cause — that every commonwealth in its external relations, i.e., as a state in reference to other states, occupies the same ground of lawless and uncontrolled liberty. Consequently each must anticipate from the other the same evils which compelled individuals to enter the social state. Nature accordingly avails herself of the spirit of enmity in man, as existing even in the great national corporations of that animal, for the purpose of attaining through the inevitable antagonism of this spirit a state of rest and security. That is, by wars, by the exhaustion of incessant preparations for war, and by pressure of evil consequences which war at last entails even through the midst of peace, she drives nations to all sorts of experiments and expedients; and finally after devastations, ruin, and exhaustion of energy, to one which reason should have suggested without the cost of so sad an experience; viz., to quit the condition of lawless power, and to enter into a federal league of nations, in which even the weakest member looks for its rights and for protection not to its own power, or its own adjudication, but to this great confederation, to the united power, and the adjudication of the collective will. Visionary as this idea may seem, it is, notwithstanding, the inevitable resource and mode of escape under that pressure of evil which nations reciprocally inflict; and, hard as it may be to realize such an idea, states must of necessity be driven at last to the very same resolution to which the savage man of nature was driven with equal reluctance — viz., to sacrifice brutal liberty, and to seek peace and security in a civil constitution founded upon law. All wars therefore are so many tentative essays (not in the intention of man, but in the intention of nature) to bring about new relations of states, and by revolutions and dismemberments to form new political bodies. These again, either from internal defects or external attacks, cannot support themselves, but must undergo similar revolutions, until at last, partly by the best possible arrangement of civil government within and partly by common concert and legal compact without, a condition is attained which, like a well-ordered commonwealth, can maintain itself.

Now, whether (in the first place) it is to be anticipated that states, like atoms, by accidental shocking together, should go through all sorts of new combinations to be again dissolved by the fortuitous impulse of fresh shocks, until at length by pure accident some combination emerges capable of supporting itself; or whether (in the second place) we should assume that nature is pursuing her course of raising our species gradually from the lower steps of animal existence to the very highest of a human existence, and that not by any direct interposition in our favor but through man's own spontaneous and artificial efforts (spontaneous, but yet extorted from him by his situation), and in this apparently wild arrangement of things is developing with perfect regularity the original tendencies she has implanted; or whether (in the third place) it is more reasonable to believe that out of all this action and reaction of the human species upon itself nothing in the shape of a wise result will ever issue, that it will continue to be as it has been, and therefore that it cannot be known beforehand but that the discord, which is so natural to our species, will finally prepare for us a hell of evils under the most moral condition of society such as may swallow up this very moral condition itself and all previous advance in culture by a reflex of the original barbaric spirit of desolation; to all this the answer turns upon the following question: Is it reasonable to assume a final purpose in all natural processes and arrangements in the parts, and yet a want of purpose in the whole?

What therefore the condition of savage life effected, viz., checked the development of the natural tendencies in the human species, but then, by the very evils thus caused, drove man into a state where those tendencies could unfold and mature themselves, that same service is performed for states by the barbaric freedom in which they are now existing — viz., by causing the dedication of all national energies and resources to war, it checks the full development of the natural tendencies in its progress; but on the other hand by these very evils and their consequences, it compels our species at last to discover some law of counterbalance to the principle of antagonism between nations, and in order to give effect to this law to introduce a federation of states and consequently an international police corresponding to national internal police.

This federation will itself not be exempt from danger, else the powers of the human race would go to sleep. It will be sufficient that it contain a principle for restoring the equilibrium between its own action and reaction, and thus checking the two functions from destroying each other. Before this last step is taken, human nature — then about half way advanced in its progress — is in the deepest abyss of evils under the deceitful semblance of external prosperity. We are at this time in a high degree of culture as to arts and sciences. We are civilized to superfluity in what regards the graces and decorums of life. But, to entitle us to consider ourselves moralized, much is still wanting. Nothing indeed of a true moral influence can be expected so long as states direct all their energies to idle plans of aggrandizement by force, and thus incessantly check the slow motions by which the intellect of the species is unfolding and forming itself, to say nothing of their shrinking from all positive aid to those motions. But all good, that is not engrafted upon moral good, is mere show and hollow speciousness — the dust and ashes of morality. And in this delusive condition will the human race linger, until it shall have toiled upwards in the way I have mentioned from its present chaotic abyss of political relations.

PROPOSITION THE EIGHTH. The history of the human species as a whole may be regarded as the unraveling of a hidden plan of nature for accomplishing a perfect state of civil constitution for society in its internal relations (and, as the condition of that, in its external relations also) as the sole state of society in which the tendencies of human nature can be all and fully developed.

This proposition is an inference from the preceding. The question arises: Has experience yet observed any traces of such an unraveling in history? I answer: Some little. The entire period of this unraveling is probably too vast to admit of our detecting the relation of the parts to the whole from the small fraction of it which man has yet left behind him.

Meantime our human nature obliges us to take an interest even in the remotest epoch to which our species is destined, provided we can anticipate it with certainty. So much less can we be indifferent to it, inasmuch as it appears within our power by intellectual arrangements to contribute something toward the acceleration of the species in its advance to this great epoch. On this account the faintest traces of any approximation in such a direction becomes of importance to us. At present all states are so artificially interconnected, that no one can possibly become stationary without retrograding with respect to the rest; and thus if not the progress yet the nondeclension of this purpose of nature is sufficiently secured through the ambition of nations. Moreover, civil liberty cannot at this day any longer be arrested in its progress but that all the sources of livelihood, and more immediately trade, must betray a close sympathy with it, and sicken as that sickens; and hence a decay of the state in its external relations. Gradually too this liberty extends itself. If the citizen be hindered from pursuing his interest in any way most agreeable to himself, provided only it can coexist with the liberty of others, in that case the life of general business is palsied, and in connection with that again the powers of the whole. Hence it arises that all personal restriction is more and more withdrawn; religious liberty is established; and thus, with occasional interruptions, arises illumination; a blessing which the human race must win even from the self-interested purposes of its rulers, if they comprehend what is for their own advantage. Now this illumination, and with it a certain degree of cordial interest which the enlightened man cannot forbear taking in all the good which he perfectly comprehends must by degrees mount upwards even to the throne, and exert an influence on the principles of government.

Finally, war itself becomes gradually not only so artificial a process, so uncertain in its issue, but also in the afterpains of in-extinguishable national debts so anxious and burthensome; and, at the same time, the influence which any convulsions of one state exert upon every other state is so remarkable in our quarter of the globe — linked as it is in all parts by the systematic intercourse of trade — that at length, those governments, which have no immedi-ate participation in the war, under a sense of their own danger, offer themselves as mediators — though as yet without any authentic sanction of law, and thus prepare all things from afar for the forma-tion of a great primary state body, such as is wholly unprecedented in all preceding ages. Although this body at present exists only in rude outline, yet already a stirring is beginning to be perceptible in all its limbs — each of which is interested in the maintenance of the whole; even now there is enough to justify a hope that, after many revolutions and remodelings of states, the supreme purpose of nature will be accomplished in the establishment of an international state as the bosom in which all the original tendencies of the human species are to be developed.

PROPOSITION THE NINTH. A philosophical attempt to compose a universal history tending to unfold the purpose of nature in a perfect civil union of the human species is to be regarded as possible, and as capable even of helping forward this very purpose of nature.

At first sight it is apparently an extravagant project — to propose a history of man founded on any idea of the course which human affairs would take if adjusted to certain reasonable ends. On such a plan, it may be thought, nothing better than a romance could result. Yet, if we assume that nature proceeds not without plan even in the motions of human free will, this idea may possibly turn out very useful; and, although we are too shortsighted to look through the secret mechanism of her arrangements, this idea may yet serve as a clue for connecting into something like unity the great abstract of human actions that else seem a chaotic and incoherent aggregate. For, if we take our beginning from Greek history; if we pursue down to our own times its influence upon the formation and malformation of the Roman people as a political body that swallowed up the Greek state, and the influence of Rome upon the barbarians by whom Rome itself was destroyed; and if to all this we add the political history of every other people so far as it has come to our knowledge through the records of the two enlightened nations above mentioned; we shall then discover a regular gradation of improvement in civil polity as it has grown up in our quarter of the globe, which quarter is in all probability destined to give laws to all the rest. If further we direct an exclusive attention to the civil constitution, with its laws, and the external relations of the state, insofar as both, by means of the good which they contained, served for a period to raise and to dignify other nations and with them the arts and sciences, yet again by their defects served also to precipitate them into ruin, but always so that some germ of illumination survived which, being more and more developed by every revolution, prepared continually a still higher step of improvement; in that case, I believe that a clue will be discovered not only for the unraveling of the intricate web of human affairs and for the guidance of future statesmen, but also such a clue as will open a consolatory prospect into futurity, in which at a remote distance we shall discover the human species seated upon an eminence won by infinite toil where all the germs are unfolded which nature has implanted — and its destination upon this earth accomplished. Such a justification of nature, or rather of providence, is no mean motive for choosing this station for the survey of history. For what does it avail to praise and to draw forth to view the magnificence and wisdom of the creation in the irrational kingdom of nature, if that part in the great stage of the supreme wisdom, which contains the object of all this mighty display — viz., the history of the human species — is to remain an eternal objection to it, the bare sight of which obliges us to turn away our eyes with displeasure, and (from the despair which it raises of ever discovering in it a perfect and rational purpose) finally leads us to look for such a purpose only in another world?

My object in this essay would be wholly misinterpreted, if it were supposed that under the idea of a universal history which to a certain degree has its course determined *a priori*, I had any wish to discourage the cultivation of empirical history in the ordinary sense. On the contrary, the philosopher must be well versed in history who could execute the plan I have sketched, which is indeed a most extensive survey of history, only taken from a new station. However the extreme and, simply considered, praiseworthy circumstantiality, with which the history of every nation is written in our times, must naturally suggest a question of some embarrassment: In what way will our remote posterity be able to cope with the enormous accumulation of historical records which a few centuries will bequeath to them? There is no doubt that they will estimate the historical details of times far removed from their own, the original monuments of which will have long perished, simply by the value of that which will then concern themselves — viz., by the good or evil performed by nations and their governments in a universal view. To direct the eye upon this point as connected with the ambition of rulers and their servants, in order to guide them to the only means of bequeathing an honorable record of themselves to distant ages, may furnish some small motive (over and above the great one of justifying providence) for attempting a philosophic history on the plan I have here explained.

READING REFERENCE. Kant's *Idea of a Universal History* was published in 1784. It was followed, in 1795 by his essay, *Toward Everlasting Peace*. This latter can be read with profit as an extension of the claims set forth in the former. Among secondary sources, the following are useful: Edward Caird's *Critical Philosophy of Kant*, Volume II, Book II, Chapter 6; and Friedrich Paulsen's *Immanuel Kant*, Part II, Book II, Section II.

READING QUESTIONS

1. What are Kant's views on history and man's free will?
2. Why must the philosopher endeavor to detect some natural purpose in human actions?
3. Be prepared to formulate each numbered proposition, e.g., Proposition the First, as briefly as you can.
4. "This would expose nature, the wisdom of whose arrangements must in all other cases be assumed, as a fundamental postulate, to the suspicion of capricious dealing with man only."
   a. What would expose nature thus?
   b. Why must the wisdom of her arrangements be assumed, in all other cases, as a fundamental postulate?
   c. What is the wisdom of her arrangements?
   d. Do you imagine that Kant would criticize the design argument in natural theology?
5. Where, do you suppose, Kant finds out that the arrangement noted in Proposition the Third is the will of nature? What does such an expression mean, if not the will of God? Can nature be said to have a will?
6. What *appears* mysterious, but *is* necessary, if we once assume what?
7. What is the means which nature employs to bring about the development of the tendencies she has laid in man?
8. "No farther, however, than to that point." What point?
9. "Man wishes for concord; but nature knows better, and she ordains discord." Why?
10. What is the highest problem for the human species?
11. "This problem is at the same time the most difficult of all." Elucidate.
12. "This problem depends upon a system of international relations adjusted to law." Elucidate.
13. "The human race will linger in this delusive condition until

it shall have toiled upwards in the way I have mentioned."
What delusive condition?   What way?

14. "The history of the human species may be regarded as the
unraveling of a hidden plan of nature."   Namely?

15. Of what value is such a history?

16. "I have no wish to discourage, under the idea of a universal
history, which is to a certain degree *a priori*, the cultivation
of empirical history."   Explain.

3. IDEALISTIC INTERPRETATION OF HISTORY — FROM G. W. F. HEGEL

FROM KANT TO HEGEL.   Kant's essay was published in
1784.   His views on history did not command much attention
at that time.   Hegel on history, however, has been much
more widely read and influential.   He is the real successor to
Augustine.   For this reason it may be well to begin with a
few remarks on the period between Augustine and Hegel, before noting the period between Kant and Hegel.

Augustine died in the year 430; Hegel, in the year 1831,
just one year over fourteen centuries later.   Into these fourteen centuries were crowded the final break-up of the Roman
Empire, the Dark Ages, the Middle Ages, the Renaissance,
the Reformation, the long religious wars, the rise of modern
science, the discovery and peopling of the New World, the
rise of modern nationalism, the American, French, and Industrial Revolutions, the career of Napoleon and the post-
Napoleonic era of conservatism symbolized by Metternich.
What was the pattern now?   What would be a nineteenth
century equivalent of Augustine's City of God?   For an answer to this question, we can most profitably turn our attention to the argument of Hegel's *Philosophy of History*, delivered
as lectures in the University at Berlin for some years prior to
his death, and published posthumously in 1837.

Between Kant and Hegel the two great historical events
were the French Revolution and the career of Napoleon.
These made a difference, for persons who lived on into the

period of reaction under Metternich, in the interpretation of history. The Revolution, which began as a demand for liberty, seemed to culminate in a demand for licence; and its licence, in turn, seemed to have invoked the heavy-handed regime of Napoleon. The result, in the sphere of practical politics, was a period of illiberalism, of distrust of revolutionary politics, and of fear of the tyranny which they seem to generate. From 1815 to 1830 was the period during which this distrust was at its height. Hegel's philosophy of history is the attempt to restate the appeal to reason, such as one meets in Kant's pamphlet, by an appeal to reason somewhat disillusioned and chastened by the events which fell between him and Kant. Three things at least Hegel had to do: save the great concept of freedom, by means of the distinction between law and licence; provide recognition of the fact that the argument of history includes a place for the great man, or hero, e.g., Napoleon, whom Hegel referred to as the world-spirit on horseback; and justify the attempt of the Reaction to save Europe from licence and tyranny in the name of "rational freedom" or freedom under law.

BIOGRAPHICAL NOTE. Georg Wilhelm Friedrich Hegel was born in 1770 and died in 1831 at the age of sixty-one. He wrote many volumes elucidating the general thesis that reality is spirit manifesting itself in nature, in man, and in their combination which is history. These books are difficult reading, partly because the thought they contain is unfamiliar and elusive, partly because the words they contain are obscure and technical. Early in life, Hegel arrived at the conclusion that the totality of things is an objectification or manifestation of "Geist" or spirit. With his reasons for this conclusion we are not here concerned. They were not similar to Berkeley's argument in support of a comparable conclusion. Hegel's writings are directed, for the most part, towards elaborating his central thesis, not proving it. In his *Phe-*

nomenology of Spirit he offered an account of nature, of man, of society, of morality, of art, of religion, of philosophy, as so many "fields" in which the nature of "Geist" is disclosed. His *Philosophy of Right* was a treatise on the state and law in which these are analyzed and described to show wherein they disclose the nature of "Geist," spirit. After his death, his disciples published his lectures in a series of volumes, *Philosophy of History*, *Philosophy of Art*, *Philosophy of Religion*, in which similarly motivated analyses and descriptions are carried out.

The external facts of Hegel's life are few and unimportant. He was trained for the church. He early became an academic. Outwardly at least, he never ceased to be one. He taught at several universities before he was called to occupy the chair of philosophy in the University at Berlin. He died, at the height of his fame, from an attack of cholera which had broken out in Berlin. His writings provided the great synthesis of European thought between the age of Newton and Kant before him, and Darwin and Marx after him.

THE ARGUMENT OF THE CITATIONS. After defending the notion of a philosophy of history against the charge of forcing facts to fit theories, Hegel proposes that history be construed as the realm of mind, in contrast to nature as the realm of matter. In history, mind, or spirit, is engaged in working out the form and substance of freedom. Freedom is the capacity to act. It presupposes rules. Rules which permit the exercise and growth of the capacity to act are rules which define freedom under law, which is true freedom, in contrast to false freedom or licence. The career of spirit has been marked with violence and conflict. This breeds pessimism and cynicism only in little men. Hegel's claim is that they are the necessary conditions under which freedom comes into being. The process is blind, in the sense that the successive steps are not marked out in advance. But it is also beneficent in the sense that each step forward, no matter what the cost in individual misery, marks an increase in the conditions which make freedom possible. The pain and sorrow which characterize the history of humanity, the conflicts within states and between states are blind stumblings toward that form of organized living in which spirit will achieve a maximum of realization in the freedom of individuals. This is a kind of long-range optimism; but in the short range it is harsh and blood-thirsty in the extreme.

The world-spirit makes use of certain individuals to initiate new and difficult turns in the history of civilization. These are the great men, or heroes, of history. They serve a power and an end which transcends them. The goal of history is the evolution of the state, that is, a union of rational wills making possible the continuous exercise and development of freedom. This is the march of God on earth. The state is the organization of the nation. Since there are many nations, war is a necessary ingredient in history. Such conflict purifies and strengthens the national state. There is no judge of the nations, beyond their survival in the strenuous march of God on earth. The world's history is the world's tribunal.

The most general definition that can be given of the philosophical treatment of history is contained in the word *rational*. The *philosophy of history* means the "rationale of history." The only thought which philosophy brings to the contemplation of history is the simple conception of reason; that reason is the sovereign of the world; that the history of the world, therefore, presents us with a "rational" process. This conviction and intuition are an hypothesis in the domain of history as such.

Before elaborating this view of history, Hegel turns to consider a possible objection. May this not lead a man to set up a plan and then force the facts to fit it?

This presupposition that history has an essential and actual goal or end is called an *a priori* view of it. Philosophy is reproached with "*a priori* history-writing." On this point we must go into further detail. This seems to be the legitimate demand that the historian should proceed with impartiality; there should be no prepossession in favor of an idea or opinion, just as a judge should have no special sympathy for one of the contending parties.

Now, in the case of the judge it is admitted that he would administer his office ill and foolishly if he had no interest in justice; indeed, if he did not have an exclusive interest in justice. That is assumed to be his one sole aim. This requirement, which we make of a judge, may be called partiality for justice.

But, in speaking of the impartiality required from an historian, this self-satisfied, insipid, chatter lets the distinction between legitimate, responsible partiality and mere subjective partiality, disappear. It demands that the historian shall bring with him no definite aim, no definite conception by which he may sort out, describe, evaluate events. It demands that he shall narrate them exactly in the casual mode he finds them, in all their incoherent and unintelligent particularity. A history must have an object, e.g., Rome and its fortunes, or the greatness and decline of Rome. This lies at the basis of the events themselves, and therefore at the basis of the critical examination into their comparative importance. A history without some such criticism would be only an imbecile mental digression — not so good as a fairy tale, for even children expect a motif in their stories, at least dimly surmisable, with which events and actions are put in relation.

To presuppose such a theme is blameworthy only when the assumed conception is arbitrarily adopted, and when a determined attempt is made to force events and actions to conform to this conception. For this kind of *a priori* handling of history, however, those are chiefly to blame who profess to be "purely historical," who raise their voice against any attempt to deal philosophically with history. Philosophy is to them a troublesome neighbor; for she is the enemy of all arbitrariness and hasty suggestion.

So much, then, for an objection to his view. He asks of history what a scientist asks of nature, namely, that it be reasonable, that the use of reason on the details of history shall not *ipso facto* mislead a man. This granted, much may be expected. However, this rationality of history is not to be confused with a pious belief in a superintending providence:

The time must come for understanding that rich product of active Reason which world history offers to us. It was for a while the fashion to profess admiration for the wisdom of God as displayed in animals, plants, and isolated occurrences. But, if it be allowed that Providence exhibits itself in such objects and forms of existence, why not also in the world history? Is this too great a matter to be thus regarded? But divine wisdom, that is, reason, is one and the same in the great as well as in the little.

In those to whom such a conception is not familiar, I may at least presume the existence of a belief in reason, a desire, a thirst, for an understanding of it. Indeed, it is the wish for rational insight, not the ambition to amass a mere heap of facts, that should be presupposed in the mind of every learner. If the clear idea of reason, of pervading rationality, is not already in our minds, in beginning the study of history, we should at least have the firm faith that it does exist there, that the scene of intelligence and conscious volition — human history — is not abandoned to chance. . . . To him who looks upon the world rationally, the world in its turn presents a rational aspect. The relation is mutual.

This conviction involves much more than the mere belief in a "superintending Providence." Pious folk are encouraged to see in particular circumstances, something more than mere chance; to acknowledge the "guiding hand" of God when help has unexpectedly come to an individual in great perplexity and need. But these instances of "providential design" are of a limited kind. They concern the accomplishment of nothing more than the desires of the individual in question. But in world history the "individuals" we have to deal with are whole peoples, e.g., the Jews, the Greeks, the Romans. We cannot, therefore, be satisfied with what we may call this "trifling" view of Providence.

But *reason*, whose presence in the world and sovereignty over the world has been maintained, is as vague and indefinite a term as

Providence. Unless we can characterize it distinctly, unless we can show wherein it consists, we cannot decide whether a thing is rational or irrational. An adequate definition of *reason* is therefore the first desideratum to an inquiry into "reason in history." Without such a definition we can get no further than mere words.

To begin with, it must be observed that world history belongs to the realm of spirit, not to the realm of matter. The term *world*, indeed, includes both physical and psychical. But our concern is not with nature at large. On the stage of world history spirit displays itself in its most concrete reality. The development of spirit is our central theme.

The nature of spirit may be understood by a glance at its direct opposite — matter. As the essence of matter is gravity, so the essence of spirit is freedom. It involves an appreciation of its own nature, a power to know itself as also an energy enabling it to realize itself, to make itself actually that which it is potentially. Accordingly it may be said of world history that it is the exhibition of spirit in the process of working out that which it is potentially.

The spirit which thinks in world history, stripping off the limitations of its several national manifestations and temporal restrictions, lays hold of its actual transcendence and universality, rises to apprehend itself for what it essentially is, while the necessity of nature and the necessity of history but minister to its revelation and are vessels of its honor.

It is the spirit which not merely broods over history as over the waters, but lives in it and is alone its principle of movement. And in the path of that spirit, liberty is the guiding principle and its development the final aim. Such a doctrine — reason in history — will be partly a plausible faith, partly a philosophical insight.

If the essence of spirit is freedom, then the history of the world, if it is the history of spirit, is none other than the progress of the consciousness of freedom.

The [ancient] Orientals had not attained the knowledge that spirit, man as such, is free. And because they did not know this, they lived in bondage. They knew only the freedom of one among the many. That one was therefore only a despot, a tyrant, not a free man. The freedom of that one was only caprice; ferocity.

brutal recklessness of passion; or, equally an accident of nature, mildness and tameness of desire.

The consciousness of freedom first arose among the Greeks. And therefore they were free. But they, and the Romans likewise, knew only that some are free, not man as such. They therefore had slaves. Their whole life, and the maintenance of their splendid liberty, was implicated with the institution of slavery. Liberty, among them, was therefore only an accidental, a transient, a limited growth; and this very fact constituted it a rigorous thraldom of our common human nature.

The Germanic peoples, under the influence of Christianity, were the first to realize that man, as man, is free; that it is freedom which constitutes the essence of spirit. To introduce this realization into the various relations of the actual world was a large problem, whose solution required a severe and lengthened process of culture. Slavery did not cease immediately upon the reception of Christianity. Liberty did not all at once predominate in states. Governments and constitutions did not all at once adopt a rational organization, or recognize freedom as their basis. The application of the principle to political relations the thorough molding and interpenetration of society by it, has been a process identical with history itself. But the history of the world has been none other than the progress of the consciousness of freedom.

In the process before us, world history, the essential nature of freedom is displayed as coming to a consciousness of itself, as realizing itself. This is the result at which the process of world history has been aiming. To this end have the sacrifices that have ever and anon been laid on the vast altar of the earth, through long lapse of ages, been offered. This is the only aim that sees itself realized and fulfilled; the only pole of repose amid the ceaseless change of events and conditions; the sole efficient principle that pervades the whole. Translating this into the language of religion, we may say that this realization by spirit of the nature and conditions of freedom is God's final aim and purpose with the world.

Freedom, the capacity to act, is the essence of spirit. Spirit is both manifested as nature and our bodies, and present

in us. This "present-in-us" part is latent. We can potentially do many things that we cannot do actually; e.g., "I
cannot, actually, play bridge; but, potentially, I can; that
is, I can develop that freedom." Now, Hegel asks: By what
means does the spirit present in humanity develop its freedoms?

If, as we have argued, the history of the world is the history of
the further and further realization of freedom, we are moved to pose
a question: By what means does freedom develop? By what means
is it brought to further and further realization?

A first glance at history convinces us that the actions of men proceed from their needs, their passions, their characters, their abilities.
A first glance impresses us, too, with the belief that these needs,
passions, private interests, are the sole springs of human action.
Here and there may be found, perhaps, some aims of a liberal kind;
benevolence, maybe; or noble patriotism. But such aims and virtues are insignificant on the broad canvas of history. They bear
only a trifling proportion to the mass of the human race, and their
influence is limited accordingly.

Passions, private aims, the satisfaction of selfish desires, are the
most effective springs of human action. Let no illusions be cher-
ished on this point. Their power lies in the fact that they respect
none of the limitations which justice and morality would impose
on them. These natural impulses have a more direct influence over
men than the artificial and tedious discipline which tends to order
and self-restraint, law and morality.

If I am to exert myself for any object, principle, aim, design, it
must in some way or other be mine. In its realization I must find
my satisfaction; although the purpose for which I exert myself includes a complication of results, many of which have no interest
for me. This is the absolute right of personal existence — to find
itself satisfied in its activity and labor. If men are to interest themselves in anything, they must find their individuality gratified by
its attainment. Nothing therefore happens, nothing is accomplished, unless individuals seek their own satisfaction in the issue.

We assert, then, that nothing has been accomplished without

interest on the part of those who brought it about. If *interest* be
called *passion*, where the whole individuality is concentrating all
its desires and powers to the neglect or exclusion of all other actual
or possible interests or claims, we may affirm without qualification
that nothing great has been accomplished in the world without
passion.

Two elements, therefore, enter into our investigation: first, the
aim, principle, destiny, namely the realization of freedom; second,
the complex of human passions. The one the warp, the other the
woof, of the vast arras web of world history.

The spirit which is both manifested as and present in
humanity must come out, must gain freedom, must achieve
the capacity to act. It must learn and master the conditions
of its freedom. Now, Hegel has it, the medium in which
this spirit works is the totality of blind drives that compose
an unenlightened and undisciplined humanity. The spirit
must achieve its freedom through and in these drives, or not
at all. In themselves these drives are neither good nor bad.
They are, it happens, necessary to that freedom which spirit
is seen as seeking in the history of humanity.

Passion is by many regarded as a thing of sinister aspect, more or
less immoral. Man is required to have no passions. We need only
repeat, to silence such pallid moralizing, that nothing great has
been accomplished without passion, without the concentration of
energy and will upon some private interests — self-seeking, if you
will — to the exclusion of all things else.

World history is controlled by a general aim — the realization of
the essence of spirit, which is freedom. In the beginning this is
only implicit — a profoundly hidden, unconscious instinct. The
whole process of history is directed to rendering this unconscious
impulse a conscious one. At the very dawn of world history,
physical craving, animal instinct, private interest, selfish passion,
prejudiced opinion, spontaneously present themselves. This vast
congeries of wills, interests, and activities, constitute the instru-

ments, the means, the media, of the world spirit for attaining its object.

At this point Hegel introduces a line of thought which is not easy to grasp at first. But it is central to his whole philosophy of history. We may approach it by way of what he has already said: The story of humanity is the story of the conquest by the spirit present in humanity of the conditions of its freedom, its power to act. The spirit which is present in man encounters no difficulty in acting, in exerting its will, in the realm of the natural order. And the reason is that "nature" is the realm of law and order. Nature is calculable. She "obeys" rules. When these are known they provide a basis for action. A law in nature is a possible basis for action by men. If there were no law, no order, no pattern, in nature, we could not act. We would be reduced to sheer guesswork; even lower, since if there were no law or order, we could not even guess. When we turn from nature to society, we turn from the realm of law to the realm of freedom. If man is to act in the "medium" of private wills, there must be something corresponding to laws as they are in nature. To this end man needs the state. The *state* may be defined as "society organized to make law possible." Some laws are left without the pressure of the state immediately behind them. Such laws are moral. Law and morality then, between them, are self-imposed limitations for which the justification is that they make it possible to act. They extend the realm of freedom, from the natural into the social order.

The concrete union of the two elements which we find in history — that freedom which is the essence of spirit, and those individual needs and desires which supply the driving power — is liberty under the conditions of law and morality in the state.

A state is well constituted and internally powerful when the private interests of its citizens are one with the common interest of the state, when the one finds its gratification and realization in the other.

The epoch during which a state attains this harmonious condition marks the period of its bloom, its vigor, its virtue and prosperity.

I will endeavor to make my point more vivid by means of an example. The building of a house is, on the one hand, a subjective aim and design. On the other hand we have, as means, the several substances required for the undertaking — iron, wood, stone, etc. The elements are used to work up this material — fire to melt the iron, wind to blow the fire, water to drive the wheels to cut the wood, and so on. The result is that the wind which has helped to build the house is shut out by the house. So also are the rains and floods which supplied the water to drive the wheels; and the destructive power of fire, so far as the house is fireproof. The stones and beams obey their law of gravity — press downwards — and so high walls are carried up.

Thus the elements are used according to their natures, and yet cooperate for a product by which their operation is limited. Thus, in the building of a state, where freedom is realized under conditions of law and order, the passions of men are gratified; they develop themselves and their aims in accordance with their natural tendencies, and build up the edifice of human society; thus fortifying a position for law and order against themselves.

Lest anyone should feel that Hegel is growing optimistic, viewing humanity and the state through rosy spectacles, he turns aside to note that the price of freedom is not merely eternal vigilance; it is eternal strife and violence.

When we contemplate this display of passions, and the consequences of their violence, the unreason which is associated with them; when we see the evil, the vice, the ruin that has befallen the most flourishing kingdom which the mind of man ever created, we can scarce avoid being filled with sorrow at this universal taint and corruption. Since, moreover, this perversion and decay are not the work of mere nature, but the work of human will, we are liable to a moral bitterness, a revolt of the good will, as a result of our reflections.

Without rhetorical exaggeration, a simple truthful account of the miseries that have overwhelmed the noblest of nations and the finest exemplars of private virtue, provides a picture of most fearful aspect, excites emotions of the profoundest and most hopeless sadness, counterbalanced by no consolatory results. History appears as the slaughter bench at which the happiness of peoples, the wisdom of states, and the virtue of individuals have been victimized.

In beholding it we endure a mental torture allowing no defense or escape save the consideration that what has happened could not have been otherwise; that it has been a fatality which no intervention could alter. We draw back at last in disgust. We turn from these intolerable sorrows, from these blackened pages of humanity's history, to the more agreeable environment of our own individual life.

The philosophy of history which Hegel has been marking out threatens to end in a kind of pessimism. Spirit is the capacity to act. It is therefore freedom. It is manifested as nature. It is present in humanity. It requires a social order comprising a moral and political order. These orders are the battleground of private passions and private wills controlled by private passions. The spirit must work out its destiny in terms of these factors, or not at all. They are the matter to which it will give the form, the form of freedom. This entails tension and conflict. We turn from it, as from a slaughter bench. But where to? To our own private selves. Only by withdrawing from humanity do we see any prospect of relief from the price which it continuously pays. But we withdraw from the human scene in the name of precisely those human values and ideals which the human scene alone makes possible, and toward which it is the endless struggle. Are we caught here in a vicious circle? The "great man" as hero is Hegel's partial answer. The "great man" is he who "breaks ground" for spirit's further advance.

But whither do we thus retreat? Into the present, formed by our own private aims and interests! In short, we retreat into the selfishness that stands on the quiet shore, enjoying thence in safety the distant spectacle of wreckage and confusion.

To what final aim have these enormous sacrifices been offered? To what paradox, moreover, have we come? We point to the gloomy facts presented by history — but we point to them as the very field which we regard as exhibiting the means for realizing what we have described as the essential destiny, the final aim, of world-history. In what terms can this paradox be resolved? We pick up our analysis again. The steps to which it will lead us will also evolve the conditions required for answering the question suggested by the panorama of sin and suffering that history unfolds.

Those manifestations of vitality on the part of individuals and nations, in which they seek and satisfy their own purposes, are at the same time the means and instruments of a higher and broader purpose of which they know nothing, which they realize unconsciously. This has been questioned, denied, condemned, as mere dreaming and "philosophy." So be it. On this point I announced my view at the very outset: Reason governs the world, and has consequently governed history. All else is subordinate to it, subservient to it, and the means for its development.

In the sphere of world history we see momentous collisions between established, acknowledged duties, laws, rights on the one hand and forces adverse to this fixed system on the other. These forces realize themselves in history. They involve principles different from those on which depend the permanence of a people or a state. They are an essential phase in the creative advance of the world spirit. Great historical men — world figures — are those in whose aims such principles are present.

Caesar belongs to this category. His enemies had the *status quo* and the power conferred by an appearance of justice on their side. Caesar was contending for his own position. But his victory secured for him the conquest of the empire. This realization of his own aim, however, was an independently necessary feature in the history of Rome and of the world. It was not merely his private gain. An unconscious impulse occasioned the accomplishment of that for which the time was ripe.

Such are all great historical men. Their own private aims involve those larger issues which are the will of the world spirit. They derive their purposes from a concealed fount, from that inner spirit still hidden beneath the surface which impinges on the outer world as on a shell and bursts it to pieces; not from the calm, regular course of things sanctioned by the existing order.

Such world figures have no consciousness of the general idea they are unfolding while prosecuting their own private aims. On the contrary, they are practical, political men, but possessed of an insight into the requirements of the time, an understanding of what was ripe for development. It is theirs to realize this nascent principle; the next step forward which their world is to take. It is theirs to make this their aim and spend their energies promoting it. They are the heroes of an epoch; must be recognized as its clearsighted ones. Their deeds, their words, are the best of their time.

World historical figures form purposes to satisfy themselves, not others. Whatever they might learn from others would limit their role. It is they who best understand. From them others learn; or with them, they acquiesce. For that spirit which, in their persons, takes a fresh step in history is the inmost soul of all individuals; but in them it is in a state of unconsciousness which great men arouse. Their fellows therefore follow them, for they feel the irresistible power of their own indwelling spirit embodied in them.

If we contemplate the fate of the world historical person, whose destiny is to be the agent of the world spirit, we find it to be no happy one. He attains no calm enjoyment. His whole life is labor and trouble, driven by some master passion. And when his object is attained, he falls off like an empty shell from the kernel. He dies early, like Alexander; he is murdered, like Caesar; he is exiled, like Napoleon. This consolation those may draw from history who stand in need of it, vexed at what is great and transcendent, striving to belittle it because it is beyond them.

The special interests of private passion are thus inseparable from the development of general principles. But the principle is not implicated in the opposition and combat through which it comes into being. It remains in the hinterland, untouched. This may be called the cunning of reason; it sets the passions to work for it, while what which develops through the conflict of passions pays the penalty and suffers the loss.

A world historical figure is not so unwise as to permit many

wishes to divide his energies. He is devoted to one aim. He frequently overrides great and sacred interests. Such conduct is indeed morally reprehensible, but so mighty a form must trample
down many an innocent flower, and crush to pieces many an object
in its path.

What pedagogue has not demonstrated of Alexander the Great, or
of Julius Caesar, that they were immoral men? Whence the conclusion follows that he — the pedagogue — is a better man than
they, because he is not driven by their passion. For proof of this
he can point to the fact that he does not conquer Asia, does not
vanquish Darius, does not subdue an empire. He enjoys life and
lets others enjoy it too.

No man is a hero to his valet. Not because he is no hero, but
because his valet is only a valet. World historical figures, waited
upon in historical literature by psychological valets, come off poorly.
They are brought down to the level — or usually a few degrees
below the level — of their biographers, those exquisite discerners
of true spirits!

Hegel returns, at this point, to his central thought about
the state. It is society organized to make law possible.
Under the shadow of state law, we can gradually get moral
law. Under the discipline of "legal" law man may rise to
"moral" law. Law is the possibility of action. It is therefore the basis of freedom, since freedom is the capacity to act.
This Hegelian freedom, with its deification of the state, is
sometimes confused with freedom in the sense of "permission"
or absence of restraint. He wishes to obviate any such confusion.

In world history, only those people can come under our notice
which form a state. For it must be understood that the state is the
realization of freedom.

The state exists for its own sake. All the worth which any human
being possesses, he possesses only through the state. Thus only is
he fully conscious. Thus only is he a partaker of morality — of a
just and moral social and political life. The state is the march of

God on earth. We have in it the object of history, that in which freedom obtains realization; for only that will which obeys law is free.

In our time various errors are current, respecting the state. We shall mention only one, but one which is the direct contradictory of our principle that the state is the realization of freedom. It is this misconception: that man is free by nature, but that in society, in the state, he must limit this natural freedom. In this sense a "state of nature" is assumed, in which mankind possess their "natural rights," with the unconstrained exercise and enjoyment of their freedom.

This assumption of "natural freedom" and "natural rights" is not, indeed, given the dignity of being an historical fact. It would be difficult to point to any such condition as existing or having existed. Examples of savage social organization can be pointed to; but not in support of this idea, for they are marked by brutal passion and violence, and, however primitive their conditions, they involve social organizations which actually function to restrain freedom.

Freedom does not exist as primitive and natural. On the contrary, freedom must be sought and won, and by an incalculable discipline of intellectual and moral powers. The "state of nature" is a state of injustice and violence, of untamed natural impulse, of inhuman deeds and feelings. Limits are certainly imposed by social organization; but they are limits imposed on emotions and instincts. In more advanced stages, they are limits imposed on self-will, caprice, passion. Limitation of this kind is, in part, the means whereby rational freedom, contrasted with unbridled license, can be obtained.

To the conception of freedom, law and morality are indispensably necessary. They are discovered only by the activity of thought, separating itself from the merely sensuous and developing itself in opposition thereto. They must be introduced and incorporated into the originally desire-controlled will, contrarily to its "natural" inclination. The widespread misapprehension of the true nature of freedom consists in conceiving it to be a constraint imposed upon desire, something pertaining to the individual as such.

Thus a limitation of caprice and selfwill is regarded as a limitation of freedom. Instead, we argue, such limitation is the indispensable proviso of freedom. Society and the state, with the law and morality upon which they rest, are the very conditions in which freedom is realized.

The state, its laws and morality, constitute the rights of its members. (Thus wide of the facts is the conception of "natural" rights.) Its natural features, its mountains, its rivers, its forests and fields, are their country, their homeland, their material property. Its history is their history. What their forefathers have produced, belongs to them and lives now in their memory. All is their possession, and they are possessed by it. It constitutes their being. This is the meaning of *patriotism*.

The state, then, is the hero of Hegel's philosophy of history. In it the spirit which is manifested as nature and present in man comes to self-realization. When these unions of wills clash, there is war. This conflict clarifies and strengthens the parties. War, like every other genuine expression of will, has its place in the growth of freedom.

In world history each nation is to be regarded as an individual. For world history is the story of the growth of spirit in its highest forms. The forms which this progress assumes are the characteristic "national spirits" of history; the peculiar tenor of their moral life, their government, their art, religion, science. To realize these successive forms is the boundless impulse of the world spirit, the goal of its irresistible longing. [The state is the march of God through the world . . . the world which the spirit has made for itself . . . a great architectonic edifice, a hieroglyph of reason, manifesting itself in reality.]

All the worth which any human being possesses, all his "spiritual reality," he possesses only through the state. For his "spiritual reality" consists in this, that his own essential nature — rationality — is objectively present to him. Thus only is he fully conscious. Thus only is he a partaker of morality, of a just and moral social and political life. For truth, in these matters, is the unity of the

objective and subjective will; and the objective will is to be found
in the state, in its laws and arrangements.

Just as the individual is not a real person unless related to other
persons, so the state is not a real state unless it is related to other
states.

The relation of one state to another presents, on the largest possible scale, the most shifting play of individual passions, interests,
aims, talents, virtues, power, injustice, vice, and mere external
chance. It is a play in which even the independence of the state is
exposed to accident.

When the wills of the particular state can come to no agreement,
the matter can only be settled by war. What shall be recognized
as a violation of treaty, of respect, of honor, must remain indefinite
since many and various injuries can accrue from the wide range of
interests and complex relations among states. A state may identify
its majesty and honor with any one of its aspects. And if a state, as
a strong individuality, has experienced an unduly protracted internal
rest, it will naturally be more inclined to irritability in order to find
an occasion for intense activity.

There is an ethical element in war. It must not be regarded as an
absolute ill, or as merely an external calamity accidentally based
upon the passions of despotic individuals or nations, upon acts of
injustice and what ought not to be.

War has the deep meaning that by it the ethical health of nations
is preserved and their finite aims uprooted. And as the winds which
sweep over the ocean prevent the decay that would result from its
perpetual calm, so war protects a people from the corruption which
an everlasting peace would bring on it.

In times of peace, civic life becomes more extended, every sphere
is hedged in and grows immobile, and at last men stagnate, their
particular nature becoming more and more hardened and ossified.
Where the organs become still, there is death. Eternal peace is
often demanded as an ideal toward which mankind should move.
But nations issue forth invigorated from their wars. Nations torn
by internal strife win internal peace as the result of war abroad.
War indeed causes insecurity of property, but this is a necessary
commotion.

From the pulpits one hears much concerning the insecurity, the vanity, the instability of temporal things. Everyone is touched by the words. Yet, let insecurity really come, in the form of Hussars with flashing sabers, and that edification which foresaw all this and acquiesced, now turns upon the enemy with curses. Wars break out whenever necessity demands them; but the seeds spring up anew, and speech is silenced before the grave repetitions of history.

The principles which control the many national spirits are limited. Each nation is guided by its particular principles. No judge exists to adjust differences, save the universal spirit of which these are but moments. Only as a particular individuality can each national spirit win objectivity and self-realization; but states, in their relation one to another, reveal the dialectic, the claims and counter-claims, which arise out of their finitude. Out of this dialectic of history rises the universal spirit, pronouncing its judgment upon the nations of the worlds. For the world's history is the world's tribunal.

READING REFERENCES. Hegel has been written about, almost as much as Kant, but the result is not encouraging. In English, there is a small volume by G. S. Morris, *Hegel's Philosophy of History*. It is more understandable, perhaps, than Hegel's own volumes, *Philosophy of History* and *Philosophy of Right*. The Hegelian conception of the state, and thus the central theme in his philosophy of history, is adopted by Bernard Bosanquet in his *Philosophical Theory of the State*. A sharply critical and not altogether satisfactory account of the Hegelian notion of the state as the significance of history may be found in L. T. Hobhouse's *The Metaphysical Theory of the State*. It should be offset by a few chapters from M. B. Foster's small volume, *The Political Philosophies of Plato and Hegel*. The fact is that Hegel is difficult to read, and that no expositor has succeeded, as yet, in translating him into the language and idiom of ordinary discourse. When that is done, it will be as though the clouds had lifted from the Matterhorn.

READING QUESTIONS

1. What is the *a priori* view of history?
2. On what grounds does Hegel defend himself against any imputation of apriorism?
3. Can you explain his use of the terms *reason, spirit, freedom?*
4. How is he led to introduce questions of private interests and passions?
5. "The one the warp, the other the woof, of the vast arras web of world history." Elucidate.
6. "The concrete union of the two elements is liberty under law and morality." Elucidate.
7. "The state is well constituted and internally powerful when. . . ."
8. "I will endeavor to make my point more vivid by means of an example." What is the example?
9. What renders us "liable to a moral bitterness, a revolt of the good will"?
10. What is the role of the great man in history?
11. "No man is a hero to his valet." Why not?
12. "In our time various errors are current respecting the state. We shall mention only one. . . ." Namely?
13. "All the worth which any human being possesses, he possesses only through the state." Elucidate.
14. "There is an ethical element in war." Namely?
15. "The world's history is the world's tribunal." Meaning?

4. THE ECONOMIC INTERPRETATION OF HISTORY — FROM KARL MARX

FROM HEGEL TO MARX. Hegel died in 1831. Seventeen years later, in 1848, Karl Marx and Friedrich Engels published *The Communist Manifesto.* This slight document, not much longer than the shorter catechism, propounded a theory of history which has since been very widely held. The theory in question is known by various names, e.g., *dialectical materialism, historical materialism, economic determinism, the economic interpretation of history.* It was proposed by the authors as an alternative to Hegel's idealism, and as a statement of the principles believed by them to be implicit in the many revolutionary movements which occurred around 1848.   Few things in modern history have exercised such an instant and persistent influence.   Tom Paine's *Common Sense*, published in this country at the time of the American Revolution, might be cited by way of a comparison.

The theory, of which this fiery pamphlet was a popular expression, is to the following effect.   Suppose you distinguish within society between the polity and the economy.   A polity is a society organized to make law possible.   An economy is a society organized to make possible production by division of labor and distribution by exchange.   Now an *economic* interpretation of political history is one which traces the events and changes in the polity to events and changes in the economy.   No changes in the polity without changes in the economy.   This is perhaps the most general meaning one can attach to the phrase *economic interpretation of history*.

More specifically, however, Marx's theory holds that within the economy the most fundamental thing is the way in which production takes place.   If a change takes place here, it will be reflected throughout the entire economy, and hence will have important consequences in the polity.   Politics mirrors economics.   The defining characteristic of any one type of economy is its method of production.

More specifically still, Marx's theory holds that among the many different *kinds* of economies, one particular kind exists in the Western world today.   It is the capitalist economy.   Capitalism is one economy among many possible economies.   He wrote his large book, *Capital*, to analyze and describe the capitalist economy.   The *Manifesto* is a brief and colorful statement of what later went into the *Capital* at great length.

The central historical thesis which Marx argues, with respect to the capitalist economy, is this: It evolved out of the feudal economy, and it will evolve into the communist economy.

BIOGRAPHICAL NOTE. Marx was born in 1818 and died in 1883 at the age of sixty-five. He was educated in the universities at Bonn and Berlin, beginning with law, but subsequently devoting his entire attention to philosophy. Hegelianism was the fashionable doctrine at the time. It found no favor with young Marx. So, when he graduated and looked about for a job teaching philosophy, he found no openings. For the next few years, amid a life of newspaper work and radical agitation, he devoted his spare time to writing a series of highly critical studies of those portions of the Hegelian philosophy which he understood and rejected. By 1848 he had joined the Communist League. For it he wrote the celebrated *Manifesto*. Exiled from Germany, from Belgium, from France, he settled in London. From here, in 1864, he organized the First International. In 1867 he published Volume One of *Capital*. The remainder was edited and published by Engels after Marx's death. In life, judged by ordinary standards, he was unhappy, unsuccessful, and largely unknown. In death he has become, like Darwin and Freud and Einstein, one of the makers of the modern mind.

THE ARGUMENT OF THE CITATIONS. The history of all hitherto existing society is the history of class struggles. In early modern times the bourgeoisie triumphed over the feudal masters. They thus became masters of the modern world. An account of their multifarious doings. They have, among other things, brought into being a new class, the proletariat. The class struggle is now between bourgeoisie and proletariat. When the latter win out, as they are destined to do, the world will see its first classless society. The bourgeoisie economy will be replaced by the communist economy. Injustices arising out of the fact that modern society has been, in respect to production and distribution, a capitalist economy, will cease to exist   To the Finland station!

Ths history of all hitherto existing society is the history of class struggles.

Freeman and slave, patrician and plebeian, lord and serf, guild master and journeyman, in a word, oppressor and oppressed, stood in constant opposition to one another, carried on uninterrupted, now hidden, now open fight, a fight that each time ended, either in a revolutionary reconstitution of society at large, or in the common ruin of the contending classes.

In the earlier epochs of history we find almost everywhere a complicated arrangement of society into various orders, a manifold gradation of social rank. In ancient Rome we have patricians, knights, plebeians, slaves; in the Middle Ages, feudal lords, vassals, guild masters, journeymen, apprentices, serfs; in almost all of these classes, again, subordinate gradations.

The modern bourgeois society that has sprouted from the ruins of feudal society, has not done away with class antagonisms. It has but established new classes, new conditions of oppression, new forms of struggle in place of the old ones.

Our epoch, the epoch of the bourgeoisie, possesses, however, this distinctive feature; it has simplified the class antagonisms. Society as a whole is more and more splitting up into two great hostile camps, into two great classes directly facing each other: bourgeoisie and proletariat.

From the serfs of the Middle Ages sprang the chartered burghers of the earliest towns. From these burgesses the first elements of the bourgeoisie were developed.

The discovery of America, the rounding of the Cape, opened up fresh ground for the rising bourgeoisie. The East Indian and Chinese markets, the colonization of America, trade with the colonies, the increase in the means of exchange and in commodities generally, gave to commerce, to navigation, to industry, an impulse never before known, and thereby, to the revolutionary element in the tottering feudal society, a rapid development.

The feudal system of industry, under which industrial production was monopolized by closed guilds, now no longer sufficed for the growing wants of the new market. The manufacturing system took its place. The guild masters were pushed on one side by the manufacturing middle class; division of labor between the different corporate guilds vanished in the face of division of labor in each single workshop.

Meantime the markets kept ever growing, the demand ever rising. Even manufacture no longer sufficed. Thereupon, steam and machinery revolutionized industrial production. The place of manufacture was taken by the giant, modern industry, the place of the industrial middle class, by industrial millionaires, the leaders of whole industrial armies, the modern bourgeois.

Modern industry has established the world market, for which the discovery of America paved the way. This market has given an immense development to commerce, to navigation, to communication by land. This development has, in its turn, reacted on the extension of industry; and in proportion as industry, commerce, navigation, railways extended, in the same proportion the bourgeoisie developed, increased its capital, and pushed into the background every class handed down from the Middle Ages.

We see, therefore, how the modern bourgeoisie is itself the product of a long course of development, of a series of revolutions in the modes of production and of exchange.

The preceding paragraphs trace the origin of the class whom Marx refers to as the *bourgeoisie*. He means the capitalists, the money masters of the modern economy. In the paragraphs which follow, he traces the influence which this class in turn has had on modern society. Before passing to the details, he pauses to note that, having become masters of the economy, they are naturally masters of the polity.

Each step in the development of the bourgeoisie was accompanied by a corresponding political advance of that class. An oppressed class under the sway of the feudal nobility, an armed and self-governing association in the medieval commune, here independent urban republic (as in Italy and Germany), there taxable "third estate" of the monarchy (as in France), afterwards, in the period of manufacture proper, serving either the semi-feudal or the absolute monarchy as a counterpoise against nobility, and, in fact, cornerstone of the great monarchies in general, the bourgeoisie has at last, since the establishment of modern industry and of the world market, conquered for itself, in the modern representative state, exclusive political sway. The executive of the modern state is but a committee for managing the common affairs of the whole bourgeoisie.

Historically the members of the bourgeoisie have played a most revolutionary part. That is the theme of the paragraphs which follow. They have "abolished the Middle Ages." They have converted the professions into trades. They have placed everything, even the family upon "a cash nexus." They found things static. They have made constant change the order of the new day. They have spread over the world in quest of materials and markets. They have given an "international" cast to modern living. And so on.

The bourgeoisie, historically, has played a most revolutionary part.

The bourgeoisie, wherever it has got the upper hand, has put an end to all feudal, patriarchal, idyllic relations. It has pitilessly torn asunder the motley feudal ties that bound man to his "natural superiors," and has left no other nexus between man and man than naked self-interest, than callous "cash payment." It has drowned the most heavenly ecstasies of religious fervor, of chivalrous enthusiasm, of Philistine sentimentalism, in the icy water of egotistical calculation. It has resolved personal worth into exchange value, and in place of the numberless indefeasible chartered freedoms, has set up that single, unconscionable freedom — free trade. In one word, for exploitation, veiled by religious and political illusions, it has substituted naked, shameless, direct, brutal exploitation.

The bourgeoisie has stripped of its halo every occupation hitherto honored and looked up to with reverent awe. It has converted the physician, the lawyer, the priest, the poet, the man of science, into its paid wage laborers.

The bourgeoisie has torn away from the family its sentimental veil, and has reduced the family relation to a mere money relation.

The bourgeoisie has disclosed how it came to pass that the brutal display of vigor in the Middle Ages, which reactionists so much admire, found its fitting complement in the most slothful indolence. It has been the first to show what man's activity can bring about. It has accomplished wonders far surpassing Egyptian pyramids, Roman aqueducts, and Gothic cathedrals; it has conducted expeditions that put in the shade all former exoduses of nations and crusades.

The bourgeoisie cannot exist without constantly revolutionizing the instruments of production, and thereby the relations of production, and with them the whole relations of society. Conservation of the old modes of production in unaltered form was, on the contrary, the first condition of existence for all earlier industrial classes. Constant revolutionizing of production, uninterrupted disturbance of all social conditions, everlasting uncertainty and agitation distinguish the bourgeois epoch from all earlier ones. All fixed, fast frozen relations, with their train of ancient and venerable prejudices and opinions, are swept away, all new formed ones become antiquated before they can ossify. All that is solid melts into the air, all that is holy is profaned, and man is at last compelled to face with sober senses, his real conditions of life, and his relations with his kind.

The need of a constantly expanding market for its products chases the bourgeoisie over the whole surface of the globe. It must nestle everywhere, settle everywhere, establish connections everywhere.

The bourgeoisie has through its exploitation of the world market given a cosmopolitan character to production and consumption in every country. To the great chagrin of reactionists, it has drawn from under the feet of industry the national ground on which it stood. All old-established national industries have been destroyed or are daily being destroyed. They are dislodged by new industries, whose introduction becomes a life and death question for all civilized nations, by industries that no longer work up indigenous raw material, but raw material drawn from the remotest zones; industries whose products are consumed, not only at home, but in every quarter of the globe. In place of the old wants, satisfied by the productions of the country, we find new wants, requiring for their satisfaction the products of distant lands and climes. In place of the old local and national seclusion and self-sufficiency, we have intercourse in every direction, universal interdependence of nations. And as in material, so also in intellectual production. The intellectual creations of individual nations become common property. National one-sidedness and narrow-mindedness become more and more impossible, and from the numerous national and local literatures there arises a world literature.

The bourgeoisie, by the rapid improvement of all instruments of production, by the immensely facilitated means of communication, draws all, even the most barbarian nations into civilization. The cheap prices of its commodities are the heavy artillery with which it batters down all Chinese walls, with which it forces the barbarians' intensely obstinate hatred of foreigners to capitulate. It compels all nations, on pain of extinction, to adopt the bourgeois mode of production; it compels them to introduce what it calls *civilization* into their midst, i.e., to become bourgeois themselves. In a word, it creates a world after its own image.

The bourgeoisie has subjected the country to the rule of the towns. It has created enormous cities, has greatly increased the urban population as compared with the rural, and has thus rescued a considerable part of the population from the idiocy of rural life. Just as it has made the country dependent on the towns, so it has made barbarian and semibarbarian countries dependent on civilized ones, nations of peasants on nations of bourgeois, the East on the West.

The bourgeoisie keeps more and more doing away with the scattered state of the population, of the means of production, and of property. It has agglomerated population, centralized means of production, and has concentrated property in a few hands. The necessary consequence of this was political centralization. Independent, or but loosely connected provinces, with separate interests, laws, governments, and systems of taxation, became lumped together in one nation, with one government, one code of laws, one national class interest, one frontier, and one customs tariff.

The bourgeoisie, during its rule of scarce one hundred years, has created more massive and more colossal productive forces than have all preceding generations together. Subjection of nature's forces to man, machinery, application of chemistry to industry and agriculture, steam navigation, railways, electric telegraphs, clearing of whole continents for cultivation, canalization of rivers, whole populations conjured out of the ground — what earlier century had even a presentiment that such productive forces slumbered in the lap of social labor?

We see then: The means of production and of exchange on whose foundation the bourgeoisie built itself up, were generated in feudal society. At a certain stage in the development of these means of production and of exchange, the conditions under which feudal society produced and exchanged, the feudal organization of agriculture and manufacturing industry, in one word, the feudal relations of property became no longer compatible with the already developed productive forces; they became so many fetters. They had to burst asunder; they were burst asunder.

Into their places stepped free competition, accompanied by social political constitution adapted to it, and by economical and political sway of the bourgeois class.

The capitalist economy makes trouble for itself. Where production is motivated by profit, overproduction is to be expected. Then the whole system buckles and staggers, only to regain its equilibrium and plunge on again. In this matter of overproduction, says Marx, the modern bourgeoisie economy is like the sorcerer. It conjures up a jinni which it is unable to control.

A similar movement is going on before our own eyes. Modern bourgeois society with its relations of production, of exchange and of property, a society that has conjured up such gigantic means of production and of exchange, is like the sorcerer, who is no longer able to control the powers of the nether world whom he has called up by his spells. For many a decade past, the history of industry and commerce is but the history of the revolt of modern productive forces against modern conditions of production, against the property relations that are the conditions for the existence of the bourgeoisie and of its rule. It is enough to mention the commercial crises that by their periodical return put on its trial, each time more threateningly, the existence of the entire bourgeois society. In these crises a great part not only of the existing products, but also of the previously created productive forces, are periodically destroyed. In these crises there breaks out an epidemic that, in all earlier epochs, would have seemed an absurdity — the epidemic of overproduction. Society suddenly finds itself put back into a state of momentary barbarism; it appears as if a famine, a universal war of devastation, had cut off the supply of every means of subsistence; industry and commerce seem to be destroyed; and why? Because there is too much civilization, too much means of subsistence, too much industry, too much commerce. The productive forces at the disposal of society no longer tend to further the development of the conditions of the bourgeois property; on the contrary, they have become too powerful for these conditions by which they are fettered, and as soon as they overcome these fetters, they bring disorder into the whole of bourgeois society, endanger the existence of bourgeois property. The conditions of bourgeois society are too narrow to comprise the wealth created by them. And how does the bourgeoisie get over these crises? On the one hand by enforced destruction of a mass of productive forces; on the other, by the conquest of new markets, and by the more thorough exploitation of the old ones. That is to say, by paving the way for more extensive and more destructive crises, and by diminishing the means whereby crises are prevented.

The bourgeoisie have not only produced an unmanageable economy, they have also produced an opposition class who will do for them what they did for the masters of the feudal order. This new class is the wage earners, the proletarians. He continues:

The weapons with which the bourgeoisie felled feudalism to the ground are now turned against the bourgeoisie itself.

But not only has the bourgeoisie forged the weapons that bring death to itself; it has also called into existence the men who are to wield those weapons — the modern working class — the proletarians.

In proportion as the bourgeoisie, i.e., capital, is developed, in the same proportion is the proletariat, the modern working class, developed, a class of laborers who live only so long as they find work, and who find work only so long as their labor increases capital. These laborers, who must sell themselves piecemeal, are a commodity, like every other article of commerce, and are consequently exposed to all the vicissitudes of competition, to all the fluctuations of the market.

Owing to the extensive use of machinery and to division of labor, the work of the proletarians has lost all individual character, and, consequently, all charm for the workman. He becomes an appendage of the machine, and it is only the most simple, most monotonous and most easily acquired knack that is required of him. Hence, the cost of production of a workman is restricted almost entirely to the means of subsistence that he requires for his maintenance, and for the propagation of his race. But the price of a commodity, and also of labor, is equal to its cost of production. In proportion, therefore, as the repulsiveness of the work increases the wage decreases. Nay more, in proportion as the use of machinery and division of labor increases, in the same proportion the burden of toil increases, whether by prolongation of the working hours, by increase of the work enacted in a given time, or by increased speed of the machinery, etc.

Modern industry has converted the little workshop of the patriarchal master into the great factory of the industrial capitalist. Masses of laborers, crowded into factories, are organized like soldiers. As privates of the industrial army they are placed under the command of a perfect hierarchy of officers and sergeants. Not only are they the slaves of the bourgeois class and of the bourgeois state, they are daily and hourly enslaved by the machine, by the overlooker, and, above all, by the individual bourgeois manufacturer himself. The more openly this despotism proclaims again to be its end and aim, the more petty, the more hateful, and the more embittering it is.

The less the skill and exertion or strength implied in manual labor, in other words, the more modern industry becomes developed, the more is the labor of men superseded by that of women. Differences of age and sex have no longer any distinctive social validity for the working class. All are instruments of labor, more or less expensive to use, according to their age and sex.

No sooner is the exploitation of the laborer by the manufacturer, so far at an end, that he receives his wages in cash, than he is set upon by the other portions of the bourgeoisie, the landlord, the shopkeeper, the pawnbroker, etc.

The lower strata of the middle class — the small tradespeople, shopkeepers and retired tradesmen generally, the handicraftsmen and peasants — all these sink gradually into the proletariat, partly because their diminutive capital does not suffice for the scale on which modern industry is carried on, and is swamped in the competition with the large capitalists, partly because their specialized skill is rendered worthless by new methods of production. Thus the proletariat is recruited from all classes of the population.

With the evolution of the capitalist economy, then, proceeds the evolution of this class which is its social antithesis. Gradually every one is drawn into one side or the other. The economy is divided into the "haves" and the "have-nots," the "masters" and the "slaves," the "bourgeoisie" and the "proletariat," the "owners" and the "workers." The new class acquires its structure gradually. He proceeds:

The proletariat goes through various stages of development. With its birth begins its struggle with the bourgeoisie. At first the contest is carried on by individual laborers, then by the work people of a factory, then by the operatives of one trade, in one locality, against the individual bourgeois who directly exploits them. They direct their attacks not against the bourgeois conditions of production, but against the instruments of production themselves; they destroy imported wares that compete with their labor, they smash to pieces machinery, they set factories ablaze, they seek to restore by force the vanished status of the workman of the Middle Ages.

At this stage the laborers still form an incoherent mass scattered over the whole country, and broken up by their mutual competition. If anywhere they unite to form more compact bodies, this is not yet the consequence of their own active union, but of the union of the bourgeoisie, which class, in order to attain its own political ends, is compelled to set the whole proletariat in motion, and is moreover yet, for a time, able to do so. At this stage, therefore, the proletarians do not fight their enemies, but the enemies of their enemies, the remnants of absolute monarchy, the landowners, the non-industrial bourgeois, the petty bourgeoisie. Thus the whole historical movement is concentrated in the hands of the bourgeoisie, every victory so obtained is a victory for the bourgeoisie.

But with the development of industry the proletariat not only increases in number; it becomes concentrated in greater masses; its strength grows; and it feels that strength more. The various interests and conditions of life within the ranks of the proletariat are more and more equalized, in proportion as machinery obliterates all distinctions of labor, and nearly everywhere reduces wages to the same low level. The growing competition among the bourgeois, and the resulting commercial crises, make the wages of the workers even more fluctuating. The unceasing improvement of machinery, ever more rapidly developing, makes their livelihood more and more precarious; the collisions between individual workmen and individual bourgeois take more and more the character of collisions between two classes. Thereupon the workers begin to form combinations (trades' unions) against the bourgeois; they club together in order to keep up the rate of wages; they found permanent associations in order to make provision beforehand for these occasional revolts. Here and there the contest breaks out into riots.

Now and then the workers are victorious, but only for a time. The real fruit of their battle lies not in the immediate result but in the ever-expanding union of workers. This union is helped on by the improved means of communication that are created by modern industry, and that places the workers of different localities in contact with one another. It was just this contact that was needed to centralize the numerous local struggles, all of the same character, into one national struggle between classes. But every class struggle

is a political struggle.   And that union, to attain which the burghers
of the Middle Ages with their miserable highways required centuries, the modern proletarians, thanks to railways, achieve in a
few years.

This organization of the proletarians into a class, and consequently
into a political party, is continually being upset again by the competition between the workers themselves. But it ever rises up
again, stronger, firmer, mightier. It compels legislative recognition
of particular interests of the workers by taking advantage of the
divisions among the bourgeoisie itself. Thus the ten hours' bill
in England was carried.

Altogether collisions between the classes of the old society further,
in many ways, the course of development of the proletariat. The
bourgeoisie finds itself involved in a constant battle. At first with
the aristocracy; later on, with those portions of the bourgeoisie
itself whose interests have become antagonistic to the progress of
industry; at all times, with the bourgeoisie of foreign countries.
In all these battles it sees itself compelled to appeal to the proletariat, to ask for its help, and thus, to drag it into the political
arena. The bourgeoisie itself, therefore, supplies the proletariat
with its own elements of political and general education; in other
words, it furnishes the proletariat with weapons for fighting the
bourgeoisie.

Further, as we have already seen, entire sections of the ruling
classes are, by the advance of industry, precipitated into the proletariat, or are at least threatened in their conditions of existence.
These also supply the proletariat with fresh elements of enlightenment and progress.

Finally, in times when the class struggle nears the decisive hour,
the process of dissolution going on within the ruling class — in
fact, within the whole range of an old society — assumes such a
violent, glaring character that a small section of the ruling class
cuts itself adrift and joins the revolutionary class, the class that
holds the future in its hands.   Just as, therefore, at an earlier period,
a section of the nobility went over to the bourgeoisie, so now a
portion of the bourgeoisie goes over to the proletariat, and in
particular, a portion of the bourgeois ideologists, who have raised

themselves to the level of comprehending theoretically the historical movements as a whole.

The bourgeois have driven the feudal society off the field. They have created the modern world. Their creation is getting out of hand. Among other things it is generating an opposition class which is slowly organizing itself for large-scale revolt.

Of all the classes that stand face to face with the bourgeoisie today the proletariat alone is a really revolutionary class. The other classes decay and finally disappear in the face of modern industry; the proletariat is its special and essential product.

The lower middle class, the small manufacturer, the shopkeeper, the artisan, the peasant, all these fight against the bourgeoisie, to save from extinction their existence as fractions of the middle class. They are therefore not revolutionary, but conservative. Nay, more; they are reactionary for they try to roll back the wheel of history. If by chance they are revolutionary, they are so only in view of their impending transfer into the proletariat; they thus defend not their present, but their future interests; they desert their own standpoint to place themselves at that of the proletariat.

The "dangerous class," the social scum, that passively rotting mass thrown off by the lowest layers of old society, may, here, be swept into the movement by a proletarian revolution; its conditions of life, however, prepare it far more for the part of a bribed tool of reactionary intrigue.

In the conditions of the proletariat, those of the old society at large are already virtually swamped. The proletarian is without property; his relation to his wife and children has no longer anything in common with the bourgeois family relations; modern industrial labor, modern subjection to capital, the same in England as in France, in America as in Germany, has stripped him of every trace of national character. Law, morality, religion, are to him so many bourgeois prejudices, behind which lurk in ambush just as many bourgeois interests.

All the preceding classes that got the upper hand sought to fortify their already acquired status by subjecting society at large to their conditions of appropriation. The proletarians cannot become masters of the productive forces of society, except by abolishing their own previous mode of appropriation, and thereby also every other previous mode of appropriation. They have nothing of their own to secure and to fortify; their mission is to destroy all previous securities for and insurances of individual property.

All previous historical movements were movements of minorities, or in the interest of minorities. The proletarian movement is the self-conscious independent movement of the immense majority. The proletariat, the lowest stratum of our present society, cannot stir, cannot raise itself up without the whole superincumbent strata of official society being sprung into the air.

When the social revolution occurs, it will involve the whole of society. It must first gather momentum in national movements, then it will spread into an international movement.

Though not in substance, yet in form, the struggle of the proletariat with the bourgeoisie is at first a national struggle. The proletariat of each country must, of course, first of all settle matters with its own bourgeoisie.

In depicting the most general phases of the development of the proletariat, we traced the more or less veiled civil war, raging within existing society, up to the point where that war breaks out into open revolution, and where the violent overthrow of the bourgeoisie, lays the foundations for the sway of the proletariat.

Hitherto every form of society has been based, as we have already seen, on the antagonism of oppressing and oppressed classes. But in order to oppress a class, certain conditions must be assured to it under which it can, at least, continue its slavish existence. The serf, in the period of serfdom, raised himself to membership in the commune, just as the petty bourgeois, under the yoke of feudal absolutism, managed to develop into a bourgeois. The modern laborer, on the contrary, instead of rising with the progress of industry, sinks deeper and deeper below the conditions of existence of his own class. He becomes a pauper, and pauperism develops more rapidly than population and wealth. And here it becomes evident that the bourgeoisie is unfit any longer to be the ruling class in society, and to impose its conditions of existence upon society as an overriding law. It is unfit to rule, because it is incompetent to assure an existence to its slave within his slavery, because it cannot help letting him sink into such a state that it has to feed him, instead of being fed by him. Society can no longer live under this bourgeoisie; in other words, its existence is no longer compatible with society.

The essential condition for the existence, and for the sway of the bourgeois class, is the formation and augmentation of capital; the condition for capital is wage labor. Wage labor rests exclusively on competition between the laborers. The advance of industry, whose involuntary promoter is the bourgeoisie, replaces the isolation of the laborers, due to competition, by their involuntary combination, due to association. The development of modern industry, therefore, cuts from under its feet the very foundation on which the bourgeoisie produces and appropriates products. What the bourgeoisie therefore produces, above all, are its own grave-diggers. Its fall and the victory of the proletariat are equally inevitable.

When the great day arrives, the new order will embody many deep-going reforms. Marx cites ten such proposals:

1. Abolition of property in land and application of all rents of land to public purposes
2. A heavy progressive or graduated income tax
3. Abolition of all right of inheritance
4. Confiscation of the property of all emigrants and rebels
5. Centralization of credit in the hands of the state, by means of a national bank with state capital and an exclusive monopoly
6. Centralization of the means of communication and transport in the hands of the state
7. Extension of factories and instruments of production owned by the state, the bringing into cultivation of waste lands, and the improvement of the soil generally in accordance with a common plan

8. Equal liability of all to labor; establishment of industrial armies, especially for agriculture

9. Combination of agriculture with manufacturing industries; gradual abolition of the distinction between town and country by a more equable distribution of the population over the country

10. Free education for all children in public schools, abolition of children's factory labor in its present form, combination of education with industrial production, etc.

When, in the course of development, class distinctions have disappeared, and all production has been concentrated in the hands of a vast association of the whole nation, the public power will lose its political character. Political power, properly so called, is merely the organized power of one class for oppressing another. If the proletariat during its contest with the bourgeoisie is compelled, by the force of circumstances, to organize itself as a class; if, by means of a revolution, it makes itself the ruling class, and as such sweeps away by force the old conditions of production, then it will, along with these conditions, have swept away the conditions for the existence of class antagonism, and of classes generally, and will thereby have abolished its own supremacy as a class.

In place of the old bourgeois society, with its classes and class antagonisms, we shall have an association in which the free development of each is the condition for the free development of all. Let the ruling classes tremble at a Communistic revolution. The proletarians have nothing to lose but their chains. They have a world to win. Workingmen of all countries, unite!

READING REFERENCES. For Marx as philosopher, one cannot do better than consult Sidney Hook's book, *Toward an Understanding of Karl Marx*. It may be supplemented by the same author's paper on "Marxism" in his recent volume, *Reason, Social Myth, and Democracy*. Bertrand Russell's *Freedom versus Organization* is also excellent on Marx as theoretical philosopher. A. D. Lindsay's little book, *Karl Marx's Capital* is well worth the effort required to read it.

For Marx as social critic, one cannot do better than consult

Edmund Wilson's book, *To The Finland Station*. This is one of the finest pieces of historical writing so far published upon the revolutionary movement. Less deftly written, but valuable, is Max Nomad's *Apostles of Revolution*.

The standard biography of Marx is by Franz Mehring. It is long and very detailed. Another, not so exhaustive, by Otto Ruhle, is good reading. A recent short work, *Karl Marx*, by I. Berlin, in the *Home University Library* series, is perhaps the best single item for busy students.

READING QUESTIONS

1. What is "the history of all hitherto existing society"?
2. Name any two pairs of "oppressor" and "oppressed."
3. He speaks of "a series of revolutions in the modes of production and exchange." Name any two.
4. "The bourgeoisie, historically, has played a most revolutionary part." Specify any three items.
5. "They had to burst asunder." What had to? Why?
6. "Modern bourgeois society . . . is like the sorcerer." Wherein?
7. "It has also called into existence the men who are to wield those weapons." What men? What weapons?
8. Mention any three items characterizing the lot of the proletarian in the modern economy.
9. "The proletariat goes through various stages of development." Cite two or three.
10. "The proletariat alone is a really revolutionary class." How so?
11. "They have nothing of their own to secure and fortify." How not? So what?
12. "What the bourgeoisie produces are its own grave-diggers." Elucidate.
13. Be prepared to cite any four of the proposed reforms.
14. And to comment in detail on any two.
15. "The public power will lose its political character." What does Marx mean by this statement? When does he say this event will take place?

16. ". . . and will thereby have abolished its own supremacy as a class." Elucidate.

17. "The free development of each is the free development of all." Elucidate.

5. CULTURES DECLINE INTO CIVILIZATIONS — FROM OSWALD SPENGLER

FROM MARX TO SPENGLER. *The Communist Manifesto* was published by Marx and Engels in 1848. It broached the theory that history discloses a pattern of class struggles moving toward a social revolution which will end the class struggle by ushering in a classless social order based upon a socialist economy. Exactly seventy years later, in 1918, Oswald Spengler published his massive work, *The Decline of the West*. The years between were crowded with events and ideas. These should be recalled to mind in passing from Marx to Spengler.

1. In the first place, the period from 1848 to 1918 was crowded with much lively history. If we recall merely wars and revolutions, the list is imposing. In the year 1848 itself, revolutionary uprisings occurred throughout Europe on an unprecedented scale. The Crimean War and the Indian Mutiny came in the 1850's; the American Civil War, in the 1860's; the Franco-Prussian War and the third French revolution, in the 1870's; a number of colonial and "imperialistic" wars, in the 1880's and 1890's, culminating in the Boer War at the opening of the new century; the Russian-Japanese War and the first Russian revolution, in 1904–1905; an intricate tangle of Balkan wars, in the years preceding 1914; the important Chinese revolution, in 1912; the World War, in 1914; the two Russian revolutions under Kerensky and Lenin, in 1917; and the German revolution in 1918. This list is representative. It is not exhaustive. These wars and revolutions formed an almost unbroken accompaniment to enormous population growth, tremendous economic expansion, vast

and complex political and social reform movements, the rise of organized labor, the formation of overseas empires by European great powers, and much more besides. Consult the table of contents of any good history of the world since 1848. The cultural history of the period is no less intense. The scientific theories of Darwin, Pavlov, Freud, and Einstein fall between Marx and Spengler. The challenging problem literature of modern England, Russia, France, Germany, and the Scandinavias falls between Marx and Spengler. The heated controversies associated with the names of Colenso, Bradlaugh, Huxley, Pasteur, Dreyfus, Pankhurst, Nietzsche, to name only a few, fall between Marx and Spengler. The movements in the arts associated with such persons as Wagner, William Morris, Rodin, Cézanne, Matisse, and others, fall between Marx and Spengler. The tendencies in modern philosophy covered by such terms as *neo-Hegelianism*, *neo-positivism*, *pragmatism*, *creative evolutionism*, *instrumentalism*, *realism*, *anti-intellectualism*, etc., fall between Marx and Spengler.

2. In the second place, the period from 1848 to 1918 was exceedingly rich in historical writing. More and, with a few notable exceptions, greater histories were written during these years than during any comparable period in the past. In Germany the latter half of the historical writings of Leopold von Ranke, the historical writings of Theodor Mommsen, of Heinrich von Treitschke, of Eduard Zeller, of Kuno Fischer, of Adolph Harnack, of Theodor Gomperz, to name only a few, fall between Marx and Spengler. So, also, in France, do the historical writings of Jean Victor Duruy, Ernest Renan, Hippolyte Taine, and others. In England the historical writings of Macaulay, Froude, Stubbs, Green, Maine, Gardiner, Lecky, Seeley, Creighton, Acton, Maitland, the Trevelyans, fall within the same period; as, also, in the United States, do the works of John Lothrop Motley, of Francis

Parkman, of John Fiske, of James Ford Rhodes, Alfred Mahan, Henry Adams, and others. The point of listing these names — no more than a selection — is to indicate that a philosophy of history formulated during or at the close of this period had to take account of a vastly increased amount of sheer data. The inviting simplicity presented by the picture of world history between Augustine and Hegel is gone. The man who proposes to discourse on these matters now, must be prepared to take account of a greater number and a larger range of facts than confronted his predecessors in other centuries.

3. In the third place, the period from 1848 to 1918 was prolific in theories or philosophies of history. In England, Carlyle's "great man" theory carried over from a previous generation. It was followed by the hypothesis of geographic determinism and the central role of intellectual progress, in the writings of H. T. Buckle. Buckle was followed by Walter Bagehot, whose *Physics and Politics* proposed an application to human history of the categories applied to natural history by Darwin. On the continent philosophies of history were set forth by Hippolyte Taine, by Friedrich Nietzsche, by Anatole France, by Benedetto Croce, by Vilfredo Pareto, and many others. And mention should be made, in the United States, of the interesting and suggestive theory advanced by Henry Adams in his two papers, "The Tendency of History" and "The Rule of Phase Applied to History,"[s] and illustrated in his two books, *Mont-Saint-Michel and Chartre'* and *The Education of Henry Adams*.

No matter who is read, following Augustine, Kant, Hegel, and Marx, the facts which comprise the history of the world since 1848 would have to be brought to mind. The problem of a philosophy of history remains what it has always been: an hypothesis in the light of which to interpret the events. But, as already noted, the number and range of events known is greater, and the tempo of reflection upon them has been stepped up. In selecting Spengler with whom to close this set of five, I do not wish to suggest that valuable alternatives are lacking. Spengler, in our own day, is worth reading, in the wake of Augustine and Kant and Hegel and Marx. But so, too, are several others, particularly Benedetto Croce, Flinders Petrie, Henry Adams, Vilfredo Pareto, Pitrim Sorokin, and Arnold Toynbee. If science has been the greatest fertilizer of modern philosophy, history runs it a close second.

BIOGRAPHICAL NOTE. Oswald Spengler was born in Germany in 1880 and died in 1936, at the age of fifty-six. He was educated in the universities at Halle, Munich, and Berlin. He studied mathematics and philosophy particularly, we are told, but, like Francis Bacon, seems to have taken all knowledge for his field. After teaching for seven years in the secondary schools of Germany, he retired to do private tutoring and to write his books. His one great work, *The Decline of the West*, was published, Volume One in 1918 and Volume Two in 1922. Over a hundred thousand copies were sold in Germany in a few years. The *Decline* was followed by two small volumes, *Man and Technics* and *The Hour of Decision*, in which the author formulates a philosophy of life and a call to action, based upon the premise that the argument of the large treatise is substantially correct.

THE ARGUMENT OF THE CITATIONS. Spengler begins with the usual questions: "Is there a logic of history? Is there, beyond all the casual and incalculable elements of the separate events, something that we may call a structure of historic humanity? Does world history present certain grand traits?" The first step toward an answer to this question is the critique of what he calls the "ancient-medieval-modern" scheme of history. Reasons for rejecting this "Ptolemaic" view of history. In place of it, the author proposes his

"Copernican" view, reminding us of an earlier "Copernican revolution" in philosophy. Granted the Copernican hypothesis in history, he pauses to emphasize the fact that analogy thereby becomes fundamental in historical thinking. The essence of Spengler's Copernican revolution in historiography is the distinction between a culture and a civilization, and the claim that history reveals many cultures maturing and declining into civilizations. The culture of the West, declining into the civilization of the West, is a case in point. The book is to tell the story of this decline, once the general theory has been established. One of the characterizing features of a culture degenerating into a civilization is the emergence of "world cities" and their contributary "provinces." Our own period is then given some attention. Finally, the futility and fate of philosophizing, in our own period, are pointed out. *Sic transit gloria mundi.*

Is there a logic of history? Is there, beyond all the casual and incalculable elements of the separate events, something that we may call a structure of historic humanity? Does world history present certain grand traits? And if so, what are the limits to which reasoning from such premises may be pushed?

The above quotation shows at once that Spengler is proposing the same question as St. Augustine, Kant, Hegel, Marx. Is there a logic of history? If so, what is it? Before presenting his own views to the reader, the author pauses to repudiate the usual textbook division of history into ancient, medieval, and modern. He calls this the *Ptolemaic* view of history, likening it to Ptolemaic astronomy according to which our earth was the center of the universe. His criticisms should be noted.

What is world history? An ordered presentation of the past, no doubt. Everyone, if asked, would say that he knew "the form" of history, quite clearly and definitely. He would be under an illusion.

The illusion is there because no one has seriously reflected upon the question of the form of world history, still less conceived any doubts as to his knowledge of it. In fact, the common notion of world history is an unproved and subjective affair handed down from generation to generation, and badly in need of a little of that skepticism which, from Galileo onward, has regulated and deepened our ideas of nature.

Thanks to the subdivision of history into "ancient," "medieval," and "modern" — an incredibly jejune and meaningless scheme, which has, however, entirely dominated our historical thinking — we have failed to perceive the true position in the general history of mankind of the little part world that has developed in Western Europe from the time of the Roman Empire, to judge of its relative importance, and to estimate its direction.

The ages that are to come will find it difficult to believe that such a scheme, with its simple rectilinear progression and its meaningless proportions, becoming more preposterous with each century, incapable of bringing into itself the new fields of history as they come into the light of our knowledge, was never wholeheartedly attacked.

The criticisms that it has long been the fashion for historical students to level at this scheme mean nothing. They have only obliterated the scheme without substituting any other for it. To toy with such phrases as "the Greek middle ages" or "Germanic antiquity" does not help us to form a clear picture in which China and Mexico, the empire of Axum and that of the Sassanids have their proper places. And the expedient of shifting the initial point of "modern history" from the Crusades to the Renaissance, or from the Renaissance to the French Revolution, only goes to show that the scheme is still regarded as unshakably sound.

It is not only that the ancient-medieval-modern scheme circumscribes the area of history. What is worse, it rigs the stage. Western Europe is treated as a steady pole, and great histories of millenial duration and mighty far-away cultures are made to revolve around this pole in all modesty. We select a single patch of ground, for no better reason, it seems, than because we live on it, and make it the center of the historical system. From it all the events of history receive their light, from it their importance is judged. But this phantom "world history," which a breath of skepticism would dissipate, is acted out only in our own West European conceit.

We have to thank this conceit of ours for the immense optical illusion whereby distant histories, such as those of China and Egypt, are made to shrink to mere episodes while in the neighborhoods of our own position the decades since Luther or Napoleon loom large as Brocken specters.

For the cultures of the West, it is evident that Athens, Florence, or Paris, is more important than Lo-Yang or Pataliputra. But is it permissible to found a scheme of world history on such estimates? The Chinese historian is equally entitled to frame a world history in which Caesar, the Crusades, the Renaissance, Frederick the Great are passed over in silence as insignificant. From the morphological point of view, why should our eighteenth century be more important than any of the sixty centuries that preceded it? Is it not ridiculous to oppose a "modern" history of a few centuries to an "ancient" history which covers as many millennia? This is no exaggeration. Do we not, for the sake of keeping the hoary scheme of ancient-medieval-modern, dispose of Egypt and Babylon as a prelude to classical history? Do we not relegate the vast cultures of India and China to footnotes? Do we not entirely ignore the great American cultures?

As mentioned above, this ancient-medieval-modern scheme is to be repudiated as Ptolemaic and replaced by a Copernican view of history.

The most appropriate designation for this ancient-medieval-modern scheme of history, in which great cultures are made to follow orbits around us, is the Ptolemaic system of history. The system that is put forward in this book, in place of it, I regard as the Copernican system in the historical sphere. It admits no privileged position to the classical culture, or the Western culture, as against the cultures of India, Babylon, China, Egypt, the Arabs, Mexico. Each of these non-Western cultures, being separate worlds, count, in point of mass for just as much in the general picture of history as the classical culture, while they frequently surpass it in point of spiritual greatness and soaring power.

I see, in place of that empty figment of ancient-medieval-modern, the drama of a number of mighty cultures, each springing from the soil of a mother region; each stamping its material in its own image; each having its own idea, its own passions, its own life, its own will and feeling, its own death. Here indeed are colors, lights, movements, that no eye has yet discovered.

Here cultures, peoples, languages, truths, gods, bloom and age as the oaks and the stone pines. Each culture has its own new possibilities of self-expression, which arise, ripen, decay, and never return. There is not just one sculpture, one painting, one mathematics, one physics, one religion, one morality, one philosophy, but many, each different from the others, each limited in duration, each having its special type of growth and decline. Each grows with the same superb aimlessness as the flowers of the field. I see world history as a picture of endless formations and transformations. The professional historian sees it as a sort of tapeworm industriously adding onto itself one epoch after another.

The substitution of the Copernican for the Ptolemaic view of history effects an unmeasurable widening of horizon. This idea once attained, the rest is easy. To this single idea one can refer all those separate problems of religion, art, philosophy, morals, politics, economics with which the modern mind has busied itself so passionately and so vainly. This idea is one of those truths that have only to be expressed with clarity to become indisputable. It is capable of transforming the world outlook of one who fully understands it. It immensely deepens the world historical picture. By its aid we are enabled to follow the broad lines into the future, a privilege till now permitted only to the physicist.

The Copernican view, then, resolves history into a number of different epochs. Each epoch, it is to be argued, begins as a "culture" and ends as a "civilization." The first step will be to clarify these terms *culture* and *civilization*. Do the epochs have any common characteristics? Does each have a "life" of its own?

Is it possible to find in life a series of stages which must be traversed? For everything organic, the notions of birth, youth, age, lifetime, death, are fundamentals. May not these notions possess, in the realm of history, a meaning which no one has yet extracted? In short, is all history founded upon general biographic archetypes?

At this point Spengler pauses to develop the thought that a history of many different epochs will inevitably develop analogies between one epoch and another. Something in one epoch will be "analogous" to something in another epoch. How reliable is the analogy?

The means whereby to identify dead forms is mathematical law. The means whereby to understand living forms is analogy.

From any technique of analogies we are far distant. It is neither a principle nor a sense of historic necessity, but simple inclination, that governs the choice of the analogies we draw. They throng up without scheme or unities. If they do hit upon something that is apt, it is thanks to luck, more rarely to instinct, never to a principle. No one has hitherto set himself to work out a technique or method for striking upon apt and revealing analogies in the region of world history. Nor has anyone had the slightest inkling that there is here a root, in fact the only root, from which can come a broad solution of the problems of history.

Insofar as they lay bare the structure of history, analogies might be a blessing to historical thought. Their technique, developing under the influence of a comprehensive idea, might eventuate in inevitable conclusions and logical mastery. But, as hitherto understood and practiced, they have been a curse, for they have enabled historians to follow their own tastes, instead of realizing that their first task was the symbolism of history and its analogies. Superficial in many cases, these analogies are worse than superficial in others, while occasionally they are bizarre to the point of perversity.

Napoleon has hardly ever been discussed without a side glance at Caesar and Alexander. Napoleon himself conceived of his situation as akin to Charlemagne's. The French Revolutionary Convention spoke of Carthage when it meant England, and the Jacobins styled themselves Romans. Cecil Rhodes, the organizer of British South Africa, felt himself akin to the Emperor Hadrian. And so on, through an indefinitely long list.

I have not hitherto found anyone who has carefully considered the morphological relationship that binds together the expression forms of all branches of a single culture; who has, e.g., gone beyond politics to grasp the ultimate and fundamental ideas in mathematics, ornamentation, architecture, philosophy, literature, craftsmanship, etc., within a single culture.

Who among historians realizes that there are deep uniformities between the differential calculus and the dynastic principle of politics in the age of Louis XIV; between the classical city state and Euclidean geometry; between the space perspective of Western oil painting and the conquest of space by railroad; between telephone and long-range weapon; between contrapuntal music and credit economics? Yet, viewed from this morphological standpoint, such things as the Egyptian administrative system, the classical coinage, analytical geometry, the cheque, the Suez Canal, the book printing of the Chinese, the Prussian army, the Roman road engineering, can be made uniformly understandable as symbols.

The historian, then, despite risks, must be prepared to make large use of analogies. He will be interested in noting what things in epoch A are "contemporary" with things in epoch B. The word *contemporary* in Spengler's use means happening in one epoch at relatively the same point as in another epoch. Two events can be contemporary, in this sense, even if the epochs in question are several centuries apart. However, the whole point of working up these analogies is to throw light on the common characteristics of an epoch. Now, an epoch, it was said, begins as a culture and ends as a civilization. Accordingly, we turn to these two key terms.

If we are to discover the form in which the destiny of Western culture will be accomplished, we must first be clear as to what a culture is. What are its relations to visible history? How far may we point to peoples, tongues and epochs, battles and ideas, states and goods, arts and crafts, sciences, laws, economic types, great men, great events, world ideas, as symbols of a culture?

Every culture has its own civilization. In this book, these two words are used in a periodic sense, to express an organic succession. The civilization is the destiny of the culture. In this principle we obtain the viewpoint from which the problems of historical morphology become capable of solution. Civilizations are the most external and artificial states of which a species of developed humanity is capable. Civilizations are a conclusion, death following upon life, rigidity following expansion. They are an end, irrevocable, yet, by an inward necessity reached again and again. They consist in a progressive taking-down of forms that have become dead.

To the culture belongs gymnastics, the joust, the tournament. To the civilization belongs sport. Art itself bcomes a sport, to be played before a highly intelligent audience of connoisseurs or buyers; and this, whether the feat consist in mastering absurd instrumental tone masses and taking harmonic fences, or in some *tour de force* of coloring. Then a new fact philosophy appears, which can spare only a smile for metaphysical speculations; and a new literature that is a necessity for the megalopolitan palate and nerves but is both unintelligible and ugly to the provincial.

What is the hallmark of a politic of civilization, in contrast to a politic of culture? It is, for the classical and the West European, money. The money spirit penetrates the historical forms of the people's existence. Though the forms persist, the great political parties cease to be more than reputed centers of decision. The decisions in fact lie elsewhere. A small number of superior heads, whose names are often little known, settle everything, while below them are the great mass of second-rate politicians selected through a franchise to keep alive the illusion of popular self-determination.

Imperialism is to be taken as the typical symbol of passing away. Imperialism is civilization unadulterated. The energy of culture-man is directed inwards; of civilization-man, outwards. In this form the destiny of the West is now set. Thus I see in Cecil Rhodes a man of the age. He stands for the political style of a far-ranging future. His phrase "expansion is everything" is the Napoleonic reassertion of the tendency of every civilization that has fully ripened. It is not a matter of choice. The expansive tendency is a doom which grips man of the world-city stage.

Rhodes is to be regarded as the precursor of a Western type of

Caesar whose day is to come, though yet distant. He stands midway between Napoleon and the force-men of the next centuries. It was only before his maps that he could fall into a sort of poetic trance, this son of a parson who, sent out to South Africa without means, made a gigantic fortune and employed it as the engine of political aims.

His idea of a trans-African railway from Cape to Cairo, his project of a South African empire, his hold on the hard metal souls of the mining magnates, his capital planned as the future residence of an all-powerful statesman who yet stood in no definite relation to the state, his wars, his diplomatic deals, his road systems, his syndicates, his armies, all this is the prelude of a future which is still in store for us and with which the history of Western man will be definitely closed.

The civilization of an epoch crystallizes always into the "world city" and "the province": megalopolis and its surrounding territory. What about these two units of social organization?

World city and province, the two basic ideas of every civilization, bring up a wholly new form-problem of history, the very problem that we are living through today with hardly any notion of its immensity. In place of a people true to a type, born of the soil and grown on the soil, there is a new sort of nomad, cohering unstably in fluid masses, the parasitical city dweller, traditionless, utterly matter-of-fact, without religion, clever, unfruitful, contemptuous of the countryman. This is a great stride toward the end. What does it signify? France and England have already taken the step. Germany is beginning to do so. After Syracuse, Athens, Alexandria, comes Rome. After Madrid, Paris, London, come Berlin and New York. It is the destiny of whole regions that lie outside the circle of one of these great cities to become "provinces."

The world city means cosmopolitanism in place of home, matter-of-fact coldness in place of reverence for tradition, scientific irreligion in place of the older religion of the heart, society in place of the state, "natural" in place of hard-earned rights. It was in the conception of money, entirely disconnected from the notion of the fruitful earth, that the Romans had the advantage over the Greeks. Thereafter any high ideal of life becomes largely a question of money. Unlike the Greek stoicism, Roman stoicism presupposes a private income. Unlike the social and moral ideals of the eighteenth century, the ideals of the twentieth century are matters for millionaires. To the world city belongs not a folk, but a mass.

The uncomprehending hostility of the mass of the world city to all the traditions of the culture — nobility, church, privilege, dynasties, conventions in art, limits of knowledge — the keen and cold intelligence that confounds the wisdom of the peasant, the new-fashioned naturalism in sex and society, the reappearance of *panem et circenses* in the form of wage disputes and large-scale organized spectator sports, all these things betoken the definite closing down of the culture and the setting in of the civilization, antiprovincial, late, futureless, but inevitable.

At this level civilizations enter upon a stage of depopulation. The whole pyramid of culture vanishes. It crumbles from the summit, first the world cities, then the provinces, and finally the land itself whose best blood has incontinently poured into the towns. At last only the primitive blood remains alive, but robbed of its strongest and most promising elements. The residue is Fellah type.

Thus far by way of preliminary: Has history a logic? Repudiation of the Ptolemaic theory of history. Proposal of the Copernican theory. History deals with great epochs. Hence analogy as the historical method. Epochs begin as cultures and end as civilizations. The world city and its province characterize the end of an epoch. With these general ideas in mind Spengler turns to the particular subject of his book: the history of our own times or, as he calls it, *The Decline of the West*. We live at the end of an epoch. We live in a civilization, not in a culture. And his massive book is an inductive survey of the evidence for this claim. He says:

Our narrow task, then, is to determine, from such a survey of world history, the state of Western Europe and America for the epoch, 1800–2000; to establish the chronological position of this period in the cultural history of the West; to indicate its significance as a chapter that is found in the story of every culture; and to make clear the meaning of its political, artistic, intellectual, and social expression forms.

Every culture is a four-act drama with an ascending movement of religion, aristocracy, and art, and a descending movement of ir-religion, democracy, socialism, and the great city. The culture of the West, whose "decline" is referred to in the title of this book, originated in that feudal system of lord and serf which Roman conquest left like a network over Europe. Its basis is a stolid peasantry, bearing on its back the economic life of the world.

Considered in the spirit of analogy the period appears as chrono-logically parallel to the epoch we call *Hellenism;* and its present culmination, marked by the World War, corresponds to the transi-tion from the Hellenistic to the Roman age. Rome, with its rigor-ous realism, uninspired, barbaric, disciplined, practical, will always give us, working as we must by analogies, the key to our own future.

Long ago we should have seen in the classical culture a develop-ment which is the counterpart of our own, differing indeed in surface detail, but similar as regards the power driving the great organism toward its end. We might have established the correspondence, item by item, from the Trojan War and the Crusades, Homer and the *Nibelungenlied*, through Doric and Gothic, Dionysian and Renais-sance, Polycletus and Bach, Athens and Paris, Aristotle and Kant, Alexander and Napoleon, to the world city and imperialism.

The transition from culture to civilization was accomplished for the classical world in the fourth century A.D.; for the Western world in the nineteenth century. From these periods onwards, the great decisions take place. And they take place in three or four world cities that have absorbed into themselves the whole content of history.

Let it be realized, then, that the nineteenth and twentieth cen-turies, hitherto looked upon as an ascending straight line of world history, are in reality a stage of life which may be observed in every culture that has ripened to its limit. Let it be realized, then, that the future of the West is not a limitless tending upwards and onwards toward our present ideals, but a single phenomenon of history, strictly limited and defined as to form and duration, covering a few centuries and, in essentials, calculated from available precedents.

He who does not understand that this outcome is obligatory, that our choice is between willing this and willing nothing, between cleaving to this destiny or despairing of the future; he who cannot feel that there is grandeur in the achievements of powerful intelligence, in the energy and discipline of metal-hard natures, in battles fought with the coldest and abstractest means; he who is obsessed with the ideals of past ages, must forego all desire to comprehend history, to live through history, or to make history.

So much, then, for a few of the analogies by means of which Spengler locates the West and the period of its decline. He turns to some of the characteristic phenomena of the period. Here we can only quote a few scattered items from an enormous mass comprising two stout volumes. For example, the press:

A more appalling caricature of freedom cannot be imagined. There is today no need to impose military service on people. Whip their souls with articles, telegrams, pictures, till they clamor for weapons and force their leaders into a conflict. In preparation for the World War the press of whole countries was brought financially under the control of a few world cities, and the peoples belonging to them reduced to an unqualified intellectual slavery.

As for the modern press, the sentimentalist may beam with contentment when it is constitutionally "free." But the realist merely asks at whose disposal it is. For the multitude, that is true which it continually reads and hears. Its "truth" is a product of the press. What the press wills is true. Three weeks of press work, and the truth is acknowledged by everybody. The press and the news service keep whole peoples and continents under a deafening drumfire of theses, catchwords, standpoints, scenes, feelings.

Or the modern omnipresent machine:

These machines become less and less human; more ascetic, mystic, esoteric. They weave over the earth an infinite web of subtle forces, currents, tensions. Their bodies become ever more immaterial, ever less noisy. The wheels, rollers, levers, are vocal no more. All that matters draws itself into the interior. The center of this artificial and complicated realm is the engineer, the priest of the machine.

Or the modern masses:

. . . the fluid megalopolitan populace; the newspaper readers of our time; the "educated" who makes a cult of intellectual mediocrity and a church of advertisement; the man of the theaters and places of amusement, of sport and "best sellers," of expressionism, the movies, theosophy, nigger dances, poker, and racing. The Roman *panem et circenses* we have in our wage disputes and football games.

Such "men" constitute the "masses." The masses reject the matured culture of our epoch. The mass is formless. It persecutes with hatred all distinctions of rank, the orderliness of tradition, of property, of knowledge. They are the new nomads of cosmopolis. They recognize no past and possess no future. They are the end.

Or modern art:

It is all irretrievably over with the arts of the West. What is practiced as art today is impotence and falsehood: a faked music, filled with artificial noisiness of massed instruments; a faked painting, full of idiotic, exotic, and show-card effects; a lying plastic that steals from Assyria, Egypt, Mexico, indifferently. For Western people there can no longer be any question of great painting or great music. We are today playing out a tedious game with dead forms to keep up the illusion of a living art.

Coming, at last, to philosophy, the story makes very unpalatable reading. To begin with, Herr Spengler dislikes and distrusts the "thinker" type:

There are born destiny men and causality men. A whole world separates the man born to prosper, to rule, to fight, to dare, to organize, from the man who is destined by the power of his mind or the defect of his blood to be an intellectual — the saint, the

priest, the scholar, the idealist.   The eye for men and situations, the
belief in his star, things which every born man of action possesses,
are something wholly different from the belief in the "correctness
of a standpoint," and are denied to the critical, meditative man.
Even the footfall of the fact man sounds different from that of the
thinker.

With that as a beginning, it is not hard to see what is likely
to follow: Modern philosophers are nobodies and busybodies:

It still remains to consider the relation of a morphology of world
history to philosophy.   For me the test to be applied to a thinker is
his eye for the great facts of his own time.   Only this can settle
whether he is merely a clever architect of systems and principles,
versed in definitions and analyses, or one in whom the soul of his
time speaks in his works and intuitions.

A philosopher who cannot grasp and command actuality will
never be of the first rank.   The early Greek philosophers were
merchants and politicians *en grande*.   The desire to put his political
ideas into practice nearly cost Plato his life.   Confucius was several
times a minister of state.   Pythagoras organized an important
political movement.   Goethe, besides being an executive minister,
was interested in the Suez and Panama Canals and their effects upon
the economy of the world.   Hobbes was one of the originators of a
plan for winning South America for England.   Leibnitz, without
doubt the greatest intellect in Western philosophy, founder of the
differential calculus and the analysis situs, conceived or cooperated
in a number of major political schemes.

Turning from men of this world to the "philosophers" of today,
one is dismayed and ashamed.   What they do not possess is real
standing in actual life.   Their personalities are poor.   Their
political and practical outlook are commonplace.   Not one of them
has intervened effectively in politics, in the development of modern
techniques, in matters of communication, in economics, or in any
other big actuality, with a single act or a single compelling idea.
Not one of them counts in mathematics, in physics, in politics.
Why is it that the mere idea of calling upon one of them to prove his
intellectual eminence in government, diplomacy, large-scale or-

ganization, the direction of any big colonial or commercial or transport concern, is enough to evoke our pity? This insufficiency indicates, not that they possess profundity but that they lack weight. I look around in vain for an instance in which a modern "philosopher" has made a name by even one deep or far-seeing pronouncement on an important question of the day. I see nothing but provincial opinions of the same kind as any one else's. Whenever I take up a work by a modern philosopher I find myself asking: Has he any idea of the actualities of world politics, world-city problems, capitalism, the future of the state, the relation of techniques to the course of civilization, Russia, science? Goethe would have understood all this and reveled in it. There is not one living philosopher capable of taking it in. This sense for actualities is, of course, not the same thing as the content of a philosophy; but, I repeat, it is an infallible symptom of its necessity, fruitfulness and importance.

We must allow ourselves no illusions as to the gravity of this negative result. We have lost sight of the final significance of effective philosophizing. We have descended from the perspective of the bird to that of the frog. We confuse philosophy with preaching, with agitation, with novel-writing, with lecture-room jargon. It were better to become a colonist or an engineer, to do something that is real and true, than to chew over once more the old dried-up themes under cover of some "new wave of philosophic thought"; better to construct an aero-engine than a new theory of apperception that is not wanted. It is indeed a poor life's work to restate once more the views of a hundred predecessors on the will or on the psychophysical parallelism. This may be a profession. It is emphatically not a philosophy. A doctrine that does not attack and affect the life of one's period is no doctrine, and had better not be taught.

To me, the depths and refinement of mathematical and physical theories are a joy. By comparison, the aesthete and the physiologist are fumblers. I would sooner have the fine mind-begotten forms of a fast steamer, a steel structure, a precision lathe, the subtlety and elegance of many chemical and optical processes, than all the pickings and stealings of present-day "arts and crafts."

This is a situation that regularly repeats itself at a certain historical level. I maintain that today many an inventor, many a diplomat, many a financier, is a sounder philosopher than all those who practice the dull craft of experimental psychology. It would have been absurd in a Roman of intellectual eminence, who might, as consul or praetor, have led armies, organized provinces, built cities and roads, to want to hatch out some new variant of post-Platonic philosophy at Athens. Consequently no one did so. It was not in harmony with the tendency of the age. Therefore it attracted only third-class men of the kind that always advances as far as the Zeitgeist of the day before yesterday.

I prefer one Roman aqueduct to all the Roman temples and statues. I love the Colosseum and the giant vault of the Palatine, for they display the real Rome and the grand practical sense of her engineers. It was not for nothing, that the genuine Roman despised the "artist" and the "philosopher." The time for art and philosophy had passed; they were exhausted, used up, superfluous, and his instinct for the realities of life told him so. One Roman law weighed more than all the lyrics and school metaphysics of the time put together.

Modern philosophy, like modern art, is played out. With Kant and Schopenhauer, the curtain went down for the last time. What remains is merely the possibility of becoming competent and understanding historians of philosophy.

Systematic philosophy closed with the end of the eighteenth century. Kant put its utmost possibilities in forms that are grand and, for the Western soul, final. He is followed, as Plato and Aristotle were followed, by a specifically megalopolitan philosophy that is not speculative, but practical, irreligious, social-moral. This philosophy begins in the West with Schopenhauer. He was the first to make the will-to-live a central thought. It is the same will-to-live that was Schopenhauer-wise denied in *Tristan* and Darwin-wise asserted in *Siegfried;* that led Marx to an economic and Darwin to a biological hypothesis which have together subtly transformed the world-outlook of the Western megalopolis; and that produced a series of tragedies from Hebbel to Ibsen and Hardy.

It has embraced, therefore, all the possibilities of a philosophy, and has exhausted them.

We have not chosen our time. We cannot help it if we are born in the early winter of a civilization, instead of in the golden summer of a culture. Everything depends upon seeing our own position clearly; on realizing that we may lie to ourselves about it but cannot evade it. He who does not acknowledge this ceases to be counted among the men of his generation.

One must begin, therefore, by asking what today is possible and what is not. In the case of a genuine adept this question is answered in advance by a kind of instinct.

Systematic philosophy, then, lies far behind us, and ethical philosophy has been wound up. But a third possibility, corresponding to the classical skepticism, still remains. And it can be brought to light by the hitherto unknown methods of historical morphology. Classical skepticism was ahistoric. Our skepticism, a symbol of the autumn of spirituality, is historical. Its solutions are got by treating everything as relative, as historical. Classical skepticism is the negation of philosophy, declaring it to be useless. Our skepticism, on the contrary, regards the history of philosophy as, in the last resort, philosophy's gravest theme. This is *skepsis* in the true sense; for, where classical skepticism is led to renounce absolute standpoints by contempt for the past, we are led to do so by comprehension of the past.

It is our task to sketch out this unphilosophical philosophy — the last that the West will know. Skepticism is the expression of a pure civilization, and it dissipates the world picture of the culture that has gone before. For us, its success will lie in resolving all the older problems into one, the historical. With that, the claim of higher thought to possess general and eternal truths falls to the ground. Truths are truths only in relation to a particular mankind. Thus, my own philosophy is able to express and reflect only the Western mind, and that mind only in its present civilized phase by which its conception of the world, its practical range, and its sphere of effect, are specified.

READING REFERENCES. The best single account of Spengler and his *Decline* is to be found in Will Durant's book *Adven-*

tures in Genius. This book was reissued under the title *Great Men of Literature.* The Spengler essay, fifty pages or so, is good. A book on Spengler's interpretation of history, *Civilization or Civilizations,* has been written by E. H. Goddard and P. A. Gibbons. A volume of selections from the *Decline,* with introduction and notes by Edwin F. Dakin, has been published under the title *Today and Destiny.* The *Decline* itself is not easy reading. The author's style and his constant stream of esoteric references slow things up considerably. The two short books, *Man and Technics* and *The Hour of Decision* are much less encumbered, and in them, therefore, the author's thought moves more swiftly and vividly.

READING QUESTIONS

1. What is the Ptolemaic view of history?
2. Why is it so named?
3. Give three of Spengler's criticisms of this view.
4. What is the Copernican view of history?
5. Why is it so named?
6. Why is Spengler led to a consideration of analogy in history?
7. Name one or two he suggests.
8. In what sense does he propose to use the word *contemporary?*
9. What distinguishes a culture from its civilization?
10. What is a world city?
11. Name two or three from history.
12. How does Spengler characterize world cities?
13. What, roughly, is the period of the decline in our case?
14. What about the press in our day?
15. Or the machine?
16. Or the masses?
17. Or the fine arts?
18. What is a causality man?
19. Some items in Spengler's appraisal of modern philosophers.
20. "A third possibility . . . still remains." Namely?
21. Can you name one or more contemporary philosophers whose influence, Spengler notwithstanding, strongly affects our time?
22. Give two or more questions you would put to Spengler.

INDEX